EU Borders and Shifting Internal Security

Raphael Bossong • Helena Carrapico
Editors

EU Borders and Shifting Internal Security

Technology, Externalization and Accountability

Springer

Editors
Raphael Bossong
Europe University Viadrina
Frankfurt, Oder, Germany

Helena Carrapico
School of Languages and Social Sciences
Aston University
Birmingham, United Kingdom

ISBN 978-3-319-17559-1 ISBN 978-3-319-17560-7 (eBook)
DOI 10.1007/978-3-319-17560-7

Library of Congress Control Number: 2015958771

Springer Cham Heidelberg New York Dordrecht London

Printed on acid-free paper

Springer International Publishing AG Switzerland is part of Springer Science+Business Media (www.springer.com)

Acknowledgements

This volume was developed on the basis of an academic workshop, held at the Europe University Viadrina, Frankfurt (O.), in autumn 2014. In this context, the "B/Orders in Motion" Centre of the Europe University Viadrina provided critical support, including a research grant (entitled "*Towards a European Internal Security Order? Exploring the Redefinition of Functional and Geographical Borders in EU Security Cooperation*") that enabled Dr. Raphael Bossong to develop a more multidimensional perspective on European borders and internal security. Dr. Helena Carrapico would also like to thank the valuable support of the Aston Centre for Europe, which has enabled her to pursue new avenues for research within internal security.

Most importantly, we are grateful to the experienced scholars, as well as upcoming Ph.D. researchers, who agreed to share their insights and expertise with us in this edited volume. It has been a truly enriching experience, as we could deepen our understanding of long-standing debates, as well as develop a range of new research agendas that should concern anyone who is interested in the trajectory of European border and internal security policy.

Contents

List of Contributors

Rocco Bellanova is Senior Researcher at the Peace Research Institute Oslo (PRIO—Norway) and Post-Doc Researcher at the Université Saint-Louis—Brussels (USL-B—Belgium). His current research focuses on the study of how humans, technologies, and regulations participate in the constitution of security practices.

Raphael Bossong is a lecturer in European Studies at the Europa University Viadrina, Frankfurt/O., and a researcher at the Institute for Peace Research and Security Policy, Hamburg. His research focuses on the intersection between EU crisis management, internal and external security policy, and public administration.

Helena Carrapico is a lecturer in Politics and International Relations at Aston University, as well as a researcher at the Centre for Social Sciences of the University of Coimbra. Her research focuses on European Union Justice and Home Affairs, in particular organised crime policies.

Denis Duez is professor of political science and director of the Institute for European Studies at University Saint-Louis—Brussels (Belgium). His research focuses on practices of border controls with regard to the issue of legitimacy of the European integration process.

Paweł Frankowski is assistant professor in the Department of International Relations and Foreign Policy, Jagiellonian University. His research interests include U.S. foreign policy, space security, federal studies, and regional integration.

Dirk Godenau is lecturer in Applied Economics at the University La Laguna (Spain) and researcher at the Observatory of Immigration in Tenerife. His research focuses on border management related to irregular international migration at the South European Border. He has published in international peer-reviewed journals, such as the *Journal of Immigration and Refugee Studies, Island Studies Journal, Comparative Populations Studies, and Shima: The International Journal of Research into Island Cultures.*

Artur Gruszczak is associate professor of International Relations at the Faculty of International and Political Studies, Jagiellonian University in Krakow, Poland. He is also Permanent Fellow at the European Centre Natolin in Warsaw where he coordinates Forum "EU Justice and Home Affairs".

Julien Jeandesboz is an assistant professor in the Department of Political Science at the University of Amsterdam. His research explores the politics of security and technology in Europe, with a focus on border control and the relation between security, surveillance, and liberties. He previously held research positions at War Studies, King's College London, and Science Po, Paris.

Anne Koch is a lecturer in political sciences at the Europa University Viadrina and a postdoctoral researcher at the Viadrina Center B/Orders in Motion. Her research is situated at the interface between Political Science, International Relations, and International Law and focuses on questions of migration control and governance.

Ana María López-Sala is Research Fellow at the Institute of Economics, Geography and Demography, Spanish Council for Scientific Research (CSIC). Her research interests revolve around comparative immigration policies, and she is extensively involved in applied projects and international expert networks in this issue area [e.g. Independent Network of Labor Migration and Integration Experts (IOM and EC), Transnational Immigrant Organizations Network (Princeton University)].

Igor Merheim-Eyre is a Ph.D. candidate within the School of Politics and International Relations (University of Kent). His general research interest lies in the area of consular affairs, including visa issuance and the assistance to one's nationals in third countries.

Maria O'Neill is senior lecturer in EU Law at the University of Abertay Dundee, who specialises in the EU's provisions on Police and Judicial Cooperation in Criminal Matters. She has a number of publications in this area, including The Evolving EU Counter-Terrorism Legal Framework, with Routledge, and two co-edited volumes with Cambridge Scholars.

Alexandra M. Schmid is a Ph.D. student in European Studies, research assistant, and lecturer at the University of Passau, Germany. Her research interests include the European migration policy, European foreign and security policy, and political risk analysis.

Irma Słomczyńska is assistant professor in the Department of Political Science, Maria Curie-Sklodowska University, Lublin. Her research interests include Common Security and Defence Policy, European Space Policy, and new forms of European governance.

Angela Tacea is adjunct Lecturer at Université Paris 2 Panthéon-Assas and a Ph. D. candidate at Centre d'études européenne, Sciences Po, Paris. Her research and teaching interests are in comparative policies, legislative studies, data protection, and border control.

Katsiaryna Yakouchyk is a Ph.D. student in European Studies at the University of Passau, Germany. Her research interests focus on democratisation, democracy promotion, and authoritarian persistence.

The Multidimensional Nature and Dynamic Transformation of European Borders and Internal Security

Raphael Bossong and Helena Carrapico

1 Introduction

Europe is currently undergoing its most serious refugee crisis since the Second World War (Amnesty International 2015). News programmes, blogs, advertisement, and public for a in general have become dominated by imagery and accounts of human tragedy, political disagreement, compassionate assistance, and populist reactions. This debate and the sometime overwhelming range of pressing humanitarian and political challenges demand our engagement, not least as all indications point to their persistence and depth. As recently expressed by German chancellor Merkel, the refugee crisis is likely to "preoccupy Europe much, much more than [. . .] the stability of the euro"(Bundesregierung 2015) and to serve as an essential test for the EU's ability to take joint action where and when it matters.

Against this background, the choice of topic of this volume may be regarded as self-evident. We simply cannot reassure ourselves that all will turn out for the best—as is often the credo of seasoned European policy-makers who point to the history of integration as being crisis-led. It may well be the case that it takes a profound moral shock to break the current mold and to set a new path for European cooperation in matters of border, migration and internal security policy. As has been discussed for a long time, "Dublin"—the code word for assigning exclusive responsibility for both identity controls and appropriate asylum process to those EU states that actually maintain an external border with third states—needs to be developed into a more flexible and solidarity-driven system. "Schengen"—the

R. Bossong (✉)
Europe University Viadrina, Logenstraße 11-12, 15230 Frankfurt Oder, Germany
e-mail: bossong@europa-uni.de

H. Carrapico
School of Languages and Social Sciences, Aston University, Aston Triangle, B4 7ET Birmingham, UK
e-mail: h.farrand-carrapico@aston.ac.uk

R. Bossong, H. Carrapico (eds.), *EU Borders and Shifting Internal Security*,
DOI 10.1007/978-3-319-17560-7_1

other ambiguous signifier for hard border security as well as freedom of movement within the EU—has to be rebalanced to allow for legal and less risky access routes to the EU.

While there is legitimate disagreement as to how one should regard the relationship between academic analysis and current political debates (Lowenthal and Bertucci 2014), it is clearly not an option to shy away from such pressing social and ethical issues. However, we also need to be clear that this book does not argue for a particular normative stance, such as in the case of critical border and/or security studies. Instead, its main aim is to deepen our understanding of the diversity, complexity and contradictory practices of EU border and internal security policies. Similarly to the need of recognising the seriousness of the current situation, it is necessary to analyse matters that fall outside the ever-shifting attention of the media, and to provide orientation on developments that cannot be neatly encapsulated in the narrative of crisis and immediate response (or lack thereof).

In pursuit of these aims, this volume adopts the following three analytical strategies. First, all contributions look beyond the intentions or interests of particular policy-makers, be they national governments or EU institutions, and instead foreground the partially unintended consequences and deficient control mechanisms of the technological, institutional and legal systems that have been increasingly put into place. This reminds us that, when criticizing or reforming the EU's regime for border and internal security, we need to address a large number of issues that cannot be reduced to the "lack of political will". Secondly, the analytical emphasis on borders is not only triggered by the current refugee crises, but also helps us to understand dynamics of change and resistance. As elaborated below, it is increasingly difficult to grasp the essential dynamics of the EU's internal security policy, or those of the Area of Freedom, Security and Justice (ASFJ). Useful insights may instead be gained by focussing on instances of transgression or transformation of borders within this long-term political project, which then reflect back on the existing order for European cooperation. Following arguments from Border Studies (Rumford 2012; Côté-Boucher et al. 2014), we go beyond the traditional understanding of the border as a clearly demarcated line, which separates two coherent territorial entities, and rather emphasise the proliferation and dialectic of bordering practices. Nevertheless, we remain dominantly interested in current empirical developments of the EU, rather than abstract arguments about the nature of contemporary borders. Therefore, the third necessary move is to link the analytical perspective on borders and decentred political practices with the ever-growing range of topics that fall under the ASFJ. For this purpose, we need to define a limited number of themes that can be distilled from the EU's increasingly complex internal security and border policy, and which can support dialogue across individual research projects. For the purposes of this book, we have identified three such themes or trends, namely 1—the growing role of technology; 2—the externalization of internal security concerns across borders; and 3—the varied patterns or perceived gaps in accountability in transnational settings.

Against this background, the following introductory chapter starts by offering an overview of the current political and operational challenges in internal security faced by the European Union. We then turn to the possible consequences for academic study and justify the organization of this volume around the themes of technology, externalisation and accountability. Finally, we shortly present each individual contribution under the three respective headings.

2 EU Borders and Internal Security in a Rapidly Changing Landscape

When trying to outline the wider current context for the contributions to this book, one is struck by the persistent high pace of change, as well as by contradictory normative developments. On the one hand, we see a continuation of threat perceptions and decision-making patterns that have repeatedly dominated the AFSJ since its inception in 1999. In January 2015, the terrorist attack on the editorial office of Charlie Hebdo led to a renewed window of opportunity for accelerating a number of controversial proposals linked to border management (Bigo et al. 2015). For instance, the European Parliament took a significant step towards the introduction of a European Passenger Name Record System that should facilitate the identification of terrorist travel patterns, which contrasts with its previous oppositional stance and emphasis on data protection (Ripoll Servent 2015). Furthermore, European member states extended the use of the Schengen Information System for capturing terrorist suspects at points of border crossing. This intersection between border security systems and the fight against terrorism is anything but new. Nevertheless, the current moves revive a particularly controversial debate on the legitimacy and possibility of developing consistent personality profiles on terrorists.

For a wider picture of the current trends in EU internal security policy, one can turn to the so-called "European Agenda on Security" (European Commission 2015a), which serves as a follow up to the EU Internal Security Strategy and its annual implementation reports (Eur-Lex 2014). These documents exemplify the continuous growth of security objectives, as well as the persistent ambition to link them together, be it across various thematic fields, such as the fight against terrorism, organised crime and border security, or across the "internal" and "external" divide that traditionally characterizes the set-up of national security systems (Cremona et al. 2011). The European Agenda on Security further documents the steady rise of technological concerns and responses in this policy field, ranging from cybersecurity to various databases or information systems for improved security cooperation.

All these trends need to be set against the wider and even more long-standing discussion on the balance of values in the EU's Area of Freedom, Security and Justice (AFSJ). Although one can point to a growing official discourse on the need to balance security with other postulated core values of the AFSJ—and the related improvements for parliamentary participation and judicial oversight since the Lisbon Treaty (Occhipinti 2014)—many observers remain convinced of the dominance of security professionals and their technocratic rationales (Eriksen 2011;

Bigo 2014). Some commentators have argued further that the EU increasingly seeks to create a clear distinction between internal and external space, focusing on the putative threats posed by outsiders (Waever 1993). In other words, the traditional security rationale of European integration, i.e., the guarantee of European peace, may have increasingly been replaced by an alternative vision of internal security and order. Nevertheless, it would be premature to speak of a truly common order of EU internal security (Kaunert 2005). The Treaty of Lisbon explicitly notes that the operational provision of internal security remains the prerogative of the member states,[1] which are often hesitant to converge at a deeper level of legal and institutional systems.

However, we can no longer be certain that familiar arguments about the driving forces and limits of the EU's engagement in these fields (Monar 2012) remain valid. The current refugee crisis has led to an unprecedented depth of politicisation and to a more uncompromising clash between security and other values, which are equally central to the official discourse on the EU's raison d'être, namely fundamental rights and freedom of movement. In 2014, the United Nations Refugee Agency estimated that there were 59.5 million forcibly displaced individuals around the globe, a figure that doubled over the past 15 years (UNHCR 2015). Although the majority of displaced people are currently hosted by Turkey, Pakistan and Lebanon, the number of individuals moving across borders has come to be understood as one of the greatest challenges currently faced by many countries: "We are witnessing a paradigm change, an unchecked slide into an era in which the scale of global forced displacement as well as the response required is now clearly dwarfing anything seen before" (UNHCR 2015: 3).

The European Union and its member states have expressed particular concern at the number of asylum seekers[2] and other migrants[3] crossing, or attempting to cross, the external border of the European Union. Although most illegal immigrants currently residing in the EU arrive through regular means of transport, with tourist visas or forged documents, the political and media attention have essentially focused on irregular undocumented entries (De Bruycker et al. 2013). Their exponential increase in the past few years probably explains such societal interest. According to Frontex, the number of detected irregular crossings almost tripled between 2009 and 2014, from 104,599 to 283,532 (Frontex 2015a). This trend was further accentuated in 2015 with the January–July period amounting to 340,000

[1] Art 4 (2) Treaty of the European Union (TEU).

[2] For the purposes of this chapter, an asylum seeker should be understood as a "person who seeks safety from persecution or serious harm in a country other than his or her own and awaits a decision on the application for refugee status under relevant international and national instruments" (IOM 2011: Glossary).

[3] Although the concept of migrant is a fuzzy one, for which there is no agreed international definition, the present chapter has chosen to understand it as "an individual who has resided in a foreign country for more than 1 year irrespective of the causes, voluntary or involuntary, and the means, regular or irregular, used to migrate" (IOM 2011: Glossary). From this perspective, asylum seekers are a specific type of migrant.

detections (Frontex 2015b). Predominantly originating in the Syrian Arab Republic, Afghanistan, and Eritrea, the large majority of migrants attempt to reach EU territory through three separate routes: the central Mediterranean (from Tunisia and Libya to Italy and Malta, and from Morocco to Spain), the Eastern Mediterranean (from Turkey to Greece), and the Western Balkan route (from Turkey to Hungary via Greece, FYROM and Serbia). The decision to leave their countries of origin has essentially been sparked by conflict, in particular the war in Syria, as well as poverty and human rights' abuse. Such motivations seem to indicate that the large majority of these migrants should be considered asylum seekers and not labour or economic migrants, given their eligibility to obtain the status of refugee (Day 2015; Geneva Convention 1951).

This label, however, remains a contested one, as numerous actors within the EU continue to produce different strategies of avoidance/ resistance to these populations' rights to claim asylum. The most visible case is probably that of the Hungarian government's decision to build a four-meter high fence, which has been accompanied by the enactment of new legislation criminalising irregular entries. Although Hungary has vowed to comply with its international obligations, the new legislation's compatibility with human rights is questionable, given that it does not foresee language translation for those charged with illegal crossing, nor special procedures for children. Other EU member states, such as the United Kingdom (UK), have adopted more subtle strategies, although their result does not differ considerably. Since 2011, the UK has actively taken part in the United Nation's resettlement programme for Syrian refugees, having granted asylum to over 5000 individuals (UK Government 2015). When faced with a larger influx directly at its borders, however, the UK Government declared that it did not intend to offer asylum to individuals already in Europe. Instead, it would continue to identify and transport refugees directly from Syria, although in numbers that hardly correspond to the scale of the challenge.

From the humanitarian perspective—and contrasting with the conventional security narrative outlined above—Europe has been faced with two main problems: the reduction of migrant and asylum seekers' deaths at sea, and the welcoming of and provision for large numbers in concentrated areas/countries of the EU. As the number of migrants attempting to cross the Mediterranean increased, so did the number of lives lost at sea. Depending on the point of departure, migrants' journeys can take between 1 to 4 days, which are usually spent in extremely crowded unseaworthy vessels with little food, water, and hygiene. Migrants not only have to survive difficult maritime conditions, but they also face different forms of abuse from smugglers, rendering their journeys even more dangerous. For the period between January and July 2015 alone, Frontex estimates that 3500 migrants perished at sea (Frontex 2015b). This figure seems to reinforce the general perception that deaths at sea have reached unprecedented levels. The IOM estimates that 40,000 have disappeared at sea since 2000, rendering the Mediterranean the most deadly border in the world (IOM 2014).

As mentioned above, providing for arriving migrants constitutes the second important challenge, one which peripheral member states were not particularly prepared for. Out of the 283,532 illegal crossings detected in 2014, the large majority took place on the central Mediterranean route (170,664 individuals), followed by the Eastern Mediterranean route (50,834 individuals), and the Western Balkan route (43,357 individuals) (Frontex 2015a). The particular intense flow on these three routes has led to large concentrations of migrants in countries such as Greece, Italy, Malta, Spain and Hungary. Local arrangements vary greatly, with some being hosted, or even held, in temporary camps, while others end up on the streets. According to Médecins Sans Frontières, 'in Greece, in particular, the situation is critical, with thousands of people scattered in different islands of the Aegean Sea, without any facilities to receive them" (MSF 2015). The financial situation in which countries like Greece and Spain find themselves in has also limited their capacity to improve their infrastructures aimed at welcoming migrants and adequately providing for them (including accommodation, food, medical assistance, administrative services and conflict—related assistance) (Park 2015).

The problem of developing infrastructures with the necessary conditions to host such great numbers has also now spread to new areas of the EU, as migrants have tended to leave the peripheral countries to reach wealthier ones, such as Germany, France, Sweden and the United Kingdom. The so-called 'Calais jungle' constitutes a representative example of such temporary camps that have mushroomed in different locations throughout the EU. The 'jungle' does not correspond to a specific camp or accommodation, but rather designates a set of different makeshift camps that are inhabited by a mix of asylum seekers and economic migrants. The largest camp gathers 3000 people who live in squalid conditions, which "are absolutely unheard of in Europe, and do not even respect the norms set by the United Nations" (Médecins Sans Frontières quoted in Mulholland 2015). They remain there in the hope to have the opportunity to cross the English Channel. The reasons for this intra- EU movement are not only related to attempts to better their lives by moving to areas where employment might be more abundant and where social benefits might be more generous, but they are also related to EU asylum policy rules. Although the Dublin II Regulation established that an asylum application should be the responsibility of the member state through which the migrant first entered the European Union, only a limited number of asylum seekers apply for asylum in Greece, Italy, Spain and Malta (UNHCR 2015; Fargues and Bonfanti 2014).

Both the degree of danger involved in migrants' journeys, as well as the issue of how to host and integrate migrants have sparked a heated political debate among member states. Regarding the first issue, countries have been faced with the growing inefficiency of search and rescue missions in the Mediterranean. The replacement of the Mar Nostrum operation with the Triton one is particularly illustrative of this point. Italy ran operation Mare Nostrum from October 2013 to October 2014, a humanitarian and surveillance mission aimed at reducing the number of ship wreckage casualties, but which was characterized by limited assets and success (Fargues and Bonfanti 2014). It was also politically unpopular due to the perceived financial burden on a single country (Katsiaficas 2014). The rapid increase in migrant numbers led to the realization that Mare Nostrum was no longer able to offer a systematic surveillance of the Mediterranean. As a result, the European Union proposed, in October 2014, to establish the Triton Joint Operation, a Frontex-led mission operating in the Italian territorial waters, with a larger pool of multi-national assets and shared financial costs (Gower and Smith 2015; Brady 2014). So far, Triton has spawn mixed reactions regarding its objectives and degree of efficiency. Criticised by some, such as the UK Minister of State, Foreign and Commonwealth, for having the potentially perverse effect of encouraging more migrants to cross the Mediterranean (House of Lords 2014), Triton has also been accused of shifting the focus of Mediterranean operations from search and rescue to border surveillance and control (Carrera and Den Hertog 2015). This operation, however, is indicative of a larger trend. Frontex has also expanded a similar surveillance operation, Poseidon Sea, which operates close to the Greek coast (Frontex 2015c). Both operations are under the umbrella of the EU Maritime Security Strategy, which was adopted in June 2014 to help secure the EU's maritime external borders, in an attempt to integrate different border sectors (Carrera and Den Hertog 2015).

Where the welcoming and hosting of migrants is concerned, this is the area where most political disagreements have taken place so far. As mentioned previously, given their role as entry gates, countries such as Greece, Italy, Spain, Malta and Hungary have had a larger share in providing for the migrants than other EU member states. As a result, they have often voiced discontent regarding the lack of solidarity within the Common asylum and Migration policies of the EU (Avramopoulos 2015). The EU countries that have traditionally given refugee status to the largest number of asylum seekers, such as Germany and Sweden, have also voiced their concerns about a lack of burden distribution (Merkel quoted in Fox News 2015). The consequences of such trend have come at a heavy cost, not only in financial terms, but also in human ones. As argued by Schulz, the President of the European Parliament, "the lack of a truly European Asylum and Migration policy is now turning the Mediterranean into a graveyard" (Schultz quoted in European Parliament 2015). Gradually, appeals for a greater balance emerged to deal with "an emergency situation for Europe that requires all EU member states to step in to support the national authorities who are taking on a massive number of migrants at its borders" (Frontex Executive Director Fabrice Leggeri quoted in Frontex 2015b).

In May 2015, the European Agenda on Migration aimed at responding to the migrant crisis with medium and long-term solutions (European Commission 2015b). The document proposed to manage migration flows as a shared responsibility of all member states, by developing an emergency relocation mechanism to alleviate southern European member states, by creating a EU—wide refugee resettlement scheme for 20,000 refugees currently still residing outside of the external border and for 40,000 refugees already living in the EU, and by investing in EUNAVFOR MED, a military operation tackling migrant smuggling. Member state reactions have been mixed or outright negative, with discussions focusing on the mandatory nature of the refugee resettlement scheme and its quotas. Countries such as the United Kingdom, for instance, have refused to take part in the initiative, claiming that it undermines individual countries' efforts to develop efficient asylum policies (Gower and Smith 2015). Others, like Poland and Slovakia, sought to limit the number of potential asylum seekers by accepting only Christian applicants (Wasik and Foy 2015). At the time of writing (October 2015), little progress had been achieved. Despite a controversial majority vote in the Council of Ministers that pushed through a European "burden-sharing" effort for 120,000 migrants (European Commission 2015c)—which would only address a fraction of the overall volume— its implementation remained highly doubtful. Overall, EU leaders' discussions seem to remain focused on keeping migrants from crossing EU borders, rather than managing their distribution and hosting (Traynor 2015).

3 Analytical Concepts

What does this empirical sketch, which is bound to be overtaken by further crises, mean for the more slow-moving process of academic study? We have clearly left the period when the first explanatory puzzle was how can EU cooperation and integration arise in Justice and Home Affairs, given the crucial roles of the 'monopoly of force' and of sovereign control over national borders for modern statehood. As already alluded to above, this debate usually revolved around the contrast between functionalist and critical arguments. To illustrate such discussions, the earlier studies of EU internal security cooperation often adapted classic spill-over arguments (Monar 2001), whereby the creation of a single market and rising personal mobility led to growing transnational security problems. This drove member states to embark on cooperation in matters of police, customs and criminal justice to compensate for the loss of their national border controls. However, this reading of the creation of Schengen, the 'Third Pillar' and the Area of Freedom, Security and Justice (AFSJ) was rejected by critical security and migration studies. They argued that politically distorted, or 'securitised' perceptions on 'organised crime' and 'illegal migration', overlaid and exaggerated the supposed needs for security cooperation (Huysmans 2004). Furthermore, professional or bureaucratic self-interests of security practitioners supported the shift to the transnational level of cooperation, as they sought after technological modernization, additional resources and emancipation from national systems of oversight (Bigo 2000; Guiraudon 2003).

Both these master-narratives on functionalist or critical sociological divers for cooperation remain pertinent—and have become ever more sophisticated with added arguments derived from new institutionalism, public policy analysis (policy entrepreneurship) or postmodern theories (governmentality, etc.). Given its focus on current empirical trends, this edited volume is not the appropriate platform to provide a broad and fair account of this proliferating scientific literature (Bossong and Rhinard forthcoming). Here, we simply argue that a more conscious change of analytical perspective beyond the classic question of political integration, or the creation of overarching systems or fields of control, may be fruitful. In very stylized terms, when faced with the current complexity and level of contestation of the EU's

AFSJ, one may opt for two broad avenues for analysis. One is to continue following the current dynamics in EU policy-making, reaching further into the analysis of cleavages, conflicts and politicisation, as one would do with other "mature" policy fields, where there is less of an assumption of steady deepening and widening. The other avenue for analysis is to foreground the diverse political and bureaucratic practices, patterns of implementation and feedback loops. Thus, one takes a deliberate step back from narratives on the broad sweep of the EU's AFSJ—be it towards an ever more securitised or a rebalanced, constitutionalised regime—and seeks more diverse insights across different aspects and sites. This is not to say that the long-term questions of the "finality" of EU integration have to be put aside as fruitless. Rather, it is to acknowledge that our understanding needs to be increasingly multi-faceted and contextualised, while we can profit from concepts and arguments beyond traditional EU studies.

For instance, analysts from border studies and political sociology have argued in recent years that the official narrative on the erosion of the abolition of borders within Europe has been somewhat illusionary, going beyond the known dialectic of the reinstallation of hard external Schengen borders in exchange for increased internal mobility. Instead, European and other Western states (also) created further virtual or networked borders, which reach both far beyond and deep inside the EU's territory (Delanty 2006; Broeders 2007). These kinds of borders are more permeable to transnational flows of goods, capitals and elites, but are less visible to public scrutiny and may be more effective at excluding disempowered or marginalized groups (Aas 2011). Thus, the rights citizen or third-country nationals to privacy, mobility, residence or refuge may be increasingly overwritten by biometric controls (Ajana 2013), technocratic risk assessments and related decisions by executive agencies (Neal 2009). A cross-cutting erosion of borders could rather be made out between different forms of data that are increasingly gathered for diffuse preventive purposes rather than for the prosecution of committed crimes (Newkirk 2010; Den Boer 2013). However, none of these potential trends can simply be assumed to dominate over the long term. We rather need to treat them as pertinent hypotheses, which need to be substantiated in different contexts.

It is against this background that the contributions to this book approach EU internal security and border management as a diverse and distributed phenomenon, which involves constantly 'shifting borders' and a growing range of actors and technologies. In the remainder of the second section, we turn to the aforementioned organising themes of technology, externalisation and accountability, and outline the individual contributions to this volume.

4 Technology

At least since the revelations by Edward Snowden, problems and risks of technological surveillance have attracted considerable public debate. Yet, in the context of European border controls, it seems to be the case that the role of technology remains underpoliticized (Leese 2014; Verburgt 2012). European citizens occasionally express their unease at the spread of full-body scanners in airports, but remain largely indifferent to more abstract measures, such as on the introduction of a European Passenger Name Record system. In the current migration crisis, there have been salient concerns about the construction of new barbwire fences in Eastern Europe and the Western Balkans. However, more technologically advanced, but less visible, systems, such as the EURODAC database for fingerprinting asylum seekers, usually escape public attention, even if they are at least as effective in obstructing migrants.

This may contribute to explaining why the EU has extended its steady financial and programmatic support for border and internal security technologies. This reflects both in the spending of the European Internal Security fund (or the previous funding lines for Justice and Home Affairs) and the EU Framework Research Programme for security. In contrast to difficult political debates on burden sharing or positive rights standards for migrants, technological research and pilot projects, and subsequent planning for standardisation and systems integration, appear as a productive field for bureaucratic management. Thus, one may detect the ever-extending use of databases for internal security management, which recently led to the creation of an entire EU Agency that should oversee their operation (EU-LISA). There are further ambitions for situational awareness and data fusion, as in the case of EUROSUR, but they also manifest themselves in other lesser known initiatives and networks.[4]

Against this background, Bellanova and Duez argue in this volume that EUROSUR should be analysed as a more complex phenomenon than a technical system, no matter how complicated this system may be. This follows Science and Technology Studies, which regard technological artefacts as intimately connected with, and directly influencing or acting upon, dominant political, social and economic (power) relations and practices. Thus, EUROSUR represents a more profound ambition to integrate a very large variety of actors, instruments and technological components in order to be able to "make sense" of the messy and elusive "reality" of European border management. In other words, it embodies an encompassing dispositive of rationalist control that seeks to transform the contingencies of individual migratory movements in space as well as the uncoordinated resources, actors and institutions of European member states for border control into "sensible" data, manageable figures and reliable indicators for priority actions. Yet Bellanova and Duez also show that this ambition is significantly more costly, challenging or elusive than initially envisaged, which may also be compared to the experiences of the US in creating "smart borders".

In the following chapter, Kuster and Tsianos similarly underline that even a long established and comparatively straightforward technological systems, such as EURODAC, remains poorly understood as a "blackbox". Instead, they trace the deeper impact of this technology on the practices of its users, as well as its targets

[4] See, in particular CISE for maritime surveillance, and other EU-sponsored projects: http://ipsc.jrc.ec.europa.eu/index.php/Projects/318/0/

(i.e., security practitioners and migrants), which took shape long before the current crisis and have challenged the very rationale and sustainability of EURODAC. Again, Science and Technology Studies provide the analytical basis, whereby security technologies construct, or fix, meaning, and transform rather than passively capture data. Thus, via EURODAC migrants can turn into data doubles and statistical artefacts that circulate across borders in a decoupled manner from the physical process of migration, or where the temporal sequencing of border crossing acquires an unprecedented importance. At the same time, Kusters and Tsianos contrast this vision with ethnographic observations from the field, which undercut this abstract logic of manageability due to the more tactical behaviour or resistance strategies of both migrants and security professionals in different countries.

While there are different political perspectives on technological projects for border security—with migration and border studies pointing to the inability to achieve much more than a diversion of migratory flows towards more costly and risky routes (Cornelius 2001)—we should recognise that their impact is not to be taken for granted. As shown by Słomczyńska and Frankowski, the integration of space assets represents a further high-tech dimension of EU internal and border security. However, for the time being, we should not entertain—nor paint dystopian—visions of real-time border surveillance from space. Technical aspects, such as the available picture resolution, the kind of imaging technology and the chosen orbit, often escape the attention of social scientists, but significantly limit the potential use the current generation of EU-sponsored satellites for security purposes, despite long-standing political ambitions in this field. Nevertheless, space-based surveillance generates questions of international law and ownership of data, which should inhibit the desired data fusion or the creation of a "patrolling power Europe".

The final contribution to the first part of this volume, by Lopez-Sala and Godenau, provides an empirical case study on the evolution of border management of Spain, which reflects, as well as embeds, the desire for technological modernisation. On the one hand, they show how technological innovations that are considered at the EU-level (EUROSUR), have been trialled in the Spanish context. On the other hand, Lopez-Sala show how this circulation of technological practices is not a self-explanatory process, but needs to be embedded in wider political trends for the communitarisation, i.e., European harmonisation, of border management as well as for their externalisation into the European neighbourhood. This should sensitise us to the diffuse origins and circulation of practices. In other words, if one seeks to criticize current developments in border management, it is clearly insufficient to focus on one level of governance or a narrow set of policymakers (in Brussels). The case study on Spain also leads to the second part of this volume, which seeks to deepen our understanding of externalisation, as one of the core drivers for change in European border and internal security policy.

5 Externalisation

Building on the increasing overlap between internal and external security, which has already been discussed since the 1990s (Lutterbeck 2005), the EU has widely been seen as a forerunner in the erosion of hard conceptual and territorial boundaries with regard to a wide-range of policies. Thus, it has become an official claim of EU foreign and security policy to pursue a "comprehensive" approach to crisis management (Kaunert and Zwolski 2013), by mobilising different instruments seeking to address security problems at their root, not least since they also spill-over into the EU. However, in the academic literature this ambition for comprehensiveness, and particularly the projection of Justice and Home Affairs concerns onto the EU's neighbourhood (Balzacq 2009), has been criticised. The main two grounds for criticism are, firstly, the erosion of the supposed international normative power of the EU, as its proclaimed universalist mission to spread democracy and human rights is subverted by external domination (Merlingen 2007) and more pragmatic interests in security and stability (Eder 2011; Börzel and van Hüllen 2014). Secondly, the externalisation of internal security measures is seen to aggravate deficits in democratic legitimacy and accountability. Controversial security measures have not only shifted "upwards" from the national to the EU level, where parliamentary and judicial actors have increasingly managed to catch up with security executives, but have also moved further "out" to the European neighbourhood (Lavenex 2006). In third states—many of which are autocracies or severely deficient democracies—there is little political oversight or very weak mechanisms for the protection of human rights. This process remains, however, invisible to European citizens who are not confronted with the unsavoury effects of such "policing at a distance" (Bigo and Guild 2005). Moreover, the EU may try to exert structural power over neighbouring states, to secure unfavourable policies, such as migrant readmission agreements, in return for financial assistance and the prospect of visa facilitation for its citizens (Wolff 2014).

These critiques remain highly pertinent in light of the current refugee crisis, as cooperation on border security and border management with various states in the EU's neighbourhood constitutes daily practice and may be further extended—as evidenced by negotiations with Turkey in October 2015. While this deserves further critical research, this volume emphasises, as explained above, less visible yet significant shifts in European border and internal security policies and practices, which essentially involves the simultaneous transcendence of borders in space.

As shown by Merheim-Eyre, for instance, the important dynamics of the externalised EU's border management cannot be solely explained by the often-critiqued rhetorical securitisation of foreigners and migrants trying to enter the EU. EU citizens themselves have become increasingly cast as reference objects of securitisation, in so far as European cooperation on consular affairs has moved beyond regular administrative assistance and towards the management of major crisis and natural disasters beyond the borders of the EU. As such, civil protection and consular affairs, which are often neglected in standard treatments of EU internal security cooperation, have become a significant component of the EU's external engagement. Furthermore, Merheim-Eyre underlines that the processing of Schengen visas of third country nationals is not only increasingly coordinated by the EU, with regard to security concerns that are clearly differentiated across geographical regions; it also involves a growing range of actors, including private ones, who are tied together in more technocratic and hidden, if nonetheless securitised, assemblages that reach beyond the EU's territory.

Schmid and Yakouchyk similarly seek to nuance or to complement dominant arguments about the externalisation of EU internal and border security policy by analysing the relations between the EU and Belarus. At first sight, this case seems to exemplify the classic critique of the EU willing to give up on its normative commitment in exchange for smooth security cooperation with third countries. However, the authors show that the EU maintains a bifurcated external engagement, with no decrease in sanctions aimed at pressuring the autocratic regime, while it simultaneously extends substantial financial assistance for reforming and professionalising Belarussian border management. While such security cooperation should be understood as limited and has not made a wider positive impact on the Belarussian state at large, it is significant that such contacts can take place in a framework that respects EU governance norms (such as transparency and accountability) and may have supported modernisation and learning among Belarussian border guards. Thus, we should pay more attention to divergent empirical developments, rather than assuming a single overarching logic behind, or effect of, the externalisation of EU internal security concerns.

The contribution by O Neill, by contrast, provides an interdisciplinary insight into other, and mostly unintentional, dynamics of externalisation, of EU internal security law. Adding to the political science literature on external governance, this author illustrates how we need to consider the further legal effects of extra-territoriality, territorial effect and the so-called Brussels effect, which lead to deeper questions on the nature and meaning of legal boundaries in our increasingly interdependent world. These dynamics not only underpin the structure of the EU's external relations across a range of issues wider than border security, but also reflect back on the EU's internal legal order and practice. This concerns, for instance, the establishment of responsible jurisdictions in transnational cases, or the approach towards private actors who are especially relevant in the field of cybersecurity. Overall, this underlines the need for a more complex understanding of the EU's shifting legal borders in internal security affairs, which will also increasingly shape the respective oversight role of the Court of Justice.

Finally, we need to recall that there is no coherent European security model, or policy, that can be projected beyond the EU's territory. This is especially the case when one takes a step back from formal legislation and programmes for financial assistance, and turns to the daily practice of internal security and police cooperation across borders within the EU. Thus, the case of Police and Customs Cooperation Centres (PCCCs) shows the possibilities and limits of experimenting with transboundary internal security cooperation "from the bottom up". These centres are not only considered as an avant-garde for national police services, but have occasionally been thought of as a possible interface for police cooperation with third countries (Council and of the European Union 2008). As shown by Gruszczak, the PCCs have grown and proliferated across the EU, and constitute important nodes for fulfilling various security dimensions of the Schengen acquis. They also represent a European manifestation of the trend towards "fusion centres" in internal security, which marks another erosion of boundaries between different kinds of intelligence and evidence for criminal investigations and police operations. However, existing PCCs have not yet converged towards a common organisational template, and remain divided on different technological data sharing standards, as well as on the extent to which national "ownership" can be transcended in favour of a fully integrated or functionalist approach to intelligence-led policing. Finally, such practical innovations in internal security cooperation, even if still incomplete, raise critical questions about appropriate control and oversight mechanisms. This leads us to the topic of accountability, the last theme of this volume.

6 Accountability

As touched upon above, internal security cooperation across borders, and the construction of the Area of Freedom, Security and Justice, has always been accompanied by strong normative debates on legitimacy (Balzacq and Carrera 2006). From a critical perspective, the EU's role in internal security entrenched a repressive policy bias is due to its limited legal competences and weak oversight mechanisms, which favour negative integration through mutual recognition (Calderoni 2010; Lavenex and Wagner 2007) and generate opportunity structures for executive empowerment.

From a more optimistic perspective, European integration processes in matters of internal security are not only a spillover of, or a necessary compensation for, the eradication of national borders in the Schengen area (Monar 2001). They are also a functional adaptation to the perpetually growing transnational dimension of organized crime and terrorism (Carrapico 2014). Furthermore, one could discern a long-drawn, but eventually significant, expansion of civil rights, political participation or judicial control mechanisms that may solidify the constitutional nature and democratic legitimacy of the European Union (Occhipinti 2014).

How do these topics relate to the heading of accountability? Accountability can be understood as a very broad notion or contemporary 'keyword' (Dubnick 2014), which ranges across multiple social, economic and political fields and organisations. More specifically, however, accountability can be understood as a control on, or requirement for justification by actors, which exercise powers that are cannot be fully defined by law—and thus invite dynamics of "agency slack" (Gailmard 2014)—or are embedded in diffuse and increasingly transnational governance networks (König-Archibugi 2010; Papadopoulos 2010; Héritier and Lehmkuhl 2011). This is especially important in the area of security (Bono 2006), where uncertainty about risks and appropriate measures to counter and prevent them, often reflects in wide institutional mandates—or provides the basis for secrecy (Rozell 1994; Curtin 2014). These considerations are already reflected in a burgeoning literature on the accountability of EU agencies (Buess 2015; Scholten 2014) and particularly the accountability of agencies in the field of internal and border security (Carrera et al. 2013), such as Europol (Busuioc and Groenleer 2013) and Frontex (Pollack and Slominski 2009).

Yet again, we need also ask further questions about neglected dimensions or processes that shape the accountability of EU internal security cooperation. Firstly, alongside the European Parliament—whose formal powers remain based on limited popular legitimacy and democratic credentials—the role of national parliaments in scrutinising the AFSJ deserves our attention. While the Lisbon Treaty generally strengthened the position of national parliaments, it provided for specific scrutiny powers in the field of internal security,[5] which reflect the normative and symbolic sensitivity of this policy field. Thus, one could expect new efforts to ensure the democratic accountability of policy-making, which could be compared to research on national parliaments' scrutiny of the EU's foreign and security policy (Wouters and Raube 2012; Huff 2015).

Therefore, the chapter by Tacea in this volume, which reviews the role of the French and Italian parliaments in the last reform of the Schengen regime, addresses a significant research gap. Similar to the European Parliament, whose shift from a "champion" of liberal civil rights to a more "pragmatic" stance on internal security has been documented (Ripoll Servent 2015), Tacea shows that the conduct of national scrutiny procedures relies on procedural as well as political constellations, rather on an inherent normative orientation or confrontational stance of parliaments towards executives. In particular, the importance of parliamentary committees for scrutiny of European issues is a mixed blessing. Committee rapporteurs may exhibit more issue-specific expertise, whereas committee procedures tend to lead to consensual decision-making or a relative suppression of dissent with the governing majority. Furthermore, standard assumptions about the importance of party-political orientations, namely of left-right cleavages on matters of "law and order", largely hold true with regard to EU issues (rather than being overridden by pro/anti-EU or parliamentary/executive cleavages). On the basis of Tacea's analysis, one could argue that the biggest potential for more democratic scrutiny of EU border and internal security lies in more plenary debates between left-wing and right-wing parties, or a classic "politicisation" that seem to develop pace in other areas of integration (Miklin 2014). The current refugee crisis should provide further ample material and render it necessity to continue exploring this ambivalent role of national parliaments, particularly if it may lead to deeper changes to the established regime of EU asylum, border management and freedom of movement.

At the same time, we should not forget about the accountability of bureaucratic actors and their routine operations that constitute the daily practice of EU border and internal security. Beyond crises or major political reforms in EU border policies, migrants are mainly concerned with how they are treated once they are inside the EU, and what regular control measures are brought to bear on them by

[5] Art 69 TFEU.

different member states. This is most clearly the case when they have been ordered to return to their country of origin or to a third state. Thus, Koch analyses how bureaucratic actors at national levels, in close conjunction with international actors and the EU, have increasingly regularised forced return operations, while formally respecting human rights standards that would traditionally have been understood as conventional restraints on such actions. This development is more complex than standard critiques of EU border and internal security policy, which revolve around the assumption of executive empowerment and neglect of migrants' rights. It also runs counter to more optimistic arguments that international law and institutions increasingly serve as "liberal constraints" on populist and repressive migration policies. In light of the current clash between the European Commission, which defends the value of freedom of movements and seeks to move member states towards a more solidarity-driven system of accepting and distributing asylum-seekers, this liberal restraint seems plausible. Yet, at least in the case of forced returns, international organisations have, formally, increased normative standards, while simultaneously supporting the "effectiveness" of such operations to justify their existence to national member states. This requires us to think about what alternative standards the authorities in charge of migration and border security should be held accountable to, if it cannot be only the formal respect for international or European law.

The answer cannot only consist in further and more demanding abstract rights for migrants, not least as many administrative actions can only be uncovered from a more embedded practice perspective. However, we can also benefit from a greater appreciation for varying, conflicting and contradictory practices when returning to the wider level of European policy-making. The ideal of accountable policy-making—if understood as a varied process between account givers and receivers (Bovens 2010)—may thus be critically linked to such a practice-based perspective on justification. In the last contribution to this volume, Jeandesboz provides a theoretically rich account of such a shift, which accentuates the inconsistencies as well as routinized nature of exchanges and 'sense-making' in the area of European border and migration policies. Policy decisions are not determined by abstract judgements on what is right, effective or legitimate, nor are entirely disregarded by hypocritical security professionals. Rather, they emerge via diverse and often incoherent practices of justification that are provided by different political and bureaucratic actors. These justifications, which are expressed in countless debates or technical reports, reflect what is considered easily justifiable, but also reveal high uncertainty und conflict. Jeandesboz illustrates this approach with reference to proceedings at the European parliament that reviewed EU border and migration policy on a wider scale and to an internal meeting with the European Commission on smart borders (which brings us back to the departure point of this edited volume). In sum, we should be more sensitive to the "labour of justification", which may occasionally expand the room for contestation and accountability beyond bureaucratic actors, but can also be directed towards normalising and de-politicising shifting practices of border control.

Thinking further, one may compare such a sociology of justification with wider arguments about the legitimacy of the EU. Neyer argued that core values of the EU, such as democracy, may be reconceptualised around the "right to justification" (Neyer 2012), which might serve as a more open-ended, but no less demanding, standard of normative evaluation. This is because the act of justification reveals our concrete commitment to universal values, or shows our respect to the affected parties that deserve a justification, or reasoned account on, why a certain course of action is taken and appropriate. In the current political climate, it remains to be seen whether such progressive norms of justification or rather reflexes to exclude and unreflexively defend the given (national or European) political order will prevail, especially towards migrants as subjects of EU internal security and border policy.

References

Aas, K. F. (2011). Crimmigrant'bodies and bona fide travelers: Surveillance, citizenship and global governance. *Theoretical Criminology, 15*(3), 331–346.

Ajana, B. (2013). Asylum, identity management and biometric control. *Journal of Refugee Studies, 26*(4), 576–595.

Amnesty International. (2015). *The global refugee crisis—A conspiracy of neglect*. London: Amnesty International.

Avramopoulos, D. (2015, August 14). A European response to migration: Showing solidarity and sharing. European Commission speech. Accessed August 24, 2015, from http://europa.eu/rapid/press-release_SPEECH-15-5498_en.htm

Balzacq, T. (2009). *The external dimension of EU justice and home affairs: Governance, neighbours, security*. Basingstoke England: Palgrave Macmillan.

Balzacq, T., & Carrera, S. (2006). *Security versus freedom—A challenge for Europe's future*. London: Ashgate Publishing.

Bigo, D. (2000). New officers in the European security field. In J. Sheptycki (Ed.), *Issues in transnational policing* (pp. 67–99). London: Routledge.

Bigo, D. (2014). The (in) securitization practices of the three universes of EU border control: Military/Navy–border guards/police–database analysts. *Security Dialogue, 45*(3), 209–225.

Bigo, D., & Guild, E. (2005). La logique du visa Schengen: Police à distance. *Cultures and Conflits, 14*.

Bigo, D., et al. (2015). *The EU counter-terrorism policy responses to the attacks in Paris: Towards an EU security and liberty agenda*. Brussels: CEPS liberty and security in Europe. 81/February.

Bono, G. (2006). Challenges of democratic oversight of EU security policies. *European Security, 15*(4), 431–449.

Börzel, T. A., & Van Hüllen, V. (2014). One voice, one message, but conflicting goals: Cohesiveness and consistency in the European Neighbourhood Policy. *Journal of European Public Policy, 21*(7), 1033–1049.

Bossong, R., & Rhinard, M. (Eds.) (forthcoming). *Theorising EU internal security cooperation*. Oxford: Oxford University Press.

Bovens, M. (2010). Two concepts of accountability: Accountability as a virtue and as a mechanism. *West European Politics, 33*(5), 946–967.

Brady, H. (2014). *Mare Europeum? Tackling mediterranean migration*. Paris: European Union Institute for Security Studies.

Broeders, D. (2007). The new digital borders of Europe EU databases and the surveillance of irregular migrants. *International Sociology, 22*(1), 71–92.

Buess, M. (2015). European Union agencies and their management boards: An assessment of accountability and demoi-cratic legitimacy. *Journal of European Public Policy, 22*(1), 94–111.

Bundesregierung, die Deutsche (2015, August 16). Refugee policy: Finding common answers. *Merkel ZDF interview*. Accessed October 20, 2015, from http://www.bundesregierung.de/Content/EN/Artikel/2015/08_en/2015-08-16-merkel-interview-zdf_en.html?nn = 392660

Busuioc, M., & Groenleer, M. (2013). Beyond design: The evolution of Europol and Eurojust. *Perspectives on European Politics and Society, 14*(3), 285–304.

Calderoni, F. (2010). *Organised Crime Legislation in the European Union: Harmonization and approximation of criminal law, national legislation and the EU framework decision on the fight against organised crime*. Berlin, Heidelberg: Springer.

Carrapico, H. (2014). Analysing the European Union's responses to organized crime through the different lenses of securitization theory. *European Security, 23*(4), 601–617.

Carrera, S., & Den Hertog, L. (2015). Whose mare? Rule of law challenges in the field of European border surveillance in the mediterranean. *CEPS Paper in Liberty and Security in Europe* 79/January.

Carrera, S., et al. (2013). The peculiar nature of EU Home Affairs agencies in migration control: Beyond accountability versus autonomy? *European Journal of Migration and Law, 15*(4), 337–358.

Cornelius, W. A. (2001). Death at the border: Efficacy and unintended consequences of US immigration control policy. *Population and Development Review, 27*(4), 661–685.

Côté-Boucher, K., et al. (2014). Border security as practice: An agenda for research. *Security Dialogue, 45*(3), 195–208.

Council of the European Union. (2008). *European best practice guidelines for police and customs cooperation centres* (Document 13815/08).

Cremona, M., Monar, J., & Poli, S. (2011). *The external dimension of the European union's area of freedom, security and justice*. Brussels: Peter Lang.

Curtin, D. (2014). Overseeing secrets in the EU: A democratic perspective. *JCMS: Journal of Common Market Studies, 52*(3), 684–700.

Day, K. (2015, July 27). These are refugees, not migrants, arriving in their thousands on Greek Shores. *The Guardian*. Accessed August 22, 2015, from http://www.theguardian.com/global-development/2015/jul/27/refugees-not-migrants-arriving-thousands-greece-shores

De Bruycker, P., Di Bartolomeo, A., & Fargues, P. (2013). Migrants smuggled by sea to the EU: Facts, laws and policy options. *MPC Research Report* 2013/09. San Domenico di Fiesole: Migration Policy Centre–European University Institute.

Delanty, G. (2006). Borders in a changing Europe: Dynamics of openness and closure. *Comparative European Politics, 4*(2–3), 183–202.

Den Boer, M. (2013). How to police a porous fortress? *Journal of Police Studies/Cahiers Politiestudies, 1*(1), 2–20.

Dubnick, M. (2014). Accountability as cultural keyword. In M. Bovens, R. E. Goodin, & T. Schillemans (Eds.), *The Oxford handbook of public accountability* (pp. 23–38). Oxford: Oxford University Press.

Eder, F. (2011). The European Union's counter-terrorism policy towards the Maghreb: Trapped between democratisation, economic interests and the fear of destabilisation. *European Security, 20*(3), 431–451.

Eriksen, E. O. (2011). Governance between expertise and democracy: The case of European security. *Journal of European Public Policy, 18*(8), 1169–1189.

Eur-Lex. (2014). *EU internal security strategy*—EUR-Lex. Accessed October 20, 2015, from http://eur-lex.europa.eu/legal-content/EN/ALL/?uri= URISERV:jl0050

European Commission. (2015a, April 28). *Communication from the Commission to the European Parliament, the Council, the European Economic and Social Committee and the Committee of the Regions—The European Agenda on Security*. COM (2015) 185 final.

European Commission. (2015b, May 13). *Communication from the Commission to the European Parliament, the Council, the European Economic and Social Committee and the Committee of the Regions—A European Agenda on Migration*. COM (2015) 240 final.
European Commission. (2015c). *Refugee crisis—Q&A on emergency relocation*. Accessed October 20, 2015, from http://europa.eu/rapid/press-release_MEMO-15-5698_en.htm
European Parliament. (2015, April 23). *Schulz: Lack of European migration policy is turning Mediterranean into a graveyard*. Press releases. REF 20150423STO45411. Accessed August 24, 2015 from http://www.europarl.europa.eu/news/en/news-room/content/20150423STO45411/html/Schulz-"Lack-of-European-migration-policy-turning-Mediterranean-into-graveyard
Fargues, P., & Bonfanti, S. (2014). *When the best option is a leaky boat: Why migrants risk their lives crossing the Mediterranean and what Europe is doing about it*. San Domenico di Fiesole: Migration Policy Centre-European University Institute.
Fox News. (2015, June 18). *Merkel presses EU partners to share burden of hosting refugees, says all have responsibility*. Accessed August 24, 2015, from http://www.foxnews.com/world/2015/06/18/merkel-presses-eu-partners-to-share-burden-hosting-refugees-says-all-have/
Frontex. (2015a). *Risk analysis 2015* (N° 4613/ 2015). Warsaw.
Frontex. (2015b, August 18). *Number of migrants in one month above 100 000 for first time*. Accessed August 21, 2015, from http://frontex.europa.eu/news/number-of-migrants-in-one-month-above-100-000-for-first-time-I9MlIo
Frontex. (2015c, June 26). *Frontex expands its joint operation Triton. News*. Accessed August 24, 2015, from http://frontex.europa.eu/news/frontex-expands-its-joint-operation-triton-udpbHP
Gailmard, S. (2014). Accountability and principal-agent models. In M. Bovens, R. E. Goodin, & T. Schillemans (Eds.), *The Oxford handbook of public accountability* (pp. 90–105). Oxford: Oxford University Press.
Gower, M., & Smith, B. (2015, July 9). *Mediterranean boat people*. Briefing Paper House of Commons, CBP 7210.
Guiraudon, V. (2003). The constitution of a European immigration policy domain: A political sociology approach. *Journal of European Public Policy, 10*(2), 263–282.
Héritier, A., & Lehmkuhl, D. (2011). New modes of governance and democratic accountability. *Government and Opposition, 46*(1), 126–144.
House of Lords. (2014). *Written answer to question by Lord Hylton*. HL 1977. Accessed August 24, 2015, from http://www.publications.parliament.uk/pa/ld201415/ldhansrd/text/141015w0001.htm
Huff, A. (2015). Executive privilege reaffirmed? Parliamentary scrutiny of the CFSP and CSDP. *West European Politics, 38*(2), 396–415.
Huysmans, J. (2004). A Foucaultian view on spill-over: Freedom and security in the EU. *Journal of International Relations and Development, 7*(3), 294–318.
IOM. (2011). *Glossary on migration* (International migration law series, Vol. 25). Geneva: IOM.
IOM. (2014). *Fatal journeys—Tracking lives lost during migration*. Geneva: International Organization for Migration.
Katsiaficas, C. (2014). *Search and rescue operations in the mediterranean—The role of Frontex Plus* (EU Migration Policy Working Paper, 13). Bridging Europe.
Kaunert, C. (2005). The area of freedom, security and justice: The construction of a "European public order". *European Security, 14*(4), 459–83.
Kaunert, C., & Zwolski, K. (2013). *The EU as a global security actor—A comprehensive analysis beyond CFSP and JHA*. Basingstoke: Palgrave Macmillan.
König-Archibugi, M. (2010). Accountability in transnational relations: How distinctive is it? *West European Politics, 33*(5), 1142–1164.
Lavenex, S. (2006). Shifting up and out: The foreign policy of European immigration control. *West European Politics, 29*(2), 329–350.
Lavenex, S., & Wagner, W. (2007). Which European public order? Sources of imbalance in the European area of freedom, security and justice. *European Security, 16*(3–4), 225–243.

Leese, M. (2014). The new profiling: Algorithms, black boxes, and the failure of anti-discriminatory safeguards in the European Union. *Security Dialogue, 45*(5), 494–511.

Lowenthal, A. F., & Bertucci, M. E. (2014). *Scholars, policymakers, and international affairs: Finding common cause*. Baltimore: JHU Press.

Lutterbeck, D. (2005). Blurring the dividing line: The convergence of internal and external security in Western Europe. *European Security, 14*(2), 231–253.

Merlingen, M. (2007). Everything is dangerous: A critique of 'normative power Europe'. *Security Dialogue, 38*(4), 435–453.

Miklin, E. (2014). From 'Sleeping Giant' to left–right politicization? National Party Competition on the EU and the Euro Crisis. *JCMS: Journal of Common Market Studies, 52*(6), 1199–1206.

Monar, J. (2001). The dynamics of justice and home affairs: Laboratories, driving factors and costs. *Journal of Common Market Studies, 39*(4), 747–764.

Monar, J. (2012). Die Gewährleistung innerer Sicherheit durch die Europäische Union: Grundlagen, Möglichkeiten und Grenzen. In T. C. G. Würtenberger & H.-J. Lange (Eds.), *Innere Sicherheit im europäischen Vergleich* (pp. 33–56). Münster: LIT Verlag.

MSF. (2015, August 19). *Mediterranean migration*. Accessed August 22, 2015, from http://www.msf.org/topics/mediterranean-migration

Mulholland, R. (2015, July 5). Calais crisis: Bicycle repair shops, mosques anda n orthodox church—the town where migrants wait to cross to Britain. *The Telegraph*. Accessed August 24, 2015, from http://www.telegraph.co.uk/news/worldnews/europe/france/11718598/Calais-crisis-Bicycle-repair-shops-mosques-and-an-Orthodox-church-the-town-where-migrants-wait-to-cross-to-Britain.html

Neal, A. W. (2009). Securitization and risk at the EU border: The origins of FRONTEX. *JCMS: Journal of Common Market Studies, 47*(2), 333–356.

Newkirk, A. B. (2010). The rise of the fusion-intelligence complex: A critique of political surveillance after 9/11. *Surveillance & Society, 8*(1), 43–60.

Neyer, J. (2012). *The justification of Europe: A political theory of supranational integration*. Oxford: Oxford University Press.

Occhipinti, J. D. (2014). Whither the withering democratic deficit? The impact of the Lisbon treaty on the area of freedom, security and justice. *Cambridge Review of International Affairs, 27*(1), 83–105.

Papadopoulos, Y. (2010). Accountability and multi-level governance: More accountability, less democracy? *West European Politics, 33*(5), 1030–1049.

Park, J. (2015, April 23). Europe's migration crisis. Council on foreign relations. Accessed August 23, 2015 from http://www.cfr.org/migration/europes-migration-crisis/p32874

Pollack, J., & Slominski, P. (2009). Experimentalist but not accountable governance? The role of Frontex in managing the EU's External Borders. *West European Politics, 32*(5), 904–924.

Ripoll Servent, A. (2015). *Institutional and policy change in the European parliament: Deciding on freedom, security and justice*. Basingstoke: Palgrave.

Rozell, M. J. (1994). *Executive privilege: The dilemma of secrecy and democratic accountability*. Baltimore: JHU Press.

Rumford, C. (2012). Towards a multiperspectival study of borders. *Geopolitics, 17*(4), 887–902.

Scholten, M. (2014). *The political accountability of EU and US independent regulatory agencies*. Leiden: Martinus Nijhoff Publishers.

Traynor, I. (2015, June 25). European leaders scrap plans for migrant quota system. *The Guardian*. Accessed August 24, 2015, from http://www.theguardian.com/uk-news/2015/jun/25/european-leaders-kill-off-plans-for-migrant-quota-system

UK Government. (2015, October 8). *Syria refugees. UK Government Response*. Accessed October 21, 2015, from https://www.gov.uk/government/news/syria-refugees-uk-government-response

UNHCR. (2015). Global trends 2014—World at war. Geneva.

United Nations. (1951). *Geneva convention*. Geneva.

Verburgt, L. (2012). A plea for technological activism at the European borders. *Science as Culture, 21*(3), 409–414.

Waever, O. (1993). *Securitization and desecuritization*. Copenhagen: Centre for Peace and Conflict Research.

Wasik, Z., & Foy, H. (2015, August 21). 'Poland favours christian refugees from Syria'. *Financial Times*. Accessed August 24, 2015, from http://www.ft.com/cms/s/0/6edfdd30-472a-11e5-b3b2-1672f710807b.html#axzz3jYXuEH3V

Wolff, S. (2014). The politics of negotiating EU readmission agreements: Insights from Morocco and Turkey. *European Journal of Migration and Law, 16*(1), 69–95.

Wouters, J., & Raube, K. (2012). Seeking CSDP accountability through interparliamentary scrutiny. *The International Spectator, 47*(4), 149–163.

The Making (Sense) of EUROSUR: How to Control the Sea Borders?

Rocco Bellanova and Denis Duez

1 Introduction

> Space is a doubt: I have constantly to mark it, to designate it. It's never mine, never given to me, I have to conquer it. (Perec 1997[1974]: 91)

The Mediterranean Sea is considered a symbolic and material site of major political issues concerning, inter alia: migration, human rights, foreign policy and European internal and external cooperation. The debates triggered by specific, and often tragic, events are mirrored by European Union (EU) and national operations that generally tackle this political space as if it were a border to be (more) efficiently patrolled. Hence, the Mediterranean Sea becomes, at the same time, a political and a controlled space, at least from a European perspective.

In this chapter, we aim at advancing an analysis of the *making (sense) of* the Mediterranean Sea as space deemed, by EU and Member States authorities, to be controlled. We focus on the set up of a specific EU project: the European Border Surveillance System, widely known as EUROSUR. EUROSUR is an information-exchange framework that aims to improve the management of Europe's external borders. It is designed to become the centrepiece of Frontex's surveillance and intervention capabilities. The stated purpose of the system is:

> the surveillance of land and sea external borders, including the monitoring, detection, identification, tracking, prevention and interception of unauthorized border crossings for

R. Bellanova (✉)
Peace Research Institute Oslo (PRIO), Hausmanns gate 3, Oslo 0186, Norway

Université Saint-Louis - Bruxelles, Brussels, Belgium
e-mail: rocco@prio.no

D. Duez
Institute for European Studies of the Université Saint-Louis - Bruxelles, Boulevard du Jardin botanique, 43, 1000 Bruxelles, Belgium
e-mail: denis.duez@usaintlouis.be

R. Bossong, H. Carrapico (eds.), *EU Borders and Shifting Internal Security*,
DOI 10.1007/978-3-319-17560-7_2

> the purpose of detecting, preventing and combating illegal immigration and cross-border crime and contributing to ensuring the protection and saving the lives of migrants. (EU OJ 2013: Art. 2(1))

While the geographical goal of this high-tech system goes well beyond the Mediterranean Sea, this space has been its initial main focus and a particularly important referent during its creation. Officially, EUROSUR has been launched immediately after the adoption of the related regulation, in December 2013 (EU OJ 2013), and it is progressively including Member States and Schengen countries (Frontex 2014b; Rijpma and Vermeulen 2015). To date, very little is publicly known about its operative status, and it is hard to say what its everyday role in the fabrication and management of a controlled space is. Yet, we can already study the different steps that brought it into being, at least as a legislatively backed program. We can understand how EUROSUR contributes to constitute the Mediterranean Sea as a space of control—what we call the "making of". Relying on few elements of information provided by Frontex, such as brief descriptions of operational trials (i.e., Frontex 2015b), we can also carry out an analysis of its operations: we can understand how EUROSUR may offer the tool-box to better understand the same controlled space—what we propose to call the 'making sense of'. Hence, even if from a limited perspective, we believe that this case study permits to provide a better account of a *methodology* of control.

We argue that the making of the sea borders operated by EUROSUR is, first and foremost, an effort to make sense of a disparate and heterogeneous ensemble of elements. This controlled space does not only concentrate on and encompass potential migrants, small vessels of smugglers, and international networks of criminals. This kind of border surveillance is also, at the same time, and somehow prominently, an effort to understand and maximize the potential use of different elements—radars, national authorities, boats, information analysis systems, etc.—already deployed for border surveillance. Hence, the set up of a surveillance system is both a matter of material and symbolic controls, and a continuous effort of *mise-en-discours* of protean elements. It is an attempted and continuous mustering of things, people, information, institutions, programs, and research. Therefore, the construction of a controlled space emerges as a dynamic, non-linear practice: not a mere site of surveillance and prohibition, but rather the set up and the articulation of enacting processes. In other words, a controlled space is a sort of productive ambition, in which all elements, both the controlled and the controlling ones, have to *make sense*, have to be rendered intelligible in order to contribute to the understanding of others. From this perspective, what is at stake in the relation between a controlled and a political space is not only the closure of the latter, but also the potential influence that the methodology of the former may have on the definition of the political issues.

In the next sections of this chapter, we first contextualize our research in relation to existing scientific literature and we present our specific research approach. Then, we briefly introduce the EUROSUR project in its EU institutional background, and we critically focus on the ways in which political goals are supposed to be achieved.

Afterward, we describe and discuss its methodology of control through the description of two sets of programmed operations. We finally present and analyze the technical and political debates concerning the feasibility of the project and, in the conclusions, we further elaborate on the *makings* of EUROSUR and the potential influence of its control methodology in the shaping of the Mediterranean Sea as a political space.

2 Borders, Technologies, and Methods

The case of EUROSUR offers the opportunity to explore the on-going re-definition of a traditional space of control: the border. Indeed, a certain consensus in both the academia and the policy-making field is growing around the idea that borders have not disappeared within globalization, but rather have undergone important transformations (Brown 2010; European Council 2010; Foucher 2007; Walters 2006). This renewed interest in borders tends to emphasize the different processes of de-bordering and re-bordering rather than their fixed, univocal forms (Newman 2006; Wilson and Donnan 2012). In particular, European and North American project on biometrics databases, automated document and identity controls, or passengers' risk-assessment have attracted the attention of researchers of critical security studies, surveillance studies, law and critical geography. Yet, while the EUROSUR project has been the object of several political debates at institutional level, and despite the fact it is supposed to become the backbone of Frontex's operations at sea, only few academic publications have engaged frontally with it (Duez and Bellanova 2014; Gabrielsen Jumbert 2012; Jeandesboz 2011; Rijpma and Vermeulen 2015).

So far, the most important transformations highlighted by scholars revolve around the borders' technological density and its effects on their spatial and temporal dimensions, their modes of operation, their referent objects and the actors concerned (i.e., Amoore 2006; Bigo and Guild 2005b). Still, in many of these accounts, technologies are taken as a 'given', a linear and powerful implementation of a will to govern and control individuals and societies. Moreover, the making sense under scrutiny is generally limited to the one operated on individuals, and not on 'things' (Aas 2011; Epstein 2007). Also, little attention is dedicated to the very articulation of the controlling elements, and their difficult implementation well beyond failures and errors (Bigo 2014; Leese and Koenigseder 2015).

To better account for the multiple efforts of making sense of different elements—humans and nonhumans—our methodology takes inspiration from Foucauldian works and from insights offered by the sociology of the translation—more widely known as actor-network-theory (ANT). We operationalize our analysis on the premises of two loose and related ANT notions: *setting* and *actant*. The first postulates that:

> [a] machine can no more be studied than a human, because what the analyst is faced with are assemblies of human and nonhuman actants where the competences and performances

> are distributed; the object of analysis is called a setting or a setup (Akrich and Latour 1992: 259).

This definition does not curtail in advance the type and quantity of elements at stake. It also obliges us to consider both linguistic and material aspects, without, by default, privileging the former over the latter. As explicitly mentioned, all elements should be considered actants, agents participating to the action even if not automatically endorsed with intentionality. Indeed, "*any thing* that does modify a state of affairs by making a difference is an actor–or, if it has no figuration yet, an actant [. . .] [t]his, of course, does not mean that these participants 'determine' the action [. . .] things might authorize, allow, afford, encourage, permit, suggest, influence, block, render possible, forbid, and so on" (Latour 2005: 71–72, emphasis in original).

The notions of setting and actant provide the tools to translate the Foucauldian emphasis on situated processes of power deployment (Foucault 1980(1976): 92–108) into an analytical description of the emergence of a program of government. In particular, through these two ANT notions we aim to engage anew with "programs, technologies, apparatuses", which both "inform individual behavior [and] act as grids for the perception and evaluation of things" (Foucault, 2003: 253–54). In this sense, we further build on the notion of *dispositifs*: these are not to be considered only as research objects which are "thoroughly heterogeneous ensemble[s]" (Foucault 1980(1977): 194), but also as methods, developed by researchers and actors alike. The main merit of the notion of setting is that it translates the attention to heterogeneity into a more practical research agenda, while the notion of actant highlights the different roles that very different elements come to play through the dispositifs. However, we still need Foucault's dispositifs to appreciate the *epistemic* dimension running through the "assemblies of human and nonhuman actants" (Akrich and Latour 1992: 259), and thus to cast a light on the double functioning of a program of control as both an apparatus and a methodology.

At the current stage of our research on EUROSUR, our approach translates into a focus on (publicly available) primary sources and documentation—impact assessments, studies, legislative proposals, road maps, reports, interviews—as well as into a stronger attention towards the description of the foreseen functioning of 'mundane' operations—information exchanges, creation of situational pictures, etc. We read, or better: de-scribe, these sources to retrace how a space of control is programmed through the tentative construction of a setting. Obviously, it should be acknowledged that proposing a new method is out of the scope of this contribution. We are all too conscious that this study represents only one of the steps needed to better grasp the role of both humans and nonhumans in border practices. Only a research that includes direct observation of the ways in which EUROSUR operations are routinely performed would permit to test, adjust and strengthen our own research *dispositif*. Furthermore, the recourse to Foucault's works in this research field is certainly not a novelty (cf. Bigo 2006; Lyon 2007; Walters 2006). Besides, several scholars have already taken inspiration from ANT literature to advance their own accounts of the role of technologies and materialities (cf. Barry 2001; Dijstembloem and Broeders 2014; Schouten 2014). Nevertheless, we believe that few elements from ANT and a return to the multiple functions of dispositifs can further enrich many Foucauldian approaches concerned with technologies and surveillance, especially for what concerns the exploration of the tension between political and controlled landscapes.

3 The EUROSUR Project

On 13 February 2008, the European Commission tabled what has been called, in the Community jargon, a 'Border Package'. This package consisted of three communications relating to integrated management of European external borders. This package was understood as an important step in a process that had already begun 7 years earlier, at the Laeken European Council in December 2001. Following the 11 September 2001 terrorist attacks, European governments and heads of state had made a solemn declaration that "[b]etter management of the Union's external border controls will help in the fight against terrorism, illegal immigration networks and the traffic in human beings" (European Council 2001: point 42). Border control was thus set very high in the political priorities of the Union.

In the Border Package, EUROSUR was granted its own communication entitled "Examining the creation of a European Border Surveillance System (EUROSUR)" (European Commission 2008c).[1] The aim of the communication was "to examine the parameters within which a European Border Surveillance System (EUROSUR), focusing initially on the southern and eastern external borders of the EU, could be developed and to suggest to Member States a roadmap for the setting up of such a system" (European Commission 2008c: 2). The immediate background of this new program was to be found in the allegedly successful implementation of the Spanish SIVE (*Sistema Integrado de Vigilencia Exterior*) along the coast of Andalusia and later in the Canary Islands. Gradually implemented by the Spanish government by means of fixed and mobile radars and sensors, the system was said, according to Spain's *Guardia Civil*, to have put an end to illegal border crossings in the Gibraltar Straight (Espinosas Navas 2003). Even if exaggerate—nearly 8000 irregular migrants were detected off the Spanish coast in 2014 (Frontex 2015a: 16)—such a claim seems to have been confirmed by subsequent evolutions in migratory routes. Within few years most of irregular border crossings shift from the Western African and Western Mediterranean routes to the Central Mediterranean route, and, eventually, the Eastern Mediterranean and Western Balkan routes.

At the end of 2011, the European Commission released a proposal for a regulation "establishing" EUROSUR (European Commission 2011c; Rijpma and Vermeulen 2015: 461–64)[2]. In the words of one of the Commission officials

[1] Hereinafter: 2008 EUROSUR Communication, or: road-map.

[2] Hereinafter: draft regulation, or: 2011 draft regulation.

responsible for this project, the 2011 draft regulation "is the result of [dozens of meetings, studies or external contractors, official documents], summarising 1500 pages of technical specifications in 21 articles" (PERSEUS Newsletter 2012: 5). Therefore, even if the draft regulation does not imply, per se, the finalization of the EUROSUR project at practical level, its text and the annexed impact assessment documents, permit an exploration of certain dynamics and solutions advanced so far. Our analysis mainly focuses on the EUROSUR draft regulation, as well as the text of the regulation finally adopted by the European Parliament on the 9th October 2013 (EU OJ 2013)[3], only 1 week after the death of hundreds migrants after a boat carrying them to Europe sank off the southern Italian island of Lampedusa.

To an even greater extent than the development of other European technological tools for border checks, such as the entry/exit system (EES), the Registered Travellers Programme (RTP) or the Electronic System for Travel Authorisation (ESTA)[4], the development of EUROSUR is revealing with regard to the trend towards the increasing role played by technology in border control at EU level. Based upon the principle of interconnecting already existing monitoring systems in the various Member States, the goal of EUROSUR is to eventually provide a shared technical environment enabling the rationalization of cooperation and communication between the relevant national authorities. The main aim of this sort of "system of systems" (European Commission 2008c: 9) is to facilitate the use of advanced technology in border monitoring.

Politically speaking, EUROSUR is a response to three different but interconnected goals (European Commission 2008c: 3–4). Firstly, EUROSUR aims to reduce the number of 'illegal' immigrants who enter the European Union undetected. The system should provide authorities responsible for border control in the Member States with more timely and reliable information. This timely information would allow them to detect, identify and intercept those attempting to enter the EU 'illegally'. Secondly, EUROSUR is supposed to increase the internal security of the EU as a whole by contributing to the prevention of cross-border crime. Consistently with the 2001 Laeken Declaration and Frontex's missions, border surveillance has not only the purpose to prevent unauthorized border crossings, but also to counter cross-border crime such as the prevention of terrorism, trafficking in human beings, drug smuggling, illicit arms trafficking, etc. Finally, in the context of increasing illegal crossings on board of unseaworthy and overcrowded boats triggered by the Arab Springs and the war in Syria, and resulting in thousands of migrants drowning in the Mediterranean Sea (Last and Spijkerboer 2014), EUROSUR is designed to reduce the number of deaths of illegal immigrants by saving more lives at sea. The capacity to detect boats in the sea is seen as

[3] Hereinafter: EUROSUR regulation, or: regulation.

[4] Parts of the Integrated Border Management strategy (IBM), the registered travellers programme (RTP) and the Electronic System for Travel Autorisation (ESTA) aim to facilitate border crossings for frequent, pre-vetted and pre-screened third country travellers. The entry/exit system (EES) should enable electronic registration of information on dates and places of entry of non-EU Member Country nationals and of the dates notified for exit from the Schengen area.

contributing to greater chances of search and rescue and thereby saving more lives (European Commission 2013a). Though, this humanitarian objective is much more frequently put forward by the Commission than by the Member States (European Commission 2013a, b, 2015), and can be considered at best "just one of the secondary aims of EUROSUR" (Rijpma and Vermeulen 2015: 467). For instance, not a single word of the statement following the Special meeting of the European Council of 23 April 2015 which aim was to prevent further loss of life at sea was dedicated to the third dimension of EUROSUR (European Council 2015). Two months later, the European Council of 25 and 26 June 2015 adopted the new European Agenda on Migration tabled by the Commission, which briefly mentions EUROSUR as a promising system for "[i]dentifying risk trends" (European Commission 2015: 11).

4 *Situational Awareness* and *Reaction Capability* at the External Borders of the EU

To achieve the said goals, the 2008 EUROSUR communication states that

> [a] European Border Surveillance System—EUROSUR—should support the Member States in reaching full *situational awareness* on the situation at their external borders and increase the *reaction capability* of their law enforcement authorities (European Commission 2008c:4 emphasis in original).

The terms *situational awareness* and *reaction capability* are conceptualized by the same Commission document as metrics. The former "measures how the authorities are capable of detecting cross-border movements and finding reasoned grounds for control measures" while the latter "measures the lapse of time required to reach any cross-border movement to be controlled and also the time and the means to react adequately to unusual circumstances" (European Commission 2008c: 4). Thus, it is interesting to note how the very general concept of EUROSUR translates de facto political goals—migration flows control, internal security and humanitarian intervention—into measurable performances which would in turn orientate the actions of socio-technical assemblages. Indeed, such a framework of control should be set up without affecting the respective areas of jurisdiction of Member States nor harmonizing or replacing any existing systems. As mentioned above, a key operational objective should be to interlink different systems, not creating a new one, while paying attention to geographical circumstances and differences between types of borders, in particular between land and maritime borders (European Commission 2008b: 4).

Interestingly, not only the space dimensions are of particular concern for the Commission, but rather the possibility to "maintain control over" them despite their challenging "nature". The temporal dimension becomes the other key element, which allows for the measurement of situational awareness and the time lapse for intervention, but also for the "quality" and relevance of the intervention, that mostly requires "near to real-time" decision making. The ability to manage both spatial and temporal dimensions is what enables forms of "control at a distance" (Bigo and Guild 2005a), but in the EUROSUR project what is particularly interesting is that such control at a distance is clearly understood in its complexity, as the fruit of multiple mediations among and actions of different heterogeneous elements. For example, the communication takes into account the lack of a unique point of decision-making which means to design the overall architecture as to include the time needed to co-ordinate it (without establishing any central database); it also identifies the possibilities and constraints of specific nonhuman elements to modify the relations between space and time in specific conditions (what are generally called "surveillance tools"); and implicitly takes into account the different meaning that the same information can acquire in different centers of decision. Such an awareness of the non-linearity and complexity of EUROSUR objectives and ambitions is made clear in the translation of the "general policy objectives" into "specific and operational policy objectives" in the text of the 2008 EUROSUR Impact Assessment (European Commission 2008a: 17–18), as well as in the specific design of the proposed setting. Indeed, one of the main features of EUROSUR is that it is presented as a project to be implemented in three different phases:

> [i] [u]pgrading and extending national border surveillance systems and interlinking national infrastructures in a communication network; [ii] [t]argeting research and development to improve the performance of surveillance tools and sensors [. . .], and developing a common application of surveillance tools [. . .]; [iii] [a]ll relevant data from national surveillance, new surveillance tools, European and international reporting systems and intelligence sources should be gathered, analysed and disseminated in a structured manner, to create a common information sharing environment between the relevant national authorities (European Commission 2008c: 5).

Furthermore, these three phases, the first two of which should be implemented in parallel, are composed of eight specific and different "steps", which range from the provision of border surveillance infrastructure at Member States' level to "research and development to improve the performance of surveillance tools", or to the establishment of an "integrated network of reporting and surveillance systems for the whole EU maritime domain" (European Commission 2008c: 5–10 and 12).

Somehow, EUROSUR can also be understood as a series of technical fixes to shortcut juridical or administrative efforts of harmonization/substitution, thus reducing the emergence of political issues in its own implementation. EUROSUR, then, would reflect a trend that has been noted by various authors (Brouwer 2008; Jeandesboz 2011), namely the tendency to seek agreement over initiatives that are deemed 'technical' in the face of persistent struggles in domains considered by Member States' governments as sovereign matters.

While this analysis provides a powerful account of the strategic role regarding the *making of* EUROSUR, it tends to overlook the (actual or future) presence of many more acting elements, as well as their operations. Thus, it keeps the participation in politics mostly limited to classical human institutions and risks losing sight of other possible sites of politics. A first possible list of EUROSUR relevant actants, or components as they are labeled in the words of the Commission, is provided in the first chapter of the 2011 draft regulation (European Commission 2011c: 9–12—Art. 4–7). They are both nonhuman and human elements, and, when we take into consideration also the rest of the Commission documentation (e.g., the 2008 and 2011 impact assessments: European Commission 2008a, 2011b), we can establish an even wider and more composite ensemble of actants, including, *inter alia*, platform for information exchange and 24/7 communication systems; satellites and satellites' high resolution data; unmanned aerial vehicles; mobile and fixed sensors; vessels and boats; private companies, national and European experts' groups; different national authorities, including National Coordination Centers (NCCs); research institutes; third countries; migrants and migrants' smugglers; commercial crews; reports; studies; risk-analysis.

To an important degree, both the effective *making of* EUROSUR and its ability of *making sense of* what is happening at the external borders are based on the relations established between this heterogeneous group of actors. The critical question thus concerns less the ability to merely un-veil institutional struggles in the policy-making, than the ability to understand the articulations proposed and their consequences on the overture and closure of the political space.

5 Two Programmed Sets of Operations

Situational awareness and reaction capability are translated, and enacted in the text of the 2011 draft regulation by two sets of operations. This can be considered the core of the program inscribed into the EUROSUR dispositif. As the analytical description below highlights, the term *program* should be understood both as a plan to follow, and as a software processing information.

For what concerns situational awareness, the relevant set concerns the production of *situational pictures*. Three types of pictures are foreseen: the National Situational Picture, the European Situational Picture and the Common Pre-Frontier Intelligence Picture (European Commission 2011c: 12–17—Art. 9–11). The structure of the three pictures is similar: each is organized in three main layers—events, operational, and analysis layers—further composed by sub-layers. Information is pooled there from sources as different as: "national border surveillance systems"; "stationary and mobile sensors operated by national authorities"; "patrols on border surveillance and other monitoring missions"; FRONTEX; "regional networks"; "ship monitoring system"; "European and international organisations" (European Commission 2011c: 12–17—Art. 9–11). The information includes elements as different as: "key developments and indicators relevant for the analysis of irregular migration and cross-border crime", "risk rating trends", "migrant profiles, routes, information on the impact levels attributed", "information with regard to natural and man-made disasters", "own assets" deployed in border areas; "geo-referenced data"; etc. (European Commission 2011c: 12–17—Art. 9–11). Apart from this feeding coming from the 'outside', there are also exchanges among the three types of pictures, and between different national pictures. It is important to note that not all potentially available

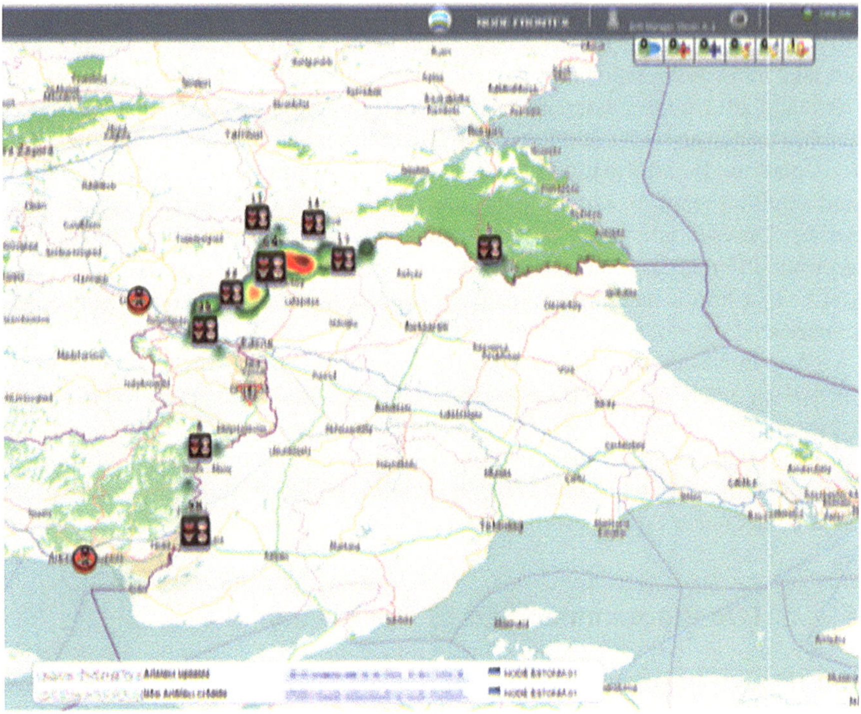

Fig. 1 The so-called "Eurosur user interface" as presented in Frontex (2014a)

information is simultaneously exchanged to all competent authorities or NCCs. Only the information which is either relevant for geographical proximity, or which reaches a specific level of alert is circulated. In this sense, the pooling of information is a real process of mediation, as the information is often partially processed before dissemination.

No formal explanation is provided in the text of the 2013 EUROSUR regulation on how this information, and the multiple pictures, will be effectively projected on the screens of the NCCs' control rooms. According to an off-the-record interview with Commission officials,[5] information will be screened on a map of Europe, in which symbols will signal the different elements, and the operators will be able to access and filter the associated information. According to the same interview, situational pictures are not, per se, a novelty in the surveillance practice of national authorities, as they are already created and screened in their centers. Hence, the specificity of EUROSUR is to streamline the way in which information is pooled, distributed and represented, and to enrich and tune its feeding. This description

[5] Off-the-record interview with DG-Home officials held on the 10th May 2012, in Brussels.

seems to be largely confirmed by the few photos provided by Frontex (cf. Fig. 1 below).

Both the continuous construction and the screening of situational pictures are a powerful example of the different declinations of *making sense of*. Not only do they contribute to making sense of still-to-be fully determined elements, but they also render different strands of information intelligible by evaluating their relevance and impact and by distributing them in a targeted way. Furthermore, when they pool data from different sources, whose primary goal is not to monitor the so-called irregular immigration or cross-border routes, the making sense of the situational pictures is, de facto, a re-enactment of these elements (as in the case of ship reporting systems). In other words, the ensemble formed by Frontex analysts, software and methodologies of risk assessment, are applying a new rationale to elements that were developed within a different discourse.

The second set of operations aims at better achieving reaction capability, and it implies three consecutive and intertwined ways of shaping the border. The first concerns consists in the splitting of the external border of each Member State into "border sections" (European Commission 2011c:18—Art. 13). This re-drawing is a sort of *quadrillage*, as it is coupled with the creation or identification of a "local or regional coordination centre ensuring the effective and efficient management of personnel and resources" (European Commission 2011c: 18—Art. 13). In line with the metrics approach of EUROSUR, the second action foresees the "attribution of impact levels" to each border section (European Commission 2011c: 18—Art. 14). This evaluation is risk assessment driven, and carried out by FRONTEX; the relevant Member States are consulted and their NCCs are expected to "regularly assess whether there is a need to adjust the impact level (. . .) [and] may invite [FRONTEX] to change the impact level by providing substantiated information on the altered conditions at the external border section concerned" (European Commission 2011c: 19—Art. 14(2)). Impact levels—low, medium or high—explicitly relate to irregular migration and cross-border crime, and are mostly calibrated on the impact of these "incidents" on border security (European Commission 2011c: 18–19—Art. 14(1)). The third action focuses on the quality and scale of the reaction to be foreseen for each border section. It creates a sort of protocol for both surveillance activities (such as patrolling) and coordination among different agencies, at national and European levels. Hence, the purpose is to tailor measures and target efforts where the impact level is higher, implicitly assuming that both resources and willingness to share information are scarce, and should be engaged according to priorities.

This second set of operations is another interesting example of making sense, not only as production of knowledge, but as channeling and tuning of controls. The purported idea is to maintain the action responsive to swift changes, and avoid the dispersion of a 'flat' or static approach. In the words of the head of unit of the Frontex Situation Centre, the goal is "to provide the right information to the right place and to the right person, at the right time, in the right format" (Frontex 2014a: 40). It is the Frontex Situation Centre that "manages data streams" for EUROSUR, enriches them with further information and "keep[s] the member states informed"

Fig. 2 Photo of the Frontex Situation Centre made publicly available on the Frontex website under the heading "Eurosur": http://frontex.europa.eu/photo/eurosur-LD3NF7

(Frontex 2014a: 43, cf. also Fig. 2 below). More importantly, through these operations, these makings of sense, the borders are represented and enacted as un-linear and dynamic spaces, which can only be tamed through differentiation and prioritization.

6 (Digital) Borders Surveillance: a *Mise-en-Discours* of Individuals, Things and Spaces

According to the Schengen Borders Code, border controls consist of: (i) *border checks* and (ii) *border surveillance* (European Parliament and Council 2010(2006)). Border checks encompass the checks carried out at border crossing points, to ensure that persons, including their means of transport and the objects in their possession, may be authorized to enter the territory of the Member States or authorized to leave it. Border surveillance refers to the surveillance of borders between border crossing points and the surveillance of border crossing points outside the fixed opening hours, in order to prevent persons from circumventing border checks (European Parliament and Council 2010(2006): Art. 2). As stated in the Commission communication, EUROSUR "focuses on enhancing border surveillance" (European Commission 2008c: 2).

In the design of EUROSUR, border surveillance is a set of practices in which space maintains a primary role. As said above, the physical features of specific spaces still seem to count. For example, concerning maritime surveillance, it is acknowledged that "[s]urveillance of the maritime areas is not surveillance of movement across a line (as in the case of land borders), but across an area which has its inner boundary at the coast" (European Commission 2008a: 22). However, this space is not empty: "[a]wareness in the maritime domain therefore requires monitoring the compliance of all activities, detecting with the help of surveillance and ship reporting systems anomalies that may signal illegal acts and generating intelligence that enables law enforcement authorities to stop unlawful entry into the EU area" (European Commission 2008a: 13).

Therefore, the government of the (maritime) space is not a mere territorialized government, but one that is able to make sense of a (scarcely) populated space, of the individuals and the things animating it. In this sense, the different operations described in the section above are crucial: the fragmentation of a single space into both meaningful and manageable sections; the population of these new spaces via the enrollment of elements that were exogenous to the surveillance practices or via the introduction of new ones; the connection of different elements to make them speak, and to prioritize some among many; the calibration of the use of limited resources; the representation of information within dynamic situational pictures.

In a sense, this ambition is one of *mise-en-discours*, and is somehow similar to that of other settings proposed at EU level, such as the EU wide project for the collection and processing of Passenger Name Records for security purposes (Bellanova and Duez 2012). This *mise-en-discours* is at the same time an incitation to discourse, to let things reveal and speak and a continuous *mise-en-relation*, connection of different elements. These related operations are often translated in institutional jargon as risk-analysis, or framed as government through risk management in academia (Aradau and Van Munster 2007; Muller 2010).

What is also particularly interesting in the EUROSUR system is that risk analysis is defined and tailored in a partially different way, as its main focus concerns explicitly both human and non-human elements in a given space rather than only individuals' behavior. Actually, single individuals are not the most relevant elements of the methodology of control. Even if they are formally and ultimately the main 'target' of surveillance, they do not 'feed' the system as such. Individuals become a source of information and a site of operation for EUROSUR only when they are in a group and when they are subsumed in specific objects (e.g., boats). In both cases, what is relevant is not their single behavior or their individual and personal characteristics, but only their statistic features and the discrepancy between the behavior of a given object and its supposedly 'normal' route. For example, in the 2008 Commission communication risk analysis is understood as recognition of patterns, analysis of trends, detection of migration routes and prediction of risks, detection of anomalies and is linked to the idea of pre-frontier intelligence picture (European Commission 2008c: 8).

7 Sweet Dreams or Reality? Technical and Political Feasibility

Beyond the analytical de-scription of its programmed operations, it is now important to explore the question of the very feasibility of EUROSUR. Analytically, the issue of the feasibility encompasses two different sets of questions: the technical ones and the political ones. Even if these two dimensions are deeply intertwined, we stick to this basic opposition in the remainder of the study. Nevertheless, we consider as granted that the distinction between what is a political and what is a technical question is often blurred. A careful analysis usually shows that technicalities are not politics-free, and that politics encompass important technical dimensions. Indeed, as we already mentioned, formally labeling a question as 'technical' is often a subterfuge of the political; an attempt to depoliticize sensitive matters (Brouwer 2008; Jeandesboz 2011). Still, even when we accept as starting point the institutional repartition of technical and political, the analysis has to face heterogeneous ensembles, which persistently defy the official repartition.

Regarding the technical feasibility, the Presidency Conclusions of the European Council meeting of the 15th–16th December 2005 (European Council, 2005) called on FRONTEX to launch two feasibility studies. The aim of the first report, called MEDSEA, was to study the reinforcement of the monitoring and surveillance of the southern maritime border of the EU, more concretely in the Mediterranean Sea, and the possibility of creating a Mediterranean Coastal Patrols Network involving EU Member States and North African countries.[6] The main conclusion of the study delivered on July 2006 was a call for setting up a two-level structure for the regular exchange of information. The first level would consist in the (already mentioned) National Coordination Centres (NCC) in each Mediterranean Member State that would be connected to a FRONTEX network to ensure the cooperation and coordination of activity at the maritime borders and areas. The second level would be based on the interconnection of each NCC with two Operational Entities (in each Operational Area "OA") at national level. The operational working concept would depend on the cooperation between them, both at national level and also between Member States. NCCs would therefore ensure the communication between the two levels.

The second feasibility study, complementary to the previous one, was called BORTEC.[7] The aim of the BORTEC study was to explore the technical feasibility of establishing a surveillance system covering the whole southern maritime border of the EU and the Mediterranean Sea. The study made an overview of the existing technologies in use, the different areas of coverage and their technical solution, and the needs and wishes for further developments. It offers definition and overview of

[6] A summary of the MEDSEA Study is available in Annex 7 of the Impact Assessment document accompanying the EUROSUR Communication (European Commission 2008a: 78–84).

[7] As for MEDSEA, a summary of the BORTEC Study is available in Annex 8 of the Impact Assessment (European Commission 2008a: 85–89).

the technical management system for different technologies and their possible compatibility. It also provides an overview of the areas which are not covered by any systems today and which systems are covering the neighboring areas. Similarly to the MEDSEA study, the BORTEC study was prepared by a team of experts from Member States and from FRONTEX. Additionally, the European Joint Research Centre (JRC) in Ispra (Italy) contributed to the Core Team with one expert. The Core Team was also assisted by a Support Group of 14 Member States, the European Commission, European Defence Agency (EDA), European Maritime Safety Agency (EMSA), European Space Agency (ESA) and European Union Satellite Centre (EUSC) (Arias Fernandez 2006: 130; European Commission 2008a: 78). The study was completed in 2006 and tabled in January 2007.

Most of the elements presented in MEDSEA and BORTEC have been included in the 2008 EUROSUR communication and the 2011 draft regulation, including the technologies to be used and the institutional structures (cf. also: Jeandesboz 2008:7). Backing these guidelines, the Justice and Home Affairs Council encourages the Commission to launch a new study concerning the key components of the EUROSUR concept, and to analyze the possibilities of using surveillance tools and satellites on reliable basis, financial consequences for the introduction of such a system and an assessment to the border surveillance infrastructure in selected third countries on the basis of an evaluation to be carried out by FRONTEX. Consequently, the Commission signed in December 2008 a contract with a private contractor for the technical study on developing concepts for border surveillance infrastructure, a secure communication network and a pre-frontier intelligence picture (European Commission 2011a: 3). Funded under the External Borders Fund, the study was carried out by the software and system company ESG, with the help of subcontractors such as EADS, SELEX and Thales. SECUNET and the University of the German Federal Army enacted as consultants (European Commission 2011a: 5, note 10).

While EUROSUR is mainly a project carried on by the Commission, in close cooperation with Member States and FRONTEX, we can see that industry and research also play an important role in developing, testing and implementing the system. We have not yet explored these aspects of the makings of EUROSUR, what we can already note that it is particularly interesting of the EUROSUR project is the acknowledged role of industry and research, which are designed to actively contribute to the production and design of the setting. The participation of private actors (industry) is not a novelty, but one of the most common features of the set up of digital borders (both as providers of technologies and information, and enactors of surveillance and control). However, their role is often left on the margin of debates, as 'incidental' actors rather than main characters. Apart from this invisibility of the private actors, it is worth to note that the EUROSUR project explicitly foresees a key role for EU-founded research projects, which formally become an important actor of the setting (European Commission 2009: 7).

The next step after the tabling of the 2011 draft regulation was to complete the legislative process through its adoption and make EUROSUR operational by 2013. EUROSUR effectively went live on December 2, 2013, and is since on trial. The system enables the NCCs to exchange—within a common sharing environment—relevant information with other communities with interests in the EU maritime domain, such as transport, fisheries, customs and defense (European Commission 2011a: 11). In the first phase of implementation, 19 Schengen countries having external land or sea borders adopted the system (Rijpma and Vermeulen 2015).

If the Commission seems quite confident about the technical feasibility of the project, what about it's political feasibility? Regarding this second dimension, the American experience can be seen as a worrying precedent for the European strategy. As mentioned before, the argument for the implementation of EUROSUR as put forward in Europe shares certain theses developed across the Atlantic, in particular by the former Democrat Governor of Arizona and current Secretary of State for Homeland Security Janet Napolitano. Her well-known formula "[s]how me a 50–foot wall and I'll show you a 51–foot ladder" was meant to give support to an alternative "virtual border" to the actual "physical" fencing of the United States/Mexico border. For Napolitano

> [b]oots on the ground definitely help, but we can shore up our border gaps with ground-based sensors, radar, and unmanned aerial vehicles for wide-area intrusive-detection. Any combination of the above will work far better than any 10 or 20 or 50 miles of wall (Napolitano 2007).

At the time, this sort of 'faith' in the potential of new technology ignored its exorbitant cost as well as its relative efficiency. According to an evaluation report by the US Department of Homeland Security, the American project for a *SBInet* virtual border developed by Boeing (Greenhouse 2011) cost almost a billion dollars for equipping a mere 53 miles of border. It was eventually abandoned in January 2011, the DHS considering that "the SBI*net* program, as originally proposed, does not meet current standards for viability and cost-effectiveness" (US Department of Homeland Security 2011).

Coming back to the European context, border control and surveillance has also turned into a costlier-than expected venture for the EU budget (Jeandesboz 2008: 13). Whilst the initial budget of FRONTEX amounted to 19.2 million Euros in 2006, the figure had risen to 94 millions by 2013 (Frontex 2014a: 30). Nevertheless, that budget still looks like a drop in the sea compared to the American SBI*net* program. Regarding EUROSUR as such, all Member States concerned have programmed relevant measures under the External Borders Fund (EBF) and the "Cash-Flow and Schengen Facility" in line with Priority 2 of the strategic guidelines (European Commission 2009: 3). These guidelines foresee Community funding up to 75 % for investments in establishing a single NCC and in establishing or upgrading a single national surveillance system. Here, much more money seems to be available, given that 1.820 million have been allocated the EBF over the period 2007–2013.

Nevertheless it is not self-evident that Member States will accept to dedicate, in the long-term, big budgets to border surveillance, especially in a context of severe financial crisis and economical downturn. For instance, the 9 million euros/month Operation Mare Nostrum (OMN), established by the Italian Government between

October 2013 and October 2014, was considered to strain the resources of its navy and coast guard, even if it permit Italy to save 150,000 migrants, mainly from Africa and the Middle East. The Italian operation was eventually replaced by Frontex Joint Operation Triton on November 1st 2014, with a monthly budget of only 2.9 million euros/month. It was only under the pressure of fast repeating tragedies at sea that the initial Triton's budget has eventually been tripled to reach the same budget that the Italian operation. The proposal includes tripling Triton's monthly budget to some 9 million euros/month so that it can lease extra military vessels and other assets pledged by member states.

In a sense, the preparatory work of the Commission on the financial consequences of EUROSUR, the long pages on costs sharing, projections of investment, policy option building and evaluation, all these multiple impact assessments could be understood as a way to reduce the political risk of the enterprise, to reassure 'classical political actors' and reduce their point of entry into the question. Similarly, the rejection of a "one size fits all" program that would be implemented by a unique private contractor, following the model of the American SBI*net*, reveals a sensitivity to cost-effectiveness. Conversely, the choice of a system of systems that integrate already existing sectoral systems, which are reporting and monitoring traffic and activities in sea areas under the jurisdiction of the Member States and in adjacent high seas into a broader network aims to reduce the overall cost of EUROSUR and avoiding useless duplications.

Beside financial considerations, relations with neighboring countries are another source of difficulties in implementing EUROSUR. As stated in the 2008 Impact Assessment, a major factor for the success of EUROSUR will be the active involvement of neighboring third countries (European Commission 2008a: 28). Moreover, the Commission acknowledges that the migration pressure presents considerable challenges not only for the Member States on the northern border, but also for the third countries located on the southern shores of the Mediterranean Sea in terms of detection, apprehension, reception and further processing and readmission of migrants. It is therefore necessary to include these areas into surveillance activities and to support and to cooperate with the countries of origin and the countries of embarkation of illegal immigrants. The development of conflict situation in Syria and Libya in the wake of 2011 Arab Springs, the emergence of new conflict areas, such as Iraq or the Horn of Africa, not only further increase war-related migration through the Eastern and Central Mediterranean routes, but also make impossible any cooperation with transit countries.

8 Conclusions

Besides being a politically important project, EUROSUR shows also interesting specificities. The most evident one is often captured and synthesized in its frequent dubbing as *system of systems*. Indeed, the ambitions are so high, the range of action so wide, and the constitutive elements so disparate that the definition of *system of the systems* surely renders the setting up of a vast, protean and complex system.

However, it is important to note that such complexity, and the many foreseeable difficulties in its implementation are mostly acknowledged in the text, to a point in which such awareness seems to influence the very design, and presentation, of the setting. This is evident in its declination as a sort of "road-map" in the 2008 EUROSUR communication. A road-map to be implemented in different steps, which should permit a both incremental and differential deployment before definitive completion. Compared to other EU proposed settings which were presented as linear implementation of new technologies to specific challenges and issues, this "road-map philosophy" appears more reflexive, and somehow pre-emptive of socio-technical controversies latent in all settings (cf. the tortuous and yet incomplete implementation of most of the other EU projects in the field, and in particular the implementation of the SIS2). In this sense, as discussed in the section above, the role of studies, experts, EU funded projects is particular important to increase the ability to muster "things" together, to effectively advance in the *making of* EUROSUR.

At the same time, speaking of a system of the systems should not obfuscate the influence of the new setting on previously existing ones. The relations established by and via EUROSUR are not a strictly vertical hierarchy with EUROSUR or FRONTEX on the top. The operations mediated by and via EUROSUR deploy a different geometry: the *platform* distributes existing information, or collects and elaborates new ones, and quickly forwards the most relevant ones to connected systems in targeted way; the *quadrillage* of the space dynamically convoys and re-directs resources and cooperation efforts. As discussed above, all these actions are possible only through the articulation and mustering of multiple and heterogeneous elements, and, to a large extend, through the introduction of new elements or the re-calibration of existing ones (surveillance devices, situational pictures interfacing information, a new spatialization of the border sections). In this sense, EUROSUR is not just an addendum or technical fix, but it is a continuous effort of *mise-en-discourse*.

Indeed, *prima facie* the role of EU-flagged actors (including the nonhuman ones) seems ancillary to Member States' governments and agencies: a sort of mere technological platform limiting its role to the establishment of connections, provision of technological tools and little else. Probably, in this sense, it can also be understood as focusing on border surveillance rather than on border checks, which apparently keeps EU actions outside Member States' borders both in spatial and temporal terms. However, the different sets of operations envisaged by EUROSUR transform the previous settings and become an (implicit) obligatory passage point. Within this new panorama, specific EU agencies, such as FRONTEX, but also those who are in charge of granting research funds, acquire an important role in the *making of* specific digital borders.

On the backdrop of these analyses, we submit that EUROSUR works as a proper *dispositif*. It does not only assemble heterogeneous elements, but it establishes a methodology to both construct and make sense of a controlled space. It attempts to bring order and to mobilize something that is perceived as messy, and too prone to generate political controversy. Through its main operations, as well as through its very development, it attempts to split a political space in two more manageable imbroglios. On the one hand: the chaotic institutional panorama of European and national agencies and border control policies; on the other hand: the challenges rising from geography and human mobility. This partition is proposed and at the same time solved through a double operation of *making sense of* what is outside or external—the migrants, the flows of smugglers, etc.—and of what is (to be) used to make this outside intelligeable—the radars, the patrolling boats, the national authorities and so on.

All in all, our analysis of the EUROSUR project does foster an understanding of a controlled space very similar to the one pictured by Perec in the quote at the beginning of this chapter. It does push this description further beyond the words of Perec: it is not only "space [that] is a doubt", but also the elements that are used for its "mark[ing]" and "conqu[est]" that are not given per se, but have continuously to be assembled and mustered together (Perec 1997(1974): 91). Two final notes for further research can be then proposed. First, even a controlled space emerges in its inherent fragility, a fragility that should be further investigated not merely in terms of efficiency and failure, but in search of the possible openings for politics. Yet, even if the controlled space remains fragile and does not foreclose the political, its methodological character may achieve a more subtle, but still far-reaching, impact on the kind of political questions that can be advanced.

Acknowledgements The authors would like to thank Helena Farrand Carrapico and Raphael Bossong for their precious comments and suggestions. An earlier version of some sections of this chapter has been published in French as: Duez and Bellanova (2014). The authors acknowledge the support of the following research projects: Actions de recherche concertées (ARC)—"Why Regulate? Regulation, De-Regulation and Legitimacy of the EU"; and NordSTEVA—"Nordic Centre for Security Technologies and Societal Values".

References

Aas, K. (2011). 'Crimmigrant' bodies and bona fide travelers: Surveillance, citizenship and global governance. *Theoretical Criminology, 15*(3), 331–346.

Akrich, M., & Latour, B. (1992). A summary of a convenient vocabulary for semiotics of human and nonhuman assemblies. In W. E. Bijker & J. Law (Eds.), *Shaping technology/building society. Studies in sociotechnical change* (pp. 259–264). Cambridge, MA: The MIT Press.

Amoore, L. (2006). Biometrics borders: Governing mobilities in the war on terror. *Political Geography, 25*(3), 336–351.

Aradau, C., & Van Munster, R. (2007). Governing terrorism through risk: Taking precautions, (Un)knowing the future. *European Journal of International Relations, 13*(1), 89–115.

Arias Fernandez, G. (2006). Frontex. The European agency for the management of operational cooperation at the external borders of the member states of the European union. In *5th International Seminar on Security and Defence in the Mediterranean. The migration flows: An opportunity for cooperation in the Mediterranean* (pp. 125–31). Barcelona: CIDOB.

Barry, A. (2001). *Political machines: Governing a technological society*. London/New York: Athlone Press.

Bellanova, R., & Duez, D. (2012). A different view on the 'making' of European security: The EU passenger name record system as a socio-technical assemblage. *European Foreign Affairs Review, 17*(Special Issue), 109–124.
Bigo, D. (2006). Security, exception, ban and surveillance. In D. Lyon (Ed.), *Theorizing surveillance. The panopticon and beyond* (pp. 46–68). Devon: Willian Publishing.
Bigo, D. (2014). The (in)Securitization practices of Thre Three Universes of EU border control: Military/Navy—Border Guards/Police—Database analysts. *Security Dialogue, 45*(3), 209–225.
Bigo, D., & Guild, E. (2005a). Policing at a distance: Schengen visa policies. In D. Bigo & E. Guild (Eds.), *Controllin frontiers: Free movement into and within Europe* (pp. 233–263). Aldershot: Ashgate.
Bigo, D., & Guild, E. (Eds.). (2005b). *Controlling frontiers. Free movement into and within Europe*. Aldershot: Ashgate.
Brouwer, E. (2008). *Digital borders and real rights: Effective remedies for third-country nationals in the schengen information system* (Immigration and asylum law and policy in Europe). Leiden: Martinus Nijhoff Publishers.
Brown, W. (2010). *Walled states, waning sovereignty*. New York: Zone.
Dijstembloem, H., & Broeders, D. (2014). Border surveillance, mobility management and the shaping of non-publics in Europe. *European Journal of Social Theory, 18*(1), 21–38.
Duez, D., & Bellanova, R. (2014). Humains et non-humains dans la fabrique des frontières de l'Europe : une approche in medias res de l'européanisation. In D. Duez, O. Paye, & C. Verdure (Eds.), *L'européanisation à la croisée des disciplines et de nouveaux enjeux* (pp. 223–252). Bruxelles: Bruylant.
Epstein, C. (2007). Guilty bodies, productive bodies, destructive bodies: Crossing the biometric borders. *International Political Sociology, 1*(2), 149–164.
Espinosas Navas, F. (2003). Le Système intégré de surveillance maritime. *La Revue Maritime, 465*, 5.
EU OJ. (2013). *Regulation (EU) No 1052/2013 of the European Parliament and of the Council of 22 October 2013 Establishing the European Border Surveillance System (Eurosur)* (pp. 11–26). Luxembourg: Official Journal of the European Union.
European Commission. (2008a). Commission staff working document. Accompanying Document to the Communication from the Commission to the European Parliament, the Council, the European Economic and Social Committee and the Committee of the Regions. Examining the Creation of a European Border Surveillance System (Eurosur). Impact Assessment. Brussels: European Commission.
European Commission. (2008b). Commission staff working document. Accompanying Document to the Communication from the Commission to the European Parliament, the Council, the European Economic and Social Committee and the Committee of the Regions. Examining the Creation of a European Border Surveillance System (Eurosur). Summary of the Impact Assessment. Brussels: European Commission.
European Commission. (2008c). Communication from the Commission to the European Parliament, the Council, the European Economic and Social Committee and the Committee of the Regions. Examining the Creation of a European Border Surveillance System (Eurosur). Brussels: European Commission.
European Commission. (2009). Commission Staff Working Paper. Report on Progress Made in Developing the European Border Surveillance System (Eurosur). Brussels: European Commission.
European Commission. (2011a). Commission staff working paper. Determining the Technical and Operational Framework of the European Border Surveillance System (Eurosur) and the Actions to be taken for its Establishment. Brussels: European Commission.
European Commission. (2011b). Commission staff working paper. Impact Assessment Accompanying the Proposal for a Regulation of the European Parliament and of the Council

Establishing the European Border Surveillance System (Eurosur). SEC. 2011. 1536 Final. Brussels: European Commission.
European Commission. (2011c). Proposal for a Regulation of the European Parliament and of the Council Establishing the European Border Surveillance System (Eurosur). COM. 2011. 873 Final. Brussels: European Commission.
European Commission. (2013a). Cecilia Malmström Welcomes the European Parliament's Vote on Eurosur. Brussels: European Commission.
European Commission. (2013b). Eurosur: New tools to save migrants' lives at sea and fight cross-border crime. Brussels: European Commission.
European Commission. (2015). A European agenda on migration. Communication from the Commission to the European Parliament, the Council, the European Economic and Social Committee and the Committee of the Regions. Brussels: European Commission.
European Council. (2001, December 14–15). Presidency conclusions. Laeken.
European Council. (2005, December 15–16). Global approach to migration; priority actions focusing on africa and the mediterranean. Annex I to the Presidency Conclusions of the European Council. Brussels.
European Council. (2010). Internal security strategy for the European Union. Towards a European security model. Brussels.
European Council. (2015, April 23). Special Meeting of the European Council, Statement. Brussels.
European Parliament and Council. (2010). Regulation (Ec) No 5622006 of the European Parliament and of the Council on 15 March 2006 Establishing a Community Code on the Rules Governing the Movement of Persons Acress Borders (Schengen Borders Code) [2010 Consolidated Version].
Foucault, M. (1980[1976]). Two lectures. In C. Gordon (Ed.), *Power/Knowledge: Selected interviews and other writings 1972–1977* (pp. 78–108). New York: Pantheon Books.
Foucault, M. (1980[1977]). The confession of the flesh. In C. Gordon (Ed.), *Power/Knowledge: Selected interviews and other writings 1972–1977* (pp. 194–228). New York: Pantheon Books.
Foucault, M. (2003). Questions of methods. In P. Rabinow & N. Rose (Eds.), *The essential Foucault. Selections from essential works of Foucault, 1954–1984*(pp. 246–258). New York: New Press.
Foucher, M. (2007). *L'obsession des frontières*. Paris: Perrin.
Frontex. (2014a). *12 seconds to decide. In search of excellence: Frontex and the principle of best practice*. Luxembourg: EU Publication Office.
Frontex. (2014b). *Eurosur goes live*. Available at: http://frontex.europa.eu/feature-stories/eurosur-goes-live-Z8ZM4f.
Frontex. (2015a). *Annual risk analysis 2015*. Warsaw: Frontex.
Frontex. (2015b, May 6). Eurosur tools play key role in boat rescue. *Frontex feature stories*.
Gabrielsen Jumbert, M. (2012). Controlling the mediterranean space through surveillance. The politics and discourse of surveillance as an all-encompassing solution to EU maritime border management issues. *Espace, Populations, Sociétés, 3*, 35–48.
Greenhouse. (2011, January 22). Legacy of a fence. *The New York Times*.
Jeandesboz, J. (2008). *Reinforcing the surveillance of EU borders. The future development of Frontex and Eurosur*. Brussels: CEPS. CHALLENGE Research Paper 11.
Jeandesboz, J. (2011). Beyond the tartar steppe: Eurosur and the ethics of European border control practices. In P. J. Burgess & S. Gutwirth (Eds.), *A threat against Europe? security, migration and integration* (pp. 111–131). Brussels: VUB Press.
Last, T., & Spijkerboer, T. (2014). Tracking deaths in the mediterranean. In T. Brian & F. Laczko (Eds.), *Fatal journeys: Tracking lives lost during migration*. Geneva: IOM.
Latour, B. (2005). *Reassembling the social. An introduction to actor-network-theory*. New York: Oxford University Press.
Leese, M., & Koenigseder, A. (2015). Humor at the airport? visualization, exposure, and laughter in the "War on Terror". *International Political Sociology, 9*(1), 37–52.

Lyon, D. (2007). *Surveillance studies. An overview*. Cambridge: Polity.
Muller, B. J. (2010). *Security, risk and the biometric state governing borders and bodies. Prio new security studies*. London/New York: Routledge.
Napolitano, J. (2007). Governor Janet Napolitano Address to the National Press Club. Regarding Immigration, Border Security. Washington, DC.
Newman, D. (2006). Borders and bordering: Towards an interdisciplinary dialogue. *European Journal of Social Theory, 9*(2), 171–186.
Perec, G. 1997(1974). *Species of spaces and other pieces*. London: Penguin Books.
PERSEUS Newsletter. (2012). Oliver seiffarth, Dg-Home—Interview. Available at: http://www.perseus-fp7.eu/wp-content/uploads/2012/02/PERSEUS_2012_02_Newsletter_n%C2%B02.pdf
Rijpma, J., & Vermeulen, M. (2015). Eurosur: Saving lives or building borders? *European Security, 24*(3), 454–472.
Schouten, P. (2014). Security as controversy: Reassembling security at Amsterdam airport. *Security Dialogue, 45*(1), 23–42.
US Department of Homeland Security. (2011). *Report on the assessment of the secure border initiative-network (Sbinet) Program*. Washington DC: Department of Homeland security.
Walters, W. (2006). Border/Control. *European Journal of Social Theory, 9*(2), 187–203.
Wilson, T. M., & Donnan, H. (2012). Borders and border studies. In T. M. Wilson & H. Donnan (Eds.), *A companion to border studies* (pp. 1–25). Oxford: Wiley-Blackwell Publishing.

How to Liquefy a Body on the Move: Eurodac and the Making of the European Digital Border

Brigitta Kuster and Vassilis S. Tsianos

1 Introduction

Using the example of Eurodac the following contribution concentrates on the digitization of European border controls. Eurodac, an information, communication and control technology, operates by means of a European database, in which the fingerprints of asylum seekers and irregular migrants are stored. Eurodac works as a so-called Automated Fingerprint Identification System (AFIS) and is applied within the areas where the rules of the Dublin III regulation are applicable. Dublin/Eurodac were designed in relation to each other and in response to the crisis of the European asylum system, which was accompanied by the construction and the use of rather lax and crude terms such as "asylum shopping."[1] The Dublin III regulation is based on the "polluter-pays" principle. It states that the Member State which has "caused" the entry of an asylum applicant (for instance by granting a visa or for lack of border security) should perform the asylum procedure. By using the Eurodac database to reconstruct the one and only responsible Member State per

[1] Same as Dublin, Eurodac is a regulation adopted by the European Council on 11 December 2000 as a Dublin-based measure. A regulation does not require parliamentary approval, but can be initiated directly by the European Commission. The Eurodac regulation provided the legal basis for the establishment of an automated European dactyloscopic system that combines biometric identification technology and information technology solutions (Council Regulation (EC) 2725/2000). The Eurodac II Regulation from February 2002 provides the legal framework for the operationalization of the technical system. It includes rules for the administrative maintenance and for the implementation such as the age limit of those to be identified by fingerprints (Council Regulation (EC) No. 407/2002).

B. Kuster (✉)
Independant researcher, Berlin, Germany
e-mail: brigittakuster@snafu.de

V.S. Tsianos
University of Applied Sciences Kiel, Sokratesplatz 1, 24149 Kiel, Germany
e-mail: vassilis.tsianos@fh-kiel.de

R. Bossong, H. Carrapico (eds.), *EU Borders and Shifting Internal Security*,
DOI 10.1007/978-3-319-17560-7_3

asylum application Dublin III regulates the mobility of non-EU-citizens without a valid visa within the EU.

In general, control technologies for border security are either assessed by their political effects or purposes and criticized accordingly—that is, disconnected from the technical infrastructures they require—or they are subject to a techno-deterministic apperception due to an axiom of technical feasibility. A digitally stabilized border is therefore usually considered to be potentially functional. In contrast, we understand the present article as an ethnographic contribution to the understanding of the socio-technological emergence of the digital border and the digitization of border conflicts.[2] Our object of study leads to the formation of both at once, society and technology, respectively migration and digital border control. In the first and second part, we expose our critique of the somewhat unsharp and blurred outlines of the idea of a new European digital border. With recourse to Bruno Latour's concepts of "blackboxing" and "immutable mobiles" we develop an analysis that in a third part allows us to describe some exemplary actor-networks of Eurodac following our multi-sited fieldwork, from Athens via Igoumenitsa to Bari and back into European control centers where digital data of fingerprints and their registration processes are stored and redistributed. We have localized the current crisis of the Schengen border regime at three different but interconnected spots that generate insights into what we call an "information and control continuum," namely the conflict and contact zones between migrants and their digital traces or their "embodied identity of migration."

2 Blackboxing and the Challenge of the Digital Border

The thesis of an increasing "securitization" of migration in the course of the Europeanization of migration policy since the 1980s and 1990s is largely uncontested within the scientific literature. Rather the debate revolves around the question how to conceptualize and analyze the securitization (cf. Krasmann 2011). Many authors in the tradition of constructivist or feminist technology studies (Topak and Ozgun 2010; Van der Ploeg 1999a, b, 2005; Amoore et al. 2008; Ceyhan 2008; Haggerty and Ericson 2000) claim that European border monitoring and control technologies, such as biometrics or information and communication technology applications, always involve social and discursive contexts that are situated beyond the literal electronic space. However, they opt for different theoretical approaches to study the "complex imbrications of technology and society" (Sassen 2002: 365).

[2] This paper is based on the field research of the border-crossing research group of the Mig@Net Project "Transnational Digital Networks, Migration and Gender" (http://www.mignetproject.eu/) funded under the European Union's Seventh Framework Programme (FP7). The findings discussed within this paper stem from the research conducted by Dr. Vassilis Tsianos and PhD. canditate Brigitta Kuster, University of Hamburg; Dr. Nelli Kambouri, PhD. canditate Olga Lafazani and Dr. Dimitris Parsanoglou, Centre for Gender Studies—Panteion University, Athens; Dr. Renata Pepicelli, University of Bologna.

Saskia Sassen distinguishes explicitly between those aspects of the digital space that are constitutive of new social dynamics and those that reproduce more traditional conditions:

> (...) digital space and digitization are not exclusive conditions that stand outside the non-digital. Digital space is embedded in the larger societal, cultural, subjective, economic, imaginary structurations of lived experience and the systems within which we exist and operate. (Sassen 2002: 369)

"Doing border"[3] from a bottom-up perspective, calls for addressing the ways how the border is constructed, determining who manages it and how it is governed. In this view, the border is conceptualized a relational field of negotiations, whereby the simple juxtaposition of institutions versus informal agents loses its validity (see Anzaldua 1987; Salih 2000).

The existing literature on database-supported border technologies, and in particular on Eurodac, however, differs markedly from this research desideratum. Like the Paris School around Didier Bigo (Bigo 2002, 2007; CASE 2006) analysts focus primarily on narratives and practices of important security policy actors, and base their work principally on policy reports such as the annual Eurodac evaluations and the accounts of European and national data protection authorities (Broeders and Hampshire 2013; Dijstelbloem et al. 2011; Aus 2006; Amoore 2006). This body of literature thus criticizes various unsatisfactory political and democratic structures, which are connected with the architecture of Eurodac in the context of the Europeanization and securitization of migration management. Rather than pointing out how the process of "doing border connects with operations that emanate from Eurodac, this body of works thus mostly elucidates how Eurodac is supposed to operate. Arguably, this is due to the fact that almost no social science contributions are based on independent field research—as if only the public administration were able to gather data and study the current and complex ways in which this European database system is working and operating on a variety of (national and local) institutional, social and geopolitical levels. In this regard the study of Gregory Feldmann which builds on his own field work to elaborate a "nonlocal ethnography of EU migration policy" (2012: 17) represents an exception, markably the chapter on biometrics (ibid.: 78ff).[4]

In sum, although the digitization of the European border is part of migration control policies, we lack theoretically and empirically sufficient analyses of their socio-technical contexts, if compared, for instance with Surveillance Studies and their discussions on control technologies such as ID cards or CCPS systems (Lyon 2007: 118ff, 2009: 19ff). Even at the level of subjects and concepts for investigation there seems to be anything but clarity. Dennis Broeders, for instance, defines the

[3] With the figure of "doing border" we associate a break with notions of geographical and sovereigntist approaches. "Doing Border" is a cultural-anthropological perspective on the border, similar to the feminist approach of "doing gender".

[4] See also the draft "The Digitalization of European Border and Migration Controls", by Hampshire and Broeders (2010). However the related research project has not been realized since.

digital border as „a network of EU databases under development" (Broeders 2011: 49) or as "ICT-enabled proliferation of border sites and pre-emptive mobility governance" (Broeders and Hampshire 2013: 1208). For Bigo and Guild (2005), the digital border is mainly seen as a contrast to physical or territorial borders, which, as also underlined by Broeders, serves to monitor the immigrant population "at-home" (Broeders 2007). Or, in another variant, the digital border emerges as a wider "Europe's technological border"and is equated with a so-called „migration-machine" (Dijstelbloem et al. 2011: 174f).[5] In contrast, Martina Tazzioli points to European "technological systems of monitoring at a distance and the mechanisms of digital traceability", which give rise to a "twofold operation of multiplication (differentiation) and invisibilization of borders" (Tazzioli 2013: 190).

All these authors share an understanding, whereby a putatively undisputable and clearly identified territorial border becomes digitally duplicated or multiplied. In other words, they locate the difference of the digital border in the digitization of the processes of demarcation. In such vague terminologies of the digital border, we see an instance of social-science oriented "blackboxing." Using this expression from the sociology of science, we want to target the technical, political and institutional operations that are rendered invisible, but significantly impact on the success and effectiveness of the digital border. According to Bruno Latour, blackboxing is

> the way scientific and technical work is made invisible by its own success. When a machine runs efficiently, when a matter of fact is settled, one need focus only on its inputs and outputs and not on its internal complexity. Thus, paradoxically, the more science and technology succeed, the more opaque and obscure they become. (Latour 1999: 304).

In our view, very often the literature on the digitization of the border results from a blackbox-epistemology, whereby the object of study, that is, the question to what extent Eurodac actually makes a difference for "doing border," remains opaque and unadressed. To open up this question to detailed inquiry and to accomplish a process of de-blackboxing, is a prerequisite for arriving at a better understanding of the digital border. Even though many existing academic accounts of the digital border regime are meant to critically confront it, they tend to a social science blackboxing and thus may paradoxically contribute to the "success" of the increasing digitalization.

Ironically, the technological proportion of the object of study, namely the Eurodac Central Unit, is literally speaking a blackbox. Formally located in Luxembourg and actually operating from Strasbourg, the EU agency for "Large-Scale Information Systems" (EU-LISA) took over the daily operational management

[5] More specific concepts such as for example the "biometric border," a portable border, carried by mobile bodies and understood as part of a "biopolitical border" (Walter 2000), or the "smart border"—a diffuse border which is not localizable in certain zones or in one place of passage only, but a border that is based on a multiplicity of physical and virtual sites of control and surveillance—are found in Louise Amoore (2006) respectively in Amoore et al. 2008.

of Eurodac from the European Commission on 1 June 2013.[6] Beyond these basic facts, only the inputs and outputs of Eurodac can be known. The central server is a fully automated lights-out system within which even the deletion of data occurs automatically. Interventions in the system and extrapolating observations adhere exclusively to input or output data.

An interview we conducted 2011 with the IT manager and pioneer architect of EURODAC Gillian Ormiston was revealing in regards to an other facet of a blackbox-epistemology. As a woman in a leading position—rather an exception in the field of IT management—, she recounted how she was managing the logistical and technical construction of Eurodac in 2003:

> It is not about IT, it is about people. People are making IT." She emphasized that the task to establish Eurodac not only comprised projects of data exchange with the then 16 Member States. She also had to establish a communications networks in parallel: "Communication is something else than data exchange.

Most obviously, the communication about which she talked here doesn't pertain to the terms of a communication theory model which implies a signal to noise ratio. Mrs. Ormiston taught us to break definitively with the idea that control technologies—in our case biometric identification technologies—are primarily technological.

3 Numbers that Matter

The fall of 2010 when we were formulating the starting points of our research coincided with the proclamation of a Schengen state of emergency. Subsequently the first Rabbit-deployment[7] of Frontex took place on the Greek-Turkish border around the Evros region. As experienced border regime-researchers concerned with an ethnographical record of the border in situ and in actu, we followed the reflex to explore the crisis deployment on site in the sense of the topological border area as soon as possible. However, we had some doubts whether such a field research would also be able to locate the digital dimension of the supposed crisis in the Evros

[6] The head office of EU-LISA is based in Tallin, Estonia, while its operational data centre is located in Strasbourg (http://www.eulisa.europa.eu/Pages/ContactUs.aspx). Technically speaking, EU-LISA manages the operations of the so-called Biometric Matching System (BMS) platform, a search engine systematizing biometric data that not only runs Eurodac data, but also that of the Schengen Information System (SIS II) and the Visa Information System (VIS). With the appearance of the platform approach, which provides an open and flexible architecture and ensures compatibility (harmonized data formats), interoperability (European standards for data storage and transmission) and expansion—i.e., allows for exchange within and between sub systems, networks and organizations, as long as the legal grounds are given—the data bank systems VIS, SIS II and Eurodac seem to be in the process of becoming virtually merged.

[7] Rabbit is the acronym for „Rapid Border Intervention Teams"(see also: Regulation (EC) No 863/2007 of the European Parliament and of the Council of 11 July 2007 establishing a mechanism for the creation of Rapid Border Intervention Teams and amending Council Regulation (EC) No 2007/2004 as regards that mechanism and regulating the tasks and powers of guest officers).

region. In other words, following Rabinow's considerations on the "anthropology of the actual" (2003), we asked ourselves about the meaning of a digital actuality of the border and about the kind of research practices that would be needed to explore it. When beginning to deal with Eurodac, we noticed that the crisis, which European political institutions had proclaimed in 2011, was already visible and readable from the numbers and interpretations published in the 2009 Eurodac activity report (European Commission 2010). Back then, a marked drop in the data curve concerning those persons who were deemed to have illegally crossed the EU external border had been registered:

> The trend regarding the number of persons who were apprehended in connection with an irregular crossing of an external border ("category 2") changed dramatically in 2009. After a rise of 62.3 % between 2007 and 2008 (to 61.945), the number of transactions fell by 50 % in 2009 (to 31.071). Italy, Greece and Spain continue to be the countries, which enter the vast majority of such data. However, Greece is now the one with most transactions—it sent 60 % of all 'category 2' in 2009 (18.714 compared to 20.012 in 2008). (European Commission 2010: 5)

This Brussels report is not about an event in the sociological sense, but it counts, combines, allocates and arranges numbers. More precisely, this numbers are digital records that simulate or sample fingertip imprints that have been made at different places in the Schengen border area, according to certain temporal and spatial categories. The figures are organized according to the sex and age as well as the whereabouts of the person at the time of the recording of his or her fingerprints. These are the basic inputs for the far-reaching Eurodac categorization of individuals: Category 1 stands for asylum seekers, Category 2 for foreigners who have illegally crossed the EU external border, and Category 3 denotes illegal migrants within the Schengen area.[8] As Irma van der Ploeg has shown incisefully, such categorizing does not increase the knowledge of third-country nationals, but results in an "informatization of the body" (Van der Ploeg 2005a) that aims to capture the volatility of moving bodies in making them machine readable (Van der Ploeg and Sprenkels 2011). This concept connects very well with the notion of "data body," a term first coined by the Critical Art Ensemble in their book "The flesh machine" (1998) and defined as the total collection of files connected to an individual in complete service to the corporate and police state (145).[9] In response to both concepts we call the result of the numbers and categories within Eurodac an "embodied identity of migration" (Kuster and Tsianos 2013), which can be verified in the Schengen area and is reflected by an annual report.[10]

---

[8] See Council Regulation (EC) 2725/2000.

[9] The horizon of meaning of the term "data body" is inspired by ideas and actual data processing operations of personal data in large data centers by the government or big companies, as they have emerged since the 1970s. However the idea of "data bodies" - particularly with regard to privacy issues—could be updated for the new circumstances in the information Society as we try to do it with our research on the digital border of Europe.

[10] In the language of programming "identification" is the one-to-many search via pattern recognition algorithms in an established database. In contrast, a "verification" is based on a one-to-one match. This distinction reflects the difference between truth and identity, as it is well established in

Unlike a field researcher looking down from the hills on the border river and the local movements of border police, Frontex and transit migrants—something we also did—this understanding led us to recombine and interpret numbers. On the basis of algorithms whose function is to calculate the connection between points—thus distances, the Eurodac report unfolds a "numerical event," which tries to determine and affect what counts "out there." Starting from the registered numbers, subsequent processes occur and events emanate that we understand with Bruno Latour's notions of inscription and grasp as the agency of "immutable mobiles" (Latour 1986). Latour refers to immutable mobiles as "objects which have the properties of being *mobile* but also *immutable*, *presentable*, *readable*, and *combinable* with one another" (Latour 1986: 6). This is largely the case for the digital representation of a living and volatile body's singularity via its fingerprints. To paraphrase Latour for our case: Digitalized fingerprint data can be transferred, translated, decoded and recoded via an algorithm, without data loss or changes and independently of their size and position in time and space.

Already for the year 2009 the EURODAC protocol inscribed a (statistically underlined) record of an anomaly on the Greek Schengen border. Its activity (in the form of Rabbits) stepped out of the transcript in 2011. Obviously the numbers—and this is crucial point—shifted on the Greek Schengen border in 2011, where as a result of their status change, they began to perform a new life as signifier, as bearers of meaning and of legitimacy for the ongoing Rabbit-intervention. Hence, we understand the Eurodac-numbers as an immutable, presentable, readable, but also mobile and rearrangeable inscription. Such inscriptions circulate as reference entities for mobile migrant identity. They do not mutate when they circulate, but what matters is their speed or slowness, as we will see further on—and their agency unfolds in relative autonomy. Embodied identity of migration is thus just another word for the emergence and disappearance of Eurodac's numerical events. In the following, we try to reconstruct some of this processes by focusing on activities and places of the Eurodac-actor-network as we researched it between 2010 and 2013.

4 The Production of Inputs and Outputs

We began our research by identifying places where the technical, political and institutional work on the successes that are achieved at the border with the Eurodac in- and output-numbers can be made visible and examined. Thus, we came across the German Eurodac Central Office in the Federal Office of Criminal Investigation (BKA) in Wiesbaden, where the large German electronic fingerprint archive is

the western (everyday) thinking. While trying to reach the truth corresponds to the attempt to liquidate the mediation and to thereby gain congruence, identity is always already confronted with the difficulty to subtract multiplicity. Authenticity in turn, tries to meet the subtraction of the multiplicity of identity in the singular. In the language of biometric matchers, on the contrary, "verification" and "authentication" have the same meaning. See also: The Biometrics Blog online at: http://www.360biometrics.com/blog/difference-between-identification-authentication/.

located.[11] During the course of our interview with the head of the German AFIS (which includes more than 3.5 million records) in June 2011, we were asked, if we, as field researchers at the southern European border, would know about the motives of Greek authorities who produced such a large number of Eurodac entries under the category 2 of "illegal border crossers. "This homo-faber-like police officer commented on counting as a reasonable practice. But he also argued that this large numbers of entries must be the result of a political compromise rather than justifiable on a technological or logical ground:

> In Italy the number of entries has meanwhile indeed decreased. It seems that there has been a change of mind ... Why does Greece not use category 3? I do not understand. Let me know if you find out something about it. If they were to use the category 3, they could get rid of many asylum applicants.

As can be seen from the considerations, people in the BKA admit a broad scope for national and institutional differences, interpretative flexibility regarding an unambiguous attribution and thus a certain constructivism regarding the three categories of entry putted at disposition when it comes to data feeding to the Eurodac Central Unit.

In line with a multi-sited ethnography, we picked up the question of the German police officer and attempted to obtain insightful access at other nodal points of the Eurodac-actor-network. This led us to a police officer in the central national Eurodac office in Athens, who explained to us the functioning of Eurodac in a different but similarly unconventional manner. While he pointed to the computer screen showing a hit message, he declared:

> For example, this person here has applied for asylum in Greece, but his fingerprints were first registered in Sweden. So it seems that this must be a case for which Sweden is responsible. The person should be sent to Sweden. But of course, this could also prove wrong, because: How could this person have reached Sweden directly? In all likelihood, he first arrived in Greece, but without being registered or being registered as a category 2 when entering. This entry has been deleted, so that his fingerprints appears for the first time in Sweden.[12]

Beyond the fact that this police officer implicitly admits that illegal entries into Europe via Greece often happen often without registration, two other aspects of his description are remarkable. On the one hand, this police officer provides us with an implicit report on a migration route to Europe, which by now has become targeted by the police. The route which is referred to in this officer's speech is, however, less of geographical nature but characterized by a time frame, since according to the rules of the Eurodac Regulation,[13] the fingerprint data recorded under category

[11] See for instance Töpfer 2008.

[12] Interview, Eurodac Central Unit Athens, 22/09/2011.

[13] The actual rules are exposed in (EU) No 603/2013. See further on the rules of Eurodac regulation Kuster/Tsianos 2013, Tsianos/Kuster 2012. (EU) No 603/2013 is coming into force in July 2015 and based on COM(2012)254 approved by the Commission on 30 May 2012 refers to the establishment of Eurodac, which was laid out in a treaty that came into effect on 1 December

2 (illegal entries across the EU's external border) will be deleted after 2 years.[14] It is not allowed to take this data as an opportunity to execute a search within the Eurodac database, but category 2 data must only serve as reference material for automated search requests, based on category 1 entries. This restriction is part of the political compromise, to which we were alluded at the BKA.[15] On the other hand, the description of the Greek official can be interpreted as a clue to the pragmatic reasons that the German officer in the Federal Criminal Police in Wiesbaden was wondering about. The self-conception of Greece still remains one of a transit country for migration, so that differences between illegal forms of popping up as having entered into the Schengen area, depending on whether they feature as related to the border or to the territory, thus to category 2 or 3, are not so crucial. Thus, the subtlety of such a distinction is eroded by reference to Europe just like Europe refers to Greece as the European border. Yet it is still possible to achieve the objective that the BKA officer postulated: To generate numbers and inscriptions that help to get rid of asylum seekers.

2009, and states that it is to operate in compliance with the European Union's directives. In other words, it is the proposal for a revision of the Eurodac Regulation that, in a single legal act, not only formulates guidelines for the comparison of fingerprint data for "establishing the criteria and mechanisms for determining that the Member State is responsible for reviewing an application for international protection lodged in one of the Member States by a third-country national or a stateless person," but also guidelines for "request[ing] comparisons with EURODAC data by Member States' law enforcement authorities and Europol for law enforcement purposes" and those relating to Regulation (EU) Nr. 1077/2011 concerning the establishment of "a European Agency for the operational management of large-scale IT systems in the area freedom, security and justice." One important new feature of Regulation (EU) No 603/2013 concerns the access rights for criminal prosecution officials and Europol). Already on 3 December 2008, the Commission presented its first proposal to revise the Eurodac legislation, which included, in particular, the implementation of a new management framework—the IT agency (COM(2008)825 final). A new version of the Eurodac Regulation was presented in September 2009 (COM(2009)342 final/COM (2009)344 final). It provided that criminal persecution officials receive access to Eurodac data. This version became obsolete, however, once the Lisbon Treaty came into effect. In October 2010, the Commission again presented another proposed revision withdrawing the motion that criminal persecution officials receive access to the system - this was especially due to the harsh criticism from the European Data Protection Supervisor, among others (COM(2010)555 final). Negotiations concerning the proposal of 2010 (which did not grant access to criminal persecution officials) ceased, because, in the meantime, the majority of Member States was reportedly in favor of granting access to criminal persecution officials and Europol as part of the negotiations on the Common European Asylum System. This was adopted in October 2008 by the European Council as part of the framework of the European Pact on Immigration and Asylum and provides that both refugees and beneficiaries of subsidiary protection be granted equal status. This short reconstruction of the actual Eurodac Regulation shall demonstrate roughly the way in which the European Commission works on migration and asylum politics: three steps ahead, one back, two to the side.

[14] See Council Regulation (EC) 2725/2000.

[15] In more detail, see: Aus 2003, 2006.

5 "The Glass Is Dangerous"

Another facet that is missing from existing analyses of Eurodac is that the subjectivity of the migrants, who are registered in Eurodac, is fully decoupled from the operations of this system of information and control. In our view this is a result of the widespread assumption of technology's neutrality and of the dominant focus on the accounts of policy makers. In particular, the knowledge and information exchange strategies of migrants on the routes is treated as largely irrelevant and hardly ever taken into account when trying to research the effects of Eurodac or the EU's digital borders. Thus, generally the literature tends to a picture of a Manichean relationship between agents and forms of "control knowledge" and subjects of this control who are rarely conceived of as being agents of "mobility knowledge". This runs the risk of contributing to an "escalating dialectic of control"—to speak with Peter Shields (2010: 277)—by playing its part in the shaping of those symptoms it most often tries to criticize, i.e., a heavy reliance on technical solutions to police borders. In contrast, to conduct research on actor-networks in which information on migration and its control also means to stick closely to all involved practices and actors, not least to the heels of migrants. In developing the method of an "(n)ethnographic border regime analysis" (Pieper et al. 2011) we have tried to cope with this complexity and to simultaneously address border control practices and migrants' agency both online and offline. The meanings that transit migrants within the Schengen territory attach in their narratives to the removal of their fingerprints played a crucial and privileged role for our actor-network-reconstruction of Eurodac. When we started our fieldwork in 2010, the border conflict that has become known today by the keyword "Dublin III" was largely absent. However, this does not mean that this conflict did not already exist. Rather, relevant knowledge on the glas circulated only among migrant's networks and more scarcely and with a time lag on a bottleneck in the production of digital data among security professionals. Today, allegations that Italian or Greek authorities do not fingerprint asylum seekers correctly are made in public, for instance by German police representatives (see for example Dahlkamp and Popp 2013). Hence, the internal complexity of and conflicts over a digital border always address us first from the perspective of migration. Migration comes first. Movement comes before its control.

In the spring of 2011 we came to Igoumenitsa for the first time. It is the last Greek port town before Italy, located close to the border with Albania. During our stay we visited the local informal camp inhabited almost exclusively by male transit migrants. Shortly after our visit in Igoumenitsa, the camp—situated on the edge of town on a slope directly above the access road to the harbor and called by the inhabitants "the mountain"—was brutally demolished by the police.[16] During the day, the transit migrants were in the streets of the town to find jobs and food. In the evening and during the night they were hanging around the harbor and trying to

[16] See for instance the report about the situation in Igoumenitsa from the end of may 2011:http://infomobile.w2eu.net/2011/05/24/igoumenitsa-mountain-jungles-threatened-by-eviction/.

seize an opportunity. When Rastaman came towards us, he asked for a cigarette, and told about his journey. He got here from Sudan, via Syria, Lebanon, Turkey, and finally in November 2009 the Greek island of Lesvos. In Mytilini, he was arrested after few days and then detained in the prison of Paganì for about a week. Like all other people there he has been interviewed, photographed, and "fingered." "Fingered" was the term in the pidgin English in which newly arrived migrants spread the words amongst them, or communicated with people like us. All the others who had been in Paganì together had been fingered on paper, too, Rastaman said. He did not know why, maybe because his prints were not clear enough. Still, he would have had to press his fingers into a rather small machine with a glass plate. He said he knows that not all fingerprints play a role. On the mountain he met two Sudanese who would have made it across the Adriatic sea and then to Germany a week ago. Obviously, there would have been no problem in Germany with their fingerprints, while he would know from many conversations and many experiences that the Greeks were not too particular in their approach to the "fingering." Rastaman wants to go to England, where he has friends and family. His eyes are fixed on the harbor. He is waiting for the right moment. There were always people who made it. If you go away from the mountain, you write your name and phone number onto the concrete wall of the bridge to the harbor.

6 The Information and Control Continuum

We came repeatedly across the indication that glass is dangerous. Such information seems to be circulating among migrants[17] and the validity of this knowledge was not necessarily invalidated in the numerous expert interviews we held.[18] Rather, the migrant's stories around the glass seem to be further evidence of the fact that migration constitutes a self-reflexive part of the border regime. This is what we address as the "information and control continuum" which, as Broeders (2011: 59) puts it, always encompasses two modes of exclusion: the exclusion from registration and documentation, and the exclusion through registration and documentation—both having eminent implications for the knowledge production on migration.

Later on, we are able to verify numerically the tacit prognosis of the BKA officer when we read the considerable decrease of category 2 entries in Greece of −58 % compared to 2012, as noted in the Eurodac 2013 annual report (published in May 2014).[19] However as a countermove, a general increase in category 3 operations can

[17] See further about the knowledge of migration as part of the "mobile commons" in: Papadopoulos and Tsianos 2013 and Trimikliniots et al. 2015.

[18] See more detailed on this aspect Tsianos and Kuster 2012.

[19] On the general European level, a rather markable increase of 23 % for category 2 transactions can be observed, to a total amount of 48,276 category 2 entries in 2013 (Annual report on the 2013 activities of Eurodac).

be observed on a European level: This operations concern persons found illegally present within a member state territory. Their data are not stored but only compared to category 1 and 2 entries. Moreover, category 3 transactions are mandatory according to the Eurodac Regulation. Such a sharp increase in numbers of +23 % compared to 2012—according to the annual report on the 2013 activities of Eurodac the total amount is 106,013 for 2013—points to an intensified border control within the Schengen territory in contrast to operations along the external border line. We tend to read this actual growth in category 3 entries as evidence for a doing border, which—since the begin of our field work in Greece and Italy between 2010 and 2013—became more and more de-territorialized.

This trend will create noticeable shifts in border conflicts, which today are markably articulated around the Dublin III regulation and its reform (Kasparek and Tsianos 2015). While we write this at the beginning of September 2015, no one really talks about any of the three Eurodac categories any more. There is a staggering evidence of the fact that the Dublin III Regulation is not a functioning regulatory European system altogether. Things are happening very fast, almost each day the border seems to shift. The system of counting is overwhelmed by the system of feet: Every day some 10,000 of people seeking refuge are arriving in Vienna, in Munich and in the Aegean Sea. . .

"Missed hits" is the technical term used amongst Eurodac experts for category 1 against 2 matchings. Hits within this data search help to reconstruct the routes of migrants once they have entered Schengen territory. The cases in point are for instance persons having applied for asylum in Germany and subsequently are controlled and registered by Greek border guards, if we follow the timeline of Eurodac entries. Under the 206 cases of such "missed hits" in 2013 202 concern Greece (Annual report on the 2013 activities of Eurodac). A second specialist jargon term—"wrong hit"—refers to a similar Eurodac accident due to time delays between the date of taking the fingerprints and their sending to the Eurodac Central Unit.[20] The corresponding numbers for 2013 are 258 cases and the related cases concern category 1 against 1 hits indicating multiple asylum applications.[21] A "wrong hit," according to the 2013 report is to be understood in the context of a scenario where

> a third-country national lodges an asylum application in Member State (A), whose authorities take his/her fingerprints. While those fingerprints are still waiting to be transmitted to the Central Unit (category 1 transaction), the same person could already present him/herself in another Member State (B) and ask again for asylum. If this Member State B

[20] For Greece the annual report highlights a peak of 148.97 days of delay in sending category 2 data to the Central unit in April 2013 whereas an average delay for category 2 transactions of category 2 45.45 days is reported.

[21] A hit category 1 against category 1 occurs when the fingerprints of an asylum seeker have been recognized by the Central Unit as a match against the stored fingerprints of another existing asylum applicant. The report indicates that the percentage of multiple asylum applications is increasing over the last 3 years. This is interesting because Eurodac and Dublin III were originally created to prevent this.

> sends the fingerprints first, the fingerprints sent by Member State A would be registered in the Central database later than the fingerprints sent by Member State B and would thus result in a hit from the data sent by Member State B against the data sent by the Member State A. Member State B would thus be determined as being responsible instead of the Member State A where an asylum application had been lodged first. (Annual report on the 2013 activities of Eurodac: 18)

Moreover, a wrong hit as we learn from the same Eurodac report is a hit "in wrong sense" (18). Wrong sense clearly refers to a territorial orientation and thus to the chronology of an immigration narrative from a European periphery (A) to a European core (B). In the architecture of Eurodac this is also understood as a temporal trajectory "by design."[22] In consequence we have to recognize the immanent time dimension of Eurodac and the consequent conflictive dynamics as they happen to unfold between the contested mobility of migrant's immigration projects and the advised smooth circulation of data relating to them - in other words the maneuverability of an embodied identity of migration.

These few hundred "wrong hits" seem to be anything but representative. But they reflect a synchronization performance of entries in category 1 and 2 as well as entries in category 1 and 1 which are diametrically opposed to the differential gap between North and South Europe, core Europe and countries of first entry. The terminology "wrong hit" however, designates that the pathways and endeavors of thousands of transit migrants should not result in hits. It does not mean that they do not take these journeys, which they actually do and often over several years. The lesson of such a mismatch and that numbers are constructs, or even simulations instead of social facts, was taught us by a police officer from the BKA. And in autumn 2015 the reality of the marked discrepancy which is represented here by the small word "wrong"—nobody wants to stay in Hungary—emerged in full, while people in search of refuge leave marks on one internal European border after the other.

But what is it then that we address when referring to an "identity" of migration? We would like to refer to Stuart Hall who advanced the concept of identity "'under erasure' in the interval between reversal and emergence", stating that the very idea of identity in its original form is no longer serviceable as a concept "good to think with" (Hall 1996: 1–2). However, it has not been superseded by an entirely different concept, while the central questions it addresses remain crucial. With this notion of identity in transition between different meanings we wish to encompass both, migrant's identifying practices and immigration projects on the one hand as well as the identification practices of control and identification technologies in service of the construction of an embodied identity of migration on the other. In this sense, identity under erasure traverses the information and control continuum and shimmers between the appearance of identity attributions and claims, on the one hand, and the refusal and rejection of a particular and given identity, on the other

[22] The idea of a temporality "by design" alludes here to the established term of "privacy by design."

hand. It is always an identity under erasure within the modulation of the two processes of exclusion, namely registration and documentation. When we apply this broader picture of identification and exclusion by Broeders on the operational functions of the Eurodac system, we encounter an astonishing coincidence with the system's own categories: Hits within the matcher searching category 1 entries against category 2 entries lead as a final consequence to an exclusion through documentation. This kind of hit is seen to capture the routes taken by migrants that run against the will of the temporal direction prescribed by the Eurodac system: As your point of entry into Schengen precedes your asylum application, the space between them is subject to a European border geography. In contrast, category 3 fingerprint scans are principally not stored. Thus, they do not concern an embodied identity of migration in the strict sense, rather they are a kind of snapshot of the fluid and illegitimate volatility of bodies on the move within Schengen territory who are suspicious to maintain an intimate relation to an embodied identity of migration and thus a fishy immigration history.[23] A hit in category 3 against category 1 helps to reconstruct and prevent a route taken by migrants on which they tend to disappear from the screen. Such hits do not relate to the temporal ordering of irregular immigration in Europe, but rather to its spatial order: Now that you are here, your presence identifies the distance to the place at which you were once registered, crossing the border or filing an asylum claim and subsequently got lost of track. Both of this system's transactions, 3 to 1 and 1 to 1 are informative for cycles of "digital deportability" (Papadopoulos et al. 2008). With this term we refer to the extension of the risks of mobility—money, perseverance, length of the itinerancy and, sometimes, life itself—to the whole area enclosed by the Schengen border and beyond. Just as you enter Schengen time/space via passing, fading and emerging on computer screens, digital deportability involves a potentially expanded ubiquity as a result of the digital liquefaction of the spatiality of the European border. However as we have shown above, this supposedly ubiquitous border is subjected to a temporal order, in other words, a timeline of the European space. [24]

[23] While most member states report to not permitting use of coercive measures to take fingerprints in category 1 with regards to category 2 and 3 the picture differs: 50 % of the responding member states admit to allow responsible authorities to use coercive measures. (Summary of European Migration Network (EMN) Ad-Hoc Query No. 588 and Eurodac Fingerprinting 2014) As a reaction the Commission published a non-paper indicating 10 steps for obtaining fingerprints in spite of refusals of data subjects to be fingerprinted which include the use of force and detention (Commission non-paper for SCIFA, 2014). See further on this also Statewatch 2015.

[24] It is interesting to relate this to the deletion of EURODAC data—which is the moment when they are not longer migration-relevant so to say. Fingerprints of in category 1 for asylum applicants have to be deleted after 10 years with the exception of for instance individuals who obtain the nationality of one of the member states. Data registered in category 2 for illegal bordercrossers have to be deleted after 18 months and instantaneously once the person in question has received a residence permit, left the territory of the member states or acquired citizenship. (See Regulation (EU) No 603/2013)

Eurodac data bodies are algorithmically converted fingerprint profiles, which visualize and project individuals and their travel routes within Schengen. Not only that they render the mobile and volatile bodies of migrants machine-readable and verifiable when enrolling their fingers and inscribing the according data, but also immutable and hypermobile. Therefore, according to Latour's concept of immutable mobiles, the embodied identity of migration represents the attempt to liquefy and freeze mutable, alterable, fluctuating, and varying corporealties: the persistence and the dynamics of bodies, things and matters involved in migration projects.

As we have seen so far, data bodies represent a circulating reference, and "immutable mobiles." The embodied identity of migration, being the sum of migrant's "data bodies" establish two-way relations with migrants on the move, namely between a corporeality and its inscription. According to Latour, the veracity of inscriptions is a result of the multiplicity of actors that can be mobilized within these two-way connections. In consequence, the growing quantity of circulating data bodies and the rising amount of hits increase the mobility and the immutability of the tracks and traces of the migrants and thus solidify and strengthen the accuracy and consistency of the embodied identity of migration. If we follow Latour's argument, the decisive factor with regard to Eurodac is not the medium—i.e., the biometric fingerprint[25] or the digital database. Instead, what makes a difference is the increasing accuracy, which can be realized through the mobilization of a multiplicity of acts and actors who operate—if necessary proactively—in Eurodac's sense. As Latour puts it in relation to books as immutable mobiles:

> the accuracy *shifts from the medium to the message,* from the printed book to the context with which it establishes a two-way connection. A new interest in 'Truth' does not come from a new vision, but from the same old vision applying itself to new visible objects that mobilize space and time differently. (Latour, 1986: 11)

That is another reason why we think identity under erasure. The concept of immutable mobiles differs markedly from a semiotic or media-theory approach. With regard to agonistic situations or more precisely formulated for our case, to the controversy between migration and its control, the concept of the immutable mobiles accentuates a shift from the medium to the message and the context in which inscriptions matter. Precisely for this reason it can be argued the other way around that, because the migrants carry the border, because they embody the border—especially in the form of their fingers—they cannot entirely cross it. However, what they do is to transgress the border at the same time than incorporating it. Only in this way—as a contempt or by trampling Schengen

[25] To this however, we may remark, that the biometric marker which is considered the ultimate, universally applicable and virtually infallible guarantee of identity, arises from two presumptions: First, an assumption based on simple empiricism, namely that fingerprints are unique and do not change during the course of life. The second assumption goes as follows: Two identical ways to produce a representation of a fingerprint must lead to identical results. Additionally, it can be said that hit within Eurodac based of the identity of two fingerprints provides all the other stored data such as sex for instance, with more authenticity and credibility.

under their feet—they re-territorialize the border and they push it deeper into the European territory as we can actually see today. In this way they challenge the limits of Europe. Eurodac's digital border as we understand it in this paper is not ubiquitous, it is not always everywhere, rather it displays a smoothening of the space while at the same time sustaining and bringing forth a temporal directionality.

7 Coda

In July 2014 we visited the newly build "first reception" screening center Moria on the island of Lesvos. As we had no permission to enter, we were hanging around on spot in classical manner of ethnographers. Eventually a man stepped out of the main entrance and set about to walk on foot to Mytilini city which is about ten km away. He did not carry a bag but was only equipped with a paper that he held in his hands. As we were by car we offered him to take him with us. He agreed and we began a conversation. He told us that he comes from Sudan. Three weeks ago he would have crossed the border to Greece via Turkey. He would have been arrested by the border police and "fingered on a glass" a first time. Afterwards they brought him to Morias and he got through extensive interviews concerning his trajectory, his traffickers, etc. They confronted him with the choice of either staying in detention for 18 months or applying for asylum. He would have opted for the second possibility, and thus would have been fingerprinted a second time. The document he got in response was an asylum claim rejection because unfounded. But the paper granted him a humanitarian short-term permit, in other words a suspended deportation order. He told us that he now wants to go to Athens. We asked him if he will stay in Greece to which he replied: "This is a good paper. I want to go to Sweden." We concernedly looked at him and explained that somehow he would have settled for Greece because of the Dublin regulation. "No Greece. No Greece. First Athens and then Sweden." he answered and left us. If we account for the fact that our conversation partner is part of the information and control continuum, it is plausible that on this short distance trip he shared an idea with us on numbers that matter and on identities under erasure that we were not able to fully understand as researchers who find themselves as well within this information and control continuum, but probably always come last.

Acknowledgements Tsianos and Kuster collaborated in the research project Mig@Net. Transnational Digital Networks, Migration and Gender at the University of Hamburg, http://www.mignetproject.eu/

References

Amoore, L. (2006). Biometric borders: Governing mobilities in the war on terror. *Political Geography, 25*, 336–351.

Amoore, L., Marmura, S., & Salter, M. B. (2008). Editorial: Smart borders and mobilities: Spaces, zones, enclosures. *Surveillance & Society, 5*(2), 96–101.

Anzaldua, G. (1987). *Borderlands—La frontera: The New Mestiza*. San Francisco, NC: Aunt Lute.

Aus, J. P. (2003). *Supranational governance in an 'Area of Freedom, Security and Justice': Eurodac and the politics of biometric control* (SEI Working Paper 72). University of Oslo: ARENA.

Aus, J. P. (2006). *Eurodac: A solution looking for a problem? Centre for European Studies* (Working Paper No. 9). Oslo: Centre for European Studies, University of Oslo.

Bigo, D. (2002). Security and immigration: Toward a critique of the governmentality of unease. Special english-language issue of cultures et conflits. *Alternatives, 27*(2(Special issue)), 63–92.

Bigo, D. (2007). Detention of foreigners, states of exception, and the social practices of control of the Banopticon. In P. Rajaram & C. Grundy-Warr (Eds.), *Borderscapes. Hidden geographies and politics at territory's edge* (pp. 3–33). Minneapolis: University of Minnesota Press.

Bigo, D., & Guild, E. (Eds.). (2005). *Controlling frontiers: Free movement into and within Europe*. Aldershot: Ashgate.

Broeders, D. (2007). The new digital borders of Europe: EU databases and the surveillance of irregular migrants. *International Sociology, 22*(1), 71–92.

Broeders, D. (2011). A European 'border' surveillance system under construction. In H. Dijstelbloem, A. Meijer, & M. Besters (Eds.), *Migration and the new technological borders of Europe* (pp. 40–67). Basingstoke: Palgrave Macmillan.

Broeders, D., & Hampshire, J. (2010). *The digitalization of European borders and migration controls. Migration to Europe in the Digital Age (MEDiA)*. Report on Work Package 2, Prepared for the the MEDiA meeting at Koc University, Istanbul, April 9–10, 2010.

Broeders, D., & Hampshire, J. (2013). Dreaming of seamless borders: ICTs and the pre-emptive governance of mobility in Europe. *Journal of Ethnic and Migration Studies, 39*(8), 1201–1218.

C.A.S.E.-Kollektiv. (2006). Critical approaches to security in Europe: A network manifesto. *Security Dialogue, 37*(4), 443–487.

Ceyhan, A. (2008). Technologization of security: Management of uncertainty and risk in the age of biometrics. *Surveillance & Society, 5*(2), 102–123.

Dahlkamp, J., & Popp, M. (2013, October 14). Asylum crisis: How many refugees can Germany handle? *Spiegel Online International*.

Dijstelbloem, H., Meijer, A., & Besters, M. (2011). Reclaiming control over Europe's technological borders. In H. Dijstelbloem, A. Meijer, & M. Besters (Eds.), *Migration and the new technological borders of Europe* (pp. 170–185). Basingstoke: Palgrave Macmillan.

European Commission. (2010). COM 2010 415 final. Annual report to the European Parliament and the Council on the activities of the EURODAC Central Unit in 2009.

European Commission. (2014, October). Commission non-paper for *Strategic Committee on Immigration, Frontiers and Asylum* (*SCIFA*) on Best Practises for upholding the obligation in the Eurodac Regulation to take fingerprints, DS 1491/14, ANNEX.

European Council. (2009). COM(2009)344 final, Proposal for a COUNCIL DECISION on requesting comparisons with EURODAC data by Member States' law enforcement authorities and Europol for law enforcement purposes.

European Union. (2000). Annual report on the 2013 activities of the Central Unit of Eurodac pursuant to Article 24(1) of Regulation (EC) No 2725/2000).

European Union. (2008). COM(2008)825 final, Proposal for a REGULATION OF THE EUROPEAN PARLIAMENT AND OF THE COUNCIL concerning the establishment of 'Eurodac' for the comparison of fingerprints for the effective application of Regulation (EC) No [../..] [establishing the criteria and mechanisms for determining the Member State responsible for examining an application for international protection lodged in one of the Member States by a third-country national or a stateless person].

European Union. (2009). COM(2009)342 final, Amended proposal for a REGULATION OF THE EUROPEAN PARLIAMENT AND OF THE COUNCIL concerning the establishment of 'EURODAC' for the comparison of fingerprints for the effective application of Regulation (EC) No [../..] [establishing the criteria and mechanisms for determining the Member State

responsible for examining an application for international protection lodged in one of the Member States by a third-country national or a stateless person].
European Union. (2010). COM(2010)555 final, Amended proposal for a REGULATION OF THE EUROPEAN PARLIAMENT AND OF THE COUNCIL on the establishment of 'EURODAC' for the comparison of fingerprints for the effective application of Regulation (EC) No [../..] [establishing the criteria and mechanisms for determining the Member State responsible for examining an application for international protection lodged in one of the Member States by a third-country national or a stateless person].
European Union. (2011). Regulation (EU) No 1077/2011 of The European Parliament and of the Council of 25 October 2011establishing a European Agency for the operational management of large-scale IT systems in the area of freedom, security and justice.
European Union. (2012). COM(2012)254, Amended proposal for a Regulation of the European Parliament and of the Council on the establishment of 'EURODAC' for the comparison of fingerprint.
European Union. (2013). Regulation (EU) No 603/2013 of The European Parliament and of the Council of 26 June 2013 on the establishment of Eurodac for the comparison of fingerprints for the effective application of Regulation (EU) No 604/2013 establishing the criteria and mechanisms for determining the Member State responsible for examining an application for international protection lodged in one of the Member States by a third-country national or a stateless person and on requests for the comparison with Eurodac data by Member States' law enforcement authorities and Europol for law enforcement purposes, and amending Regulation (EU) No 1077/2011 establishing a European Agency for the operational management of large-scale IT systems in the area of freedom, security and justice (recast).
Feldmann, G. (2012). *The migration apparatus. Security, labour, and policy making in the European union*. Standford: Standford University Press.
Haggerty, K. D., & Ericson, R. V. (2000). The surveillant assemblage. *British Journal of Sociology, 51*(4), 605–622.
Hall, S. (1996). Introduction: Who needs 'identity'? In S. Hall & P. D. Gay (Eds.), *Questions of identity* (pp. 1–17). Sage: Thousand Oaks.
Hampshire, J., & Broeders, D. (2010). *The digitalization of European borders and migration controls, migration to Europe in the Digital Age (MEDiA)*, Report on Work Package 2, Prepared for the MEDiA meeting at Koc University, Istanbul, 9–10 April 2010.
Kasparek, B., & Tsianos, V. S. (2015). Back to the future. Blair-Schily reloaded. Movements. *Journal für kritische Migrations- und Grenzregimeforschung, 1*(1).
Krasmann, S. (2011). Der Präventionsstaat im Einvernehmen. Wie Sichtbarkeitsregime stillschweigend Akzeptanz produzieren. In L. Hempel, S. Krasmann, & U. Bröckling (Eds.), *Sichtbarkeitsregime. Überwachung, Sicherheit und Privatheit im 21. Jahrhundert*, (pp. 7–24). Leviathan Special Issue 25.
Kuster, B. & Tsianos, V. S. (2013). *Erase them! Eurodac and digital deportability, transversal/ EIPCP multilingual webjournal*. http://eipcp.net/transversal/0313/kuster-tsianos/en
Latour, B. (1986). *Visualization and cognition: Thinking with eyes and hands* (Article no. 21). http://www.bruno-latour.fr/sites/default/files/21-DRAWING-THINGS-TOGETHER-GB.pdf
Latour, B. (1999). *Pandora's hope: Essays on the reality of science studies*. Cambridge, MA: Harvard University Press.
Lyon, D. (2007). *Identifying citizens. ID cards as surveillance*. Cambridge: Polity Press.
Lyon, D. (2009). *Surveillance studies: An overview*. Cambridge: Polity Press.
Papadopoulos, D., Stephenson, N., & Tsianos, V. (2008). *Escape routes. Control and subversion in the 21th century*. London: Pluto Press.
Papadopoulos, D., & Tsianos, V. S. (2013). After citizenship: Autonomy of migration and the mobile commons. *Citizenship Studies, 17*(2), 42–73.
Pieper, M., Kuster, B., & Tsianos, V. (2011). "Making connections". Skizze einer net(h) nografischen Grenzregimeanalyse. In O. Leistert & T. Röhle (Eds.), *Generation facebook. Über das Leben im Social net* (pp. 221–248). Transcript Verlag: Bielefeld.

Rabinow, P. (2003). *Anthropos today: Reflections on modern equipment*. Princeton, NJ: Princeton University Press.

Salih, R. (2000). Towards an understanding of gender and transnationalism: Moroccan migrant women's movements across the mediterranean. *AJEC: The Mediterraneans: Transborder Movements and Diasporas, 9*(2), 75–92.

Sassen, S. (2002). Towards a sociology of information technology. *Current Sociology, 50*(3), 365–388.

Shields, P. (2010). ICTs and the European Union's evolving border surveillance architecture: A critical assessment. *Observatorio Journal, 4*(1), 255–288.

Statewatch. (2015, March 10). Fingerprinting by force: Secret discussions on "systematic identification" of migrants and asylum seekers including '"fingerprinting [with] the use of a proportionate degree of coercion" on "vulnerable persons, such as minors or pregnant women". Press release.

Summary of European Migration Network (EMN). (2014, September). Ad-Hoc Query No. 588, Eurodac Fingerprinting. http://statewatch.org/news/2015/mar/eu-com-compulsory-fingerprinting-asylum-applicants-ms-responses-summary.pdf

Tazzioli, M. (2013). *Arab uprisings and practices of migration across the mediterranean*. (Doctoral thesis). Goldsmiths, University of London. [Thesis]: Goldsmiths Research Online. http://research.gold.ac.uk/9607/

Topak, O. E. (2010, September 9–11). *The new borders of EU: Surveillance, security and European citizenship*. Paper prepared for SGIR 7th Pan-European International Relations Conference, Stockholm.

Töpfer, E. (2008). Mobile Daten—begrenzte Kontrolle. Auf dem Weg zum europäischen Informationsverbund. *Bürgerrechte & Polizei/CILIP, 91*(3), 19–32.

Trimikliniots, N., Parsanoglou, D., & Tsianos, V. S. (2015). *Mobile commons, digital materialities and the right to the city. Migrant digitalities & social movements in three arrival cities—Athens, Istanbul, Nicosia*. London: Palgrave-Pivot Series Mobility and Politics.

Tsianos, V. S., & Kuster, B. (2012). *mig@net—Transnational digital networks, migration and gender*. Thematic report "Border Crossings". http://www.mignetproject.eu/?cat= 5

Van der Ploeg, I. (1999a). Written on the body: Biometrics and identity. *Computers and Society, 29*(1), 37–44.

Van der Ploeg, I. (1999b). The illegal body: "Eurodac" and the politics of biometric identification. *Ethics and Information Technology, 1*, 295–302.

Van der Ploeg, I. (2005). *The politics of biometric identification. Normative aspects of automated social categorization*. Biometric Technology and Ethics, BITE Policy Paper 2.

Van der Ploeg, I., & Sprenkels, I. (2011). Migration and the machine-readable body: Identification and biometrics. In H. Dijstelbloem, A. Meijer, & M. Besters (Eds.), *Migration and the new technological borders of Europe* (pp. 68–105). Basingstoke: Palgrave Macmillan.

Walter, W. (2000). Mapping schengenland: Denaturalizing the border. *Environment and Planning D: Society and Space, 20*(5), 561–580.

Patrolling Power Europe: The Role of Satellite Observation in EU Border Management

Irma Słomczyńska and Paweł Frankowski

1 Introduction: Orbit-Based European Security—Ideas and Possibilities

As a global actor, the European Union not only seeks to expand its external activities, but also to enhance its instruments. Space assets have became important in this context, allowing to support objectives of foreign and security policy and to promote its values in a coherent and much more autonomous manner (cf. Algieri 2015). Coherence of external actions, highlighted in the list of principles of the EU, links EU space policy to other actions taken in the international arena. Improving the use of resources and technological capabilities is crucial for the effectiveness of EU external and internal security. It should be noted, however, that the European Space Policy is still in the early stages of development. Thus, its impact on European security needs to be assessed on the basis of the *possibilities* of the use of space assets.

Space policy and space assets used for border management, like Copernicus initiative, partially result from the EU's desired holistic approach to international affairs, aiming to shape international standards (cf. normative power (Manners 2008; Larsen 2014; Birchfield 2013; Eriksen 2014)), global trade relations (see market power Europe (Damro 2012; Meunier and Nicolaïdis 2006)) and economic and social problems within the EU and third countries (cf. regulatory power (Genschel and Jachtenfuchs 2014)). However, the current academic debate on the role of the EU tends to unnecessarily separate these different agendas and power resources, i.e., normative, market and regulatory power, ignoring important points

I. Słomczyńska (✉)
Maria-Curie Skłodowska University, Plac Litewski 3, 20-080 Lublin, Poland
e-mail: irma.slomczynska@umcs.edu.pl

P. Frankowski
Jagiellonian University, ul. Gołębia 24, 31-007 Kraków, Poland
e-mail: pawel.frankowski@uj.edu.pl

R. Bossong, H. Carrapico (eds.), *EU Borders and Shifting Internal Security*,
DOI 10.1007/978-3-319-17560-7_4

of interaction between substantive norms and institutions of regulation. As a result, analysts frequently overestimate the EU's influence and are unable to make sense of important empirical observations of practices on border management across time, geographical areas and involved parties. Patrolling power Europe, as another element of European identity, built on similarities with national state, is based on supposed relinquishment of border control, in broader sense, by EU member states. The European agenda on border protection, based on an assumption that EU member states cannot, and should not protect European borders themselves gives powerful tool for European Commission for seeking new technological solutions for such problems as irregular migration, smuggling or transborder environmental pollution. Patrolling power Europe reaches another level of EU identity and legitimacy, but technological limitations to far extent undermine this very ambitious and ground-breaking project.

The goal of this chapter is to examine the nature, as well as the potential concerns and challenges satellite technology used for European external border surveillance. The article finds that despite having a clear agenda in foreign affairs and border protection, the European Union action is more limited by technology and legal constraints, than by the agency and preferences of member states. Thus, the success of its activities in the area of border management is dependent on the EU overcoming technological challenges, while the use of resources would also have to be improved. The authors of this chapter argue that in order to deal with the lack of technical resources in border management, more thought should be given to the question of political responsibility in surveillance, and whether states have or should have sovereignty over their border management. Finally, we suggest that the EU tends to use the notion of "border management" to increase its competences in this area, although technological capabilities are still in the hands of the states.

The chapter proceeds in the following manner. Part one surveys the field of actors and the ideas behind the provision of European security from space. It also assesses the milestones of the European Space Policy in relation to border protection, and identifies a number of technological variables that condition the emergence of border management from space. Part two focuses on possibilities and obstacles for using satellite applications for border management by discussing the European External Border Surveillance System (EUROSUR) as a comprehensive European approach to border management. This part reviews recent propositions about border control, and analysing the relations between different agencies responsible for space activities in Europe. In Part three, we argue that, despite very ambitious EU goals in the area of pre-border management, European capabilities are still limited and there is a lack of coherence between military and civilian dimensions of EU space policy.

2 The Conceptual Basis for EU Space and Security Policy

Many actors are involved in the formation of a European space policy and European border management. This includes the European Commission, the European Parliament, the European Council, the European Space Agency, FRONTEX, the EU Satellite Centre, non-state actors involved in the space industry, the rotating Council Presidency and the EU Member States—in particular those countries that pursue space policy as a political priority, including when holding the Presidency, as France, Italy and Greece. In addition, one has to consider the role of non-EU member states, which are in the Schengen area and further institutional or political legacies that developed before the EU, such as the previous role of the Western European Union that laid the foundation for the EU's Common Foreign and Security Policy. Despite this complexity, the majority of representatives in these institutions include the same EU Member States. Moreover, given the traditional intergovernmental nature of foreign and security policies, it could be argued that the European Space Policy and border management result from the interests of Member States, implemented at the level of the European Union. Yet this would be an oversimplification, as the objectives pursued by individual member states and institutional actors are not always convergent. As a result, the EU's evolving space policy and border management has its own dynamics.

From a historical perspective, the use of space assets for European international relations and foreign policy can be traced back to the 1960s. With the first artificial satellites in orbit, such technological progress became a symbol of state power and of the changing ability to influence the international environment, which obviously had strong security implications during the Cold War (Moltz 2014; Remuss 2012). Thus, long before the European countries had the physical and technological capabilities to use space for their security, policy discussion started in a specific geopolitical context. In particular, it led to a separation between civilian and military aspects of space use. The European Space Agency was founded to pursue exclusively peaceful projects in space, whereas activities of a military nature of took place outside the structures of the European Communities.

In 1984, the WEU Parliamentary Assembly adopted a recommendation on the military use of space (WEU 1984). Also after the end of the Cold War, reports and resolutions discussed the potential military dimension of European activities in space. In 1998, the Ministerial Council of the WEU pointed to the creation of a Space Policy (WEU 1998), and that any space activity can affect vital security interests. In 2001, the WEU Assembly adopted the report "A joint European space strategy: security and defense aspects," which argued that to fulfill the objectives of the European Headline Goal, i.e., the military capacity goals of the newly created European Security and Defence Policy—it would be necessary to use space resources. Satellites would not only help to predict weather conditions for military operations, but are also needed to pinpoint targets and guide missiles, to monitor the movement of the civilian and military units, to allow an assessment of actions taken and to provide intelligence on potential adversaries, including electronic surveillance and observation (WEU 2001: 8). These arguments were underlined in a further WEU Assembly report from 2004, entitled "The space dimension of the ESDP," which proposed the creation of comprehensive EU structures, including ground stations, satellite data centers, telecommunications systems, satellite navigation and weather reconnaissance systems (Western European Union 2004: 5). Moreover, the European Union Satellite Centre in Torrejon (EUSC—EU SatCen), transferred from Western European Union in 2002, was tasked with creating a special military unit. Originally the EUSC was established by the Western European Union in 1992, as an independent capability for WEU member states to assess the international situation through the usage of space assets. The centre was declared operational in 1997, and provided specific information for all WEU member states on crisis management. Due to changes in the EU structure, however, when the EU took over WEU activities on crisis management in 2002, the WEU Satellite Centre in Torrejon was transferred as well. This important step for building EU space assets gave a new impetus for space-based observation and space surveillance in the EU. By 2008, the EUSC special unit would reach the target of obtaining satellite imagery for EU foreign missions around the world in less than 44 h (Asbeck 2008: 22).

Similarly, the European Parliament and the European Commission emphasized the need to take space assets into account in the development of the European Security and Defence Policy. In 2003, the European Commission published two papers (European Commission 2003a, b) on European Space policy that emphasized that the development of European security requires space resources and also drew a connection to European border management, by indicating that space-based assets with surveillance power "allow for a better enforcement of border and coastal restrictions and, therefore, more effective controls on illegal immigration and trafficking" (European Commission 2003a: 19). In November 2004, the Council identified the need to support the implementation of the European Security Strategy with the use of space capabilities that are controlled by Member States (European Council 2004). Detailed arrangements that specify related military resources were adopted on February, 7th 2006 in the document "Generic Space Systems Needs for Military Operations" (6920/06) (Council of the European Union 2006), and supplemented by the classified document "Space System Requirements" (Kolovos 2009: 9). These resources provide image acquisitions on any location on Earth in a timely manner to satisfy the decision making process. Imager requirements vary between low resolution panchromatic and multispectral mosaics, providing background geographic information through Synthetic Aperture Radar (SAR) images,[1] independent from daylight and weather, and very high resolution, including extreme high resolution imagery for reconnaissance and identification of military significant objects, as well as stereoscopic imagery for Digital Elevation Models (DEMs) for 3D viewing. Further proposals on border management could be found in the 2009 parliamentary Report on the

[1] For example for the detection of half-buried infrastructures, the detection of camouflaged infrastructures, and the characterization of troop deployments.

European Security Strategy, which emphasized that space assets create "new opportunities to exploit synergies and enhance interoperability between armed forces and security forces," which includes border surveillance (European Parliament 2009).

3 Technical Systems and Capacities for EU Space Policy

Overall, the specific contribution of space assets consists in

1. Earth observation and reconnaissance,
2. Telecommunications,
3. Navigation,
4. Positioning and timing.

However, even nowadays only the first two systems are partly usable, mainly due to the lack of technical capacity of the European Union, and its member states. Currently, space assets at the EU disposal can be divided into four types of satellites: observation, communications, positioning and early warning satellites. Observation capabilities give the EU satellite imagery for advance strategic planning, regular, precise and detailed situation assessments, as well as collection of geospatial data, provided by EUSC. Communication capabilities are provided by commercial operators, including very high rate communication, interconnection, videoconferencing and other data services (such as medical data). The global positioning system "Galileo" is still in nascent phase, and with twelve positioning satellites (December 2015) the desired independence of European capabilities from the US-based GPS system is still non-existent. Early warning services, such as for missile defence, are used by the EU in a pre-crisis situation to monitor the activities of potentially proliferating countries.

Earth observation and positioning satellites form the basis of the European Galileo and Copernicus, which are only in the development stage and have not yet been verified in practice (Giannopapa 2012; Gleason 2009; Von der Dunk 2006; Rohner et al. 2007). The following paragraph provides further details on these systems in so far as they relate to EU security policy.

Earth observation and reconnaissance can be provided by *Copernicus*. This system, formerly known as GMES, was initially created to ensure the monitoring of environmental change. The concept was later extended to a wider "European Earth observation capacity" (Rohner et al. 2007; European Commission 2009) to deliver services in the environmental and security fields. The reason behind this change is that European space capabilities, from the very beginning, were planned as dual use systems, but gaining legitimacy on the European level for building space military assets was almost impossible when idea of civilian power Europe were widely promoted. Copernicus differs from similar monitoring activities undertaken by European countries, as it is designed as a comprehensive system that will not only gather information from reconnaissance satellites, but also classify and supplement data obtained from other sources, namely border surveillance and traditional intelligence sources. Therefore, in addition to the original idea of climate change monitoring and early warning about environmental threats, the Copernicus system will support border monitoring, movements of people, as well as support for conflict prevention, crisis management, verifying treaties and arms control agreements and environmental agreements, thus ranging across the divide between internal and external security. The aforementioned document, "Generic Space Systems Needs for Military Operations" provides clear guidelines for future EU capabilities. Copernicus, with Sentinel satellites, will provide end users all-weather, day and night SAR imaging and high-resolution optical imaging for emergency services.

Against this background, two types of data are currently provided by the European Union Satellite Centre (EUSC) in the context of the CSFP. The first type of data is satellite imagery (IMINT) derived from European countries under special agreements concluded between the EU and the countries having the resources to provide this kind of data. Currently EUSC uses data from satellites Helios intelligence (Belgium, France, Greece and Spain), SAR-Lupe (Germany), TerraSAR-X (Germany), COSMO-SkyMed (Italy) and Pléiades (France). These systems are equipped with both optical systems and synthetic aperture radar (SAR) providing images of the ground in all weather conditions.

The first satellite as part of an independent space program of the European Union, Sentinel-1, was launched on 3 April 2014, and is equipped with synthetic aperture radar that allows to obtain images with a resolution of 5 m. Another satellite, Sentinel-2A, the first of a pair of satellites, was launched on 23 June 2015, and provides images with a resolution of 10 m. The launch of Sentinel satellites theoretically allows the EU to achieve autonomy in the use of space assets, be it for the purposes of the Common Security and Defense Policy or EUROSUR. Nevertheless, technical capabilities of Sentinels are not sufficient for gathering advanced intelligence, and therefore there will be a need to supplement data from other satellites on the behalf of EU member states.

The second type of data provided by the EUSC is geospatial intelligence (GEOINT), which combines images obtained with the data of other types in order to monitor and anticipate developments in the area of conflict (Jentzsch 2010). Data of this type are particularly useful in areas where existing maps are inaccurate or outdated. Furthermore, satellite observation reduces the need for the introduction of forces (observers) in the area of conflict, which not only limits the possible loss of life, but also contributes to a neutral approach to conflict resolution. A physical presence of troops or civilian observers, instead, increases the possibility of being accused of encouraging conflict, or of supporting specific groups.

This brief overview of EU space policy regarding security and space assets suggests that the EU has the potential to provide border surveillance using space assets, with legitimacy, and support of EU member states. Nevertheless, EU technical capabilities are still limited, since services provided by satellite imagery operators do not entirely correspond to the generic needs concept proposed in 2006. However, before drawing out the direct implications for EU border management, it is important to identify the ideas behind EUROSUR. Therefore, the next part of this chapter will be devoted to role of EUROSUR in the overall EU security strategy, to identify the key elements of this concept.

4 EUROSUR as Comprehensive European Approach to Border Management

The EU has 7400 km of external land borders and 57,800 km of external maritime borders. The European Border Surveillance System (EUROSUR) has been planned to reinforce the control of the Schengen external border, especially on the southern European flank (maritime realm) and eastern borders. The JHA Council Conclusions of June 2008 (Council of the European Union 2008) and February 2010 (Council of the European Union 2010), as well as the Stockholm Programme, and the European Council of June 2011 confirmed that EUROSUR should reinforce the management of the external border. The main goals for EUROSUR are to reduce the loss of lives at sea and the number of irregular migrants entering the EU undetected, and to increase internal security by preventing cross-border crime such as terrorism, trafficking in human beings, smuggling of weapons and drugs (European Parliament 2011). In order to achieve such ambitious and far-reaching goals EUROSUR should provide EU Member States[2] with advanced technical capabilities and an operational framework for border monitoring, situational awareness and reaction capacities. EUROSUR is technically connected with FRONTEX, which also aims to support national authorities on border security (European Parliament 2013).

The legal basis for EUROSUR is Article 77(2)(d) of the Treaty on the Functioning of the European Union (TFEU), which allows the EU to adopt any necessary measures for the establishment of an integrated management system for external borders. This integrated management should encompass "situational awareness," which means the ability to monitor, detect, identify, track and understand cross-border activities. Such awareness should include, according to article 3d of the EUROSUR regulation (European Parliament 2013a)

> graphical interface to present real-time data, information and intelligence received from different authorities, sensors, platforms and other sources, which is shared across communication and information channels with other authorities in order to achieve situational awareness and support the reaction capability along the external borders and the pre-frontier area.

Although surveillance of external borders is seen as normal and even desirable, the notion of "pre-frontier areas" is opaque and problematic. In the proposal for the EUROSUR regulation, "pre-frontier areas" are defined as the "geographical area

[2] EUROSUR applies to the Schengen countries plus Bulgaria, Romania, and Croatia. Two EU member states, Ireland and the United Kingdom, which are not taking part in the Schengen cooperation, have been excluded from EUROSUR, however specific provisions have been included in the EUROSUR Regulation, to allow them for cooperation.

beyond the external border of Member States, which is not covered by a national border surveillance system." (European Commission 2011: 873, 3f) Even if the document underlines that situational pictures will as "a general rule not involve personal data but rather the exchange of information on incidents and depersonalised objects, such as the detection and tracking of vessels," it creates a very broad array of possible activities. Incidents may be traced, taped, collected, and analysed through sophisticated software, "to understand" cross-border activities. Therefore, by defining pre-frontier areas in such a wide fashion, EUROSUR evolved from a border management and surveillance system to wider tool for intelligence collection, a tendency that is particularly noticeable in the original legal proposal for EUROSUR. The final EUROSUR regulation, however, differs from the original proposal, in the sense that "any exchange of personal data in the European situational picture and the common pre-frontier intelligence picture should constitute an exception."

As some authors suggest, EUROSUR has been designed as a system for "supranational extraterritorial surveillance" instead of simple border management (Mitsilegas 2015: 18). New methods of border control, using remote technology and delegating tasks to individuals who are not present at European borders, paves the way to intelligence activities, where different standards, norms, and laws are applied. Pre-border intelligence, which is necessary to create a complete and updated "situational picture," can be collected from three systems and platforms: (1) ship reporting systems in accordance with their respective legal bases; (2) satellite imagery; (3) sensors mounted on any vehicle, vessel or other craft (European Parliament 2013, para. 12). Both ship reporting systems and sensors mounted on means of transportation, however, demand very detailed legal bases, related to relevant national provisions and international law.

When it comes to satellite imagery, such limits are less important. The only explicit legal basis for satellite reconnaissance can be found in the UN Resolution A/RES/41/65 adopted in 1986 concerning remote sensing (United Nations 1986; Christol 1988; Feder 1990; Harris 2008). The rules allow, not only optical devices—based observation, but also the usage of data obtained through the reception of reflected waves, emitted or diffracted by objects on the surface of the globe. In accordance with the principles of titles I and IV of the UN resolution, remote sensing should be conducted in the interest of all countries. Moreover, the UN privileges the framework of regional agreements for data collection, processing, and interpretation in principle VI. Thus, if we assume that such actions are in the interest of all states, then remote sensing observation becomes a foreign policy tool of the European Union.

Yet as Von der Dunk notes, the legal situation remains complicated, since various Member States, the ESA, the European Union and private operators currently provide services for Copernicus, including remote sensing (Von der Dunk 2008: 400). The existence of a multitude of actors in the field raises problems of accountability and authorization. The Program Committee Earth Observation (PB-EO) of the European Space Agency recently regulated access to system data from Copernicus Sentinel, while Regulation No 1159/2013 of the Commission

(Commission of European Union 2013) introduced significant limitations to the use and application of the data supplied by Copernicus. In particular, the Commission reserved the right to assess the sensitivity of any data to control "the use of information from GMES services for tactical or operational activities detrimental to the security interests of the Union, its Member States and international partners" (art. 14).

In sum, from the perspective of international and European law, EUROSUR and the European space policy are perceived as legitimate and useful tools for supporting European security. Nevertheless, the lack of coherence among EU policies, the practical realities of technologies at the EU's disposal, and the considerable differences between public and private interests are crucial to understand the contested role of space assets and border management.

5 Patrolling Power Europe? Policy Expectations and Technical Capabilities

The existing institutional framework for space applications and the European space policy as such were not mentioned in the EUROSUR proposal (Kolovos 2013: 167). Similarly, the EUROSUR final regulation (European Parliament 2013) makes no references to existing documents on space and security, possible space applications, or programs, such as the ones reviewed in the first part of this chapter. Therefore, from a legal point of view, the European space policy has been excluded from border management. Space applications and institutions are mentioned only three times in the EUROSUR regulations: the European Union Satellite Centre is alluded to in the preamble, as the last actor on the list of cooperating bodies, and then in the body of the text as providing common applications for surveillance tools (art. 18.2.b). "Satellite imagery" is also mentioned as source of information (art. 12.3.b).

More details on the role of European institutions, as well as requirements for satellite applications necessary for EUROSUR's functioning, can only be found in secondary documents. An example of such material can be found in the common applications of surveillance tools supporting Border Surveillance (CONOPS), prepared as orientation material for the EU Framework Research Programme, which also includes Border Surveillance (European Commission 2011). The 2013 EU Concept on CSDP Support to Integrated Border Management largely omits the role of satellite imagery, and only refers briefly to the European Satellite Centre (EUSC) as an institution which "can be used to provide border related surveillance and provide pre-frontier intelligence subject to specific arrangement to this end" (Council of the European Union 2013: 43).

This somewhat tenuous or underspecified relationship between space capacities and EU border security needs to be critically discussed. In general, one can identify a noticeable connection between CSDP and the external dimension of border management. On an abstract level, analysts tend to agree that European security requires a mixture of different instruments and that internal security and external security are increasingly linked (Koutrakos 2013:226–227; Wolff et al. 2009). This was underlined in the 2010 EU Internal Security Strategy, where the interdependence between internal and external security, the external dimension of the Area of Freedom, Security and Justice, and information management are key elements of the European model of security (Council and European Parliament 2010:19; Duke and Ojanen 2006). Furthermore, new technologies should play a key role in border management, which is one of the five strategic objectives of the EU Internal Security Strategy.

However, in 2015, border management was deleted from the list of priorities of the EU Agenda on Security (European Commission 2015b), and was moved to the EU Agenda on Migration (European Commission 2015a). Adopted in May 2015, the EU Agenda on Security focuses on risk trends, and on anticipating crises, rather than just reacting to them. Pre-border intelligence, emphasized in previous documents, was replaced by more neutral expressions, such as "an effective situational picture". However, the notion of a situational picture, created to a large extent from satellite imagery, has remained a key element of pre-border intelligence. But again, border management, when border "is moved beyond its legally defined definition" (Jeandesboz 2012: 126), raises the issue of internal security, when non-European actors can use this concept for building pre-border intelligence on European soil.

At the same time, space, as well as border technologies, are seen by private companies as potential sources of profit. For example, the funding of EUROSUR and COPERNICUS has been rendered possible thanks to the FP7 and Horizon 2020 programmes. In 2015, seven COPERNICUS projects have be supported with 36 EUR million (Hallinan and Friedewald 2015: 239). The FP7 and Horizon 2020 programmes should generate results available to the broader public or serve the public interest. Nevertheless, as some media report, it is not clear if the projects can effectively detect small boats. "Frontex's deputy director has said that the myriad surveillance tools that make up EUROSUR do not provide information quickly enough to save lives" (Statewatch 2015). Two research projects, SAGRES and LOBOS, are aimed to implement and test the high time critical, intelligence driven maritime surveillance component of EUROSUR. The projects will address two scenarios dealing with the tracking of vessels on the high seas and the punctual monitoring of third country ports and coasts. LOBOS will also provide "low time critical" pre-operational services corresponding to monitoring the pre-frontier land areas. The LOBOS report summary (European Commission 2015c), however, barely provides any usable results for future space applications for EUROSUR.

Information, acquired from satellite imagery must provide accurate and verifiable information, given that border management relies on the concept of quick response and protection of life at sea. These objectives could be achieved by frequent overflights of satellites and adequate resolution of satellite imagery. "Air Standard 80/15" (Minimum Resolved Object Sizes For Imagery Interpretation) prepared for NATO forces gives five levels of minimum resolution required to perform numerous activities, from detection to identification, precise identification, description and technical analysis. For example, surface ships can be detected with a 7.5 m resolution, but identified only with a 0.6 m resolution or higher (European Parliament and Council of the EU 2014). For border management, however, in order to trace small boats and individuals with greater accuracy, the minimum measurements require at least a 0.5 m resolution (European Commission 2011: 21). Higher resolutions are classified, but another parameter (tasking) is also important. Quick tasking time and orders at short notice (from 6 to 12 h) is much more expensive. In sum, technical possibilities available to EUROSUR, such as the COPERNICUS system or the regular satellite imagery that can be provided by the EU Satellite Centre with the help of members state, are arguably of limited use for many goals in EUROSUR, in particular with regard to the protection of lives. European satellites cannot provide high resolution on demand, when any successful action at sea requires almost on-line coverage. Furthermore, while EUROSUR services include automated *large* vessel tracking and detection capabilities. For example, the seizure of illegal guns on the Greek vessel Haddad-1 was presented as a success (Frontex 2015), but this size of this ship (66 m × 11 m) is already visible with basic satellite imagery capabilities. In contrast, most refugees and migrants are travelling on small 5–7 m long boats, which are usually not picked up by satellites. Most ships on European waters are traced via other systems, like Automatic Identification System (AIS), and data could be accessed via websites open to general public (FleetMon, Vessel, MarineTraffic).

6 Normative Debates Over Satellite-Based Surveillance and Border Management

Apart from technical limitations and questions over the political or commercial motivation of EU space policy, other ethical problems arise with regard to border surveillance from outer space. First, satellite surveillance is not individualized, since technical limitations do not allow for precise action, surveillance, nor quick action to seek and capture possible migrants, suspected criminals or just people crossing border. Tracking individuals, trucks or small boats via satellite images (or videos) delivered on demand, in high quality as seen in action movies, does not occur in practice. In most cases, evidence becomes available after four or more hours, when migrants or vessels are already miles away from their previously observed position. Algorithms and software developed by EUROSUR allow for the prediction of shipping ways based on earlier satellites images and weather conditions, but such computer-assisted trajectories on a map of the Mediterranean are not necessarily helpful for border guards, who may not share the same vision of risk assessment. As pointed out by Bigo, border guards, who are dispatched to patrol and intercept, might be afraid to be "mere operators who obey other actors" (Bigo 2014: 216), and might just choose to ignore any data obtained from space and analysed by EUROSUR.

Two logics of action play out—(1) direct control of strategic areas/fields thanks to satellite images and imagery intelligence (IMINT) and (2) surveillance oriented towards indirect actions and of predictability of behaviour. These logics are connected with different satellite technologies. Whereas direct control demands almost live coverage of movement/mobility provided by IMINT, indirect control removes responsibility from border guards and places it on distant analysts who can trace, predict and estimate the risk based on more complex Digital Intelligence Signals (DIGINT). DIGINT combined with geospatial intelligence (GEOINT), that allows to obtain detailed geographical indications like maps of pre-border areas or urban areas and morphological information, builds "an effective situational picture", where *picture* is only a substitute for *intelligence*. It is worth noting that indirect logic de-territorializes border management, where people, objects, vessels, vehicles and other physical bodies are only statistical numbers. Didier Bigo aptly points out that "for practical sense of mobility and real-time traceability", computer analysts and operators then try to predict and anticipate "in the name of a preventive agenda" (Bigo 2014: 211). It is an invitation for reshaping the meaning of border, from border control to border management. Moreover, bordering spaces, which transcend the internal/external divide, are more important than lines on the map. In this sense, satellite data—and operators or algorithms working on this data-project the EU border outwards, thus contributing to the merging of external and internal security.

Such practices of bordering and de facto surveillance raise further questions about the right to privacy. The EU expressly guarantees this right in other contexts in the EURSUR regulation. As mentioned before, the regular does not allow for the regular exchange personal data in the context of continuous information exchanges on the "European situational picture and the common pre-frontier intelligence picture." However, the regular practice of satellite-based surveillance may conflict with the right to be forgotten, when data on daily activities of individuals—collected from satellite signals and processed by sophisticated software—could be stored for any purpose without any right to access. Intelligence gathered by creating pre-border situational pictures can contain sensitive data, however, some authors argue that current resolution possibilities of satellite images are too limited to "reveal sufficient detail to become an intrusion on privacy" (London Institute of Space Policy and Law 2012: 378). Nevertheless, this last point can be countered by pointing to the fact that SAR images can highlight traces on grass, due to different angle of radar wave reflection, while analysts can predict habits and behavior of inhabitants with algorithms. In other words, people living in certain areas could be systematically observed and their everyday life could be dominated by distrust, or "withdrawal of trust," as extensively discussed with regard to CCTV and urban surveillance (Van der Ploeg 2006; Zedner 2009; Andersen and Möller 2013). Reliance on technology may also dehumanize mobility and flows (Aas et al. 2009: 10–11) and obscure political assessments or judgment. Images provided by satellites can only be analysed by technically specialized experts, as they are not self-evident documents, requiring instead substantial evaluation of evidence. For instance, satellites equipped with SAR can provide information, but not evidence, and detected objects, which look like boats, can include waves, wind, algae or other natural phenomena (London Institute of Space Policy and Law 2012: 317). For the purposes of border management, this kind of data could be counterproductive. In other words, the comprehensive monitoring of SAR signals may give rise to conflicting data, which also requires expert evaluations, rather than clearly bringing out the desired trends and information about particular migratory movements or vessels necessary on demand.

7 Conclusion

By using space resources for border management and border security, the EU is clearly attempting to establish itself as a regional and global technological leader. With satellite systems, possibilities for surveillance, reconnaissance, and border management seem to be unlimited. However, questions of technological possibilities as well as the coherence of the EU's external actions remain relevant. Initially, the EU space policy was mainly connected to CSDP. Its extension to border management is less clear or coherent than expected. This is mainly due to the fact that EU technological capabilities are still limited. In fact, data for geospatial intelligence provided by the EUSC comes from European satellites, but also from Indian and Taiwanese sources. Furthermore, any independent European capabilities are still in the pipeline.

Since no reliable results have been presented so far by EUROSUR, and the numbers of lives lost at sea remain high, the future of EUROSUR does not look so promising. Especially, the lack of European action at the level of southern maritime borders, in the context of the current refugee crisis in Europe, raises the question of coherence of actions, effectiveness of EUROSUR, and pushes EU member states to start independent policies on border management. Combined with legal challenges, as the right to privacy (Deibler 2015: 91), and the redefinition of European borders, border management with satellite applications may encounter more challenges in the near future than originally predicted. Moreover, there is a clash between the image that the EU wishes to project in the world, namely as a normative actor in the regional and global orders, and the gradual creation of capacities for actively managing the pre-border environment, with unlimited competences for gathering intelligence. With more surveillance at European borders, and unlimited data collection from satellite imagery, one could thus expect the evolution of the familiar critical debate on "Fortress Europe"—which implies a static image—to a newer, technologically modern negative vision of "Patrolling Power Europe."

Acknowledgements This contribution draws on wider research projects. Dr. Słomczyńska received financial support by the Polish Ministry of Science and Higher Education for the project "European Space Policy", N N116 321638. Dr. Frankowski received the 2014 Sorensen Grant of the European University Institute, Florence, where he pursued the project "Tracing the origins of space security".

References

Aas, K. F., Gundhus, H. O., & Lomell, H. M. (2009). Introduction. In K. F. Aas, H. O. Gundhus, & H. M. Lomell (Eds.), *Technologies of inSecurity: The surveillance of everyday life* (pp. 1–18). Abingdon-NewYork: Routledge-Cavendish.
Algieri, F. (2015). In search of shared autonomy: The EU as a restricted foreign, security and defence political actor. In C. Al-Ekabi (Ed.), *European autonomy in space* (pp. 93–103). Vienna: Springer International Publishing.
Andersen, R. S., & Möller, F. (2013). Engaging the limits of visibility: Photography, security and surveillance. *Security Dialogue, 44*(3), 203–221.
Asbeck, F. (2008). EU satellite center—A bird's eye view in support of ESDP operations. *ESDP Newsletter, 8*, 22–23.
Bigo, D. (2014). The (in) securitization practices of the three universes of EU border control: Military/Navy–border guards/police–database analysts. *Security Dialogue, 45*(3), 209–225.
Birchfield, V. (2013). A normative power Europe framework of transnational policy formation. *Journal of European Public Policy, 20*(6), 907–922.
Christol, C. Q. (1988). Remote sensing and international space law. *Journal of Space Law, 16*(1), 21–44.
Council and European Parliament. (2010). *The EU internal security strategy in action: Five steps towards a more secure Europe.* Available at http://eur-lex.europa.eu/legal-content/PL/TXT/HTML/?uri=CELEX:52011DC0152andfrom=PL. Brussels
Council of the European Union. (2006). *Generic space systems needs for military operations.* Accessed January 11, 2015, from http://www.europarl.europa.eu/meetdocs/2004_2009/documents/dv/st6920_/st6920_en.pdf
Council of the European Union. (2008). *Council conclusions on the management of the external borders of the member states of the European union, 9873/08.* Accessed September 14, 2015, from http://register.consilium.europa.eu/doc/srv?l = ENandf = ST%209873%202008%20INIT
Council of the European Union. (2010). *Council conclusions on 29 measures for reinforcing the protection of the external borders and combating illegal immigration.* Accessed August 14, 2015, from http://www.consilium.europa.eu/uedocs/cms_data/docs/pressdata/en/jha/113065.pdf
Council of the European Union. (2013). *Revised draft EU concept on CSDP support to integrated border management.* 16044/2/13 REV 2.
Damro, C. (2012). Market power Europe. *Journal of European Public Policy, 19*(5), 682–699.
Deibler, D. (2015). EUROSUR-Sci Fi border zone patrolled by drones. In J. Camenisch, S. Fischer-Hübner, & M. Hansen (Eds.), *Privacy and identity management for the future internet in the age of globalisation* (pp. 87–109). Cham: Springer.
Duke, S., & Ojanen, H. (2006). Bridging internal and external security: Lessons from the European security and defence policy. *Journal of European Integration, 28*(5), 477–494.
Eriksen, E. O. (2014). *The normativity of the European Union.* Basingstoke: Palgrave Macmillan.
European Commission. (2003a). *European space policy.* Green Paper. COM(2003) 17 final.
European Commission. (2003b). *White paper on space: A new European frontier for an expanding union—An action plan for implementing the European Space policy.* COM(2003) 673 final.
European Commission. (2009). *Global monitoring for environment and security (GMES): Challenges and next steps for the space component.*
European Commission. (2011). *Application of surveillance tools to border surveillance "Concept of Operations"*. Available at http://ec.europa.eu/enterprise/policies/security/files/doc/conops_gmes_en.pdfBrussels
European Commission. (2013). *COMMISSION DELEGATED REGULATION (EU) No 1159/2013 of 12 July 2013 supplementing Regulation (EU) No 911/2010 of the European Parliament and of the Council on the European Earth monitoring programme (GMES) by establishing registration and licensing conditions for GMES users and defining criteria for restricting access to*

GMES dedicated data and GMES service information. Available at http://eur-lex.europa.eu/legal-content/PL/TXT/HTML/?uri = CELEX:32013R1159andfrom = EN Brussels
European Commission. (2015a). *The European agenda on migration*. Available at http://eur-lex.europa.eu/legal-content/PL/TXT/HTML/?uri=CELEX:32013R1159andfrom=ENBrussels
European Commission. (2015b). *The European agenda on security*. Available at http://eur-lex.europa.eu/legal.content/PL/TXT/HTML/?uri=CELEX:32013R1159andfrom=ENBrussels
European Commission. (2015c). *FP7–Space, LOBOS (LOw time critical BOrder Surveillance) Report Summary*. Accessed May 6, 2015, from http://cordis.europa.eu/result/rcn/155588_en.pdf
European Council. (2004). *ESDP and space*. 11616/04 REV3.
European Parliament. (2009). Report on the European security strategy and ESDP.
European Parliament. (2011). Establishing the European border surveillance system (EUROSUR).
European Parliament. (2013). Regulation (EU) No 1052/2013 of the European Parliament and of the Council of 22 October 2013 establishing the European Border Surveillance System (Eurosur),
European Parliament and Council of the EU. (2014). *Proposal for a directive of the European parliament and of the council on the dissemination of Earth observation satellite data for commercial purposes*. Accessed September 13, 2014, from http://eur-lex.europa.eu/legal-content/PL/TXT/HTML/?uri = CELEX:32013R1159andfrom = EN
Feder, H. (1990). Sky's the limit—Evaluating the international law of remote sensing. *The New York University Journal of International Law and Politics, 23*(2), 599–670.
Frontex. (2015, March 9). Frontex|News—Greeks seize illegal guns on ship monitored by Frontex. Accessed September 15, 2015, from http://frontex.europa.eu/news/greeks-seize-illegal-guns-on-ship-monitored-by-frontex-KcJsMr
Genschel, P., & Jachtenfuchs, M. (2014). Beyond market regulation. Analysing the European integration of core state powers. In P. Genschel & M. Jachtenfuchs (Eds.), *Beyond the regulatory polity?: The European integration of core state powers* (pp. 1–23). Oxford: Oxford University Press.
Giannopapa, C. (2012). Securing Galileo's and GMES's place in European policy. *Space Policy, 28*(4), 270–282.
Gleason, M. P. (2009). *Galileo: Power, pride, and profit. The relative influence of realist, ideational, and liberal factors on the galileo satellite program, DTIC document*. Accessed August 1, 2014, from http://www.dtic.mil/cgi-bin/GetTRDoc?AD = ADA495023&Location = U2&doc = GetTRDoc.pdf
Hallinan, D., & Friedewald, M. (2015). Economic costs of surveillance technologies. In D. Wright & R. Kreissl (Eds.), *Surveillance in Europe* (pp. 230–239). Oxon: Routledge.
Harris, R. (2008). Current status and recent developments in UK and European remote sensing law and policy. *Journal of Space Law, 34*(1), 33–44.
Jeandesboz, J. (2012). Beyond the Tartar steppe: EUROSUR and the ethics of European border control practices. In J. P. Burgess & S. Gutwirth (Eds.), *A threat against Europe?: Security, migration and integration* (pp. 111–132). Brussels: VUB Press.
Jentzsch, J. (2010). Use of satellite data for treaty monitoring. In M. Sánchez Aranzamendi, R. Sandau, & K.-U. Schrogl (Eds.), *Current legal issues for satellite earth observation* (pp. 27–30). Wien: ESPI.
Kolovos, A. (2009). The European space policy-its impact and challenges for the European security and defence policy. *European Space Policy Perspectives, 27*, 1–17.
Kolovos, A. (2013). Space-Based capabilities for internal security operations: A critical assessment of the case of land border surveillance. In P. Hulsroj, S. Pagkratis, & B. Baranes (Eds.), *Yearbook on space policy 2010/2011: The forward look* (pp. 159–174). Wien: Springer.
Koutrakos, P. (2013). *The EU common security and defence policy*. Oxford: Oxford University Press.
Larsen, H. (2014). The EU as a normative power and the research on external perceptions: The missing link. *Journal of Common Market Studies, 52*(4), 896–910.

London Institue of Space Policy and Law. (2012). *Evidence from space*. London: London Institue of Space Policy and Law.
Manners, I. (2008). The normative ethics of the European Union. *International Affairs, 84*(1), 45–60.
Meunier, S., & Nicolaïdis, K. (2006). The European Union as a conflicted trade power. *Journal of European Public Policy, 13*(6), 906–925.
Mitsilegas, V. (2015). The law of the border and the borders of law: Rethining border control from the perspective of the individual. In L. Weber (Ed.), *Rethinking border control for a globalizing world: A preferred future*. Oxon: Routledge.
Moltz, J. (2014). *Crowded orbits: Conflict and cooperation in space*. New York, NY: Columbia University Press.
Remuss, N.-L. (2012). Space and security as an identity forming element—meeting Europe's external and internal security through space applications. In C. Venet & B. Baranes (Eds.), *European identity through space: Space activities and programmes as a tool to reinvigorate the European identity* (pp. 132–144). Vienna-NewYork: Springer.
Rohner, N., Schrogl, K.-U., & Cheli, S. (2007). Making GMES better known: Challenges and opportunities. *Space Policy, 23*(4), 195–198.
Statewatch. (2015). *News Online: EU: Frontex budget: €17 million increase puts agency on "cruising speed."* Accessed July 4, 2015, from http://www.statewatch.org/news/2015/feb/eu-frontex-budget%202015.htm
United Nations. (1986). *Principles relating to remote sensing of the earth from space. A/RES/41/65*. Accessed July 4, 2015, from http://www.un.org/documents/ga/res/41/a41r065.htm
Van der Ploeg, I. (2006). Borderline identities: The enrollment of bodies in the technological reconstruction of borders. In T. Monahan (Ed.), *Surveillance and security: Technological politics and power in everyday life*. New York: Routledge.
Von der Dunk, F. G. (2006). Towards Monitoring Galileo: The European GNSS Supervisory Authority in Statu Nascendi/Zur Kunftigen Uberwachungsagentur des Galileo Systems/Vers une Autorite de Surveillance du Systeme Galileo. *Zeitschrift für Luft- und Weltraumrecht, 55* (1), 100–117.
Von der Dunk, F. G. (2008). European satellite Earth observation: Law, regulations, policies, projects, and programmes. *Creighton Law Review, 42*(3), 397–446.
Western European Union. (1984). The military use of space. In *Proceedings Vol. I, Thirtieth Session, First Part*, June 1984 (Assembly document 976).
Western European Union. (1998). In *Proceedings Vol. I, Forty-Fourth Session, First Part*, May 1998 (Assembly document 1612). WEU Council of Ministers 11–12 May 1998, Rhodes Declaration.
Western European Union. (2001). *A joint European space strategy: Security and defence aspects. Assembly of Western European Union. Forty-seventh session* (Document A/1738).
Western European Union. (2004). The space dimension of the ESDP. In *Proceedings Vol. III, Fiftieth Session, First Part*, November–December 2004 (Assembly document A/1881).
Wolff, S., Wichmann, N., & Mounier, G. (2009). The external dimension of justice and home affairs: A different security agenda for the EU? *Journal of European Integration, 31*(1), 9–23.
Zedner, L. (2009). The inescapable insecurity of security technologies. In K. F. Aas, H. O. Gundhus, & H. M. Lomell (Eds.), *Technologies of inSecurity: the surveillance of everydaylife* (pp. 257–270). Abingdon-NewYork: Routledge-Cavendish.

Integrated Border Management and Irregular Migration at the South European-North African Border: The Case of Spain

Ana López-Sala and Dirk Godenau

1 Introduction

Just as in other European and North American countries (Huysmans 2000; Andreas 2000; Adamson 2006), irregular migration in Spain was labelled as a security issue in the 1990s. Immigration appeared on the Spanish security agenda due to the intensification of irregular border crossings by land and sea and because of growing fears regarding the vulnerability and physical integrity of the country's southern border. In fact, over the past two decades the Spanish government has come to view irregular migration from Africa as its greatest threat and controlling these flows has become the primary way it demonstrates its ability to protect the country's borders and exercise its sovereignty. This has resulted in the border adopting new functions through the creation of an asymmetric border control regime, in which differentiated and hierarchical migration control actions have been implemented at land, maritime and airport borders.

Against this backdrop, the objective of this chapter[1] is to analyse how Spanish policy on migration control at the southern border has been constructed within the context of the implementation of European border policy. The analysis shows that Spain's approach is characterized by processes of externalization, communitarization and technologization in which the borders have adopted new

[1] Research developed in the framework of MIND Research Project (grant number CSO2014-53680) funded by the Spanish National Research Program (Programa Excelencia), 2015–2017.

A. López-Sala (✉)
Institute of Economics, Geography and Demography, Spanish Council for Scientific Research (CSIC), Center for Human and Social Sciences, C/Albasanz, 26-28, Madrid 28037, Spain
e-mail: ana.lsala@cchs.csic.es

D. Godenau
Department of Applied Economics and Quantitative Methods, University La Laguna, Campus de Guajara, 38071 La Laguna, Spain
e-mail: dgodenau@ull.es

R. Bossong, H. Carrapico (eds.), *EU Borders and Shifting Internal Security*,
DOI 10.1007/978-3-319-17560-7_5

roles and functions. In the Spanish case, the objective of containing irregular immigration has been put into practice through a dynamic strategy that combines, in a flexible and interactive way, these three processes in response to migration contingencies. As a result, controlling irregular immigration has taken the form of political embeddedness in which these instruments have been implemented with varying levels of intensity and progressed in a complementary way as part of a single border-enforcement system.

Spanish border territories have also been used to test new approaches to migration control that have later been applied to the entire European outer perimeter (European Commission 2011). As we shall see, European and Spanish border policies have adapted to changes in migration dynamics and reflect the tensions between the principles of protecting state interests and protecting the rights of immigrants. In fact, the control practices that have been implemented have led some parliamentary groups and civil society organizations to question the legitimacy of this restrictive migration regime and to try and mobilize public opinion in the defence of migrant rights. However, the scope and effectiveness of this critical response have been constrained by the parliamentary majority of the conservative government.

The chapter proceeds in four parts. The first part centres on the embeddedness of irregular migration control practices into the state logics of containing such flows, giving rise to conflicts between security issues and the fundamental rights of migrants. The second part offers a synoptic vision of the main tendencies in irregular migration in the Mediterranean, in general, and of flows heading to the Spanish coasts, in particular. The third describes the changes that stem from the adaptation of Spanish policy on migration control and the progressive implementation of the Integrated Border Management (IBM) of the European Union. The fourth and final part focuses on the Spanish cities of Ceuta and Melilla, the most "visible" sectors of the Spanish perimeter, to analyse the wider response to this kind of border management, which has generated an intense and heated public debate on the fair limits of state control policies (Weber 2013).

2 Bordering Irregular Migration: Struggling for Control and Fundamental Rights

Borders are socially constructed rules that condition the flow of people, goods, capital and information between states. In this sense, they can be considered mechanisms that regulate bilateral and multidimensional permeability. Borders are not only restrictive, they also promote certain kinds of flows that are considered desirable, such as highly skilled workers. In other words, borders function selectively, distinguishing between regular (legal) and irregular (illegal) flows. Therefore, border management must meet the challenge of impeding undesirable mobility without creating obstacles for desirable mobility (Wonders 2006; Mau et al. 2012; Kinnvall and Svensson 2014). The restrictive immigration policies of rich countries predominantly implement measures that make their borders more impermeable. In this regard, the southern border of the European Union is a type of border referred to by Walters as the "limes"[2] (2004, p. 690), a kind of wall constructed to impede unauthorized access.

In terms of state security and the pursuit of national interest the function of the European Union's border is tied to the risks and dangers associated with the entrance of undocumented population, international terrorism and the fight against organized crime (Pickering and Weber 2006; Adamson 2006; Rudolph 2003; Guild 2009). While one aspect of security is to effectively and substantially reduce security risks, a more discursive dimension is related to the public perception of threats to society (Andreas 1998). In this second aspect, perceived security, and the implementation of border control technologies in particular, symbolizes the state's efforts to ensure security, simultaneously serving as proof that everything possible is being done to reduce exterior threats.

The area of human security, a dimension of security focusing on individuals (King and Murray 2001), examines how state intervention to control migration affects the physical integrity of the migrants themselves while they are in transit or crossing borders (Eschbach et al. 1999; Meneses 2003; Grant 2011; Weber and Pickering 2011; Ferrer-Gallardo and Van Houtum 2014; Basaran 2014). For example, implementing technology is dynamically linked to human security, in that it can save the lives of migrants or put them at greater risk. In this sense, the relationship between technology and the security of the migrants is ambiguous and conditioned by how it is used. At the same time, highly effective border control technologies can also indirectly affect the risks associated with migration, because they may cause migration routes and modes of entry to shift in ways that make the process more dangerous. Protecting the lives of migrants has recently become a focus of some international bodies and international civil society. A good example of this is the UNHCR "Rescue at Sea" initiative, a 2-year initiative launched to limit the loss of life and foster international cooperation (Newland 2014). The European Union has recently included migrant protection and security as an inherent part of border management. This concern for the fundamental rights of migrants has also been formally acknowledged by the inclusion of a "fundamental rights officer" in the organization chart of Frontex (2014d).

Externalization, communitarization and technologization are some of the traits that have characterized the management of irregular immigration in the European

[2] In a 2004 article, Walters proposed four analytics to conceptualize different facets of the EU's changing borders and argued that each of these analytics could be associated with a particular "geo-strategy". Inspired by Michel Foucher's work, he referred to one of these analytics as "limes", in reference to the border defense or "strategic figure" of Ancient Rome which marked the boundaries of the Roman Empire. Foucher describes limes as "essentially a strategy aiming both at containing unwelcome migrants and at organizing trade with Romanized peoples (Foucher 1998). "The strategy of limes does not envisage a progressive or eventual subsumption of the exterior territory and its inhabitants. Instead, it effects the institutionalization of asymmetries of economy, culture and order [...] It is an asymmetrical relationship which remains a permanent source of tension" (Walters 2004).

Union and Spain (Lahav and Guiraudon 2000; Zolberg 2003; Wolff 2012; Dijstelbloem and Meijer 2011). Both externalization and communitarization involve formal cooperation mechanisms between states. Externalization involves the partial transfer of migration control to countries of origin and transit and includes a wide range of measures. For example, from 2004 onwards the formal collaboration between Spanish and Moroccan and Mauritanian authorities has included the creation of bi-national coordination commissions on immigration and the deployment of joint surveillance patrols at sea. Since 2006 this collaboration has been strengthened and broadened, first with the creation of the Seahorse Program and later the Seahorse Network.[3] Externalization has been particularly evident on the southern border of the European Union because it includes large interstitial maritime regions, physical and jurisdictional spaces where surveillance requires additional coordinated efforts (López-Sala and Esteban 2010; Baldacchino 2014).

Communitarization involves the joint design and application of immigration policies by different members of the European Union (see the contribution on EUROSUR in this book) including legal and operational measures. Our focus on the control of maritime borders within the general process of communitarization highlights elements linked to the surveillance of maritime flows in transit, including initiatives such as Frontex joint operations, the implementation of EUROSUR or the investment in remote sensing technologies using shared budget instruments, as in the Closeye project. From this perspective, the communitarization of border control implies the homogenization of permeability, although the effort required to implement these conditions is highly variable depending on the geopolitical context. In the case of the European Union, the common policy and joint management is gradually being developed, with Spain playing an active role in this process, particularly through its pilot experience in the prevention of irregular maritime migration (Godenau 2014; López-Sala 2015a).

Despite the advances in communitarization, it is worth noting that the member states of the European Union still have a great deal of freedom to act as they see fit to safeguard and condition their national borders. In the Spanish case the measures that fall under the process of communitarization have supplemented the initiatives adopted at the national level and it can be stated that no significant tension has arisen between the principles of national autonomy and communitarization. On the contrary, during the "cayuco crisis"[4] the Spanish government demanded that other European countries take a larger role in controlling the southern border of the EU

[3] Seahorse Network is a safe regional satellite communications network coordinated by Spain, to exchange information on maritime irregular immigration in which police authorities from Mauritania, Morocco, Cape Verde and Senegal participate.

[4] During 2006 more than 30,000 irregular migrants arrived at the shores (when not intercepted) and ports (after being intercepted) of the Canary Islands. The term "cayuco" refers to a type of wooden fishing boat used in Western African countries. This event was labelled as a "crisis" because there was a sudden amplification of the Atlantic route from Africa to Spain that implied the geographical extension of control efforts beyond the Mediterranean route (Godenau and Zapata 2008).

and an intensification of the communitarization processes in order to have effective subsidiary action. However, tension between these two principles has emerged during the past few years due to the actions carried out on the land borders of Ceuta and Melilla, as will be explained further in the last section of this chapter.

The third tendency is the technologization of border management. Despite appearances, it is not easy to define what border technologies are and what they are not. In a broad sense, the concept of technology refers to a "design for instrumental action that reduces the uncertainty in the cause-effect relationships involved in achieving a desired outcome" (Rogers 2003, p. 13). Under such a broad definition, all means employed for a certain end are technology. In this sense, a physical obstacle placed in a border post to stop entrance is technology, as are the intelligence services when they provide information about the movement of migrants in border areas. However, in literature dealing with borders, and in the approach that we use in this article, the term technology is normally used more restrictively, referring only to information and communication technologies and instruments that are based on them (such as satellites, drones, night vision cameras, radars, etc.). Technology has diverse functions in controlling migration: it contributes to detection, interception, identification and derivation (Godenau and López-Sala 2016). These new technologies play a larger role in detection and interception, while "traditional" technologies are more common in identification and derivation (passports, interviews, means of transportation). The effectiveness and efficiency of these border management technologies depend on how they are embedded into a specific context. The physical context (land, maritime or airport borders), the geographic location (borders that separate spaces that have high or low levels of inequality), and the socio-political context (the degree of conflict between states) shape the way technology is implemented.

Technology also plays an important role in the bottom-up visibilization of government practices, because the miniaturization and portability of new information technologies allow incidents that had once been opaque to be easily recorded and disseminated. In this kind of restrictive border, which blocks mobility and generates irregular crossings, the praxis of border management has been under increasing scrutiny by the migrants, the organizations that represent them, NGOs and the general public. This means that accountability and the need to legitimize the sovereign actions of the state in the management of its borders go hand in hand with the growing pressure of information provided by the migrant actors themselves and the NGOs that support their demands. It should be mentioned that to some degree greater transparency might increase the externalization of border control, because shifting control measures to other countries may help western societies feel less exposed to criticism for implementing highly visible restrictive measures at their own borders. In this sense, the availability of information and different levels of visibility can produce differentiated practices and patterns of protest in several parts of Europe.

Spain is a good example of the gradual construction of Integrated Border Management on the southern border of the European Union. This process has advanced in stages and is based on the contribution of national initiatives carried out by Border States and European Union itself. The rest of this chapter will analyse in detail how Spain, part of the complex Mediterranean scenario of irregular maritime migration, has combined externalization, communitarization, cooperation with countries of origin and transit and the implementation of new technological resources to manage its borders and examine the difficulties of politically and socially justifying these measures in the face of growing protests by civil society.

3 The Embeddedness of Irregular Migration From Africa to Spain

The irregular migration scenario at the southern EU border is a complex of interconnected routes, where national control practices and extraordinary political and economic events in origin and transit countries are intertwined and lead to a dynamic pattern that must be described in order to understand Spain's relative position within the system. The empirical pattern of irregular migrations from Africa to the European continent can be summarized by the following: (a) over the years there have been pronounced oscillations in the total volume of arrivals and interceptions; (b) at the same time the pattern of the most used routes has also changed,[5] specifically, there has been a shift from western routes to other routes in the centre or east of the Mediterranean; (c) the means used for transport have diversified, with migrants using everything from individual transports (small rubber dinghies) to old merchant ships; (d) the composition of the origins of the immigrants has also diversified, most recently incorporating a large contingent from the Middle East (especially Syria); (e) the smuggling "industry," and intermediaries in general, have organized themselves in various formats depending on the context in which they operate; (f) the resources dedicated to measures of detection, interception and acceptance/derivation have increased, their financing has been internationalized and their forces have been partially integrated.

This complex and dynamic pattern is caused by many factors. In order to systemize this group of interrelated factors, we can distinguish between those that generate a greater or lesser affluence of people prepared to undertake irregular maritime migration to the European Union; those that condition the probability of opting de facto for this option; and those that affect the probability of being intercepted during the trajectory. In the first group of factors there are phenomena related to geopolitical instability in certain countries and historical periods, as armed conflicts and poverty generate pressure to immigrate to the nearest stable countries. The conflict in Syria is a recent example. The second group of factors is related to the range of organizational alternatives available to potential emigrants. Their decisions are affected by the possibility of entering other countries legally;

[5] The routes are: the Western Africa route, the Western Mediterranean route, the Central Mediterranean route, the Apulia and Calabria route, the Circular Albania-Greece route, the Western Balkans route, the Eastern Balkans route and the Eastern Border route (Frontex 2014a, see Fig. 1).

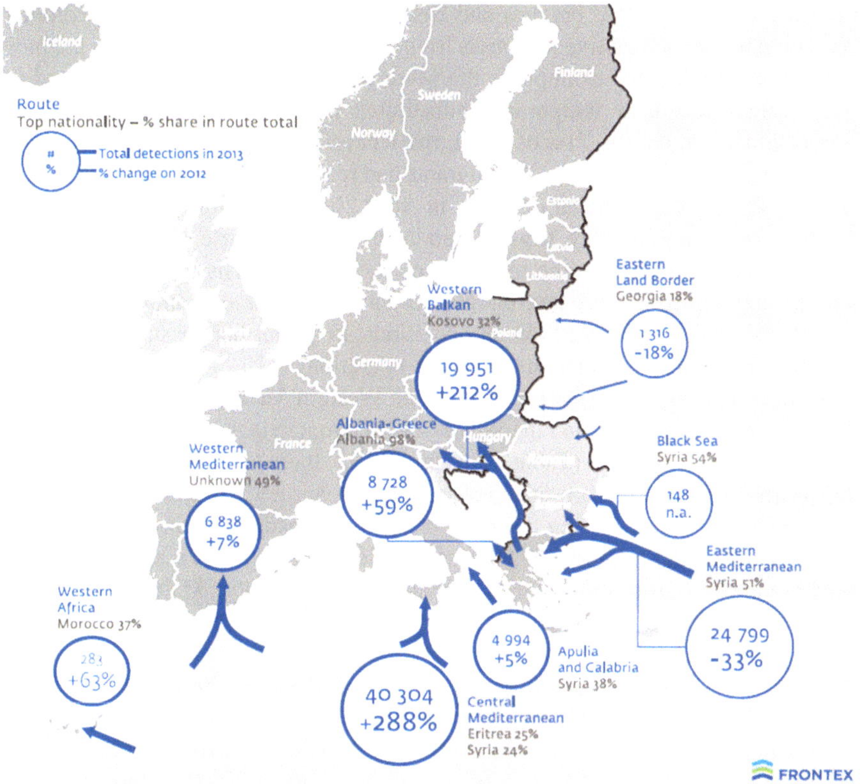

Fig. 1 Detections of illegal border-crossing in 2013 with percentage change from 2012 by route and top nationality detected. *Source*: Frontex (2014a, p. 33)

their ability to finance the different options; and the information available to them to take their decision. Finally, the probability of interception is affected by the level of impermeability of the border according to places and seasons, the efficacy of the smugglers and the consequences of interception. These consequences can vary from rescue and asylum to immediate expulsion.

The statistical data on interceptions provided by Frontex (2014a, b, c) indicate that in 2013 and 2014 there was a clear increase, reaching an annual total greater than 150,000 intercepted people, a volume even greater than during the Arab Spring (107,000 in 2011). This increase is due in particular to the political instability in Eastern Mediterranean regions, with a growing affluence of emigrants from these areas (e.g., Syria) and lesser controls in some of the countries of transit (e.g., Libya and Egypt). A large part of these immigrants used the Central and Eastern Mediterranean routes (see Fig. 1). Among the countries of origin, there was a substantial increase in Syrians, Eritreans, Afghans and Albanians, reducing the proportion of sub-Saharan migrants (Frontex 2014a). The intensification of irregular maritime immigration has been accompanied by greater risks for the immigrants (Brian and

Laczlo 2014; FRA 2013; Fargues and Bonfati 2014; Fargues and Di Bartolomeo 2015) and has led to reactive responses from the European Union and from the most affected countries. One example is the Mare Nostrum operation implemented by Italy, which was later temporarily substituted by the Triton operation of the European Union. On the 21st of April, the UN refugee agency UNHCR reported that in 2015 so far a total of 36,390 migrants had reached Italy, Greece and Malta by sea. The dramatic events that occurred in April 2015, with more than 800 migrant deaths at sea in a single day, triggered an institutional response (with an extraordinary meeting of the EU prime ministers on the refugee crisis on the 23rd of that month) that tripled the Frontex budget dedicated to these operations but did not change the basic objective: Frontex operations are about border surveillance and not about humanitarian corridors or rescue operations.

Unlike the Central and Eastern routes, the Western Mediterranean route, whose main destination is Spain, and the Western Africa route via the Canary Islands have diminished in volume (Table 1). In 2013, there were only 6838 and 283 interceptions on these routes, respectively. Spain reached these low levels of maritime arrivals after having been one of the main destinations in earlier periods: of the accumulated total of 850,000 interceptions between 1998 and 2014 in the Mediterranean European countries (including Spain, Italy, Malta and Greece) (Fargues and Bonfati 2014), around 200,000 (25 %) arrived by maritime routes to Spain (López-Sala, 2015a). The timing of these occurrences on the routes to Spain can be divided into various phases: the first includes the 1990s to 2000, during which the Western Mediterranean route predominated; a second from 2001 to 2008, when there was an intense increase, with more than 30,000 arrivals in 2006 during the cayuco crisis in the Canaries (Godenau and Zapata 2008), followed by the collapse in the Western Africa route via the Canary Islands; and a third phase after

Table 1 Maritime irregular immigration routes to Spain

Western Mediterranean route	Western Africa route
Migration corridors	
North African-Iberian Peninsula countries Strait of Gibraltar route Ceuta and Melilla land route Algiers and Northern Morocco-Balearic Islands and south-eastern provinces route	Northwest African countries—Canary Islands Eastern island route Western island route
Origin	
Morocco, Algiers and sub-Saharan countries (Mali, Senegal, Gambia, Ghana, Ivory Coast, Nigeria, Benin, etc.)	Morocco, Algiers and sub-Saharan countries (Mali, Senegal, Gambia, Ghana, Ivory Coast, Nigeria, Benin, etc.)
Destination	
Andalusian and south-eastern Spanish provinces and the Balearic Islands	Eastern and Western Canary Islands
Main transit countries	
Morocco, Algiers, Mali and Niger	Morocco, Mauritania and Senegal

Source: Authors

2008 in which the Mediterranean route again becomes the focus, but with decreasing numbers of immigrants intercepted. One of the most important reasons for the gradual reduction in the volume of arrivals has been the "sustained high levels of surveillance (ensuring early detections) and collaboration with third-country authorities" (Frontex 2014c, p. 20). Given the increase in arrivals through the Western Mediterranean route in 2014, Frontex (2014c, p. 6) warns that "several indicators point to a continued increase in migration along this route."

The western route has also shifted toward a greater percentage of immigrants intercepted at the land borders of Ceuta and Melilla. In 2013 they accounted for two thirds of the total interceptions on this route. The territories of Ceuta and Melilla can be entered by land, scaling the fences that protect the border or by sneaking past border-crossing control posts, as well as by sea, usually by swimming while avoiding the physical obstacles (breakwaters) and surveillance along the sea coast by Moroccan and Spanish authorities. In the last decade, a total of 28,000 irregular immigrants have entered by land, becoming the largest flow after 2010. Currently (data of the second 4-month period of 2014; Frontex 2014c) 80 % of arrivals to Ceuta and Melilla are of sub-Saharan origin, primarily from Cameroon, Guinea and Mali, but this route has also been increasingly used by Syrian refugees. The increase in arrivals through this route is related to greater control in the other (maritime) routes and the escalation of internal control in Morocco, which pushes migrants in transit to leave that country. Frontex (2014c, p. 19) also alludes to the fact that "Ceuta and Melilla are preferred destinations because they do not require the costly involvement of a facilitation network." The growing pressure on this fortified part of the land border has led to its reinforcement using physical and organizational measures. The control actions implemented on this segment of the Spanish border site have triggered public protest and sparked a debate about the accountability of the control practices employed by the Spanish government, which has had some resonance in the European debate. At the same time, this greater impermeability is being contested by the immigrants through changes in their entrance strategies (attempts to cross in massive simultaneous waves at various points of the perimeter) and the reconsideration of alternative maritime trajectories to continental Spain (Frontex 2014c, p. 6). These trajectories have once again increased their volumes, accounting for up to 45 % of the Western route during 2014.

The determinants of these flow patterns in the Mediterranean in general, and the Spanish case in particular, are related to political events and economic hardship in origin and transit countries, but also to changes in migration control policies. The impact of policy measures should not be underestimated. Externalization, technologization and communitarization are the labels for three basic trends underlying these changes. Spain's temporary success in irregular maritime migration control is not only due to the "luck" of having stable and cooperative neighbours, it is also a consequence of an early implemented multi-layered deterrence strategy. The next section will focus on these trends in detail.

4 Integrated Border Management at the Spanish Southern Borders. Externalization, Communitarization, Technologization

Throughout the past two decades controlling irregular immigration to Spanish territory through the southern Spanish border has been the focus of intense state intervention. This action, based on securitization and the criminalization of irregular migration, was implemented through a progressive and comprehensive multi-layered deterrence strategy combined the use of barrier, surveillance and detection technologies (technologization) with creative and innovative forms of government at and beyond the border (externalization), both as national initiatives or in cooperation with the EU (communitarization). The Spanish case demonstrates that all these trends are combined under the common objective of deterrence and that they evolve adaptively over time.

Over the years the Spanish deterrence strategy has changed along three fluid spatial and political lines: (a) a gradual externalization and geographical extension of the action, revealing the novel multiple and multi-sited character of migration control policies; (b) the consolidation of bilateral and multilateral cooperation with countries of origin and transit; and (c) the progressive Europeanization or communitarization of Spanish migration control policy, incorporating new forms of institutional design and border management at a supranational scale. This intervention, increasingly complex in its objectives and spatial dimensions, has evolved along with the migration dynamics of the diverse border corridors.

In the second half of the 1990s the implementation of new technologies to contain migration flows to Spain became more important. At first, the intervention was focused on blocking the periphery land borders. During this period security fences were built and the first infrared cameras and motion detectors were installed in Ceuta and Melilla. More recently, the intensification of migration flows through these enclaves located in African territory has led to the barrier instruments being reinforced with the installation of anti-climbing fences and the controversial concertina wire. The Moroccan border perimeter has also been reinforced. At the start of the last decade, the increase of irregular immigration by sea led to the implementation of long-distance surveillance and remote control technologies better suited to the physical characteristics of maritime borders. Between 2000 and 2007 the Integrated Surveillance System (SIVE) was designed and implemented on the Western Mediterranean route, in the Strait of Gibraltar and the Western Atlantic route, in the Canary Islands. SIVE is a radar-based system of interception and detection of maritime routes and crossings that allows remote detection in Spanish coastal areas. Spain's experience with SIVE has served as a bench test for the development and implementation of EUROSUR (Godenau 2012, 2014; Jeandesboz 2011).

Since the end of the last decade, the southern Spanish border has been used to experiment with more innovative technological detection mechanisms. The application of this experimental technology has taken place in the context of the increasing communitarization of migration control policy and has allowed surveillance to be extended to more remote maritime areas. Drones were used in 2008 to measure their effectiveness in maritime surveillance of irregular migration. This previous experience resulted in the implementation of the CLOSEYE Project in 2013, a project coordinated by the Spanish Civil Guard, which uses UAVs to monitor Europe's maritime borders.[6] In 2008 the AMASS project (Autonomous Maritime Surveillance System) was installed in the water around the Canary Islands. This is a system of maritime buoys located at high sea that allow for more thorough surveillance of remote maritime areas.[7] In sum, in the last decade Spanish migration borders became technical landscapes of control and surveillance (Paasi 2014).

The use of border control technologies has been embedded in bilateral and multilateral initiatives with countries of origin and transit. These initiatives demonstrate that Spanish policy is strongly oriented toward externalization mechanisms. The objective has been to improve the effectiveness of surveillance procedures through early detection and prevention, including actions in the interior or in coastal areas of transit countries. Bilateral cooperation was materialized through the "Africa Plan" (Alcalde 2007), an instrument that has converted migration cooperation with African countries into one of the priorities of Spanish foreign policy since 2006. Other instruments included the creation of binational surveillance patrols with Mauritania and Morocco, the expansion of the network of liaison officials, and the development of the Atlantic Seahorse programme and the Sea Horse Network, a national security network to exchange information on irregular migration by sea with police forces from Mauritania, Morocco, Cape Verde and Senegal (López-Sala 2012; Casas et al. 2014).[8] The bilateral initiatives have also extended the reactive mechanisms used to deal with irregular migration flows through the signing of readmission and repatriation agreements with African countries, including Morocco, Mali and Guinea Bissau (Asín 2008). The main deterrence effects of these measures are the prevention of departures, an increased likelihood of detention in transit, and readmission or repatriation after border crossing.

An additional layer of migration control management at the Spanish borders has been implemented by initiatives adopted through the European common borders policy. These initiatives are complementary, but they are directed at the common goal of containing migration flows that cross the southern border. Among the most notable initiatives on the Western Africa and Western Mediterranean routes are the

---

[6] See http://www.closeye.eu/index.php/the-project

[7] Other European technological projects implemented since 2011 in which Spain actively participated are WIMAS, OPARUS, SEABILLA and PERSEUS (see Godenau 2014).

[8] The positive results of the Atlantic Seahorse project have led to the creation of a new multilateral Seahorse network in the Mediterranean, which is currently being implemented and in which participate Spain, Italy, France, Malta, Portugal, Cyprus, Greece and Libya, with the support of the European member states and the European Commission. It is also expected that Algiers, Tunis and Egypt will join this network. The creation of Atlantic Seahorse is another example of the influence of the initiatives developed by Spain on the adoption of multilateral and communitarian measures at the European level.

joint Frontex operations (Hera, Indalo and Minerva) and the implementation of technological surveillance projects, such as those mentioned above, using European finance mechanisms, such as the European External Borders Fund. The experience gained by Spain since 2004 in joint maritime surveillance operations, such as Operation Nobel Sentinel, Guanarteme and the Atlantis Project, was key to the implementation of the joint Frontex operations starting in 2006. This process was similar to Spain's prior experience with SIVE, which had served as a test bench for the development and implementation of EUROSUR (Jeandesboz 2011). However, the most important Integrated Border Management (IBM) initiative driven by the European Union has been the implementation since 2013 of EUROSUR, an information-exchange system designed to improve the management of EU external borders, creating what is known as a Common Information Sharing Environment.

The effects of these political and technological mechanisms to control irregular immigration to Spain have been highly varied. First of all, they have deviated the migration flows to other sectors of the national border[9] and other European countries like Italy and Greece (De Bruycker et al. 2013; Triandafyllidou and Dimitriadi 2013; Morehouse and Blomfield 2011). Second, various adaptive and reactive changes were made in the modus operandi of the smuggling networks and in the entrance strategies employed by the migrants. Among them was an increase in the use of falsified documents (Frontex 2014a, p. 29) and the use of new kinds of vessels to make the sea voyages (Frontex 2014a, p. 34). There was also an increase in the risk to the migrants in transit, as well as in the cost of irregular crossings.

In addition to those mentioned above, there were also dissuasive and selective effects produced by the application of this migration control regime in the Spanish case. Regarding the dissuasive effects, the big question posed by this kind of intervention is just how effective it is in containing, or at least reducing irregular flows; it is valid to question the efficiency of this strategy considering the large volume of investment it requires. Regarding the selective effects, the application of a spatially differentiated impermeabilization policy that is especially strict on the southern maritime border, compared to, for example, the Spanish airport borders, has made access to opportunities for migrants dependent on their nationality and resources. In this sense, technologies are not neutral. Their invention and implementation are socially selective and reveal, as in the Spanish case, the permeability regulation function of bordering.

[9] As evidenced by the intensification of the Ceuta and Melilla route after the maritime perimeter was reinforced; see Koslowski 2011, p. 7, about "squeezing the balloon" at the US border.

5 Contesting Migration Control in Spain? The Scope and Limitations of the "Humanitarian Border"

Irregular migration is a central aspect in the dilemma of how to maintain security—defending the territory and sovereignty of States—while also protecting the fundamental rights of irregular migrants and asylum seekers at borders and in transit. In the sphere of migration control, this paradox has produced deep tensions between states and the civil organizations that defend human rights. These human rights groups are developing novel approaches, alone or in collaboration with other international actors, to organize opposition against what they consider to be increasingly repressive policies. These approaches are directed at immobilizing migrants considered undesirable and are thought to be creating a new form of global apartheid (Balibar 2004; Van Houtum 2010). The analysis of the Spanish case provides a good illustration of the emergence of a novel response in defence of the human rights of migrants, questioning restrictive migration regimes (Nyers and Rygiel 2012) that violate the physical integrity of the migrants (FRA 2013; Brian and Laczlo 2014) and casts doubt on the legitimacy of migration control.

This kind of public and social scrutiny of the praxis of migration control and the parallel construction of supervision mechanisms around the forms that migration control has adopted is well covered by the concept of "humanitarian borders", coined by Walters (2011). In the opinion of Walters, migration and border studies have extensively focused on analyses of the new rationales underlying the political measures and objectives of border control and on the securitization and technologization associated with them. However, an analysis that seeks to reflect the functional and symbolic transformation of the borders in the sphere of human mobility must also consider what Walters has referred to as the "birth of the humanitarian border" or the reinvention of the borders as a space of humanitarian government[10] (Walters 2011). The humanitarian border is less interested in military or political security concerns, and instead focuses on a perspective of migrants as victims (de Genova et al. 2015). The Spanish border meets the conditions that could explain the emergence of this kind of humanitarian border, mostly due to geographic, political and economic factors. More specifically, it is a location where the sharp inequalities between the Global North and South converge; a scenario in which political migration control practices seriously jeopardize the lives and physical integrity of the migrants; a space where the border is defined by a dynamic, fluctuating and contingent nature shaped by the changes in the dynamics and routes of irregular migration flows; and finally, a geographic context for migration control in which humanitarian engagement is articulated through political struggles and the action of diverse actors.

[10] To construct this concept Walters uses the definition of humanitarian government mentioned by Fassin "as the administration of human collectivities in the name of a higher moral principle which sees the preservation of life and the alleviation of suffering as the highest value of action" (Fassin 2007).

The proposal of this section is to map and analyse these emerging dynamics in the response to state migration control practices, using the Spanish case as the example and, in particular, the protest that has developed in reaction to control practices at the territorial limits of Ceuta and Melilla (López-Sala 2015b). Although the earlier sections of this chapter have analysed the main characteristics of the management of irregular immigration (externalization, communitarization and technologization), it is important to highlight that current border dynamics in Europe and Spain cannot be understood without considering the emergence of these new forms of protesting control practices.

Despite the scope and complexity that migration control and border action have acquired in Spanish immigration policy, they have not been broadly questioned until recently. For two decades the agenda of social organizations regarding irregular immigration centred on different areas of internal control, such as documentation campaigns, or the lack of transparency in migration management and the vulnerability of migrant rights in internment camps. Since the middle of the past decade, only a limited number of organizations in the vibrant Spanish pro-immigration world have focused on the effects of border policy on the human rights of irregular migrants and individuals applying for asylum seekers in transit.[11]

However, in the past 2 years migration control at Spanish borders has been widely contested by a growing number of organizations and has provoked significant rejection among various sectors of civil society and public opinion, leading to an intense social debate that is still underway. This change was caused by a new increase, since 2013, of unauthorized border crossings at Ceuta and Melilla and the severe response of the Spanish government to contain this flow. This change has also been facilitated by the physical visibility and media exposure of these land borders, compared to the inaccessible and diffuse Spanish maritime borders,[12] where photographers and press cameras from around the world have repeatedly recorded and distributed images of migrants who have been injured or killed while attempting to reach Spanish territory. Although most of the visibility and social attention is raised by the mass media, grass root initiatives such as documentaries produced by NGOs[13] or independent artists[14] should not be undervalued as a pool of information from which the mass media frequently obtains material instead of investing in their own fieldwork. Additionally, social networks integrating migrants

[11] Among them the Pro-Human Rights Association of Andalusia (APDHA), CEAR, SOS Racismo, Amnesty International or the Acoge Network.

[12] A large part of the migration control actions have been implemented over the past decade in Spanish maritime borders. However, the peripheral geography of this kind of intervention has transformed these kinds of control sites into what Coutin denominates "spaces of noexistence" (Coutin 2003).

[13] See, for example, PRODEIN videos at vimeo (https://vimeo.com/108211634)

[14] See, for example, "*The Land Between*", a film by David Fedele (http://thelandbetweenfilm.com/) or "*Ceuta douce prison*" by Jonathan Millet and Loic H. Rechi (http://ceuta-douce-prison.tumblr.com/)

and the local population in border areas are an important source of data for professionals interested in documenting border events.

As we pointed out in the previous sections, externalization, communitarization and technologization are the basic lines along which Spanish border management of irregular immigration has developed under the fundamental goal of deterrence. Has social protest of bordering in Spain been directed equally at all three developments? As we will show, current societal response in Spain is centred on the treatment migrants receive at the border, particularly in recent years, in Ceuta and Melilla. What happens "beyond the border" (externalization, remote control) is not receiving much public attention, neither is EU participation in control initiatives run by Frontex. In the case of externalization, the opacity of control practices in origin and transit countries facilitates attitudes like "not in my backyard;" in the case of communitarization, public attention is only captured when extraordinary events occur (like the "cayuco crisis" in the Canaries in 2006) and are channelled towards the national request for more EU funds and cooperation. The technology present in border control practices is highly visible through the mass media (radars, planes, drones, satellites), but societal response is not focused on the technology itself, but rather on how it is used.

After mentioning these aspects that are (significantly) marginal to public attention, we will now concentrate on the issues that do attract social responses, all of which are directly related to control practices at the border. There are three elements of social debate articulated by the opposition to the actions of the current Spanish government: first, the use of contention equipment on border perimeters, in particular concertina wire; second, pushback deportations criticized as irregular return practices; and third, the treatment received by asylum seekers at these land borders.

The concertina wire was installed in the border perimeters of both Ceuta and Melilla after the incidents in August and September 2005 (Ferrer-Gallardo 2011; López-Sala 2012). Pressure from various political groups and social organizations forced this kind of razor wire to be removed in 2007, but after the increase in collective attempts to enter Spanish territory they were again installed on different sections of the fence at the end of 2013. Rejection of the use of the concertina wire has been unanimous, due to the injuries it causes to the migrants. Among those who have been openly against the use of concertina wire are all of the opposition parliamentary groups, the office of the Ombudsman, police unions and Civil Guard associations, the State Attorney General, religious organizations and the Episcopal Conference, as well as authorities from the European Commission and the Council of Europe. The position of the government on this issue has been, however, unyielding and emphatic. In June of 2014, the Spanish Ministry of the Interior dismissed the proposal of the Ombudsman to substitute the concertina wire with other kinds of non-cutting mechanisms. In addition, in September of the same year MPs of the Popular Party blocked a motion in the Interior Commission of the Parliament to remove the concertina wire.[15]

[15] Diario de Sesiones. Congreso de los Diputados, Comisiones, núm. 637, de 24/09/2014.

A second debate has been centred on irregular pushback practices, which return immigrants who have reached diverse sectors of the border perimeters of Ceuta and Melilla. For various years the Spanish government has denied using these kinds of summary deportations, but in the summer of 2014 the debate heated up when the press disseminated various videos recorded by a Spanish NGO that showed these practices. The videos provoked social outrage, even leading to a lawsuit that ended with the indictment of the head of the Civil Guard in Melilla (APDHA 2015).

The position of the Ministry of the Interior is that these practices are not illegal and that they are not returns "per se," but rather they argue that the area between the two fences[16] is not Spanish territory and therefore they fall in the category of what Spanish legislation refers to as "border rejections" or refusals of entry. The Spanish government has used its majority in the Congress to give legal coverage to these practices through the controversial inclusion of an article in the reform of the Citizen Security Act, which is currently in the approval stage in the Senate. The social and political response has been strongly against the legalization of the pushback policy. Although the law was approved by the Congress thanks to the ruling party's majority, it was rejected by every other political group. These groups, along with diverse social organizations, including the Episcopal Commission on migrations, the immigration sub-commission of the General Council of Spanish Advocacy and diverse legal organizations, such as Judges for Democracy or the Progressive Union of Public Prosecutors, have formally requested that it be repealed. The European commissary for immigration, Dimitris Avramopoulos, stated in November 2014 that the European Commission would act against Spain if this reform was shown to violate European legislation.[17] In addition, in January 2015 the commissary of Human Rights of the Council of Europe, Nils Muiznieks, affirmed that this reform violated international law and puts the asylum system at risk.[18] Muiznieks' conclusion is particularly concerning at this moment, when an increasing number of nationals from African countries in conflict, such as Mali, have been added to the heavy flow of Syrian refugees.

Therefore, another dimension of the primacy of the contention principle over the principle of protection in Spanish migration control practice, which has been emphatically contested by social organizations and international organizations like the Council of Europe and the Council of Europe for Refugees, is the erosion of the fundamental rights of many asylum seekers who enter Spanish territory via this route. Since 2010 access to the Spanish mainland has been restricted for asylum seekers whose application is processed in one of these cities. In practice, their stay in Melilla or Ceuta can be prolonged for months, producing not only a serious

[16] The Spanish border fences at Ceuta and Melilla include several internal razor wire barriers set up on Spanish soil. See http://politica.elpais.com/politica/2014/03/03/actualidad/1393857848_793887.html

[17] Debates on the EU approach to migration and the expulsion of migrants from Spain. Plenary sessions [26-11-2014], Press Release, European Parliament.

[18] http://ecre.org/component/content/article/70-weekly-bulletin-articles/943-muinieks-urges-spain-to-withdraw-amendment-giving-legal-cover-to-pushbacks-in-ceuta-and-melilla.html

limitation of their freedom of movement, but also recurring overpopulation problems in the Temporary Holding Camps. In the middle of 2014, the government had to explain the situation of asylum seekers in the autonomous cities to the Parliament in response to questions asked by various political parties.[19]

However, despite the broad social and political backlash the Spanish government has maintained an inflexible position regarding the practices implemented in both cities, using all of the political resources at its disposal to maintain them. At the same time, the government has promoted a fear-mongering narrative of chaos and crisis (Mountz and Hiemstra 2014; Mainwaring 2012), arguing that "waves of migrant invasions" are becoming increasingly violent in their massive attempts to cross the border or that there is an alarming number of irregular immigrants in Morocco waiting for their chance to enter Spanish and European territory. These arguments, which can be boiled down to the reinforcement of state sovereignty, have resulted in Ceuta and Melilla being placed in a permanent "state of emergency" (Bigo 2006; Agamben 2005) as a way to justify using measures that are controversial in legal terms, and that have led to strong legal debates on their legitimacy and accountability.

6 Conclusion

Spain has implemented a progressive and comprehensive multi-layered deterrence strategy to control unwanted migration at its borders. This strategy has evolved along three basic lines. Cooperation with African countries (externalization) has been key to fostering fast return procedures, whereas cooperation with the EU (communitarization through joint Frontex operations) has only been complementary to national border control initiatives driven by technological innovation (technologization). Spain's experience and innovation in border control has served as a test run for initiatives that have later been implemented along the entire European perimeter through its Integrated Border Management. Among the political and technological mechanisms used to control irregular immigration, the most notable effects on the dynamics of migration flows have been caused by deviation, dissuasion and selection.

An additional aspect analysed in this chapter is the emergence of a humanitarian border in the Spanish case, a scenario in which new forms of civil mobilization in defence of the human rights of migrants have emerged reactively. Particularly at the land borders in Ceuta and Melilla, the highly visible and well-documented border control practices have raised growing concerns and public debate about the violation of fundamental rights, such as non-refoulement and asylum. Despite social protest against these practices, which has been supported by broad social and political sectors, the current Spanish government has used its parliamentary majority to impose a policy that prioritizes the protection of the national borders over the

[19] Boletín Oficial de las Cortes Generales, 18 de septiembre de 2014, página 241.

fundamental rights of migrants and asylum seekers. It is plausible that in the current situation of political majority, the only way to contain these kinds of practices will be found in the international community and the European institutions.

References

Adamson, F. (2006). Crossing borders: International migration and national security. *International Security, 31*, 165–199.

Agamben, G. (2005). *State of exception*. Chicago: University of Chicago Press.

Alcalde, A. (2007). The spanish action plan for Africa. *Review of African Political Economy, 34* (1), 194–198.

Andreas, P. (1998). The escalation of U.S. immigration control in the post-NAFTA era. *Political Science Quarterly, 113*(4), 591–615.

Andreas, P. (2000). *Border games. Policing the US-Mexico divide*. Ithaca: Cornell University Press.

APDHA (Asociación proderechos humanos de Andalucía). (2015). *Derechos Humanos en la Frontera Sur*. Sevilla.

Asín, A. (2008). Acuerdos bilaterales suscritos por España en materia migratoria con países del continente africano. Especial consideración de la readmisión de inmigrantes en situación irregular. *Revista de Derecho Constitucional Europeo, 10*, 165–188.

Baldacchino, G. (2014). Islands and the offshoring possibilities and strategies of contemporary states: Insights on/for the migration phenomenon on Europe's southern flank. *Island Studies Journal, 9*(1), 57–68.

Balibar, E. (2004). *We, the people of Europe? Reflections on transnational citizenship*. Princeton: Princeton University Press.

Basaran, T. (2014). Saving lives at sea: Security, law and adverse effects. *European Journal of Migration and Law, 16*(3), 365–387.

Bigo, D. (2006). Security, exception, ban and surveillance in theorizing surveillance. In D. Lyon (Ed.), *The panopticon and beyond* (pp. 46–68). Devon: Willan Pb.

Brian, T., & Laczlo, F. (Eds.). (2014). *Fatal journeys. Tracking lives lost during migration*. Ginebra: International Organization for Migration.

Casas, I., Cobarrubias, S., & Pickles, J. (2014). Good neighbours make good fences: Seahorse operations, border externalization and extra-territoriality. *European Urban and Regional Studies, 14*, 1–20. doi:10.1177/0969776414541136.

Coutin, S. (2003). Illegality, borderlands, and the space of nonexistence. In R. Perry & B. Maurer (Eds.), *Globalization under construction: Governmentality, law, and identity* (pp. 171–202). Minneapolis: University of Minnesota Press.

De Bruycker, P., Di Bartolomeo, A., & Fargues, P. (2013). *Migrants smuggled by sea to the EU: Facts, laws and policy options*. Florence: Migration Policy Centre.

De Genova, N., Mezzadra, S., & Pickles, J. (2015). New keywords: Migration and borders. *Cultural Studies, 29*(1), 55–87.

Dijstelbloem, H., & Meijer, A. (2011). *Migration and the new technological borders of Europe*. London: Palgrave.

Eschbach, K., Hagan, J., Rodríguez, N., Hernández-León, R., & Bailey, S. (1999). Death at the border. *International Migration Review, 33*(2), 430–454.

European Commission. (2011). Communication from the Commission to the European Parliament, the Council, The European Economic and Social Committee and the Committee of the Regions, *The Global Approach to Migration and Mobility*. Brussels, 18.11.2011 COM(2011) 743 final.

Fargues, P., & Bonfati, S. (2014). *When the best option is a leaky boat: Why migrants risk their lives crossing the Mediterranean and what Europe is doing about it*. Florence: European University Institute Migration Policy Centre.

Fargues, P., & Di Bartolomeo, A. (2015). *Drowned Europe*. Florence: Migration Policy Centre.
Fassin, D. (2007). Humanitarianism: A nongovernmental government. In M. Feher (Ed.), *Non-governmental politics* (pp. 149–160). New York: Zone Books.
Ferrer-Gallardo, X. (2011). Territorial (Dis)Continuity dynamics between Ceuta and Morocco: Conflictual fortification Vis-Á-Vis Co-operative interaction at the EU border in Africa. *Tijdschrift voor Economische en Sociale Geografie, 102*(1), 24–38.
Ferrer-Gallardo, X., & Van Houtum, H. (2014). The deadly EU border control. *ACME, An International E-Journal for Critical Geographies, 13*(2), 295–304.
Foucher, M. (1998). The geopolitics of European frontiers. In M. Anderson & E. Bort (Eds.), *The frontiers of Europe* (pp. 235–250). London: Pinter.
FRA. (2013). *Fundamental rights at Europe's southern sea borders*. Vienna: European Union Agency for Fundamental Rights.
Frontex. (2014a). *Annual Risk Analysis 2014*. Warsaw
Frontex. (2014b, August). *FRAN Quarterly 1* (Frontex Risk Analysis Network). Warsaw.
Frontex. (2014c, October) *FRAN Quarterly 2* (Frontex Risk Analysis Network). Warsaw.
Frontex. (2014d, June). *Frontex report to the Office of the High Commissioner for Human Rights on its activities aimed at protecting migrants at international borders, including migrant children*. Warsaw.
Godenau, D. (2012). An institutional approach to bordering in islands: The Canary Islands on the African-European migration routes. *Island Studies Journal, 7*(1), 3–18.
Godenau, D. (2014). Irregular maritime immigration in the Canary Islands: Externalization and communautarisation in the social construction of borders. *Journal of Immigrant and Refugee Studies, 12*, 123–142.
Godenau, D., & López-Sala, A. (2016). Multi-layered migration deterrence and technology in Spanish maritime border management. *Journal of Borderlands Studies* (forthcoming)
Godenau, D., & Zapata, V. M. (2008). The Canary Islands. A transit region between Africa and Europe. In Documento CIDOB n° 17, *Immigration flows and the management of the EU's southern maritime borders*. Barcelona: CIDOB.
Grant, S. (2011). Irregular migration and frontier deaths: Acknowledging a right to identity. In M. Dembour & T. Kelly (Eds.), *Are human rights for migrants?* (pp. 48–68). New York: Routledge.
Guild, E. (2009). *Security and migration in the 21st century*. Cambrigde: Polity Press.
Huysmans, J. (2000). The European Union and the securitization of migration. *Journal of Common Market Studies, 38*, 751–777.
Jeandesboz, J. (2011). Beyond the Tartar steppe: EUROSUR and the ethics of European border control practices. In J. P. Burgess & S. Gutwirth (Eds.), *Europe under threat? security, migration and integration* (pp. 111–132). Brussels: VUB Press.
King, G., & Murray, C. (2001). Rethinking human security. *Political Science Quarterly, 116*, 585–610.
Kinnvall, C., & Svensson, T. (2014). *Governing borders and security: The politics of connectivity and dispersal*. London: Routledge.
Koslowski, R. (2011). *The evolution of border controls as a mechanism to prevent illegal immigration*. Migration Policy Institute: Washington D.C.
Lahav, G., & Guiraudon, V. (2000). A reappraisal of the state sovereignty debate. The case of migration control. *Comparative Political Studies, 33*(2), 163–195.
López-Sala, A. (2012). The political design of migration control in Southern Europe. In C. Gortázar, C. Parra, B. Segaert, & C. Timmerman (Eds.), *European migration and asylum policies: Coherent or contradiction* (pp. 209–223). Brussels: Bruylant.
López-Sala, A. (2015a). Exploring dissuasion as a (geo)political instrument in irregular migration control at the southern spanish maritime border. *Geopolitics, 20*(3), 513–534. doi:10.1080/14650045.2015.1025384.
López-Sala, A. (2015b). La inmigración irregular en Ceuta y Melilla en 2014: prácticas de control y debate público. In J. Arango, D. Moya, J. Oliver, & E. Sánchez (Eds.), *Anuario de la Inmigración en España 2014* (pp. 170–191). Barcelona: CIDOB.

López-Sala, A., & Esteban, V. (2010). La nueva arquitectura política del control migratorio en la frontera marítima del suroeste de Europa: los casos de España y Malta. In E. Anguiano & A. López-Sala (Eds.), *Migraciones y fronteras. Nuevos contornos para la movilidad internacional* (pp. 75–102). Icaria Editorial: Barcelona.

Mainwaring, C. (2012). Constructing a crisis: The role of immigration detention in Malta. *Population, Place and Space, 18*, 687–700.

Mau, S., Brabant, H., Lause, L., & Roos, C. (2012). *Liberal states and freedom of movement. Selective borders, unequal mobility*. New York: Palgrave-MacMillan.

Meneses, G. (2003). Human rights and undocumented migration along the Mexican-U.S. Border. *UCLA Law Review* 267.

Morehouse, C., & Blomfield, M. (2011). *Irregular migration in Europe*. Washington: Migration Policy Institute.

Mountz, A., & Hiemstra, N. (2014). Chaos and crisis: Dissecting the spatiotemporal logics of contemporary migrations and state practices. *Annals of the Association of American Geographers, 104*(2), 382–390.

Newland, K. (2014). *Protection at sea: Addressing irregular maritime migration*. Washington: Migration Policy Institute.

Nyers, P., & Rygiel, K. (2012). *Citizenship, migrant activism and the politics of movement*. London: Routledge.

Paasi, A. (2014). The shifting landscape of border studies and the challenge of relational thinking. In M. Bufon, J. Minghi, & A. Paasi (Eds.), *The new European frontiers: Social and spatial (re) integration issues in multicultural and border regions* (pp. 361–376). Newcastle: Cambridge Scholars Publishing.

Pickering, S., & Weber, L. (Eds.). (2006). *Borders, mobility and technologies of control*. Dordrecht: Springer.

Rogers, E. (2003). *Diffusion of innovations*. New York: Free Press.

Rudolph, C. (2003). Security and the political economy of international migration. *American Political Science Review, 97*(4), 603–620.

Triandafyllidou, A., & Dimitriadi, A. (2013). Migration management at the outpost of the European Union. *Griffith Law Review, 22*(3), 598–618.

Van Houtum, H. (2010). Human blacklisting: The global apartheid of the EU's external border regime. *Environment and Planning D: Society and Space, 28*(6), 957–976.

Walters, W. (2004). The frontiers of the European Union: A geostrategic perspective. *Geopolitics, 9*(3), 674–698.

Walters, W. (2011). Foucault and frontiers: Notes on the birth of the humanitarian border. In U. Bröckling, S. Krasmann, & T. Lemke (Eds.), *Governmentality: Current issues and future challenges* (pp. 138–164). New York: Routledge.

Weber, L. (2013). Visible and virtual borders. *Griffith Law Review, 22*(3), 666–682.

Weber, L., & Pickering, S. (2011). *Globalization and borders. Death at the global frontier*. New York: Palgrave-MacMillan.

Wolff, S. (2012). La gestión integrada de las fronteras de la UE después de Lisboa. Contrastando políticas y prácticas. In R. Zapata-Barrero & X. Ferrer-Gallado (Eds.), *Fronteras en movimiento. Migraciones hacia la Unión Europea en el contexto Mediterráneo* (pp. 57–78). Barcelona: Bellaterra.

Wonders, N. (2006). Global flows, semi-permeable borders and the new channels of inequality. In S. Pickering & L. Weber (Eds.), *Borders, mobility and technologies of control* (pp. 63–86). Dordrecht: Springer.

Zolberg, A. (2003). The archaeology of "Remote" control. In A. Fahrmeir, O. Faron, & P. Weil (Eds.), *Migration control in the North Atlantic World. The evolution of state practices in Europe and the United States from the French Revolution to the Inter-War Period* (pp. 195–221). New York: Berghahn Books.

Protecting Citizens, Securitising Outsiders? Consular Affairs and the Externalisation of EU's Internal Security

Igor Merheim-Eyre

1 Introduction

> Every citizen of the Union shall, in the territory of a third country in which the Member State of which he is a national is not represented, be entitled to protection by the diplomatic or consular authorities of any Member State, on the same conditions as the nationals of that State. Member States shall adopt the necessary provisions and start the international negotiations required to secure this protection (Consolidated Treaties, Article 23)

> The abolition of internal border controls cannot come at the expense of security. Since no checks are carried out at the borders between Schengen states, EU states have decided to join forces to attain dual objective of improving security through more efficient external border controls, while facilitating access of those having a legitimate interest to enter the EU territory (EU Action in Response to Crisis in Lebanon 2014)

As Marx often liked to remark, everything moves. Long before the existence of the Westphalian state and the rise of European style of diplomacy (Der Derian 1991), Greek city-states used consuls as emissaries (a less privileged version of the modern ambassador) while the Christendom employed them to protect their merchants in the Ottoman Empire. In the history of consular affairs, the role of the consul has gone through huge transformations, taking on new roles and representing polities of all kinds.

As Brian Hocking and David Spence note, the European Union "is a laboratory for students of modern diplomacy. . .a telling reflection of major adaptations to the notions of representation and diplomacy in the international relations of the twenty-first century" (2005: 2). For its part, the European Union (EU) represents a challenge to consular affairs and highlights the changes to this specific area of diplomacy. Not merely a responsibility of a sovereign state, the creation of a European citizenship along with the removal of internal borders and the creation

I. Merheim-Eyre (✉)
School of Politics and International Relations, Rutherford College, University of Kent, Canterbury, Kent CT2 7NX, UK
e-mail: im507@kent.ac.uk

R. Bossong, H. Carrapico (eds.), *EU Borders and Shifting Internal Security*,
DOI 10.1007/978-3-319-17560-7_6

of common external borders has resulted in the emergence of new actors and discursive and non-discursive practices, not traditionally associated with the consular sphere.[1]

To some, the use of the word "externalisation" (Balzacq 2009) may seem inappropriate in the case of consular affairs. Consular affairs are, after all, an "external" dimension for managing relations with the wider world. To this extent, consular affairs are permanently "externalised". Yet, as Fernandez notes, the process of European integration has caused changes for the external administration of the Member States (2006: 1). This chapter, however, seeks to push one's imagination of diplomatic practices a little further, by tracing how internal security of the European Union is gaining an external dimension, securitising consular affairs as a result of a widening field of actors, changing practices and subjectivities. This is produced through diffused security governmentality, emphasising crises and structural insecurity, exemplified through two very different strands of consular affairs: the protection of EU citizens outside of the European Union, and the issuance of Schengen visa.

Over the past two decades, Member States of the European Union have been developing a framework within which a citizen in distress may seek assistance from consular or diplomatic representatives of another Member State if his/her State is not represented in a particular third country outside of the Union. In 2009 alone, over 90 million citizens of the European Union (EU) travelled to third countries outside the EU. From the earthquakes in Haiti (2010) and Japan (2011), to the Icelandic volcanic ash (2010) and conflicts across the Middle East and North Africa, over 100,000 citizens were present when these emergencies occurred, often requiring immediate assistance from the nearest consular missions (European Commission 2011). In this context, consular protection of citizens takes place in the form of evacuations, immediate humanitarian or medical assistance through EU-funded or individual Member States' responses. This is a significant shift from the original rationale for cooperation, which was focused towards daily assistance to EU citizens in areas such as loss of passport or imprisonment.

The coming into effect of the Lisbon Treaty opened new opportunities and challenges for EU level cooperation in this regard. This concerns consular protection during emergency situations (Articles 23 and 35, Consolidated Treaties 2008), including the strengthening of cooperation between Member States' consulates, the creation of the European External Action Service (EEAS), the development of the Union's rescue and military capabilities for the protection of citizens and, thus, the reinforcement of the concept of European citizenship.

Overall, the consular protection of EU citizens can be linked to a general shift within the EU towards "soft" security issues, such as man-made and natural disasters (Booth 1991: 318; Merheim-Eyre in Janułewicz et al. 2014), but also on post-disaster resilience (Aradau and Van Munster 2011; Lundborg and Vaughan-

[1] Balzacq (2014: 378), for example, attempts this through triangulation of discourse analysis and process tracing.

Williams 2011; Heath-Kelly 2015). So although consular assistance has always been an external dimension to a polity's protection of citizens, the increased discursive and non-discursive focus on the protection of EU citizens has firmly placed consular protection in the sphere of EU internal security. This means that EU citizens are not merely protected, but they are also treated as reference objects in relation to the securitisation of potential man-made or natural threats (Merheim-Eyre 2014b).

Issuance of Schengen visa to non-EU citizens is another consular dimension that has known a shift towards growing competencies at the European level and towards externalisation beyond the physical border of the Union. However, externalisation in this case refers to the use of new surveillance tools and performative action, as well as to the increasing participation of third countries in the management of EU external borders, exerting considerably more structural power on the eastern neighbourhood than individual national policies. The externalisation of EU border management through visa issuance (and gradual visa liberalisation) is, unlike in the case of consular protection of EU citizens, about the prevention of potential risks reaching the borders of the EU, consequently treating third country nationals as potential threats. Its task is to manage EU external borders through politics of inclusion and exclusion (Smith 1996; Andreas in Andreas and Snyder 2000: 2). It acts as a filter, managing access by sorting desirable migrants from undesirable while, through externalisation, also attempting to increase the capacity of its neighbours' in judicial and police affairs, creating a buffer zone between itself and what Smith called "the real outsiders" (1996: 7).

This is particularly visible in the EU's eastern neighbourhood, where the EU is increasingly offering a process of visa liberalisation as an incentive for greater convergence with EU norms and practices—affected, but not determined by the various unresolved conflicts and the war in eastern Ukraine. People-to-people contact is strengthened while, ironically, the EU simultaneously constructs an "exclusionary" zone by externalising the regulation of risks beyond the EU's borders. For example, the EU offers visa liberalisation to Georgia, but Georgia must comply with EU-set conceptual parameters (Visa Liberalisation Action Plans/VLAPs) on migration, policing, or issuance of passports.

To simplify such diverging and complex issues, this chapter is divided into three sections. The first part sets out a theoretical framework situating consular affairs as the external dimension of EU internal security through two very different strands of consular affairs: protection of EU citizens and the filtering of non-EU citizens. This chapter builds on the bourgeoning literature in critical security studies and wider post-structuralist approaches (C.A.S.E. 2006; Foucault 2007; Balzacq 2009) by exploring the problematisation of consular affairs and the development of EU level synergies to mitigate internal (in)security.

The second part of the chapter empirically traces (i) the shift from focus on daily consular assistance to EU citizens to civilian protection in emergencies, and (ii) the role of Schengen visa in the EU's eastern border management. The final part will deal with consequences of externalisation, providing a synthesis of the conceptual framework and the empirical analysis. This includes: (i) the growing complexity of the field due to the rise of EU competencies, participation of third countries, rescue teams and private companies; (ii) changes in consular practices stemming from new security pressures and the rise of new actors and; (iii) the differentiation between EU citizens as victims of insecurity and non-EU citizens as potential threats, highlighting the expansion of "social sorting" (Lyon 2003) through and beyond the digital.

Finally, it should be mentioned that latest developments in the field of consular affairs on the European level have also presented cases that may be seen as challenging the present framework. For example, the controversy over Hungary's wall on the border with Serbia challenges the notion of "inclusive" borders. However, this is not the case. Rather, this author argues, the problem in the Western Balkan does not lie with "inclusive" border management, but the failure to extend the same technical security governmentality that is present in the eastern neighbourhood to regulate the "inclusion" which, in itself, was developed from the shortcomings in the Western Balkans. Similarly, the new Council Directive on Consular Protection (Council of the European Union 2015) presents some indicators that the Union's concerns are once again turning towards daily assistance, such as the loss of passports (Merheim-Eyre 2015). In this case, the new Directive rather represents a consensus after 3 years of negotiations over financial and legal technicalities rather than a shift in security rationalities.

2 Situating Consular Affairs in EU Internal Security

Studies of international relations are dotted with disputes of what constitutes security or what does not. Taking a post-structuralist approach based around the Foucauldian concept of governmentality (see Dean 2010: 17), security is perceived as a wide concept with calculated rationalities. Security governmentality becomes an assemblage of four dimensions needed for governing: milieu (space/territory), population, circulation ("movement, exchange, contact" within the milieu) and contingency (projection into future) (Foucault 2007: 45). Security, in short, emerges out of insecurity (Balzacq et al. 2010) as an assemblage of the four dimensions, conditional on "things, events and elements" (Foucault 2007: 6) in a given milieu.

While, according to Foucault, its outcome is never guaranteed, its function is to allow "circulation to take place, of controlling them, sifting the good and the bad, ensuring the things that are always in movement, constantly moving around, continually going from one point to another, but in such a way that the inherent dangers of this circulation are cancelled out" (2007: 65). As Dillon notes, the organisation of security or contingency within the milieu is not just a matter of chance but "complex discourse-set of truth-telling practices-about the knowledge of uncertainty" (2007: 45). It is a calculated possibility, but also a means of deciding on who and what should be protected, or who is to be excluded by a dominant group (Balzacq et al. 2010).

However, according to Dillon and Lobo-Guerrero (2008), such wide approach to security is only valuable as long as it is problematic. This can, for instance, concern the problematisation of geopolitical insecurities as was the case during the Cold War, or by putting an emphasis on the individual, and on "soft security" threats (Booth 1991). The question, then, is how a particular referent object becomes a subject of security, and what impact this has on the practices and tools employed. As Edkins (1999) and Balzacq (2008) point out, the very understanding of securitisation should be re-examined. The most widely used definition of securitisation is that of Buzan, Waever and de Wilde (1998). Firstly, for an issue such as consular protection or cross-border mobility to become securitised, it must pass through a speech act as recognition of a threat. As Balzacq notes, however, this gives an "incomplete picture of what a threat is at any given time, because it fails to account for variations of intensity within the process of securitisation" (Balzacq 2008: 78). Instead, he advocates a further analysis of practices which, in the context of securitisation, can be defined as "an identifiable social and technical *dispositif* or device embodying a specific threat image through which public action is configured in order to address a security issue" (2008: 79). For example, the EU's reconfigured Civil Protection Mechanism thus responds to man-made and natural disasters within and outside the Union.

Therefore, securitisation should be seen as an intervention through discursive and non-discursive practices because, as Foucault notes, security allows for the organisation of "ever wider circuits", bringing together various discourses and instruments. Balzacq further argues that an instrument is not simply a policy nor a programme. Instead, an instrument is a collection of policy activities that show similar characteristics focused on influencing and governing social purposes" (Ringeling in Balzacq 2008: 79) and, as a result, "can be brought to bear on particular fields or problems by different programmes" (Balzacq 2008: 79). For example, the relationship between the EU and the Eastern Partnership countries is not merely securitised in the sense that the EU's eastern border is a point of on-going/existing insecurity (such as the conflict in eastern Ukraine). Rather, it is further securitised in the sense that the border constellations are configured through the use of specific instruments of control to prevent potential threats reaching the EU's physical border. The difference between the EU's eastern and southern neighbourhoods is that, whilst on the southern border (including the Western Balkans) the EU is reacting to the states' failure to manage their own borders through exclusionary practices, in the east constellations are set to mitigate risks externally, either through extra-territorial surveillance instruments or through the third countries' convergence with EU norms and practices in matters of border management or law enforcement.

Secondly, in order to understand security practices, we must also re-assess the realm of "the political". Any issue, such as assistance to EU citizens in third countries, may be politicised or not—i.e., being part of public policy and discussion, requiring action. However, when an issue becomes securitised, it is "presented as an existential threat, requiring emergency measures and justifying actions outside the normal bounds of political procedures" (Waever et al. 1998: 23–24).

Therefore, according to Buzan et al., securitisation is an extreme version of "politicisation" and removed from regular public debate by being labelled a threat (1998: 24). Yet, as Edkins notes, "much of what we call 'politics' is in this sense 'depoliticised' or technologised: the room for real political change has been displaced by a technology of expertise or the rule of bureaucracy" (1999: xii). Therefore, what the Copenhagen school calls politicisation is in fact extreme "depoliticisation" because securitised issues become "even more firmly constrained within the already accepted criteria of a specific social form" (Edkins 1999: 2). Consequently, issues such as visa issuance or the protection of civilians are not only removed from the public sphere, but "decisions about them are taken in technical terms, following the advice of experts" (Edkins 1999: 11).

This depoliticisation points us to new experts beyond the traditional knowledge or existing practices of consular officers, becoming a matter of "technical efficiency" (Edkins 1999: 4), widening the field of actors, but also injecting knew rationalities and practices into the performance of tasks which, in themselves, are changing due to a changing environment. As Kevin Stringer notes, "the consular dimension of diplomacy has often taken the backseat to the political and military aspects of foreign policy in the past. This situation has changed dramatically with the end of the Cold War and the rapid globalisation of the world economy" (2004: 2).

For example, in the case of consular assistance cooperation the Commission interpreted the opportunity of post-Lisbon Treaty institutional changes as offering "opportunities to improve consistency between disaster response and possible political and security related elements of the EU's overall crisis response" (European Commission 2010b). This further rationalises enhanced cooperation and the role of EU institutions to mitigate potential threats to EU citizens in third countries and produces knowledge about "best practices". It is, as Edkins concludes, "a search for order, discipline, and regulation" through expert knowledge over emerging practices (Edkins 1999: 1). Securitisation in itself is subjective, depending on different perceptions (Cotey 2007: 8), but in this diffused process of governmental rationalities, it is also productive, widening the field, introducing new actors, changing practices and creating knowledge about potential threats and victims.

Finally, it is also worth conceptualising how security practices are externalised. As the EU's Stockholm Programme notes: "security is interlinked with the external dimension of the threats. In a global world, crime knows no borders. As the policies…gradually reach maturity, they should support each other and grow in consistency" (Council of the European Union 2010). Against this background, externalisation is defined simply as the attachment of internal security priorities to external affairs (Rijpma and Cremona 2007), with consular affairs providing an example par excellence. This chapter also considers Schengen tools such as databases having equally an external or, more precisely, an extra-territorialised dimension (Bigo and Guild 2005), since they are neither defined nor limited to a given space. Whether it is the shift of assistance priorities for EU citizens in crises or prevention of potential risks through a regulated border regime, EU consular affairs thus highlight the growing scope and application of internal security priorities externally.

In short, what is new is not only the development of new EU level synergies, but the growing connection between the two very different dimensions of consular affairs with the discursive and non-discursive practices of the EU's internal security. As a result, the internal pressures to regulate the milieu (within EU-28) are shifted outwards, widened to new actors, subjected to new rationalities, and connected with security tools to mitigate insecurity beyond the borders of the EU. Consular affairs are no longer simply including or excluding third country nationals, nor merely providing daily "desk" assistance to EU citizens. Instead, they filter foreigners using new instruments, provide post-crises protection to EU citizens and, above all, shift security pressures beyond the borders of the EU. Thus, the internal security gains a further external dimension, securitising and de-politicising consular affairs and injecting it with new expert knowledge. This evolving security governmentality, however, requires a more detailed empirical analysis.

3 Rationalities of Security Governmentality

3.1 Consular Protection for EU Citizens in Third Countries

European citizens travel farther and in larger numbers than ever before to all corners of the globe. Natural and man-made disasters, such as the Asian tsunami (2004), can leave citizens in distress, who in turn are becoming increasingly demanding of assistance.[2] At the same time, European states have become increasingly attentive to new security threats beyond the traditional politico-military sphere, requiring new contingency strategies and instruments to protect civilians. This recognition gained momentum since the tragic events of September 11 in the United States. As discussed in further detail below, transforming security threats, together with greater exposure and public pressure (Okano Heijmans 2010), stimulated the development of an (i) EU level legal framework, (ii) burden-sharing in post-crises response and (iii) local consular cooperation.

In its November 2001 Communication the European Commission already stated that, "in the aftermath of the unprecedented and tragic terrorist attacks in the USA, governments at all levels have been prompted to reconsider how ready and able they are to prevent or mitigate the impact of these threats to our society" (European Commission 2001). It was only as part of this partial post-9/11 climate that the Member States rushed the Council decision regarding protection for EU citizens

[2] According to the Conflict Barometer, in 2005 there were 249 conflicts globally. See *Conflict Barometer 2005: Crisis—Wars—Coups d'états—Negotiations—Mediations—Peace Settlements*; 14th Annual Conflict Analysis, Heidelberg Institute of International Conflict Research; University of Heidelberg, Heidelberg.

(95/553/EC) through their legislatures, a point of deadlock since 1995. The EU's response further corresponded with the Council review of the Union's Civil Protection Mechanism (CPM) in October 2001. The Commission implemented a re-organisation of the CPM by bringing under a single "Community" umbrella the various instruments and programmes that have been created to mitigate both natural and man-made disasters (Merheim-Eyre in Janułewicz et al 2014: 20). Thus, as the Care Project's Final Report concluded, "the need to provide for the right to consular protection derives not only from evolution of European law, but also from obvious substantial/factual reasons. . .made it obvious that even the best, widest and most resourceful consular services could not cope on their own" (2010).

Almost a year after 9/11 came the Bali bombings, with over 30 European dead and many injured. The 2004 Tsunami resulted in thousands of Europeans dead, injured or in need of immediate humanitarian assistance and repatriation across the Indian Ocean. The European effort here was dire or, as Michel Barnier, the Council's rapporteur on civil protection and former French Foreign Minister, argued in his 2006 Report, practically non-existent (in Merheim-Eyre 2014a: 3). As one eyewitness put it, "it is impossible really to get an accurate picture of the number of casualties. . .there are no kind of emergency services here, there are no helicopters thumping through the sky to come to save people. It is a do-it-yourself rescue." (BBC News 2004).

The year 2005 brought further drama with Hurricane Katrina in the US, the Sharm-el Sheik bombing, second bombing in Bali and, finally, in 2006 came what has been described as the biggest evacuation since the Second World War (Merheim-Eyre 2014b: 3). The 2006 Lebanese War trapped over 22,000 French nationals alone, with French, British and Italian navies cooperating to evacuate EU citizens and dual nationals to safety. The then-High Representative Javier Solana and the Finnish Presidency worked with the Israeli military to open an evacuation corridor into southern Lebanon, whilst the Civil Protection Mechanism was triggered to help with the logistical issues surrounding the transfer of evacuees to Cyprus (European Commission 2006). Further, on the request of the High Representative, the British "Operation Highbrow" with 2500 personnel and 6 navy vessels led the joint EU effort (Jureidini in Koser & Martin 2011), although wider coordination was relatively limited up until the later stages of the evacuation.

All these post-9/11 crises showed that consular cooperation was reactive, rather than focused on long-term planning. For example, the mentioned Council Decision on consular protection (95/553/EC) was adopted shortly after the Treaty of Maastricht that created the notion of European citizenship and related notions of common European rights for assistance under Art.20. Yet it took 7 years to be ratified. By 2006, only 4 years after coming into effect, the Commission's Green Paper on consular protection (European Commission 2006) critically reviewed the 1995 Decision and argued that the experience of crises made its substance dealing with daily tasks such as the loss of passport largely inadequate. Ignasi Guardans Cambo, a former Member of the European Parliament who was caught up in the 2008 Mumbai terror attacks, expressed this most dramatically:

> the European Commission has the obligation...to implement Article 20, to make European citizens proud of their passport and to make sure that certain officials understand that...Europe does exist whenever a European citizen is in trouble in New Delhi, Beirut or wherever else (2009).

The first step in this direction took place before the hostage crisis. In 2007, the Council clarified that the recast Community Mechanism (under section 18) 'could also be used for supporting consular assistance to EU citizens in major emergencies in third countries, regarding civil protection activities, if requested by the consular authorities of the Member States' (Council of the European Union 2007). As a result, the CPM could now be activated to complement Member States' wider crisis response efforts under leadership of the Council Presidency or a Lead State responsible for unrepresented EU citizens in a particular location. This Lead State would identify, dispatch and coordinate required capabilities provided by other Member States. If required, "double-hatted" rescue teams were made available for rescue missions inside and outside the EU, bearing the EU flag and "European Civil Protection" on their clothing in order to create a sense of joint effort, adding a new dimension to the changing field of consular assistance but, in themselves, acting as agents of securitisation.

One of the major issues at stake remains representation. Since all 28 Member States have diplomatic and consular missions in only three third countries (Russia, China and the US), European citizens can be caught in situations not of their own making, requiring immediate assistance from the nearest embassy or consulate. At a time when budgets across the Member States are strained and Foreign Ministries are having to cut on their activities,[3] cooperation in the sphere of consular protection is becoming increasingly important, as burden-sharing is becoming recognised as a tool for strengthening citizens' security beyond the EU's borders without adding extra pressure on Foreign Ministries' budgets (Merheim-Eyre 2014b: 2). As the 2011 Libyan evacuation showed, the European External Action Service (EEAS) also plays vaguely defined role in representing European citizens, highlighting that "a big chunk of today's diplomatic agenda focuses on the physical and economic security of the individual within the state, rather than of the state itself" (Melissen et al. 2012). According to Kristi Raik, "consular tasks of the EEAS are already being gradually strengthened, as the Service and its network of 141 EU Delegations abroad is building up its coordinating role with respect to the national diplomacies of the member states. First and foremost, the EEAS's consular coordination role in crisis situations is being enhanced" (2013: 4). This included the creation of a Consular Crisis Management Unit within its Crisis Response Department, but also attempts at establishing the practice of chairing local consular meetings by Heads of Delegations or their deputies.

---

[3] For example, the debt-ridden Spain went as far as to cut its Foreign Ministry budget by 54 % in 2012 compared to 2011, See Molina, Ignacio and Sorroza, Alicia. Spain and the European External Action Service in Balfour, Rosa and Raik, Kristi (eds.) (2013). 'The European External Action Service and National Diplomacies'; *European Policy Centre*, EPC Issue Paper No. 73.

Further, emergencies as those highlighted above no doubt existed before however, the post-9/11 era highlighted a significant increase in the number of man-made and natural disasters, as well as the general inability to respond in line with citizens expectations and travel patterns to third countries (from 50 million in 2005 to over 90 million in 2008, European Commission 2011). Therefore, new contingency plans and new frameworks for joint response have been developed, requiring new discursive practices and instruments, especially in delivering immediate humanitarian and medical assistance, followed by evacuations. This also legitimised the merger of the integration of the EU's Civil Protection Mechanism with DG-ECHO in 2010, but further highlighted the need to widen the field from national consular officers, to civilian or military rescue teams that could respond across the globe (Merheim-Eyre 2014b: 6).

Such framework of cooperation challenges the more traditional beliefs, such as that of Martin Wight, that only sovereign states can be engaged in diplomacy (Melissen et al. 2012). The fact that the European institutions are being given roles in this sphere (albeit vague and informal) shows that consular affairs are taking on a new symbolic and expert-driven dimension. As the Commission's 2010 Citizenship Report notes, the raison d'être of EU level consular protection is to 'increase the effectiveness of the right of EU citizens' (2010) but, consequently, securitising and depoliticising the sphere of consular affairs.

3.2 Visa Issuance: The Case of the EU's Eastern Partnership (EaP)

Similarly to consular assistance, visa issuance also underwent a comparable transformation stemming from securitisation, and resulting in the externalisation of internal (in)security problems through (i) development of local consular cooperation and the harmonisation of practices at the European level, (ii) advancement of surveillance technology as further securitising tools and (iii) the participation of third countries in EU border management. The eastern neighbourhood became a laboratory for the EU on all these fronts.

The common management of Schengen external borders primarily emerged in response to the removal of internal borders between its members, but also underlined the need to regulate potential external insecurities. In the 1990s, the swift disintegration of the Soviet Union created fears of ethno-political conflicts, economic collapse and westward migration, a sitution not dissimilar to that in the EU's southern neighbourhood today. While the situation eventually stabilised on the eastern border, the Yugoslav wars created huge migratory pressures. In 1992 alone, Germany took in 350,000 refugees and was processing further 438,000 applications. In addition, it was estimated that up to 500,000 illegal migrants entered Italy via North Africa and the Balkans (Torpey in Andreas and Snyder 2000: 44–45), while the spill over of Algerian terrorism to France raised further fears over migration.

Commencing at the local level in third countries, cooperation between Member State consular services became regarded "as complementary means of achieving integrated management of external borders" (Fernandez 2006: 10). This justified calls to increase coordination and harmonise practices (such as the introduction of a European Visa Code; European Parliament and the Council of the European Union 2009) and develop joint tools and frameworks, especially to enhance information-sharing on individual visa applicants. Following a French initiative, the practice of mutual representation of Schengen Member States for visa application purposes was introduced (Council of the European Union 2003). External visa cooperation, therefore, became an important aspect of monitoring access, and controlling the inflow of potential insecurities.

Eastern Europe, where visa applications for Schengen visa rose dramatically (see below) as a result of the 2004 enlargement, became a laboratory for new approaches. In 2007 Hungary opened the first EU Common Visa Application Centre in Chisinau, Moldova, representing 14 Schengen states. Simultaneously, the out-sourcing of the visa application process to private companies started to spread. Both trends highlighted the growing need for burden-sharing and cooperation in consular affairs at a time of increasingly constrained national budgets and calls for better coordination of Schengen visa application as an integral part of the common external border.

In 2008, the European Union launched the Eastern Partnership initiative[4] (EaP) as an ambition to bring the eastern neighbourhood closer to the EU. As in the case of the European Neighbourhood Policy, the aim was cooperation and convergence without the promise of accession, but with an increased emphasis on cross-border mobility. Around the same time, the southern Mediterranean region also saw a new initiative, namely the French-sponsored Union of the Mediterranean, but which failed to develop. Even before the 2011 Arab spring, serious doubt over the North African countries' abilities to manage their own security, let alone migration into the EU, dominated discussions and generally led to exclusionary policies (Youngs 2008: 167). In the EaP the problem and trend are of a somewhat different nature, whereby increasing expectations for a more inclusive approach to cross-border mobility by the EU were linked with the increasing inclusion of these states' physical borders and institutions in the EU's management of its external borders. For example, in 2012 alone, out of 2.1 million multiple entry "C" Schengen visas, over a million (52 %) were issued by the consulates of the Visegrad countries.[5] Of the 700,000 "C" visas issued by the Visegrad states' consulates in Ukraine, over 200,000 were issued by the Polish consulate in L'viv (European Commission 2013). In 2013, there was over 2.6 million "C" visa applications throughout the Eastern Partnership making it (with the exception of Russia) the busiest area for Schengen visa applications anywhere in the world (European Commission 2014).

As Anderson notes, the EU's eastern border is not simply a physical wall, separating one part of the continent from another. Instead, it is "porous"

[4] Armenia, Azerbaijan, Belarus, Georgia Moldova and Ukraine. Although Belarus is part of the Eastern Partnership, it does not formally participate in its initiatives.

[5] Czech Republic, Hungary, Poland and Slovakia; traditionally, given the geographic proximity and ethnic minorities, the busiest Schengen consulates in the EaP.

(in Andreas and Snyder 2000: 22), filtering wanted from unwanted migrants, giving the EU greater flexibility on managing access. As the case of the EaP shows, the increasing reliance on digital technology in surveillance systems (Lyon 2003) has significantly changed access management to the Schengen area, diminishing the importance of more physical obstacles, such as the once-important visa interview. While the rise of digital technology is not just a European phenomenon, the Schengen area is increasingly *avant-garde* in both the development of these instruments, but also through the structural impact its border management practices have on the eastern neighbourhood. The technique of visa issuance has altered significantly, relying on new technology and methods of control, which in themselves are adding a new securitising rationale. This includes a regulated Local Border Traffic (LBT) regime, the Registered Traveller Programme (RTP), the Visa Information System (VIS), the Schengen Information System (SIS) I and II, the European Image Archiving System (EIAS), the European Database of Asylum Applicants (EURODAC), the European Border Surveillance System (EBSS), the Agency for large-scale IT systems and the European Agency for the Management of Operational Cooperation at the External Border (FRONTEX).[6]

So even before an individual reaches the external border of the EU, there is a complex system of pre-screening and a scrutiny of applications. Background checks at consulates make use of the VIS and the SIS while relevant information submitted by applicants is stored in the EIAS (Europa.eu 2014). Further, the Schengen Information System I and II, as well as connecting all Member State consulates and border crossings, has now developed a capacity to store biometric data (Balzacq 2008: 85). Together with the VIS, it contains information on persons involved in serious crime, missing persons or stolen property.

The problem for policy-makers and security practitioners is that, whatever technical systems are put in place, the EU's external borders cannot be adequately protected, let alone to function as filters, without the assistance of third countries, particularly those bordering the EU. As Andreas notes, "not only has the EU external frontier come to resemble a state border, in effect it extends outward into neighbouring countries" (Andreas in Andreas and Snyder 2000: 3). As a result, the EU has come to diffuse security governmentality approaches to governing its external borders. For example, the Visa Liberalisation Action Plans (VLAPs) with the eastern neighbourhood countries are dominated by conditions on improving third countries' law enforcement and border management, seeking to create a sort of cordon sanitaire around the Union that would see less unwanted migrants reaching the physical borders, while maintaining and legally facilitating visa-free access for citizens of the eastern neighbourhood countries meeting EU standards.

The most important part of the visa liberalisation process is the fulfilment of EU-set conceptual parameters and the convergence with "European and international" norms and practices. For example, in the case of the EU's Association Agreement with Armenia, the EU speaks of "political support towards visa

[6] Meanwhile, negotiations about a common European Passenger Name Record (PNR) are still on-going.

liberalisation of the visa regime in a secure environment" (Council of the European Union 2013). It is the kind of discourse that highlights that visa liberalisation can only take place within the remits of EU-set conceptual parameters, involving the security of Armenia's external borders (under EU supervision) to prevent any potential transit of unwanted migrants attempting to reach the EU.

In 2008, the Council agreed on the so-called "Return Directive", which set common standards for readmission and return and, most importantly, sought to provide new incentives on readmission of illegal migrants to third countries, particularly those bordering the European Union (Council of the European Union 2008). The readmission agreements signed with individual third countries in the eastern neighbourhood have become tied with the Visa Facilitation Agreements and, henceforth, the VLAPs, as one of the instrumental parts towards visa liberalisation between the EU and the Eastern Partnership countries. Thus, in its Visa Facilitation Agreements, the Union emphasised the desire to increase people-to-people contact, but under set-conceptual parameters (Kurki 2011) that further include the strengthening of law enforcement institutions, border management, and democratic governance.

The VLAP concluded with Moldova in 2014 provides an instructive case on how these conditions, as part of the process of externalising EU security governmentality, are translated into technical calculability. Prior to the establishment of a visa-free regime with Moldova, annual progress reports published by the Commission required an extensive list of reforms. This included document security (including the introduction of biometric technology), strengthened management of Moldova's physical borders, migration management, asylum policy, preventing and fighting organised crime, terrorism, corruption, judicial cooperation in criminal matters, law enforcement cooperation, data protection, conditions and procedures for the issue of identity documents, and citizens' rights including the protection of minorities. The EC's fifth and final progress report (European Commission 2013) then concluded that Moldova reached the necessary benchmarks for visa liberalisation in four areas: the reform of the Interior Ministry, judicial cooperation with the EU Member States, improvement of international police cooperation and strengthened cooperation with Ukraine on border management.

This shows that EU external border management is not merely about surveillance technology or the "fences" of Fortress Europe, but also about the increasing participation and security of neighbouring countries. Under these set conceptual parameters, the EU is managing its dialogue with eastern neighbours, while at the same time creating a "buffer-zone". By mixing conditions such as the Readmission Agreements with visa liberalisation for citizens of the EaP, countries such as Georgia have, despite internal opposition, created new structures for managing migration (Delcour 2013) and, "thereby providing an additional control zone between the refugees' countries of origin and potential destination countries in western Europe" (Colinson 1996: 82). In sum, the EU is able to project its security governmentality into a wider field that includes third countries, creating an external regulatory system that filters access towards the EU's internal milieu.

4 Conclusion: Consequences of Externalisation

This chapter traced the externalisation of EU internal security through two very different strands of consular affairs: the protection of EU citizens in third countries, and the issuance of Schengen visa. The chapter conceptualised this externalisation using a post-structuralist "governmentality" approach to security, and the securitisation of consular affairs through both discursive and non-discursive practices. The chapter then empirically explored the ways in which the EU's security governmentality is produced by externalising internal security concerns and merging it with consular affairs, specific instruments and programmes. The first major result of externalisation is the growing field of actors and its complexity, understood as "a configuration of objective relations between positions" (Bourdieu and Wacquant 1992: 94). The shifting and externalising field of internal security involves actors and structures, and the relations of power between them shapes what does or does not constitute a security threat. In the case of consular protection, securitisation dynamics in the aftermath of major crises increased the pressure to pool both civilian (rescue) and military resources to provide post-crises relief in third countries.

On the level of formal EU structures, the Lisbon Treaty promoted further reforms of the Union's crisis management structures. In particular, the Civil Protection Mechanism was strengthened and merged into DG ECHO for humanitarian assistance, while the European External Action Service added a Crisis Management Division to its structures (including a Consular Crisis Unit). The practical impact of these changes was clearly demonstrated during the 2011 Libyan crisis (Merheim-Eyre 2014b). On the other hand, Gorgio Porzio, who headed the EEAs' Consular Crisis Unit, made it clear that the EU institutions "do not—and cannot—have direct consular dealings with the public" (2008). Therefore, roles of EU institutions may be also largely informal or not publicly recognised, but they are part of a growing number of actors, ranging from national consular officers to civilian-military teams, entering the field as a result of securitisation. They also act as securitising agents, shifting internal (in)security rationalities into new areas of government, and beyond the borders of the EU.

In the case of visa issuance, EU institutions have gained an important (but not decisive) role in determining internal security threats. The process is, still, essentially Member State-driven, uploading their policy preferences on what constitutes a security risk and what does not (Merheim-Eyre in Janułewicz et al. 2014). Despite the pilot Visa Application Centre in Chisinau, competencies are also increasingly outsourced to private companies. Especially in the eastern neighbourhood of the EU, this is becoming a standard practice, owing to financial constraints and processing pressures due to increasing number of visa applicants. Consequently, private actors in many instances under-take the "processing" tasks, although final decisions on issuance are still a competence of the individual Member States.

The most striking aspect of widening the field, however, lies in the EU's externalisation of responsibilities for border management to third countries. In the case of the eastern neighbourhood, third countries are offered a more "inclusive" approach to mobility through visa liberalisation. However, conceptual parameters are set in the VLAPs, which include conditions for the rule of law, issuance of passports, and the adoption of new migration laws. As a result, the EU's eastern neighbourhood, widens the field of EU internal (in)security, providing an additional space for mitigating potential risks that might reach the borders of the European Union.

Building on the growing number of actors and complexities within the field of consular affairs, new practices and tools are produced and re-produced. These tools and practices can in themselves "transform the image" of a particular threat (Balzacq 2008: 77). Tools are not merely responsive, but they evolve according to need. They can be securitised, but they can also securitise. For example, the continuous externalisation of EU borders into the eastern neighbourhood has reconfigured the way the EU has engaged with its neighbours, adopting a more inclusive approach to mobility through visa liberalisation. On the other hand, an inclusive approach only takes place as long as it is managed, through extra-territorial surveillance technology and the willing participation of third countries to participate in EU border management. Most significantly, EU level synergies such as the EU Consular Code or Frontex Common Curriculum Course for Border Guards attempt to harmonise national (and third countries') practices, producing knowledge about best practices, levels of quality, and terms of exceptions or cooperation between consulates as well as outsourced visa application centres.

However, the EU institutions do not directly provide formal consular protection, and neither has it formally agreed to conduct consular relations with third countries under the 1963 Vienna Convention.[7] Prior to the Lisbon Treaty, numerous EU institutions gained some form of limited role in consular protection, justified through security-driven discourse. Since Lisbon, however, these have shifted as a result of institutional changes. The Member States' Ministries of Foreign Affairs, in particular, are increasingly coordinating with other Member States through EU Institutions, dealing with consular cooperation matters in all areas, including the financing of missions, the pooling of suitable civilian-military capabilities and the repatriation of EU citizens, insisting on the security dimension of consular protection (European Parliament 2013). The bulk of the legislation on consular protection, therefore, is still that of the Member States[8] but, as in the case of consular protection, the EU is increasingly setting conceptual parameters for "best standards" through harmonisation and enhanced cooperation, involving the "supportive" role of the EU institutions, including the securitising Civil Protection Mechanism.

[7] Such scenario is considered highly unlikely even by the EEAS, who lack the funding or expertise.

[8] This legislation has been collected under the Database of the EU-funded CARE Project. See CARE—Citizens Consular Assistance Regulation in Europe; *Consular and Diplomatic Protection: Legal Framework in the EU Member States*, Project No JLS/2007/FRC-1/50 30-CE-0226854/00-31 2010.

Finally, the externalisation of EU internal security impacts on the way we subjectivise both EU and third country citizens. The growing focus on protection in crises highlights how securitisation has reconfigured the conception of EU citizens as victims. In other words, if the Member States cannot guarantee citizens' security beyond the Union, which is impossible on a global scale, changing expectations about the need for post-crises assistance thus highlights victimisation of citizens. Consular protection, therefore, becomes an external means of mitigating post-crises scenarios, requiring new kind of expert knowledge beyond the traditional tasks, and leading towards the emergence of new discursive and non-discursive practices of security governmentality. Rescue teams and contingency planning shift the focus of expert technical knowledge to the necessity of protection, producing new perceptions of consular priorities beyond the more traditional daily tasks, such as loss of passports. This shift does not imply that these tasks are no longer an important part of the practice. In fact, statistically, they form the most significant part of consular assistance to citizens. Visas also maintain similar security-dominated subjectivities.

Finally, third country nationals continue to be regarded as potential threats to the EU (Balzacq 2008: 89), producing the need to regulate, check and filter desirable from undesirable elements. Even visa liberalisation, suggesting an inclusive approach, is managed and conditioned upon a "safe environment" that the EU defines within its own conceptual parameters. Therefore, the visa document as a securitising tool does not only manage inclusion or exclusion, but also subjectivises the perception of third country nationals. Thus overall, the emergence of new practices and subjectivities in consular protection and issuance of visa provides a highly instructive case for exploring the shifting and externalising governmentality attached to EU internal security.

References

Andreas, P., & Snyder, T. (Eds.). (2000). *The Wall around the West: State borders and immigration controls in North America and Europe*. Lanham: Rowman and Littlefield Publishers.

Aradau, C., & Van Munster, R. (2011). *Politics of catastrophe: Genealogies of the unknown*. Abingdon: Routledge.

Balfour, R., & Raik, K. (Eds). (2013). *The European external action service and national diplomacies* (EPC Issue Paper No. 73). European Policy Centre.

Balzacq, T. (2008). The policy tools of securitisation: Information exchange, EU foreign and interior policies. *Journal of Common Market Studies, 46*, 1.

Balzacq, T. (Ed.). (2009). *The external dimension of EU justice and home affairs: Neighbours, governance, security*. New York: Palgrave Macmillan.

Balzacq, T. (2014). The significance of triangulation to critical security studies. *Critical Studies on Security, 2*, 3.

Balzacq, T., Basaran, T., Bigo, D., Guittet, E.-P., & Olsson, C. (2010). *Security practices*. International Studies Encyclopaedia Online. Blackwell Publishing.

Barnier, M. (2006). *For a European civil protection force: Europe aid*. Brussels: European Commission.

Bigo, D., & Guild, E. (Eds.). (2005). *Controlling frontiers: Free movement into and within Europe*. Aldershot: Ashgate.

Booth, K. (1991). Security and emancipation. *Review of International Studies, 17*, 4.
Bourdieu, P., & Wacquant, L. (1992). *An invitation to reflexive sociology*. Cambridge: Polity Press.
Buerk, R. (2004, December 26). Eyewitness: Sri Lanka Tsunami. *BBC News*. Accessed May 21, 2014, from http://news.bbc.co.uk/1/hi/world/south_asia/4125581.stm
Buzan, B., Waever, O., & de Wilde, J. (1998). *Security: A new framework for analysis*. London: Lynne Rienner Publishers.
Citizens Consular Assistance Regulation in Europe (CARE). (2010). *Consular and diplomatic protection: Legal framework in the EU Member States*. Project No JLS/2007/FRC-1/50 30-CE-0226854/00-31.
Colinson, S. (1996). Visa requirements, carrier sanctions, "safe third countries" and "readmission": The development of an asylum "buffer zone" in Europe. *Transactions of the Institute of British Geographers, New Series, 21*, 1.
Consolidated Versions of the Treaty on European Union and the Treaty on the Functioning of the European Union. (2008/C 115/01). *Official Journal of the European Union C115, 51*.
Cotey, A. (2007). *Security in the New Europe*. Basingstoke: Macmillan.
Council of the European Union. (2003). *A secure Europe in a better world: European Security Strategy*. Brussels: Council of the European Union.
Council of the European Union. (2007). Council Decision establishing a Community Civil Protection Mechanism (recast), Decision (2007/779/EC Euratom). *Official Journal of the European Union, L, 314*, 9–19. Brussels.
Council of the European Union. (2008). *Report on the implementation of the European Security Strategy—Providing security in a changing world, (S407/08)*. Brussels: Council of the European Union.
Council of the European Union. (2010a). *Internal security strategy for the European Union: Towards a European security model*. Brussels: Council of the European Union.
Council of the European Union. (2010). The Stockholm Programme—An open and secure Europe serving and protecting citizens (2010/C 115/01). *Official Journal of the European Union, C115/1*. Brussels.
Council of the European Union. (2013). Agreement between the European Union and the Republic of Armenia on the facilitation of the issuance of visas. *Official Journal L, 289*, 2–11.
Council of the European Union. (2015). Council Directive on the coordination and cooperation measures to facilitate consular protection for unrepresented citizens of the Union in third countries and repealing Decision 95/553/EC (2015/637). *Official Journal of the European Union, L, 106*. Brussels.
Critical Approaches to Security in Europe (C.A.S.E. Collective). (2006). Critical approaches to security in Europe: A networked Manifesto. *Security Dialogue, 37*, 4.
Dean, M. (2010). *Governmentality: Power and rule in modern society* (2nd ed.). London: Sage.
Delcour, L. (2013). Meandering Europeanisation: EU policy instruments and policy convergence in Georgia under the Eastern Partnership. *East European Politics, 29*, 3.
Der Derian, J. (1991). *On diplomacy*. Oxford: Blackwell.
Dillon, M. (2007). Governing through contingency: The security of biopolitical governance. *Political Geography, 26*, 1.
Dillon, M., & Lobo-Guerrero, L. (2008). Biopolitics of security in the 21st century: An introduction. *Review of International Studies, 34*, 265–292.
Edkins, J. (1999). *Poststructuralism and international relations: Bringing the political back in*. London: Lynne Rienner Publishers.
EU Action in Response to Crisis in Lebanon (2006). *European Union Joint Press Release 25/07/2006*. Brussels. Accessed May 22, 2014, from http://www.consilium.europa.eu/ueDocs/cms_Data/docs/pressData/en/er/90662.pdf
European Commission. (2001). *Civil protection—State of preventive alert against possible emergencies*. Communication from the Commission to the Council and the European Parliament. COM(2001) 707 Final. Brussels.

European Commission. (2006). Green paper: Diplomatic and consular protection of Union citizens in third countries. COM(2006) 712 Final. Brussels.
European Commission. (2010a). EU citizenship report: Dismantling the obstacles to EU's citizens' rights. COM(2010) 603 Final. Brussels.
European Commission. (2010b). *Communication from the Commission to the European Parliament and Council: Towards a stronger European Disaster response: the role of Civil Protection and Humanitarian Assistance*. COM(2010) 600 Final. Brussels.
European Commission. (2011). Communication from the Commission to European Parliament and the Council - Consular protection for EU citizens in third countries: State of play and way forward. *COM* (2011), 149 Final.
European Commission. (2013). *Complete statistics on short-stay visas issued by Schengen consulates 2012*. Brussels: European Commission.
European Commission. (2014). *Complete statistics on short-stay visas issued by Schengen consulates 2013*. Brussels: European Commission.
European Parliament. (2009). *Debate of the European Parliament concerning Consular protection of citizens of the European Union in third countries*.
European Parliament. (2013). Workshop: The role of the European external action service in consular protection and services for EU Citizen's. EXPO/B/AFET/FWC/2009-01/Lot2/12 PE 433.808. Brussels.
European Parliament and the Council of the European Union Regulation. (2009). (EC) No 810/2009 establishing a community Code on Visas (Visa Code). *Official Journal of the European Union L, 243*. Brussels.
Fernandez, A. M. (2006). *The Europeanisation of consular affairs: The case of visa policy* (Discussion Papers in Diplomacy). The Hague: Netherlands Institute of International Relations 'Clingendael'.
Foucault, M. (2007). *Security, territory, population: Lectures at the Collège de France 1977–78*. Basingstoke: Palgrave Macmillan.
Heath-Kelly, C. (2015). Securing through the failure to secure: The ambiguous resilience of the Bombsite. *Security Dialogue, 46*, 1.
Hocking, B., & Spence, D. (2005). *Towards a European diplomatic system?* (Discussion Papers in Diplomacy). The Hague: Netherlands Institute of International Relations 'Clingendael'.
Janułewicz, Ł., Merheim-Eyre, I., & van Gils, E. (Eds). (2014). *'All things to all people?' Internal and external approaches to Europeanisation* (Global Europe Centre Working Paper)
Koser, K., & Martin, S. (Eds.). (2011). *The migration-displacement nexus*. Oxford: Berghahn Books.
Kurki, M. (2011). Democracy through technocracy? Reflections on technocratic assumptions in EU democracy promotion discourse. *Journal of Intervention and Statebuilding, 5*, 2.
Lundborg, T., & Vaughan-Williams, N. (2011). Resilience, critical infrastructure and molecular security: The excess of "Life" in biopolitics. *International Political Sociology, 5*, 4.
Lyon, D. (Ed.). (2003). *Surveillance as social sorting; privacy, risk and digital discrimination*. Abingdon: Rourtledge.
Melissen, J., Hocking, B., Riordan, S., & Sharp, P. (2012, November 14). A Europe in crisis in need of diplomatic reform. *The Japan Times*. Accessed November 25, 2014, from http://www.clingendael.nl/media/?id=9126
Merheim-Eyre, I. (2014a). *Strengthening the security of UK nationals in third countries FCO consular services in the emerging European consular cooperation*. Evidence to the UK Parliament House of Commons Foreign Affairs Committee (CON0016).
Merheim-Eyre, I. (2014b). *Towards a more ambitious framework for cooperation? FCO Consular Services, the European Union and the challenges of consular protection*. Evidence for the Foreign and Commonwealth Office BoC Semester 4.
Merheim-Eyre, I. (2015). Consular protection to EU citizens in third countries: A loss of interest? *Vocal International*. Accessed July 07, 2015, from http://vocalinternational.com/?p=1758

Okano Heijmans, M. (2010). *Change in consular assistance and the emergence of consular diplomacy* (Clingendael Diplomacy Papers No. 26).
Porzio, G. (2008). Consular assistance and protection: An EU perspective. *The Hague Journal of Diplomacy, 3*, 1.
Raik, K. (2013). Serving the citizens? Consular role of the EEAS grows in small steps. *European Policy Centre Policy Brief.*
Rijpma, J., & Cremona, M. (2007). *The extra-territorialisation of EU migration policies and the rule of law* (EUI Law Working Paper).
Smith, M. (1996). The European Union and changing Europe: Establishing the boundaries of order'. *Journal of Common Market Studies, 34*(1), 6–28.
Stringer, K. D. (2004). *The visa dimension of diplomacy* (Discussion Papers in Diplomacy). The Hague: Netherlands Institute of International Relations "Clingendael".
Youngs, R. (2008). Fusing security and development: Just another Euro-platitude? *European Integration, 30*, 3.

EU-Belarus Cooperation in Border Management: Mechanisms and Forms of Norm Transfer

Katsiaryna Yakouchyk and Alexandra M. Schmid

1 Introduction

Irregular migration is one of the core security concerns of the European Union (EU) (European Council 2003: 4). To cope with the irregular migration pressure, the EU cooperates with neighbourhood countries and helps them to build the capacities for an effective protection of the common border (European Council 2010). Through different projects, the EU seeks to diffuse its own standards of border management to neighbours (e.g., Hernández i Sagrera 2014). Yet since not all of the EU neighbours are democratic, the EU faces some fundamental challenges in this regard. Thus, Belarus is excluded from major EU neighbourhood projects, and its ruling elites are banned from entering the EU. Nevertheless, security cooperation with the regime is deemed necessary as Belarus and the EU share about 1200 km of borders. For instance, for 2012–2013 Belarus experienced a sixfold increase in European funding for different kinds of projects (among them border management projects) when compared to the period from 2007 to 2011 (Korosteleva 2015).

Various scholars (e.g., Bosse 2012), journalists[1] and policy makers (German Bundestag 2014) have raised concerns over this kind of cooperation with Belarus, and emphasized the poor human rights situation in the country. Specifically, they accused the EU of supporting projects aimed at strengthening the Western border of the country, which would also reinforce the Belarusian security forces and its

[1] For example, see "EU Passes British Aid to Belarus Dictator". The Telegraph. 10 October 2013. http://www.telegraph.co.uk/news/worldnews/europe/10391006/EU-passes-British-aid-to-Belarus-dictator.html (accessed on 20 August, 2014). See also an investigation made by Radio Svaboda on EU development aid in Belarus. http://www.svaboda.org/archive/foreign-aid-belarus/latest/17344/17344.html (in Belarusian) (accessed on 11 January 2015).

K. Yakouchyk (✉) • A.M. Schmid
University of Passau, Dr. Hans-Kapfinger-Straße 14b, 94032 Passau, Germany
e-mail: yakouc01@stud.uni-passau.de; Alexandra.m.schmid@posteo.de

R. Bossong, H. Carrapico (eds.), *EU Borders and Shifting Internal Security*,
DOI 10.1007/978-3-319-17560-7_7

capabilities to intimidate domestic opposition. Does the EU indeed face this insurmountable normative conflict in its border and migration management cooperation? Or can we observe a pragmatic approach, which includes both hierarchical sanctions and networked cooperation with Belarus, and can be reconciled with the overarching aim of democratization?

From a more conceptual perspective, this chapter contributes to two major debates: (i) the presumed conflict between the EU declared ambitions to promote democracy and its practical realization in light of internal strategic security interests (Boswell 2003), and (ii) the capacity of the EU to export democratic governance provisions through technocratic aid (Freyburg et al. 2009; Freyburg 2015; Korosteleva 2015). Hence, this chapter proceeds in two main parts. First, based on process tracing and textual analysis of EU documents and reports, we provide a survey of the EU's overall political strategy towards Belarus. Second, we analyze the case of functional cooperation between the EU and Belarus on border and migration management in order to explore whether the EU is practicing a Janus-faced policy. While we need to recognize the EU's security interests, which may undermine its wider normative stance on Belarus, we also need to look more closely at the content and implementation of border management projects, which has been missing from the current literature. For this purpose the chapter analyses official documents of the EU and other organizations involved in border management projects, as well as press-releases and websites of relevant projects. These primary data have been completed by semi-structured interviews conducted in Belarus in 2014.[2] In conclusion, we argue that although EU-Belarus border management cooperation did not lead to wider governance improvements, this cooperation neither directly supports the wider repressive tendencies of the Belarusian political-security apparatus, as the EU funded projects are largely accountable.

2 The EU's Approach Towards Belarus: An Overview

Relations between the EU and Belarus started to deteriorate shortly after the first presidential elections in the post-Soviet state. President Lukashenko moved quickly to restrict media freedom, civil society and political opposition, and passed reforms to extend his presidential mandate (e.g., Bosse 2012). In 1996, the questionable legitimacy of a referendum on constitutional amendments,[3] which concentrated power in the hands of Lukashenko, led the EU to freeze official bilateral relations with Belarus. In the following year, the EU decided to freeze the conclusion and ratification of the Partnership and Cooperation Agreement along with an Interim agreement, signed in 1995 (European Commission 2006). Since then, the EU has

[2] Five semi-structured interviews were conducted in Minsk in May 2014, three of them with local experts, and two with EU officials.

[3] As a result of the 1996 referendum, the mandate of Lukashenko's presidency was extended and the president gained additional powers. For more details see, for example, Silitski (2005).

made the resumption of normal bilateral relations and further cooperation conditional on "clearly identified steps towards democratization" (European Commission 2006: 7). In response to human rights violations, the EU furthermore began to impose sanctions against Belarusian officials and companies connected with the regime.

When drafting the European Neighbourhood Policy (ENP) in the early 2000s, the EU decided to include Belarus only on the condition of free and fair elections (European Commission 2004). Therefore, Belarusian participation in the ENP remained declaratory and no corresponding ENP Action Plan was developed. As Yeliseyeu (2013) claims, between 2004 and 2007 Belarus repeatedly proposed the European Commission to start negotiations on visa facilitation, whereas the Commission refused because of human rights problems. In 2006, the EU issued a Non-Paper with a list of democratizing measures to be implemented by Belarusian authorities if they sought closer cooperation. Among other things, this included democratic elections, the abolition of the death penalty, and media freedom.[4]

Thus, the EU apparently maintained a clear line with regard to fundamental rights and democracy promotion. Yet in the Country Strategy Paper 2007–2013, the EU did not only underline the need to "respect democratic values and the rule of law," (European Commission 2006: 6) but also acknowledged that there is a "strategic interest to continue assistance programmes in certain areas which require the assent of the Belarusian authorities [...] such as migration management [.]"(-European Commission 2006: 6). The strategy paper went on to argue that low-level contacts with Belarusian officials would increase their understanding of the EU and its values.

In fact, EU-Belarus bilateral relations started to improve gradually in 2007 (e.g., Dura 2008). Positive developments in Minsk, such as the release of political prisoners and changes in electoral legislation, led to a 6-month suspension of the EU's visa-ban for high-ranking officials and the president (Rotman and Veremeeva 2011). As a next step in the logic of positive conditionality, Belarus was included in the Eastern Partnership program (EaP). Whereas the ENP tried to encompass the entire EU neighbourhood, the EaP's launch in 2009 signalized the EU's deeper engagement with Eastern countries.[5] The EaP aims to lead the participating states towards a legal approximation with the EU and to develop institution-building programs for each country that would improve their administrative capacities. So even if the EaP raised the profile of civil society actors in target states, its overall character remained state-centered (e.g., Börzel and Lebanidze 2015).

Moreover, both normative and security concerns underpin this policy framework. On the one hand, the EaP is officially based on commitments to "democracy,

[4] For the full list see the Non-Paper "What the European Union could bring to Belarus". http://eeas.europa.eu/delegations/belarus/documents/eu_belarus/non_paper_1106.pdf (accessed on 19 March 2014).

[5] The EaP covers three Eastern neighbours of the EU and three republics of South Caucasus: Ukraine, Moldova, Belarus, Armenia, Georgia, and Azerbaijan.

the rule of law and the respect for human rights and fundamental freedoms, as well as to market economy, sustainable development and good governance." (Council of the European Union 2009: 5). On the other hand, the importance of the EU's internal security and the role of Eastern neighbours can be detected. Questions of EU energy security receive particular attention, as some Eastern European countries are either direct suppliers (e.g., Azerbaijan) or host critical transit routes (e.g., Belarus, Ukraine) for fossil fuels. Thus, deepening relations with EaP countries is "both a strategic imperative and a political investment for the EU, which will pay dividends to Europe's citizens" (European Commission 2008: 13–14).

This increasingly pragmatic rhetoric may explain why Belarus was initially interested in active participation in the EaP. Rotman and Veremeeva (2011) report that Belarusian representatives initially participated in all EaP platforms and submitted many project proposals for funding along with other EaP partners. Nevertheless, the country could only participate in some sectoral projects of the multilateral track of the EaP.[6] Minsk underlined its readiness to become a full participant of the EaP, if the EU was ready to treat it on equal terms and to prioritize joint interests rather than political values (Korosteleva 2011).

In any case, the limited approximation under the EaP was soon cast into doubt. On the eve of the 2010 presidential elections, the EU promised to provide financial assistance if democratic standards were met (Rettman 2010). Yet mass protests erupted in Minsk after the announcement of Lukashenko's renewed victory. Police cracked them down hard and hundreds of protesters, among them candidates for presidency, were arrested and sentenced. In response, the EU extended visa bans to several hundred officials, and froze assets of numerous Belarusian companies connected with the regime. In addition, the EU imposed an arms embargo, which has been prolonged several times (and is currently valid until 29 February 2016).[7] However, EU economic sanctions did not have a marked effect on prosperity, such that Belarusian authorities would be ready to comply with democratic conditionality. Personal entry-bans might instead have an adverse effect: being on the EU "black list" is considered as the expression of loyalty to the president (interview with a local expert 2014) and sanctions, at least temporarily, triggered political defiance. When the Commission invited Belarus to start negotiations on visa

[6] The institutional setting of the EaP framework is divided into two platforms: a bilateral and a multilateral track. The bilateral track is the heart of the EaP and was designed to develop relations between the EU and each of the partner countries. The Bilateral track leads towards upgrading contractual agreements from the Partnership and Cooperation Agreements (PCA) to more inclusive Association Agreements. Negotiations on free trade areas, visa-liberalization, and cooperation in energy security issues are incorporated into the bilateral track. The multi-lateral dimension is constituted by both political and expert meetings and should be a platform for dialogue and exchange. However, its operational scope is limited and dissociated from highly sought-after benefits, such as visa-liberalization.

[7] "EU Arms Embargo on Belarus". Stockholm International Peace Research Institute. http://www.sipri.org/databases/embargoes/eu_arms_embargoes/belarus (accessed on 31 August 2015).

facilitation in 2011, Belarus refused due to the suspension of official top-level contacts (Yeliseyeu 2014).

Nevertheless, some improvements in the EU-Belarus relations have taken place since 2013. In the wider context of the EaP, Belarus ratified the readmission agreements with Russia (the source of the most irregular migrants) and Kazakhstan.[8] Belarusian delegation participated in the EaP Vilnius Summit in November 2013 and declared its readiness to start EU visa-liberalization negotiations (Astapenia 2013). In this improving climate, expectations were raised that a respective agreement could already be signed at the next major EaP Summit in May 2015 (Gubarevich 2015). This proved not to be the case, reportedly due to disagreements on the regulation for diplomatic passports (Gubarevich 2015), while the Belarusian Foreign Minister maintained afterwards that negotiations were in the final stages (Korovenkova 2015). Moreover, these steps also have to be understood against the background of the Euromaidan in Ukraine, the war in Donbass, and Belarusian role in hosting the cease-fire negotiation. To support these processes, the EU intensified official contacts with Belarusian authorities, eased sanctions against some corporations and removed 24 persons from the entry ban list (Kulakevich 2015). On the side of the Belarusian regime, there seems to be an interest in putting some distance between itself and Russia.

Summing up, Belarus remains the only EU's Eastern neighbour under sanctions,[9] and where the EU made a full use of political conditionality (Börzel and Lebanidze 2015). Sanctions were lifted for a short time as a response to some positive developments between 2007 and 2009, but quickly re-introduced as Belarus continued its authoritarian course. At the same time, the EU has long recognized the need of cooperating with the country's authorities in areas of mutual interest. Beyond the more recent crisis in Ukraine, this includes, in particular, migration and border management. At the time of writing, further improvement in mutual relations seemed possible, as Belarus released a number of political prisoners in August 2015. The critical test has been the conduct of the presidential elections in October of the same year. In fact, a few weeks after these elections the EU suspended most of sanctions against Belarus. The following section of this chapter deepens this recurrent contrast between security interests and the twists and turns, as well as potential effects, of political conditionality in the EU's external relations.

[8] "Senators Approve Ratification of Belarus-Kazakhstan Readmission Agreement". Belarusian Telegraph Agency. 30 May 2014. http://goo.gl/Ks596l and "Belarus Completes Internal Proceedings to Ratify Readmission Agreement with Russia". Belarusian Telegraph Agency. 24 July 2014. http://goo.gl/T9bVNw (both accessed on 8 September 2015).

[9] As for 2014, 232 individuals and 25 companies are targeted with a travel ban and asset freeze, respectively. ENP Package—Belarus. European Commission—MEMO/14/222. 27 March 2014 (accessed on 19 June 2014).

3 Border Management as a Proxy of EU Security Interests

Ten years after the launch of the ENP there is a consensus that the policy failed in bringing the participating states on the democratization path (e.g., Börzel and van Hüllen 2014), although it was modelled as an alternative for enlargement (Kelley 2006).[10] Whereas scholars agree on the overall success of democratic conditionality in countries with a EU membership perspective (e.g., Dimitrova and Pridham 2004; Schimmelfennig and Scholtz 2008), this model has had only a limited success in non-accession states. Incentives offered by the ENP, such as free trade agreements and visa facilitation, are rarely appealing to elites of concerned countries because the alleged benefits do not outweigh possible disadvantages (i.e., losing power).[11]

Another possible reason for the EU's inability to promote democratic governance beyond its borders is the lack of coherence in formulating the aims of its neighbourhood policies. European neighbourhood projects, as a means to guarantee primarily European internal security, have attracted scholarly attention in the recent years (e.g., Del Sarto and Schumacher 2005; Lavenex and Wichman 2009). Scholars highlight that the EU democracy promotion paradigms are vaguely defined and often incoherent, whereas the EU is much more precise with regard to internal security issues (e.g., Bosse 2011). High-level policy makers, too, underline the EU's interest in secure and stable neighbouring countries. For example, the former EU Commissioner for External Relations and Neighbourhood Policy, Benita Ferrero-Waldner, acknowledged that: "[T]he EU's interests are tightly bound up with developments in its eastern and southern borders and that we need stable and predictable relationships with our neighbours. In short: if we don't 'export' stability, we risk 'importing instability'" (Ferrero-Waldner 2009).

This set of arguments can be condensed into the so-called democratization–stabilization dilemma (e.g., Jünemann 2003; Jünemann and Knodt 2008; Schlumberger 2006). As any regime change is often a long and unpredictable process, its outcomes are uncertain. The transition process might involve conflicts, civil wars and, in turn, mass migration and trans-border crime. The Arab uprisings and the Ukrainian crisis are two recent examples of unpredictability of a regime change. For the EU, instability is a direct opposite of what it seeks to promote in neighbouring countries (Börzel and van Hüllen 2014). Hence, the EU clearly tends, in some cases, to prefer authoritarian stability over democratization in its neighbourhood.

Indeed, Bosse (2009) claims that, in case of Belarus, the EU has failed to bring about democratic changes because of the pursuance of own security interests. Furthermore, Bosse (2012) argues that there has been a gradual shift from the

[10] On the various instruments and strategies of the EU democracy promotion see, for example, Schimmelfennig and Scholtz (2008), Knodt et al. (2011), and Lavenex and Schimmelfennig (2011).

[11] Notice that factors such as the influence of other (non-democratic) states might also diminish the impact of EU policies in its neighbourhood. For the Belarusian case see Yakouchyk (2015).

democracy promotion approach towards the interest-based functional cooperation with Belarus. The author mentions border management as a proxy of the EU policy concerned with its own security interests. Cooperating with an authoritarian regime on soft security issues and financing projects in which the EU's self-interest is evident is, in her view, problematic with regard to the EU as a normative actor and diverges from the official rhetoric on democracy promotion.

Finding the right balance between "sticks and carrots" as a strategy of democracy promotion, and a more network-based functional cooperation with authoritarian regimes is especially evident in migration and border management. To begin with, the European Commission underlines that Belarus is an important transit country for trade and financial flows between the EU, Russia, Kazakhstan, and China (European Commission 2011). This requires state borders with modern infrastructure, both for facilitating international trade and containing irregular migration. However, Hernández i Sagrera (2014) underlines that the main goals of the EU border management agenda towards its neighbours, in particular the Eastern ones, are information exchange on irregular migration flows and capacity-building programmes for the purposes of a security-driven migration policy.[12] When promoting the EU standards for border management or the integrated border management (IBM) in Eastern Europe, the EU thus concentrates on modernization and technologization of border equipment (Hernández i Sagrera 2014).

Against this background, Belarus can be considered a very important partner for Brussels in combating irregular migration, since the EU and Belarus share 1200 km of border. Whereas on the Eastern EU border Ukraine remains the main transit route for irregular migrants from both CIS and non-CIS countries, "Belarus is gaining importance as a hub for mixed (complex population movements including refugees, asylum seekers and economic migrants) migratory flows originating from Caucasus" (Jaroszewicz and Kindler 2015: 6). Migrants transiting Belarus are mainly economic migrants from Georgia and Russia (citizens originating from North Caucasus) who either arrive by air or cross the uncontrolled Belarusian-Russian border (Jaroszewicz and Kindler 2015). In addition, migrants from Afghanistan and Vietnamese labour migrants moving from Russia often choose Belarus for their route (Jaroszewicz and Kindler 2015).

Migrants of Belarusian citizenship, in contrast, mostly enter the EU in a legal fashion. Belarus is even the world leader in the per capita number of Schengen visas

[12] Irregular migration as a threat to European internal security has taken an important room in the European policy discourse on migration (e.g., Vollmer 2011). Before the first Eastern enlargement became reality in 2004, Lavenex (2001: 24) pointed out that the EU was "captured between realist fears and liberal values" and that "extension of asylum and immigration policies to the Central and Eastern European countries [...] is dominated by the imperative to secure the new border against unwanted immigration." The perception of threat coming from irregular migration resulted in the introduction of common legislation at the EU level. In the Treaty of Amsterdam (Article 1, clause 5), the EU called upon the maintaining itself as an "area of freedom, security and justice in which the free movement of persons is ensured in conjunction with appropriate measures with respect to external border controls, asylum, immigration and the prevention and combating of crime."

(Yeliseyeu 2015). Irregular migrants from Belarus are mainly labour migrants who are engaged in undeclared employment on tourist visa and often overstay the validity period of visa (Jaroszewicz and Kindler 2015). Although the numbers of irregular migrants from Belarus in the EU are difficult to estimate (Yeliseyeu 2015), they seem to be rather low. For example, in the period between 2009 and 2012 78 Belarusians were found to be employed in Poland without work permits (Jaroszewicz and Kindler 2015). At least until the recent decline of Russian economy, most Belarusians chose Russia as a destination country for labour migration due to the geographical proximity, absence of language barriers and higher wages (Yeliseyeu 2014).

As already documented above, the EU's relations with Belarus reflect the underlying tension between political conditionality with respect to fundamental rights and the perceived needs to cooperate on border management. Most surprisingly, the Council of the EU authorized the Commission to start talks on visa facilitation and readmission agreement with Belarus in February 2011, i.e., shortly after the brutal suppression of domestic protests (Council of the European Union 2011). As Delcour (2013) argues, the EU sought to fill the gap with the only Eastern partner without readmission agreement negotiations, even though this move contrasted poor state of diplomatic relations with Belarus. If such a readmission agreement could be concluded, the EU would be able to send back not only irregular migrants of Belarusian nationality, but migrants who transited through the territory of Belarus, too (e.g., Hernández i Sagrera and Korneev, 2012). This raises a normative problem of its own. In Belarus, irregular migrants are detained in poor conditions, while procedures of state bodies lack transparency and are often hidden from public (Viasna Human Rights Center 2014). Nevertheless, we need to investigate further, whether the ensuing conflicts or dilemmas between normative and security concerns cannot be mitigated. Evidently, the EU is ready to cooperate with Belarus despite existing problems in the human rights situation. Yet the bilateral cooperation could also positively contribute to the improvement of the migrant detention conditions in Belarus, in case the EU demands approximation to its own standards.

In the following part, we trace in more empirical detail how increased security cooperation with Belarus has been spelt out in practice and has led to an externalization of EU border control. At the same time, we also argue that this cooperation may be regarded as a relatively effective program for security sector reform, and not directly support the wider repressive tendencies of the Belarusian political-security apparatus. This corresponds to wider arguments that ENP programmes may not directly advance democratization, but may indirectly contribute to more accountable governance (e.g., Freyburg et al. 2009).

4 The EU-Belarus Border and Migration Management Cooperation

Cooperation in technical sectors and contacts among officials between Brussels and Minsk are more intense than among politicians. This two-track approach of the EU policy towards its neighbours, or the division between democracy promotion and functional cooperation are evident from the EU documents. As the EU acknowledges, "assistance in a sensitive area such as border management needs to be developed through a constant and often time-consuming dialogue with beneficiary governments" (European Commission 2013). A closer look at financial transfers that the EU has made available for capacity-building measures at its external borders shows, that the EU puts a major emphasis on questions of its internal security, allocating the majority of the EU funds to projects aimed to strengthen the capacities of the Belarusian border.

Increased cooperation between the EU and Belarus in border management issues already started well before as well as in anticipation of the 2004 Eastern enlargement, which would dramatically shift the EU's external borders. After the dissolution of the Soviet Union, only the Belarusian-Polish border was relatively well equipped (European Union External Action Service 2013). The borders with Baltic countries, Ukraine, and Russia were largely open or without technical installations for border security (European Union External Action Service 2013). In 1996 the first steps were taken to address this situation, when the EU (through Technical Assistance to the Commonwealth of Independent States—TACIS) allocated financial aid to Belarus for the reconstruction of three border crossing points with Latvia, Lithuania, and Poland (European Union External Action Service 2013). Many large-scale projects were carried out with the EU financial help, such as the demarcation of the Belarusian state border with Lithuania and Latvia. The project stretched over 10 years, and finished only in 2012.[13] Building on this investment, the EU has allocated more than 80 million Euros to borders assistance since 2001, with the Belarusian State Border Committee (SBC) and State Customs Committee (SCC) being the main beneficiaries. The majority of financial sources comes from the TACIS and since recently from the European Neighbourhood Policy Instrument (ENPI).

Specifically, from 1999 to 2014 the EU has implemented 26 border management projects in Belarus. A visible increase in the number of projects started in 2005, reflecting the changed situation after Eastern enlargement. The average duration of a project is about 24 months.[14] Border management projects are either nationally (bilateral EU-Belarus) or regionally (other EaP countries involved) implemented.

---

[13] Another major bilateral project is the enhancement of the carrying capacity of the Kozlovichi border crossing point at the Polish-Belarusian border, an important access for transportation of goods from the EU to post-Soviet countries.

[14] For more details see: European Union External Action Service. Europeaid Activities in Belarus. See "EU Activities in Belarus" http://eeas.europa.eu/delegations/belarus/documents/eu_activities_in_belarus.pdf (accessed on 12 January 2015).

Many projects are delegated to third organizations, which are permanently present on the ground, and have expertise in a particular area, whereas the EU is merely financing the project. In particular, border management projects are often carried out either by the Belarusian office of the International Organization for Migration (IOM) or Belarusian office of the United Nations Development Programme (UNDP Belarus). Delegating competences to such organizations helps to depoliticize cooperation and to benefit from long-term ties between the organization and beneficiaries. In case of the EU, Belarusian authorities might have mistrust due to problematic political relations with Brussels. When a project is carried out by an organization in which Belarus is a full member,[15] Belarusian stakeholders do not perceive a political context of cooperation (Interview with a local expert 2014).

At the same time, EU and Belarus also maintain a policy dialogue on customs, integrated border management and law enforcement, as well as combating illegal migration and smuggling (Bakowski 2012). Furthermore, a working arrangement between FRONTEX and the SBC has been signed (Frontex 2009). The document has a soft-law character and is not considered as an international treaty, only establishing a general framework for technical cooperation.[16] Yet Hernàndez i Sagrera (2014: 175) reports that “the Working Arrangement with the Belarusian Border Guard Service has, it seems, not materialized in any concrete measures”. This arguably reflects the point just made about the use of third organizations in the context of EU-Belarus border cooperation.

In terms of content, the majority of projects are intended to (i) finance the infrastructural capacities of the common border, such as administrative buildings, (ii) design border demarcations, (iii) construct border crossing points, (iv) provide equipment such as computers, inspection devices, and (v) provide training for border guards.[17] Overall, the EU widely finances projects aimed at preventing irregular migration and protection of migrants’ rights, as well as strengthening the Belarus-Ukraine border, which is poorly guarded and weakly equipped. A low level of border protection, difficult border terrain, and a part of the border situated in the zone contaminated after the Chernobyl disaster, create favorable conditions for smugglers and organized gangs. Besides that, the number of illegal border crossings at the Belarus-Ukraine border is the highest in the region, thus making the border one of the most problematic in the EU neighbourhood (European Commission 2013: 18).

According to the four-tier access control model presented in the Schengen Catalogue, effective border controls need to start prior the external EU border, namely in countries of origin and transit countries. In this regards, the SURCAP

[15] For example, Belarus is a full member of the IOM since 2005.

[16] Generally, the FRONTEX working arrangements do not legally bound the parties. They are flexible and adaptable to the interest of the signatories (e.g., Hernández i Sagrera 2014). For the debate on the working arrangements in general see, for example, Fink (2012).

[17] EU Activities in Belarus. http://eeas.europa.eu/delegations/belarus/documents/eu_activities_in_belarus.pdf (accessed on 12 January 2015).

(Strengthening Surveillance Capacities on the "Green" and "Blue" Border between the Republic of Belarus and Ukraine) project is worth having a closer look, as it aims to "help increase efficiency and effectiveness of the work of the Belarusian and Ukrainian border services in central and western areas of the countries' joint border" (European Commission 2013: 17). A closer investigation of a particular project allows observing the mechanisms and tools of EU's standards and norms promotion to Belarus. The SURCAP project contains two parts: (i) training, provision of expertise, study visits, exchange of expertise, and (ii) procurement of equipment (European Commission 2013: 20, 22). In the case of procurement of equipment and technical tools such as radars, boats, vehicles, we do not expect neither any direct promotion of values, nor direct support of the political regime of the country. What might be more important when speaking about norms promotion are the direct collaboration and exchange between European and Belarusian border guards. During the SURCAP project many training sessions for Belarusian and Ukrainian border guards were organized. Topics of the training sessions covered both technical aspects of border protection and issues of good governance and human rights, such as migration management, involvement of local population, and anti-corruption mechanisms (International Organization for Migration 2013). In the framework of the project, border guards from Belarus and Ukraine visited various EU countries to learn the local border management (International Organization for Migration 2013). Regional meetings periodically happened both in Ukraine and Belarus, involving police experts from the EU. The training sessions were focused on narrow technical issues, such as document security and identification of falsified documents (International Organization for Migration 2013), but attention was also devoted to raising anti-corruption awareness (International Centre for Migration Policy Development 2014). Besides purely technical training sessions, occasional anti-corruption training sessions for border management officials from Belarus have been organized in cooperation with FRONTEX.[18]

Whereas regime critics might be skeptical about any positive sides of such a cooperation, scholars suggest that cross-national activities, in particular trans-governmental networks, could have a socializing effect on state officials in non-democratic countries, and influence their attitudes towards democratic governance (e.g., Freyburg 2015; Korosteleva 2015). For example, Freyburg (2015) shows, on the basis of a survey of 150 Moroccan state officials, that those who participated in interpersonal and structural activities organized by established democracies, show a greater attitude towards democratic administrative governance than their colleagues who have not participated in such activities. Although functional cooperation is unlikely to generate a substantive change of the system in the host country and is not aimed to support democratization, it could prepare the bureaucratic basis and create necessary links for a future transition (e.g., Freyburg et al. 2009). Freyburg et al. (2009) argue that in the cases of Morocco, Moldova, and

[18] For more details, see the Eastern Partnership Visa Liberalisation Index. http://monitoring.visa-free-europe.eu/belarus (accessed on 11 January 2015).

Ukraine, the EU was capable to transfer democratic governance provisions even without an accession perspective.

For the purposes of this investigation, we could not systematically analyze the effect of socialization on the Belarusian state officials involved in the European projects. However, different interviewees in Belarus highlighted the socialization effects of working on European projects with European partners. Such a cooperation fosters contacts among both officials and citizens of the involved countries. As an example, the 2007 to 2013 Cross-Border Cooperation Program Latvia–Lithuania–Belarus includes not only projects aimed at strengthening the surveillance capacity of the border, but also numerous initiatives aimed to create and enhance people-to-people contacts in the border regions.[19] So one can regard the EU's external border as the "discriminatory division between peoples (in visa policy), but also as something to be overcome (through cross-border cooperation, for example)" (Grabbe 2000: 520).

A joint EU/UNDP project "Supporting the Republic of Belarus in Addressing Irregular Migration and Promoting Human Rights of Vulnerable Migrants" (AMBEL), is promising in this regard, since it explicitly aims to improve the human rights record in Belarus. In issues of irregular migration and respect of the migrants' rights, Belarus still faces significant challenges (Viasna Human Rights Center 2014). The project started in 2013 and runs for 3 years. Besides technical issues, such as modernizing the Smorgon Border Training Centre, the project aims to improve "the institutional and technical facilities of the Psychological Support Service of the SBC" and to introduce "the procedures to prevent and respond to issues of sexual and gender-based violence (SGBV) and trafficking in human beings (THB) among and towards migrants" (Anifer 2013). In the framework of the project, border guards could take an English course with a specialization in the field of combating human trafficking and illegal migration.[20] Additionally, 14 representatives of the border service of Belarus participated in a workshop on development of human resources and training strategies, as well as EU requirements on border personnel recruitment and training systems.[21]

Nevertheless, it is generally difficult to trace whether any European practices and norms have been adopted into the national legislation. For example, an Integrated Border Management (IBM) strategy has been drafted with the support of the EU funded initiative, and presented to the leadership of the SBC, but it is

[19] See, for example, the list of the projects: http://www.enpi-cbc.eu/go.php/eng/PROJECTS_BY_PRIORITY_AND_MEASURE/1059 (accessed on 28 December 2014).

[20] Within the Framework of the Joint Project "Ambel" Border Service Officers Have Successfully Completed a Foreign Language Course. State Border Committee of the Republic of Belarus. http://gpk.gov.by/news/gpk/17502/ (in Russian) (accessed on 23 May 2015).

[21] The workshop on development of human resources and training strategies and EU requirements/practice on border personnel recruitment and training systems will hold within the joint EU/UNDP Project AMBEL. http://un.by/en/undp/news/belarus/02–06–2014–n1.html (accessed on 23 May 2015).

unknown when the strategy will be adopted.[22] According to one interviewee, Belarusian authorities are eager to learn European practical solutions to existing problems. Yet those changes to border management practices and legislation that occur as a result are rather minor, focused on technical issues and remain within hierarchical bureaucratic departments. In project evaluation documents, the EU assesses implementation of most of its projects on the ground as satisfactory and highlights a "particular showed great commitment" of the SBC for the strict implementation of all contract stipulations (European Court of Auditors 2008: 31). Nevertheless, unsatisfactory implementation of some projects, with delays and reduced scope of works, is also highlighted (European Court of Auditors 2008: 31). A more critical review is provided by the European Court of Auditors (CoA) Special Report No. 9 of 2008 "The Effectiveness of EU Support in the Area of Freedom, Security and Justice for Belarus, Moldova and Ukraine," stating that "[T]he long term goal of a modern system of border management approximating European good practice is still some way off" (European Court of Auditors 2008: 31) .

Local experts are also skeptical about the proposed visa liberalization between the EU and Belarus. According to some interviewees, Belarusian authorities are currently not interested to go beyond the visa facilitation process, as visa liberalization would require major reforms. The opening of negotiations on the visa facilitation and readmission agreement in 2013 could also be tactically connected with the approaching presidential elections in 2015, rather than reflect a deeper willingness to reform. A successful ratification of the agreement before the elections might have been perceived as beneficial for the current elites and to increase popular support, since Belarus lagged behind all other EaP countries (Interview with a local expert 2014). According to the Belarusian Foreign Minister Makei, Belarus was ready to sign the agreement during the Riga Summit, but the EU found some "technical hitch", which postponed the finalization of negotiations (Korovenkova 2015).

In general, Belarus avoids making the bilateral sectoral cooperation known to the broader public (Interview with a local expert 2014). The visibility of the projects financed by the EU is at a low level. Newspapers and TV channels minimize positive depiction of the EU involvement, preferring to represent the EU as a rather "bad guy" sanctioning Belarus (Interview with a local expert 2014). Minsk also plays the border security card to get more financial aid from the EU, by threatening it with weakening border surveillance from the Belarusian side as a response to sanctions. As a result of a unilateral relaxing of border surveillance in March 2012, an increasing number of illegal border-crossing in Lithuania and Poland were registered. As Frontex reports, compared to 2011, detections increased by 52 % (Frontex 2013: 8).

[22] Annex 1 of the Commission Implementing Decision on ENPI East Regional Action Programme 2013 Part II. Action Fiche for Eastern Partnership Integrated Border Management Capacity Building Project): 20, 22.

5 Conclusion

Scholars increasingly point out a presumed conflict of goals in the European democracy promotion. The wish to be surrounded by democratic neighbours clashes with the reality, in which many of the EU neighbours are authoritarian regimes that are guarantors of stability—at least over short term. The contrast between EU soft security interests and the problematic human rights situation in the country, as well as the EU's existing sanctioning regime, have been criticised by scholars and journalists. They suspect that supplying and cooperating with Belarusian border security forces might strengthen the capacities of the regime to intimidate the opposition. Yet no in-depth study on the EU-Belarus border management cooperation has been carried out so far. We therefore traced the EU approach towards Belarus over the last 20 years and observed a rather coherent EU policy based on negative conditionality. Unlike Bosse (2012), we do not detect a major shift in EU policy towards Belarus. Border management cooperation with Belarus already started before the Eastern enlargement and gradually proceeded since then. Due to the geographical closeness of Belarus and practical difficulties to exclude fully the country from regional integration projects, some intensification of functional engagement was, in our view, unavoidable.

We could not establish a direct link between the functional cooperation in border and migration management and the strengthening of the authoritarian regime either. Whereas the EU has indeed spent considerable sums on projects to strengthen the EU-Belarus border (in which Belarusian state border authorities were aid recipients), no strong evidence points out an eventual misuse of the EU funds. On the contrary, according to the EaP Index, Belarus has the highest score for what concerns the management of the EU assistance on the ground.[23] Whereas 80 million Euros disbursed by the EU to the border management projects in more than 10 years in Belarus is a great amount of money, it is comparable to similar projects in other EaP countries. For example, the budget of the European Union Border Assistance Mission to Moldova and Ukraine (EUBAM) is 21 million Euros.[24] Technical cooperation on border security does not have to be considered an outright externalisation of the EU border management, as is typically argued by critical observers (Boswell 2003). Furthermore, the projects undertaken are largely accountable and are not only focused on the increase of security border technology. Although some bilateral projects deal with the questions of migrants' rights, the EU should devote more attention to the situation with migrants' detention in Belarus when signing the readmission and visa-facilitation agreements with Minsk.

Thus, the EU combines negative conditionality and pragmatic cooperation at the same time. Pursuing both goals in cooperation with third states is clearly not mutually exclusive. Whereas the political dialogue between the EU and Belarus

[23] Eastern Partnership Index. http://www.eap-index.eu/ (accessed on 20 August 2014).

[24] See the website of the EUBAM. http://www.eubam.org/en/about/overview (accessed on 12 January 2014).

has been reduced to a minimum, at least before the diplomatic initiatives surrounding the Ukrainian conflict, technical cooperation between Brussels and Minsk is notable, not least as there are no contractual relations between the EU and Belarus. The EU continues to follow a hard line in questions of democracy and human rights issues, while sectoral cooperation in less politicized areas might positively affect bilateral cooperation, leading to spill-overs in other policy areas. In countries where the EU leverage is insufficient to influence the cost-benefit calculations of the ruling elites, sectoral cooperation might be a promising, though a more time and investment consuming way to promote European values (e.g., Freyburg et al. 2009).

Yet this mixed conditionality principle is incomparable with accession conditionality, but follows a more practical, efficiency-based logic. The EU demands for the adoption and implementation of technical standards and practices, and provides funds for modernizing Belarusian border infrastructure. Belarus is, in turn, interested in foreign financial aid without any strings attached. Border and migration management issues are the areas in which both sides find a common language. Our analysis shows that wider governance improvements as a result of border management projects in Belarus are still far away. Belarus does not show any initiative to apply externally imposed deeper changes. Still, changes may be forthcoming and build on an improved administrative infrastructure, once the wider political context transforms. In particular, the changing situation in Ukraine might encourage Belarusian authorities to move closer to the European Union.

Acknowledgements We wish to thank for useful comments and suggestions Raphael Bossong, Rudy Colacicco, Martin Brusis, and participants at the 22nd Tagung Junger Osteuropa-Experten 2014 (Berlin), ECPR General Conference 2014 (Glasgow), and Workshop "The Shifting Borders of European Internal Security" (Frankfurt am Oder, Germany). Katsiaryna Yakouchyk wishes to thank the Bavarian Academic Center for Central, Eastern and Southeastern Europe (BAYHOST) for the mobility grant for a research stay in Belarus.

References

Anifer, A. (2013, December 12). *New joint EU/UNDP project officially launched in Smarhoń Border Training Center*. Accessed May 23, 2015, from http://www.by.undp.org/content/belarus/en/home/presscenter/pressreleases/2013/12/12/new-joint-eu-undp-project-officially-launched-in-smarho-border-training-center.html

Astapenia, R. (2013, November 29). *EaP summit in Vilnius: Week but positive signals on Belarus*. BelarusDigest. Accessed August 31, 2015, from http://belarusdigest.com/story/eap-summit-vilnius-weak-positive-signals-belarus-16298

Bakowski, B. (2012, June 21). Justice and home affairs and the EU's eastern partners. *Library Briefing*. Library of the European Parliament.

Börzel, T., & Lebanidze, B. (2015). *European Neighbourhood Policy at the crossroads. Evaluating the past to shape the future* (MAXCAP Working Paper 12).

Börzel, T., & van Hüllen, V. (2014). One voice, one message, but conflicting goals: Cohesiveness and consistency in the European Neighbourhood Policy. *Journal of European Public Policy, 21*, 1033–1049.

Bosse, G. (2009). Challenges for EU governance through Neighbourhood Policy and Eastern Partnership: The values/security nexus in EU–Belarus relations. *Contemporary Politics, 15*, 215–227.

Bosse, G. (2011). From 'Villains' to the new guardians of security in Europe? Paradigm shifts in EU Foreign Policy towards Libya and Belarus. *Perspectives on European Politics and Society, 12*, 440–461.

Bosse, G. (2012). A partnership with dictatorship: Explaining the paradigm shift in European Union Policy towards Belarus. *Journal of Common Market Studies, 50*, 367–384.

Boswell, C. (2003). The "external dimension" of EU immigration and asylum policy. *International Affairs, 79*, 619–638.

Council of the European Union. (2009, May 7). 8435/09 (Presse 78). Joint Declaration of the Prague Eastern Partnership Summit. Brussels, Prague. Accessed August 31, 2015.

Council of the European Union. (2011, January 31). *Council conclusions on Belarus.* 3065th Foreign Affairs Council meeting Brussels. Accessed 25 August, 2014.

Delcour, L. (2013). The EU: Shaping migration patterns in its neighbourhood and beyond? In D. Kochenov & F. Amtenbrink (Eds.), *European Union's shaping of the international legal order* (pp. 261–282). Cambridge: Cambridge University Press.

Del Sarto, R. A., & Schumacher, T. (2005). From EMP to ENP: What's at Stake with the European Neighbourhood Policy towards the Southern Mediterranean? *European Foreign Affairs Review, 10*, 17–38.

Dimitrova, A., & Pridham, G. (2004). International actors and democracy promotion in Central and Eastern Europe: The integration model and its limits. *Democratization, 11*, 91–112.

Dura, G. (2008). *The EU's limited response to Belarus' Pseudo "New Foreign Policy"* (Working Paper 151). Brussels: Centre for European Policy Studies.

European Commission. (2004, May 12). *Communication from the Commission.* European Neighbourhood Policy. Strategy Paper. Brussels. COM(2004) 373 final. Accessed September 8, 2015, from http://eur-lex.europa.eu/legal-content/EN/TXT/PDF/?uri=CELEX:52004DC0373&from=EN

European Commission. (2006). *European Neighbourhood and Partnership Instrument.* Belarus. Strategy Paper 2007–2013 and National Indicative Programme 2007–2011. Accessed September 8, 2015, from http://eeas.europa.eu/enp/pdf/pdf/country/enpi_csp_nip_belarus_en.pdf

European Commission. (2008, December 3). *Communication from the Commission to the European Parliament and the Council.* Eastern Partnership, Brussels. COM(2008) 823 final. Accessed August 31, 2015, from http://eur-lex.europa.eu/legal-content/EN/TXT/PDF/?uri=CELEX:52008DC0823&from=EN

European Commission. (2011). *A study on common border crossing points management between Schengen area and Russia/Belarus.* Accessed January 30, 2015, from http://www.ndptl.org/c/document_library/get_file?folderId=16355&name=DLFE-1603.pdf

European Commission. (2013). *Annex 1 of the Commission implementing decision on ENPI East Regional Action Programme 2013 Part II. Action Fiche for Eastern Partnership Integrated Border Management Capacity Building Project.*

European Council. (2003, December 12). *A Secure Europe in a Better World.* European Security Strategy, Brussels. Accessed June 2, 2015, from https://www.consilium.europa.eu/uedocs/cmsUpload/78367.pdf

European Council. (2010). *The Stockholm programme—An open and secure Europe serving and protecting citizens.* 2010/C 115/01. Accessed January 14, 2015, from http://eur-lex.europa.eu/LexUriServ/LexUriServ.douri=OJ:C:2010:115:0001:0038:en:PDF

European Court of Auditors. (2008). *The effectiveness of EU support in the area of freedom, security and justice for Belarus, Moldova and Ukraine* (Special Report No. 9). Accessed June 2, 2015, from http://www.eca.europa.eu/Lists/ECADocuments/SR08_09/SR08_09_EN.PDF

European Union External Action Service. (2013). EU-Belarus. Borders that Unite. *Eurobulletin*. Accessed August 20, 2014, from http://eeas.europa.eu/delegations/belarus/documents/press_corner/eurobulletin/the_eurobulletin_special_issue_december1_2013.pdf (in Russian).

Ferrero-Waldner, B. (2009, October 13). *Wider Europe—The last five years*. Speech at the American Chamber of Commerce's Plenary Meeting. Brussels. Accessed September 8, 2015, from http://europa.eu/rapid/press-release_SPEECH-09-467_en.htm?locale=en

Fink, M. (2012). Frontex working arrangements: Legitimacy and human rights concerns regarding 'technical relationships'. Mercourios. *Utrecht Journal of International and European Law, 28*, 20–35.

Freyburg, T. (2015). Transgovernmental networks as an apprenticeship in democracy? Socialization into democratic governance through cross-National activities. *International Studies Quarterly, 59*, 59–72.

Freyburg, T., Lavenex, S., Schimmelfennig, F., Skripka, T., & Wetzel, A. (2009). EU promotion of democratic governance in the neighbourhood. *Journal of European Public Policy, 16*, 916–934.

Frontex. (2009). *Working arrangement on the establishment of operational cooperation between the European Agency for the Management of Operational Cooperation at the External Borders of the Member States of the European Union (Frontex) and the State Border Committee of the Republic of Belarus*. Warsaw: Frontex.

Frontex. (2013). *Annual risk analysis 2014*. Warsaw: Frontex.

German Bundestag. (2014). *Answer of the Federal Government to the minor interpellation tabled by the members of the Bundestag Andrej Hunko, Wolfgang Gehrcke, Annette Groth, Inge Höger, Ulla Jelpke, Petra Pau, Kathrin Vogler, Halina Wawzyniak and the Left Party Parliamentary Group*. Bundestag Printed Paper 18–1196 of 11.04.2014.

Grabbe, H. (2000). The sharp edges of Europe: Extending Schengen eastwards. *International Affairs, 76*, 519–536.

Gubarevich, I. (2015, January 19). *Belarus-EU visa-free travel: An unrealistic prospect?* BelarusDigest. Accessed August 31, 2015, from http://belarusdigest.com/story/belarus-eu-visa-free-travel-unrealstic-prospect-21134

Hernández i Sagrera, R. (2014). Exporting EU integrated border management beyond EU borders: Modernization and institutional transformation in exchange for more mobility? *Cambridge Review of International Affairs, 27*, 167–183.

Hernández i Sagrera, R., & Korneev, O. (2012). *Bringing EU migration cooperation to the Eastern Neighbourhood: Convergence beyond the acquis communautaire?* (EUI Working Paper RSCAS 2012/22).

International Centre for Migration Policy Development. (2014, February 17). *EU-funded "SURCAP" project provides workshop on document security for border guards*. International Centre for Migration Policy Development. Accessed June 2, 2015, from http://www.icmpd.org/EU-funded-SURCAP-project-provides-workshop-on-document-security-for-border-guards.2530.0.html

International Organization for Migration. (2013). *"Strengthening surveillance capacity on the green and blue border between the Republic of Belarus and Ukraine" SURCAP*. Accessed May 10, 2015, from http://iom.by/data/uploads/2013/03/Newsletter-SURCAP.pdf

Interview with a local expert. (2014, May). Minsk.

Jaroszewicz, M., & Kindler, M. (2015). *Irregular migration from Ukraine and Belarus to the EU: A risk analysis study* (CMR Working Paper 80/138).

Jünemann, A. (2003). Security-Building in the Mediterranean after September 11. *Mediterranean Politics, 8*, 1–20.

Jünemann, A., & Knodt, M. (2008). EU external democracy promotion: Approaching governments and civil societies. In B. Kohler–Koch, D. De Bièvre, & W. Maloney (Eds.), *Opening EU-Governance to civil society: Gains and challenges* (pp. 259–293). Mannheim: CONNEX.

Kelley, J. (2006). New wine in old wineskins: Promoting political reforms through the New European Neighbourhood Policy. *Journal of Common Market Studies, 44*, 29–55.
Knodt, P., Kotzian, M., & Urdze, S. (2011). Instruments of the EU's external democracy promotion. *Journal of Common Market Studies, 49*, 995–1018.
Korosteleva, E. (2011). The Eastern Partnership Initiative: A new partnership for neighbours? *Journal of Communist Studies and Transition Politics, 27*, 1–21.
Korosteleva, E. (2015). The European Union and Belarus: Democracy promotion by technocratic means? Democratization (forthcoming) DOI: 10.1080/13510347.2015.1005009
Korovenkova, T. (2015, June 25). *Belarus and EU continue visa facilitation talks, Foreign Ministry Spokesman says*. Accessed August 31, 2015, from http://belapan.com/archive/2015/06/25/en_12180625H/
Kulakevich, T. (2015, July 31). *Belarus-EU thaw: Will it last this time?*. Accessed 6 September 6, 2015, from http://belarusdigest.com/story/belarus-eu-thaw-will-it-last-time-22930
Lavenex, S. (2001). Migration and the EU's New Eastern border: Between realism and liberalism. *Journal of European Public Policy, 8*, 24–42.
Lavenex, S., & Schimmelfennig, F. (2011). EU democracy promotion in the neighbourhood: From leverage to governance? *Democratization, 18*, 885–909.
Lavenex, S., & Wichmann, N. (2009). The external governance of EU internal security. *Journal of European Integration, 31*, 83–102.
Rettman, A. (2010, November 4). *Poland puts €3 billion price tag on democracy in Belarus*. EUobserver.com. Accessed March 6, 2014, from http://euobserver.com/foreign/31203
Rotman, D., & Veremeeva, N. (2011). Belarus in the context of the Neighbourhood Policy: Between the EU and Russia. *Journal of Communist Studies and Transition Politics, 27*, 73–98.
Schimmelfennig, F., & Scholtz, H. (2008). EU democracy promotion in the European Neighbourhood: Political conditionality, economic development and transnational exchange. *European Union Politics, 9*, 187–215.
Schlumberger, O. (2006). Dancing with Wolves: Dilemmas of democracy promotion in authoritarian contexts. In D. Jung (Ed.), *Democratization and development. New political strategies for the Middle East* (pp. 33–60). Basingstoke: Palgrave Macmillan.
Silitski, V. (2005). Preempting democracy: The case of Belarus. *Journal of Democracy, 16*, 83–97.
Viasna Human Rights Center. (2014, August 27). *"Analytical report: Aspects of migrants' detention in Belarus" Prepared by the local initiative-Campaign "No people are illegal" with the support of the Human Rights Center Viasna*. Accessed September 6, 2015, from http://spring96.org/files/misc/analytical-report-aspects-of-migrants-detention-in-belarus.pdf
Vollmer, B. (2011). Policy discourses on irregular migration in the EU—'Number games' and 'political games'. *European Journal of Migration and Law, 13*, 317–339.
Yakouchyk, K. (2015). The good, the bad, and the ambitious: Democracy and autocracy promoters competing in Belarus. *European Political Science Review* (forthcoming). doi:10.1017/S1755773914000459.
Yeliseyeu, A. (2013). EU visa facilitation: Consequences and prospects. *Belarusian Institute for Strategic Studies*, BB #16/2013EN.
Yeliseyeu, A. (2014). *Migration between the EU, V4 and Eastern Europe: The present situation and the possible future. The perspective of Belarus*. Warsaw: Center for Eastern Studies.
Yeliseyeu, A. (2015). Visa statistics 2014: More visas, less refusals. *Belarusian Institute for Strategic Studies*, BB #02/2015EN.

The Legal Reach of Police and Judicial Co-operation in Criminal Matters (PJCCM) Measures Across EU Borders: Extraterritoriality, Territorial Extension and the "Brussels Effect"

Maria O'Neill

1 Introduction

It has often been remarked that "internal security" increasingly requires measures that transcend political and legal boundaries. For instance, in the fast-moving areas of cyber-crime and complex financial crime, even the EU as a whole is too limited for establishing effective jurisdiction. However, despite some efforts to establish global conventions with regard to such security issues, one cannot anticipate an integrated body of international law that would be sufficiently precise and operational for guiding the actions of national criminal justice authorities. Against this background, it is necessary to examine alternative models and frameworks to understand the extension of jurisdiction across borders. This can be likened to the debate on the territoriality of legal systems in commercial law, which has been ongoing for some decades.

Of importance in linking these two areas of law is the fact that the EU remains primarily a project of market integration, where most central principles of the EU legal order stem from. More specifically, the Court of Justice of the European Union (CJEU), which became fully responsible for adjudicating on cross border law enforcement and security measures at the end of 2014, has a lengthy track record in handling a wide variety of commercial law cases. And unlike most national jurisdictions, where judges are either commercial or criminal lawyers, the CJEU will be staffed by exactly the same, predominantly commercial, judges when a security or justice case comes before it. As much of the following discussion is based on judge made law at the CJEU, the transfer of theories from the commercial to the criminal and law enforcement world within the EU therefore needs to be examined. In particular, this chapter focuses on the concepts of extra territoriality

M. O'Neill (✉)
University of Abertay Dundee, Bell Street, Dundee, Scotland DD1 1HG, UK
e-mail: m.oneill@abertay.ac.uk

R. Bossong, H. Carrapico (eds.), *EU Borders and Shifting Internal Security*,
DOI 10.1007/978-3-319-17560-7_8

and extra-territorial effect (Scott 2014: 123), and the Brussels effect (Bradford 2012).

These effects need to be placed in the context of the exportation of EU norms for what was formerly legally defined as Police and Judicial Cooperation in Criminal Matters (ex. PJCCM)—or used to be known as the "third pillar", post Amsterdam. As has been discussed in a growing literature from EU studies and political science, norm transfer in this area usually happens within the context of its bi-lateral treaty based agreements on the European Neighbourhood Policy (ENP) or the Euro-Mediterranean (Euro-Med) policy. Yet EU law jurisdiction has also been substantially extended by these treaty-based agreements with third countries, which deserves further attention from a legal perspective. Moreover, the classification of what is EU law is broadening, in order to include the CJEU definition of "unconditional and sufficiently precise"[1] provisions in treaties with third countries. Therefore, this chapter introduces a further type of legal analysis, which links extra-territorial effects with the internal evolution of the EU legal order and to ex. PJCCM measures. The proper functioning of a legal system is particularly important in the context of the ex. PJCCM measures, as they involve law enforcement activities, leading to arrest and detention, bringing with them not just due process issues, but also issues of human and fundamental rights.

In sum, this chapter will address extra-territoriality, territorial effect and the Brussels effect, examining their underlying concepts, and their relevance in the context of ex. PJCCM law that increasingly diffuses beyond EU borders. This complements the existing political science literature on EU external governance or the externalisation of internal security. Furthermore, the related impact of the external agreements of the EU on its internal legal framework will be examined. In this context, the South Eastern European Law Enforcement Centre[2] (SELEC) is covered as an illustrative case. Overall, the observed patterns of shifting legal boundaries on the basis of the three identified mechanisms, or the complex interaction effects between the EU legal order and its external relations, raises questions of legal accountability and sufficient precision.

2 The Debate on EU External Governance from a Multi-Disciplinary Perspective

The political science literature to grapple with external governance (Lavenex and Schimmelfennig 2009) partly overlaps with related legal debates, as exemplified in Lavenex's (2014) reliance on Scott (2014). The global effects that legal scholars associate with the EU economic regulation is also alluded to by Lavenex and

[1] Most recently Case C-135/10; *Società Consortile Fonografici (SCF)* v. *Marco Del Corso* [2012] ECR 0000, at paragraph 43 of the ruling.

[2] Its membership comprising Albania, Bosnia Herzegovina, Bulgaria, Croatia, Greece, Hungary, FYR Macedonia, Moldova, Montenegro, Romania, Serbia and Turkey. See http://www.selec.org/

Schimmelfennig (2009: 779), when they talk about the market being the "third basic mode of external governance" and indirect adaptation to EU rules. But whereas the political science and the external governance debate mainly focusing on the transferral of norms outwards from the EU, this contribution emphasises a distinct legal angle by tracing the extension of the EU's legal jurisdiction through its *internal* or dogmatic dynamics.

In particular, the political science literature has long recognised the efforts of the EU to export its policies, both globally and to specific third countries or groups of third countries. Yet Müller et al. (2015) pointed out that this policy export is "occurring less frequently than is commonly assumed", so that we need to be more precise about drivers and dynamics in different contexts. The EU has engaged in extra-territoriality and territorial extension in the ex. PJCCM policy areas, in contrast to the commercial world, not in order to project its own standards into the global arena or onto third countries, but in order to protect itself. Security and law enforcement threats are seen as coming from outside the EU, requiring engagement with, in particular, those countries that are its immediate neighbours. These neighbouring countries are typically members of either the European Neighbourhood Policy (ENP) or the Euro-Mediterranean Policy. These third countries are also typically seeking good relations with the EU and access to the EU markets for their goods and services (Lavenex 2014). Conversely, as the EU has developed novel ways of tackling cross border law enforcement for its own benefit, neighbouring countries are interested in learning from the EU in order to be able to assist in securing their own jurisdictions.[3]

Another important dynamic that emerges from a legal perspective is that the case law of the CJEU in commercial matters will inform that same court's rulings in ex. PJCCM matters now that the transition period foreseen by the Lisbon Treaty has expired (December, 2014)[4] and the EU is operating on the basis of a unitary legal framework. As stated by the United States (US) First Circuit Court of Appeals in the anti-trust case of *Nippon Paper*, "We live in an age of international commerce, where decisions reached in one corner of the world can reverberate around the globe in less time than it takes to tell the tale".[5] The same can be said for certain types of crime. How jurisdictions have reacted to the commercial challenge helps to establish how they will react to similar criminal and law enforcement challenges. It is in this context that the concepts of extraterritoriality, territorial effect and the Brussels effect—all currently being used in the context of transnational commercial law—become relevant to transnational justice and law enforcement, and go beyond, or take a different view on, political science assumptions about drivers of external governance.

---

[3] The SELEC, which is discussed in more detail further below, provides the most advanced example of this kind of ex. PJCCM norm transfer.

[4] Article 10.3 of Protocol no. 36 on Transitional Provisions attached to the TEU and TFEU.

[5] *U.S.* v. *Nippon Paper Industries Co., Ltd.* 109 F.3d 1, C.a.1 (Mass.), 1997, March 17, 1997, 403.

In particular, the internal development of the EU has led to greater coherence and leverage in the commercial world. Legal scholars have shed light on how the EU has been increasingly confident to influence other highly developed regulatory spaces. The intention of the EU is not to take over the global regulatory space, but with the EU's "primary objective" being "to create and guard the single market" an "ancillary effect" has been "establishing the EU as a global regulatory hegemon" (Bradford 2012: 42). In the commercial field, EU competition/anti-trust law is the most developed in cross border law enforcement, with some commentators calling on the need for "Washington to wake up to Europe's regulatory imperialism" (Wall Street Journal 2008).

In sum, we need to keep two issues or perspectives in mind, namely norm transfer from inside to outside the EU, which can be referred to as "state socialization" (O'Neill et al. 2004: 164), and the flexibility of boundaries of the EU's legal jurisdiction itself, which has attracted increasing attention from legal scholars. Scott points out that "the outer limits of the legitimate authority of a state has long been in doubt", with the term "interdependence" failing to "do justice to the vulnerability experienced by states to events that take place outside of their territory" (Scott 2014: 123). Against this background, the extra territoriality and extra-territorial effect of EU law, the bi-lateral agreements under the EU's European Neighbourhood Policy (ENP), Euro-Mediterranean (Euro-Med) policy, and the Brussels effect concept as developed by Bradford (2012), should together shed light on the impact which the exportation of EU ex. PJCCM norms are having on the shifting borders of European internal security.

3 Extra Territoriality and Territorial Extension

As stated by Scott, relying on Buxbaum, "notions of territoriality and extraterritoriality are legal constructs", requiring the reader to "look beneath the surface of labels and categories" recognising that "territorial connections are a matter of degree" (Scott 2014: 89). Extraterritoriality is a long established legal concept, which presumed that a particular national law applies outside its home jurisdiction. This legal concept is followed by territorial extension, i.e., the extension of a particular legal system outside the boundaries of that state in certain circumstances. These notions are more familiar and commented upon in the US legal system than with regard to the EU legal system. In particular, US courts have accepted the extraterritoriality of US law, using the so-called effects-based jurisdiction: if action outside the US is expected to have an effect within the US, then the US has the power to intervene. The establishment of the "effects" doctrine goes back to the International Court of Justice[6] ruling in *The SS Lotus (France* v. *Turkey)* in 1927,[7] which, while discussing the territorial limitations of criminal law, accepted that it

[6] http://www.icj-cij.org/homepage/

[7] The *SS Lotus (France* v. *Turkey)* (1927) PCIJ ser.A, 10.

was normal for jurisdiction to be established once the effect of a criminal action was felt within the jurisdiction, even if the criminal act had occurred elsewhere. This case involved the collision of two ships, a criminal act having occurred on a French ship, the effect of which was felt on the Turkish ship.

There is, however, a presumption that operates against extraterritoriality. The traditional notion of *comity* is the respect that senior judges have for senior judges of another jurisdiction, which have led to a number of constraints on the practice of legal extraterritoriality. Still, many non-US lawyers would argue that such informal professional constraints are not sufficiently tight (Griffin 1998). For example, conflicting rulings in the US case of *United States* v. *ICI Ltd.*[8] led the judge in the English case *British Nylon Spinners Ltd.* v. *ICI Ltd,*[9] to grant a decree of specific performance[10] blocking the US ruling, stating that the "US judge 'was applying an enactment of Congress, which has no application to the United Kingdom.'"[11] The UK legal system then had to pass the Protection of Trading Interest Act 1980, which is still in force, in order to prevent the encroachment of US law into UK law.

Traditionally the EU has maintained an "aversion to extraterritoriality" (Scott 2014: 95), and—similarly to the UK, has been less in favour of a territorial effects doctrine. In fact, there has been a lengthy tension in EU competition law between the "effects" and "implementation" doctrine. This is illustrated by the case on the "effect" of a non-EU merger, such as the *Gencor/Lonrho* merger,[12] which was implemented and approved between two South African companies in South Africa. The two companies had a substantial proportion of the relevant metals markets and their financial turnover with respect to the EU would regularly become subject to, and in breach of the then in force EU merger regulation. Despite the use of the "effect" test for merger cases, the "implementation" test is generally considered more acceptable for the EU territorial extension in commercial matters. The key EU competition case was *Woodpulp I*,[13] where none of the defendants were based in the then EC, but they were still subject to EC anti-cartel law as then were engaged in importing paper pulp into the then EC. The companies were held liable for activities which were directly connected to the importation into the EC, even for those US companies in the cartel, which engaged in activities which were permitted, but not required, under US law.

However, beyond commercial law as well as with regard to details of commercial practice problems remain. The CJEU has "not yet clarified what position it

[8] *United States of America* v. *Imperial Chemical Industries Ltd. and others, U.S. District Court for the Southern District of New York* [1952] Civil Action no. 24-13.

[9] *British Nylon Spinners Ltd.* v. *ICI Ltd* [1955] Ch 3.

[10] An order of specific performance is an order to do something, normally given in an emergency situation. It is based on the English law of Equity.

[11] Dankerwerts J., in *British Nylon Spinners Ltd.* v. *ICI Ltd.* [1955] Ch 37, 47.

[12] Judgment of the Court of First Instance of 25 March 1999 in Case T-102/96: *Gencor Ltd* v. *Commission of the European Communities*, OJ C 160, 05/06/1999, 18.

[13] Joined Cases 89/85, 104/85, 114/85, 117/85 and 125/85 to 129/85 *Ahlström Osakeyhtiö and Others* v *Commission* [1988] ECR 5193.

would take where there is no clear evidence of EU-based implementation [of an agreement], but merely evidence of (direct, substantial and foreseeable) EU-felt effects" (Scott 2014: 96). In contrast to the "most recent U.S. sanctions against Iran", the EU does not adopt "non-nationality based extraterritorial measures of its own" (ibid: 94), with its own sanctions being based on "national and legal persons who enjoy the nationality of an EU Member State" (ibid: 95). This can be likened to the notion of an implementation test, namely that there must be a physical connection with the jurisdiction, and not just an effect for the assuming extra-territorial jurisdiction. So following Scott, the "presence [of an individual] as opposed to conduct" (ibid: 92) is used to found a jurisdictional base within the EU, with the consequent "regulation of the foreign conduct of persons present in the EU" is implying "the exercise of territorial jurisdiction" (ibid: 91).

These debates over extra-territoriality and territorial extension are not to be confused with the exportation of norms, which the EU actively engages in. The EU's exportation of norms typically occurs in its bi-lateral treaty based agreements with individual third states. This bases the norm transfer within a legal framework, be it initially at the international law level. As pointed out by Flockhart (2006: 89), this normative process needs to be internalised within the state, which lawyers would understand as through being implemented into national laws, in order for the norms in question to be adopted into "daily practice at both the state and mass level" (ibid.). IR scholars also recognise the importance of law in the process of norm diffusion as "it is generally regarded as inappropriate to breach the law, and because breaches are sanctioned" (ibid.). While the EU strives to integrate certain core principles into its external agreements, such as equality between men and women and respect for human rights, the details or legal codification vary in the EU's relationships with one state to the next. This is clearly observable even when these relationships can be packaged into groups, such as the ENP agreements[14] or the more legally detailed Euro-Med agreements with Mediterranean neighbours.[15]

[14] Thirteen ENP agreements are currently fully active, including the new agreements that have been signed and adopted with Georgia and Moldova on the 27th June 2014 (final signed texts still to be made publically available). At the same meeting the political provisions of the Association Agreement (AA) with Ukraine was signed.

[15] Russia, not wanting to be the recipient of this exportation of EU norms, has (or at least had until the recent sanctions) a different and less detailed arrangement with the EU in the form of the so-called four common spaces. Two of these are of direct relevance to the subject matter of this contribution, the Common Space of Freedom Security and Justice (CSFSJ) and the Common Space of External Security (CSES).

4 Contractual Extension of EU Law and Complex Dynamics in the Neighbourhood

Yet precisely for this reasons, various legal agreements are a good example of how the EU contractually exports its norms in ex. PJCCM matters. A comprehensive analysis is provided in Balzacq (2009), where a number of the contributors highlighted the express self-protection intention of the EU in developing its external relations with different neighbours. Similar security provisions were also included in the most recent Association Agreements with Georgia, Moldova and the Ukraine,[16] referring to human trafficking,[17] anti-money laundering and terrorism financing,[18] co-operating in the fight against drug trafficking,[19] more general provisions on the fight against crime and corruption,[20] and cooperation in the fight against terrorism,[21] to include (unspecified) co-operation with Europol[22] and Eurojust.[23]

The EU Ukraine ENP is currently the most sensitive and security related ENP agreement. The most immediately relevant security issues of this agreement would relate to the EU's Common Foreign and Security Policy, [24] rather than ex. PJCCM provisions.[25] Yet it should also be noted that despite serious set-backs before the signing of the recent EU Ukraine Accession Agreement, ex. PJCCM issues appear to have been addressed to the EU's satisfaction (European Commission 2014). This may be seen as further evidence of the importance of these security norms with regard to the EU's general influence over its neighbourhood. At the same time, the effective exportation of EU norms could not be claimed on the basis just of the signature of the Association Agreements, with Stone talking about "different 'orders'" of learning ranging from "shallow, tactical or instrumental learning as

[16] Association Agreement between the European Union and its Member States, of the one part, and Ukraine, of the other part, OJ L 161/3, Association Agreement between the European Union and the European Atomic Energy Community and their Member States, of the one part, and Georgia, of the other part, OJ L 261/4, and Association Agreement between the European Union and the European Atomic Energy Community and their Member States, of the one part, and the Republic of Moldova, of the other part, OJ L 260/4.

[17] Articles 61.1 and 16.2.b, Ukrainian AA, Article 16.1 Moldova AA, Article 15.2.d Georgia AA.

[18] Article 20 Ukrainian AA, Article 18 Moldova AA, Article 19 Georgia AA.

[19] Article 21 Ukrainian AA, Article 17 Moldova AA, Article 18 Georgia AA.

[20] Article 22 Ukrainian AA, Article 16.1.e Moldova AA, Article 20 Georgia AA.

[21] Article 23 Ukrainian AA, Article 19 Moldova AA, Article 20 Georgia AA.

[22] Article 22.3 Ukrainian AA, Article 16.2 Moldova AA, Article 17.2 Georgia AA.

[23] Article 20.2 Moldova AA, Article 24.3 Ukrainian AA, Article 21.2 Georgia AA.

[24] Title II Political Dialogue and Reform, Political Association, Cooperation and convergence in the field of Foreign and Security Policy of the draft EU-Ukraine Association Agreement.

[25] A question might arise as to what type of terrorism is covered in Article 23 of the agreement, whether this would be a CFSP approach to terrorism, thereby bringing in the current military issues in Eastern Ukraine, or whether the anticipated engagement is more ex. PJCCM style terrorism, and therefore of only relevance to law enforcement in the more peaceful areas of the country.

opposed to deeper social or policy learning" (Stone 2004: 549). A poor transfer of norms could result in just the "transfer of policy knowledge but not a transfer of policy practice" (ibid.). Writing before the recent major political shifts, Dragneva and Wolczuk (2012) point to the "problem of insufficient adaptation to local conditions and the appreciation of the differences in, or indeed the lack of, demand for law" (ibid: 221) in Ukraine. With this critique, they not only target the heritage of a post-Soviet state but also "vested interests which were successful in capturing the state" in earlier EU attempts to influence change within the Ukrainian legal system.[26] In short, there are numerous reasons to deepen critical political analyses of the EU's actual impact and approach to its neighbourhood.

Yet of primary interest to this chapter is the legal nature of the EU's relationships, with the then ECJ in the *Demireil* case[27] stating that ENP agreements create "special, privileged links with a non-member country which must, at least to a certain extent, take part in the Community system."[28] This clearly extends the legal borders of the EU beyond what was originally envisaged. This reference to taking part in the Community system implies that the third country is not just contracting on the basis of the provisions within the treaty, but also the EU *acquis* which goes with those provisions, within which those provisions are embedded within EU law. This represents a significant level of territorial extension, all be it contractually based, of EU law. In addition, the then ECJ has regularly found[29] that the EU's external association agreements have internal direct effect (Hillion 2008: 332), thereby changing the internal law of the EU itself. While predominantly commercially based, both the ENP and Euro-Med agreements have a direct connection with ex. PJCCM law. A number of the Euro-Med partnership agreements make express references, at the political level, to the development of cross-border law enforcement provisions, as in the case of Morocco[30] and Algeria,[31] with regard to drug-trafficking and manufacture, or the lengthy references by Egypt[32] to many

[26] At the EU level such an exportation of norms under the association agreements would require also, in the case of Ukraine, Moldova and Georgia, the still to be drafted supporting action plans, and their implementation, which would be reviewed, and reported on by the EU on a regular basis. It would be anticipated that there would be further deepening of the relationship with all three countries, as there has been under older AA's with other third countries, including the exportation of further EU ex. PJCCM norms.

[27] Case 12/86 *Meryem Demirel* v *Stad Schwäbisch Cymünd* [1987] ECR 3719.

[28] Ibid. para 9 of the ruling.

[29] Case 192/89 *Sevince* [1990] ECR 3461, Case C-63/99 *Gloszckuk* [2001] ECR I-6369, Case C171/01 *Wählergrupe Gemeinsam* [2003] ECR I-4301 and Case C-265/03 *Simunteknov* [2005] ECR I-2579.

[30] Mid-Term Review of the country Strategy Paper Morocco 2007–2013 and National Indicative Program 2011–2013, 2.2 Changes in Horizontal External EU Policies or unforeseen events, 5, paragraph 6.

[31] Instrument Européen de voisinage et de partenariat Algerie Programme Indicatif National 2011–2013, 2 Changements dans les politiques externs horizontals de l'UE, 4, sixth paragraph.

[32] EU/Egypt Action Plan, 2 Actions, 2.4 Migration, social integration, justice and security, (b) Law enforcement cooperation, 28.

of the crimes of interest to the EU's own law enforcement legal framework. The technical and practitioner work in filling in the detail of how these relationships are to develop is ongoing through, for example Euro-Med Police III[33] and Euro-Med Justice III[34] programmes.[35]

Thus, EU law jurisdiction has clearly been extended by these treaty-based agreements with third countries. While the EU is engaged in the express exportation of norms, as discussed above, it is also broadening the classification of what is EU law, to include the CJEU definition of "unconditional and sufficiently precise"[36] provisions in treaties with third countries. The *Pokrzeptowicz-Meyer* case[37] held that the then Europe Agreement between the EU and pre-accession Poland could be directly applicable within EU law,[38] regardless of the fact that there was "an imbalance in the obligations assumed by the Community".[39] While the Europe Agreement was a pre-accession agreement, there is nothing to distinguish it from the ENP and Euro-Med agreements with regard to the direct applicability of their legal provisions within EU law. This analysis was confirmed in *Simutenkov*,[40] which dealt with the direct effect within EU law of the provisions of the EU-Russia agreement, in the context of labour law, with the Advocate General also discussing the impact of the EU cooperation agreements with Algeria and Morocco.

In *Air Transport Association of America*,[41] the CJEU was clear that the EU was "free to agree [with third states] what effect the provisions of the agreement are to have in the internal legal order of the contracting parties."[42] In the absence of such

[33] http://www.euromed-police3.eu/

[34] http://www.euromed-justice.eu/

[35] Separate from all these relationships on internal security and the ENP, the EU is also a significant contributor to Security Sector Reform (SSR) programmes, under its CFSP justice and security programme to a much wider range of countries. While the SSR programmes are beyond the scope of this paper, this is another way in which the EU, and its individual member states, engage in the exportation of norms in the area of policing, justice, and also the CFSP related military reform. EU member states are also active contributors to the Organisation for Security and Cooperation in Europe (OSCE) which also runs police and justice reform programmes, in addition to specific programmes focused on particular security threats, such as terrorism and human trafficking. However the export of EU norms, through either the EU's own SSR activities, or indirectly through the OSCE, is likely to have a different type of impact than those under the ENP or Euro-Med agreements.

[36] Most recently Case C-135/10; *Società Consortile Fonografici (SCF)*, above.

[37] Case C-162/00; *Land Nordrhein-Westfalen* v. *Beata Pokrzeptowicz-Meyer*, [2002] ECR, I-01049.

[38] As paragraph 19 of the judgment of the court. *Beata Pokrzeptowicz-Meyer.*

[39] Paragraph 27 of the ruling *Beata Pokrzeptowicz-Meyer.*

[40] Case C-265/03; *Igor Simuntenkov* v. *Ministerio de Educación y Cultura and Real Federación Española de Fútbol*, ECR 2005, I-02579.

[41] C-366/10; *Air Transport Association of America and Others* v. *Secretary of State for Energy and Climate Change*, [2011] ECR, 0000.

[42] Ibid. para 49.

agreement, however, the legal effect of the agreements was "to be decided by the courts having jurisdiction in the matter, and in particular by the Court of Justice."[43] Here the CJEU is anticipating that the EU agreements would have a direct legal impact, and not just a political impact, within third states, should the courts of that country so decide. It is difficult however, to say with any level of clarity just what that impact of EU law is in third states independent of an examination of the law of that third state, and its reactions to the consequent importation of EU law. However the boundary line of EU law itself has clearly shifted, with international agreements being binding on the EU, and its institutions, and "they prevail over acts of the European Union,"[44] in line with Article 216(2) TFEU. Neither *Pokrzeptowicz-Meyer* nor *Simutenkov* had a direct impact on either the pre-accession Polish jurisdiction or on the Russian jurisdiction. They did however have considerable and ongoing effect within the EU legal jurisdiction. The logic underpinning these cases is likely to continue to have reverberations in the context of ENP and Euro-Med justice and law enforcement measures, once an EU jurisdictional connection can be established, using either residence, domicile, or establishment within the territory of the EU, of a natural or legal person.

Consequences of this shifting of the EU legal system will also be felt in the application of legal accountability, given that the CJEU has long been understood to have its own "*certaine idée de l'Europe*" (Rasmussen 1988: 32). The CJEU's monitoring (Bovens 2010: 55) of EU agencies and institutions, whether this reviewing is viewed through an intergovernmental, supranational or regulatory perspective (Bovens et al. 2010: 180), will be affected by this dynamic. Already now, accountability forums such as the CJEU are "actively and in fact proactively… expanding their monitoring roles" (Busuoic 2010: 114). A legal person likely to be affected by this dynamic is Europol. If Europol is acting on the basis of EU legal or policy provisions when conducting transnational law enforcement, then "the foreign conduct of [one of the EU's] own nationals" (Scott 2014: 94) under the provisions of a legally binding external agreement with non-EU countries would in turn also directly impact EU internal law and become subject to review. Europol itself already has a number of operational agreements with third counties.[45] In addition, Europol will increasingly be mandated to cooperate with third countries with which the EU has detailed bi-lateral or multi-lateral arrangements, such as under the Euro-Med and the ENP. This development is anticipated as agreements with the relevant neighbouring third countries move from the current police and justice internal reform programmes to transnational operational programmes.

---

[43] Ibid.

[44] Ibid. para 50.

[45] Albania, Australia, Canada, Columbia, FYR Macedonia, Iceland, Norway, Switzerland, Liechtenstein, Monaco and the USA. Further so-called strategic agreements are made with partners that are not yet at the stage of direct operational cooperation (currently Bosnia Herzegovina, Moldova, Russian Federation, Turkey, Serbia, Montenegro and Ukraine), but may progress to this stage.

The South Eastern European Law Enforcement Centre (SELEC) exemplifies this possible trend. SELEC shares four member countries with the EU, and was originally set up with external support from both the EU and the US-FBI.[46] It is a very clear example of norm export by the EU in the context of cross border law enforcement. Formerly known as SECI, SELEC is comprised of either EU member states or EU candidate or pre-candidate countries for EU membership, with Moldova being the SELEC member with the least developed relationship with the EU. Cross-border law enforcement had begun to change in this region with the signing of the South-Eastern Europe Police Cooperation Convention in 2006. SELEC has been working on developing "strategic analysis, concerning the regional situation", with support, *inter alia*, from Europol and Interpol. Bilateral intelligence exchange agreements have been signed, and "intelligence exchange" and "international police operations through the SECI Centre, mirror investigations and study visits" have already been undertaken (Council of the European Union 2011). In addition, work has developed to such an extent in the context of South-Eastern Europe that a project has been initiated to introduce "the requirements for establishing Joint Investigation Teams (JIT) to fight trafficking in human beings" in the region (ibid: 25), JITs being one of the main cross border operational tools in use within the EU. The Council of Europe has also been providing assistance to SELEC, for "the development of codes of ethics for the police and for prosecutors" (European Commission 2010: 7). Further potential for EU norm transfer has been signalled with the Secretariat of SELEC visiting the EU's police college, CEPOL on the 23rd January 2012, with a view to accessing and developing police training programmes.[47] Also worth noting is that SELEC, like the Europol/Eurojust relationship, is supported by the Southeast European Prosecutors Advisory Group (SEEPAG). The extent of norm transfer from the EU (and its four shared member states) and US, to SELEC and SEEPAG would merit further study.

5 Shifting Boundaries of EU Law Beyond Contractual Obligations

While the contractual exportation of norms through ENP and Euro-Med agreements, discussed above, can be classified as EU treaty based contractual territorial extension, there is a further element of territorial extension of EU law, which falls outside such contractual arrangements with third countries. Scott points out that while the EU, more broadly, frequently bases its jurisdiction on residence, domicile or establishment within the territory of the EU, thereby providing a "relevant territorial connection" (Scott 2014: 98), it also often establishes jurisdiction over "the foreign conduct of its own nationals" (ibid: 94). This approach can be

[46] For a further analysis of the role of the SELEC centre in the context of trafficking in human beings see O'Neill (2013).

[47] http://www.cepol.europa.eu, accessed 26th January 2012, Ref: 05/2012/CEPOL.

seen in the drafting of the ex. PJCCM framework decisions and recent directives, such as the Framework Decision on drug trafficking,[48] Article 8 of which requires the founding of jurisdiction on the basis of the offence being "committed in whole or in part" within the particular EU member state, or "the offender is one if its nationals," or "the offence is committed for the benefit of a legal person established in the territory of that Member State". This is a much broader founding of jurisdiction than would have been traditional under most national criminal law.

Similarly, the more recent post Lisbon directive on human trafficking[49] bases its jurisdiction in Article 10.1 on the offence being "committed in whole or part" within an EU member state, *or* that the offender is one of the nationals of an EU member state. The option for extraterritorial reach is anticipated, but not required by the directive. Article 10.2 states that a member state is to establish jurisdiction over "offences... committed outside its territory" where, *inter alia*, "the offence is committed against one of its nationals or a person who is an habitual resident in its territory", *or* the "offence is committed for the benefit of a legal person established in its territory", *or* "the offender is an habitual resident in its territory". Under this "non-contractual" extra-territorial reach EU criminal law provisions are not therefore confined to within the EU, but extend, in principle, to criminal offences defined by EU law, but committed outside the EU.

How the provisions of either the framework decision or directive is to be implemented in practice with this extended extra-EU territorial reach has yet to be established. These issues will arise repeatedly in the future, particularly in the context of the very fast moving crimes of cyber-crimes and financial crimes. Issues such as the establishment of jurisdiction in order to investigate and prosecute are important here, and can be highly problematic. The speed at which these issues can be resolved will also be important, particularly when considering the speed at which a cyber-crime or complex financial crime can move from one legal jurisdiction to the next, facilitated by internet service providers[50] or multi-national banks.

---

[48] Council Framework Decision 2004/757/JHA of 25 October 2004 laying down minimum provisions on the constituent elements of criminal acts and penalties in the field of illicit drug trafficking, OJ L 335, 11/11/2004, 8.

[49] Directive 2011/36/EU of the European Parliament and of the Council of 5 April 2011 on preventing and combating trafficking in human beings and protecting its victims, and replacing Council Framework Decision 2002/629/JHA, OJ L 101, 15/04/2011, 1.

[50] The ex. PJCCM law still has to clarify the duties and obligations of internet service providers. EU commercial law is still evolving in this area, particularly in the context of intellectual property protection. At the fundamental rights level Article 11 of the EUCFR protects the right of freedom of expression and information, which needs to be balanced with the Article 6 right to liberty and security, with any limitation of rights needing to meet the being "provided for by law" test in Article 52.1. Case C-70/10 *Scarlet Extended* [2011] ECR I-11959, threw up a number of specific legal and technical obstacles to internet service providers operating filtering systems, to include data protection issues. However the later C-314/12 UPC *Telekabel Wien* case held that those restrictions did "not preclude a court injunction prohibiting an internet service provider from allowing its customers access to a website". It is likely that EU criminal law will develop in a similar way, with a failure to follow a court order (assuming that court order is valid in a

Non-contractual territorial extension also needs to be examined beyond such express references in new or revised EU legal provisions for criminal offences. This relates to the contrast between effects-based and implementation-based tests for the assumption of extra-territorial jurisdiction discussed earlier. A possible example of this would be a cyber-attack from the US territory into China, the effects of which are felt in the EU. The analogy needs to be reflected upon in the context of EU ex. PJCCM law. As the EU and its member states attempt to grapple with serious transnational crimes, such as cybercrime and complex financial crime, the use of either the effects or implementation doctrine for founding extra treaty based jurisdiction to proceed after criminals, might prove fruitful. In addition, those who "aid and abet" a crime might be more easily targeted from inside the EU legal jurisdiction, such as multi-national financial service providers, or for anticipated crimes, internet service providers, particularly if the suspect of the main criminal offence is based in a legally difficult to get to jurisdiction, such as Syria or Libya. For example, and recognising that cyber security is not the same as cybercrime, Directive 2013/40/EU on attacks against information systems[51] speaks of establishing jurisdiction. It provides, in addition to the usual tests, that an offence is committed when the offender is "physically present on its territory, whether or not the offence is against an information system on its territory,"[52] with the extended jurisdictional requirements being that if the offence is "against an information system" based in the territory of and EU member state, "whether or not the offender commits the offence when physically present on its territory."[53]

Similar issues on the enforceability of EU laws have also arisen in EU Competition law, leading to "positive comity" agreements with jurisdictions such as the US.[54] "Positive comity" is a more advanced form of comity mentioned earlier, namely the mutual respect that senior judges in one jurisdiction have for senior judges in another jurisdiction, in the absence of any formal treaty agreement. Positive comity, in contrast, is based on either a bi-lateral or multi-lateral treaty in a subject area where both jurisdictions are aiming at the same objectives, to date normally in anti-trust/competition law. In this context, the US stated that "when possible, the decisions of foreign tribunals should be given effect in domestic

transnational setting, an issue likely to be addressed either by EU law or by an international treaty, depending on the location(s) for judicial proceedings of the internet service provider) to limit such access likely to give rise to criminal liability.

[51] Directive 2013/40/EU of the European Parliament and of the Council of 12 August 2013 on attacks against information systems and replacing Council Framework Decision 2005/222/JHA, OJ L 218/8.

[52] Article 12.2(a) of Directive 2013/40/EU.

[53] Article 12.2(b) of Directive 2013/40/EU.

[54] Includes the EU-USA Positive Comity Agreement 1998, 98/386 (1998) OJ L 173/28, the Competition Laws Cooperation Agreement 1999 (EC/ECSC/Canada) 1999/445 (1999) OJ L 175, and the Decision Concluding the Agreement between the European Community and Japan Concerning co-operation on anti-competitive activities 2003/520 (2003) OJ L183.

courts, since recognition fosters international cooperation and encourages reciprocity, thereby promoting predictability and stability."[55]

As such, positive comity can also be labelled as agreements for mutual legal assistance (MLA), which has already found a first prominent application in ex. PJCCM law in the case of the 2003 EU-US agreement (Council Decision 2003). It is reasonably foreseeable that both the EU and the US, would be interested in deepening this arrangements and in proceeding against, for example, cyber-crime and complex financial crime, assuming that the crimes and evidence gathering mechanisms can be defined to meet the requirements of both jurisdictions (and for the EU, its member states). Issues such as accountability and legal certainty would be addressed by the need for these positive comity agreements to be treaty based, those treaties being negotiated, approved and activated in accordance with the usual legislative frameworks of the relevant parties. Thus, the well-developed area of extra-EU competition law enforcement may provide parallels for the further development of extra-ex. PJCCM enforcement.

6 The "Brussels Effect"

The third method for analysing the shifting borders of EU law, introduced by Bradford, is the "Brussels effect" (Bradford 2012). Political scientists have acknowledged that the indirect adaptation to EU rules is the "third basic mode of external governance" (Lavenex and Schimmelfennig 2009: 779). In the commercial field while the EU is regulating for its own internal market, "multinational corporations often have an incentive to standardize their production globally and adhere to a single rule. This converts the EU rule into a global rule" what Bradford has referred to as "de facto Brussels Effect" (Bradford 2012: 6). Equally, given the need by global commercial business to adjust to the "EU's strict standards", they then "have the incentive to lobby their domestic governments to adopt these same standards in an effort to level the playing field against their domestic, non-export-oriented competitors" what Bradford has classified as "de jure Brussels Effect" (Bradford 2012: 6). While it would be possible for any of the dominant commercial countries to set the highest standards, in practice this is very often the EU. The Brussels effect relies on neither cooperation nor coercion (ibid: 9). When the EU imposes its standards "equally on domestic and foreign players" (ibid: 36) within its own market or jurisdiction, the foreign companies need to decide whether to produce products or services following a number of different regulatory standards, or to the highest set of standards.

While the Brussels effect does have considerable traction in commercial law, it has to date had less traction in ex. PJCCM matters. Cross-border crime and its ancillary law enforcement and justice mechanisms cannot develop organically, as in the case of decentralised market dynamics, but need to be expressly provided for

[55] *Lake Airways* v. *Sabena, Belgian World Airlines* 731.F.2D 909 (1984), 932.

in treaty provisions. However, as already alluded to above, commercial/private actors, such as internet service providers and multinational financial service providers are increasingly involved in cross-border law enforcement and related EU internal security policies (Bossong 2016: 2). Their involvement needs to be understood in the context of commercial operators greater sensitivity to competing regulatory provisions, and their need to minimise costs when operating in a for profit basis.

Currently, the most prominent example of the "Brussels effect" in the context of EU internal security is that of data and data protection. This is a major issue in the EU-US legal, and practice relationship, given that the concept of data protection, as understood in the EU, is alien to the US legal system. This is evidenced by the lengthy PNR saga, and a variety of other issues, such as, at the EU member state level, the activities of the US National Security Agency and the UK's GCHQ use of the PRISM surveillance programme. As Bradford has pointed out "internet companies find it difficult to create different programmes for different markets" and therefore apply the "strictest international standards across the board" (Bradford 2012: 25). She cites both Google and General Motors amending their global privacy policies to the EU standards (ibid: 6). How far the Brussels effect will extend into ex. PJCCM matters will depend on two factors, the extent to which there is a privatisation of security and the "privatisation of the police",[56] and whether the EU's standards are higher or lower than other commercially large regulatory players in this area, for example, the US.

7 Conclusion

Political scientists have debated the EU's external governance for years. In contrast, this chapter has taken a legal approach and developed the concepts of extra-territoriality, territorial effect and the more recent Brussels effect. This legal perspective adds more nuance, since "territorial connections are a matter of degree" (Scott 2014: 89). While political scientists concerns with the EU's active exportation of norms typically occurs in bi-lateral treaty based agreements with third states, a legal analysis base leads to different and complementary insights. In addition to treaty contract extension of territoriality, non-contractual territorial extension is also examined in the context of the "effects" and "implementation" doctrine. The Brussels effect approach in law is more closely connected to the indirect adaptation to EU rules, acknowledged by the political scientists, Lavenex and Schimmelfennig (2009: 779) as being the "third basic mode of external governance."

In practice, these three effects are not clearly delineated, with shades of grey between the different classifications and in particular legal circumstances. With much of the dynamic analysed here being the result of the EU's own legal framework and the role of the CJEU, issues of not only accountability, but also of

[56] See for example, in the context of money-laundering, Egan (2010).

legal certainty and liability arise. This is especially pressing in the area of ex. PJCCM provisions, which involve the arrest, detention, and possible imprisonment of individuals, together with their due process, human and fundamental rights.

In conclusion, the borders of European internal security shift not just in a geographic context. Not only do countries enter (and in the case of the UK may possibly leave) the EU internal security space, but physical borders are also often not where they are expected to be found. As examined by this chapter, the EU legal system itself is partly responsible for some of these shifts, so that it is not possible to draw a thick black line between where EU law stops and starts. One is confronted with eddies and whirlpools around EU based natural or legal persons acting criminally abroad, or the effects or implementation of foreign behaviour of foreign nationals within the EU. This adds to the web of formal external treaty based agreements, which increasingly include detailed and operational ex. PJCCM provisions, as evidenced by the SELEC centre activities discussed above. Finally, new trends with regard to the involvement of private commercial actors in internal security, especially in the cyber and financial business, give rise to a very complex picture from a legal perspective. More academic attention needs to be focused on all these areas. To tackle the resulting complexity and constantly shifting borders, one could build on the three underlying principles discussed in the chapter, namely that of treaty contract extension, non-contractual territorial extension and the Brussels effect, with a view to making these phenomena more predictable and accountable.

References

Association Agreement (AA) between the European Union and its Member States, of the one part, and Ukraine, of the other part. *OJ L, 161/3*.

Balzacq, T. (2009). *The external dimension of EU justice and home affairs governance, neighbours, security*. Basingstoke: Palgrave Macmillan.

Bossong, R. (2016). Critical infrastructure and critical information infrastructure protection—The new frontier of EU internal security? In M. O'Neill & K. Swinton (Eds.), *Challenges and critiques of the EU internal security strategy: Rights, power and security* (forthcoming)

Bovens, M. (2010). Studying the real world of EU accountability: Framework and design. In M. Bovens, D. Curtin, & P. t'Hart (Eds.), *The real world of EU accountability* (pp. 31–62). Oxford: Oxford University Press.

Bovens, M., Curtin, D., & t'Hart, P. (2010). The real world of EU accountability: Comparisons and conclusions. In M. Bovens, D. Curtin, & P. t'Hart (Eds.), *The real world of EU accountability* (pp. 174–197). Oxford: Oxford University Press.

Bradford, A. (2012). The Brussels effect. *Northwestern University Law Review, 107*(1), 1–68.

British Nylon Spinners Ltd. v. *ICI Ltd* [1955] Ch 3.

Busuoic, M. (2010). European agencies: Pockets of accountability. In M. Bovens, D. Curtin, & P. t'Hart (Eds.), *The real world of EU accountability* (pp. 87–116). Oxford: Oxford University Press.

C-366/10; *Air Transport Association of America and Others* v *Secretary of State for Energy and Climate Change*, [ECR] 2011, 00000.

Case 12/86 *Meryem Demirel* v *Stadt Schwäbisch Cymünd* [1987] ECR 3719.

Case 192/89 *Sevince* [1990] ECR 3461.

Case C-135/10; *Società Consortile Fonografici (SCF)* v *Marco Del Corso* ECR 2012 00000.

Case C-162/00; *Land Nordrhein-Westfalen* v *Beata Pokrzeptowicz-Meyer*, ECR 2002, I-01049.

Case C-171/01 *Wählergrupe Gemeinsam* [2003] ECR I-4301.
Case C-265/03; *Igor Simutenkov* v *Ministerio de Educación y Cultura and Real Federación Española de Fútbol*, ECR 2005, I-02579.
Case C-314/12 *UPC Telekabel Wien GmbH* v *Constantin Film Verleih GmbH*, [2014] ECR page 0000.
Case C-63/99 *Gloszckuk* [2001] ECR I-6369.
Case C-70/10 *Scarlet Extended SA* v *Société belge des auteurs, compositeurs et éditeurs SCRL (SABAM)*, [2011] ECR page I-11959.
Case T-102/96: *Gencor Ltd* v. *Commission of the European Communities*, OJ C 160, 05/06/1999, 18.
Competition Laws Cooperation Agreement 1999 (EC/ECSC/Canada). 1999/445 1999. *OJ, L175*.
Council Decision of 6 June 2003 concerning the signature of the Agreements between the European Union and the United States of America on extradition and mutual legal assistance in criminal matters; OJ L181 of 19/07/2003, 25.
Council Framework Decision 2004/757/JHA of 25 October 2004 laying down minimum provisions on the constituent elements of criminal acts and penalties in the field of illicit drug trafficking, OJ L 335, 11/11/2004, 8.
Council of the European Union. (2011). *Action-Oriented Paper (AOP) on strengthening the EU external dimension on action against trafficking in human beings; towards global EU action against trafficking in human beings, 12401/11*. Brussels.
Instrument Européen de voisinage et de Partenariat Algerie Programme Indicatif National 2011–2013. http://eeas.europa.eu/enp/pdf/pdf/country/2011_enpi_nip_algeria_fr.pdf
Decision Concluding the Agreement between the European Community and Japan concerning co-operation on anti-competitive activities 2003/520 2003. OJ L183.
Directive 2011/36/EU of the European Parliament and of the Council of 5 April 2011 on preventing and combating trafficking in human beings and protecting its victims, and replacing Council Framework Decision 2002/629/JHA, OJ L 101, 15/04/2011, 1.
Directive 2013/40/EU of the European Parliament and of the Council of 12 August 2013 on attacks against information systems and replacing Council Framework Decision 2005/222/JHA, OJ L 218/8.
Dragneva, R., & Wolczuk, K. (2012). EU law export to the Eastern neighbourhood. In P. J. Cardwell (Ed.), *EU external relations law and policy in the post-Lisbon era* (pp. 217–240). The Hague: T.M.C. Asser Press.
Egan, M. (2010). The role of the regulated sector in the UK anti-money laundering framework: Pushing the boundaries of the private police. *Journal of Contemporary European Research, 6* (2), 272–288.
European Commission. (2010). Commission staff working document accompanying the communication from the Commission to the European Parliament and the Council—Taking stock of the European Neighbourhood Policy (ENP)—Implementation of the European Neighbourhood Policy in 2009. Progress Report Republic of Moldova, SEC 2010. 523. Brussels.
European Commission. (2014). *Joint staff working document: Implementation of the European Neighbourhood Policy in Ukraine progress in 2013 and recommendations for action, SWD 2014*. 96 final. Brussels.
European Union External Action. EU/Egypt Action Plan. http://eeas.europa.eu/enp/pdf/pdf/action_plans/egypt_enp_ap_final_en.pdf
Flockhart, T. (2006). 'Complex socialization': A framework for the study of state socialization. *European Journal of International Relations, 12*(1), 89–118.
Griffin, J. P. (1998). Foreign governmental reactions to US assertions of extraterritorial jurisdiction. *European Competition Law Review, 19*(2), 64–73.
Hillion, C. (2008). The EU's neighbourhood policy towards Eastern Europe. In A. Dashwood & M. Maresceau (Eds.), *Law and practice of the EU external relations: Salient features in a changing landscape*. Cambridge: Cambridge University Press.

Joined Cases 89/85, 104/85, 114/85, 116/85, 117/85 and 125/85 to 129/85 *Ahlström Osakeyhtiö and Others* v *Commission* [1988] ECR 5193.
Lake Airwarys v. *Sabena, Belgian World Airlines* 731.F.2d 909 1984), 932.
Lavenex, S. (2014). The power of functionalist extension: How EU rules travel. *Journal of European Public Policy, 21*(6), 885–903.
Lavenex, S., & Schimmelfennig, F. (2009). EU rules beyond EU borders: Theorizing external governance in European politics. *Journal of European Public Policy, 16*(6), 791–812.
Mid-Term Review of the country Strategy Paper Morocco 2007–2013 and National Indicative Program 2011–2013.
Müller, P., Kudrna, Z., & Falkner, G. (2015). EU–global interactions: Policy export, import, promotion and protection. *Journal of European Public Policy, 21*(8), 1102–1119.
O'Neill, M. (2013). Trafficking in human beings and the Eastern Neighbours: New challenges for the EU justice and law enforcement framework. In M. O'Neill, K. Swinton, & A. Winter (Eds.), *New challenges for the EU internal security strategy* (pp. 188–217). Newcastle upon Tyne: Cambridge Scholars Publishing.
O'Neill, K., Balsiger, J., & Van Deveer, S. D. (2004). Actors, norms and impact: Recent international cooperation theory and the influence of the agent–structure debate. *Annual Review of Political Science, 7*, 149–175.
EU-USA Positive Comity Agreement 1998, 98/386 1998. OJ L 173/28.
Rasmussen, H. (1988). Between self-restraint and activism: A judicial policy for the European Court. *European Law Review, 13*(1), 28–38.
Scott, J. (2014). Extraterritoriality and territorial extension in EU law. *American Journal of Comparative Law, 62*(1), 87–125.
Stone, D. (2004). Transfer agents and global networks in the 'Transnationalization' of policy. *Journal of European Public Policy, 11*(3), 545–566.
The *SS Lotus (France* v. *Turkey)* 1927. PCIJ ser.A.
Treaty on European Union.
Treaty on the Functioning of the European Union.
U.S. v. *Nippon Paper Industries Co*., Ltd. 109 F.3d 1, C.A.1 (Mass.), 1997, March 17, 1997, 403.
United States of America v. *Imperial Chemical Industries Ld. and Others*, U.S. District Court for the Southern District of New York [1952] Civil Action No. 24-13.
Wall Street Journal. (2008, January 17). *Editorial. Europe v. U.S. Business*. Accessed July 5, 2015, from http://online.wsj.com/news/articles/SB120053154686996085

Police and Customs Cooperation Centres and Their Role in EU Internal Security Governance

Artur Gruszczak

1 Introduction

Police and Customs Cooperation Centres (PCCCs) have been established throughout the Schengen area as an important institution reinforcing mechanisms and procedures of cross-border law enforcement cooperation. Since the first PCCC became operational in Offenburg in 1999, about 40 centres have emerged, performing various functions and tasks in the area of internal security and law enforcement and constituting a valuable local tool of direct cross-border cooperation. PCCCs represent an important yet understudied aspect of EU internal security. They epitomize the institutional and functional answer to the real challenge accompanying the "dissolution of borders" within the Schengen area. They also manifest considerable diversity of national views on their roles and tasks to be fulfilled by respective authorities of the participating member states. Often left at the margin of EU internal security governance, they nevertheless represent the usual and evolving practice of cross-border cooperation between national law enforcement agencies.

The issue of internal security and public order was present since the very beginning of the negotiations and preparations to conclude Schengen agreements on the gradual abolition of checks at the signatories' common borders. Fear of intensified criminal activities, flow of illicit goods through "porous" borders, trafficking in illegal migrants and human beings and—last but not least—the expansion of terrorist networks underpinned the debate on benefits and costs of the free movement across internal borders (Bonnefoi 1995; Genson 1998; Corrado 1999; Den Boer 2000). PCCCs were created as one of the compensatory measures to the abolition of the internal border control enabling free movement of persons and goods across the Schengen zone.

A. Gruszczak (✉)
Jagiellonian University, ul. Jablonowskich 5, 31-114 Kraków, Poland
e-mail: artur.gruszczak@uj.edu.pl

R. Bossong, H. Carrapico (eds.), *EU Borders and Shifting Internal Security*,
DOI 10.1007/978-3-319-17560-7_9

The primary mission of the PCCCs was to support the operational services and facilitate cross-border exchange of information among the member states. In addition, PCCCs strongly support daily cross-border co-operation and provide quick replies to other law enforcement authorities. Since their inception in the late 1990s, the PCCCs were evolving towards an important bi- and multinational form of practical cross-border law enforcement cooperation. They were consolidated as platforms for mutual assistance and operational support creating thereby a secure environment for officers and specialists in a variety of law enforcement areas.

In the reflection period preceding the 2009 Stockholm Programme, the so-called Future Group (High Level Advisory Group on EU Internal Security) suggested that the EU should establish a model of PCCC applicable to all member states and serving as "real police-customs centres of crisis management capable of handling events on an international scale." (Council of the EU 2008a: 4). Having passed several years from then, the call for a model PCCC is still actual. It is owing to the fact that the development of the centres across the Schengen area has given rise to questions about their utility and appropriateness to the changing landscape of EU internal security as well as the member states' national security policies. The crux of the matter lies in functionalities of the PCCCs and deliverables resulting from their overall performance. Divergent national views and the lack of a follow-up to the Future Group's model solution have contributed to the competing approaches to the PCCCs.

The first, traditional stance is close to the realist view at international cooperation, underlining the primacy of national security interests over potential values added by transnational cooperation. It prefers limited engagement of national institutions and resources in operational activities and in information exchange and analysis. The question of effectiveness and accountability is subject to political guidelines and legal regulations adopted by the participating member states. An alternative approach consists in the constant widening of the area of cooperation covering not only simple mechanisms of mutual assistance but also more advanced forms of collaboration, especially in the field of information exchange and analysis. This functionalist attitude is based on supranational preferences and readiness of national actors to increase the level of cooperation sticking to the principle of reciprocity. The emphasis is put on the quality of deliverables from the cooperating actors and capacity to fuse all available information in a PCCC. The matter of efficiency and accountability still rests with the relevant authorities of the participating states, however they are more disposed towards finding conciliatory solutions and adopting joint positions.

The arguments developed throughout this chapter support a thesis that the prospects for a real contribution of the PCCCs to EU internal security governance are definitely associated with the functionalist model. As a result of the increasing movement of people and goods across the common borders, the PCCCs have gradually been transformed into information gathering centres, developing knowledge management and intelligence capabilities, at least in some areas and to the extent permitted by the member states. They can contribute to general crime intelligence pictures and overall situational assessments. The old realist model of intergovernmental collaboration solely enables a limited transfer of information upon request from an authorized national law enforcement service. It is increasingly obsolete, given the emerging threats and challenges to EU internal security as well as national security interests of the member states. Certainly, both models will coexist within the Schengen area but the functionalist option offers much more opportunities to enhance security mechanisms, mainly through data fusion and intelligence-led criminal analysis. This chapter, thus, claims that some PCCCs have gradually evolved into a transnational fusion centre operating as an information management hub on a meso-level of EU internal security governance. This tendency, however, needs to be critically evaluated from different angles.

This chapter proceeds as follows: in Sect. 2, a short evolution of PCCCs is presented, focusing on legal and organizational frameworks and practical arrangements implemented by the cooperating state authorities. Practical challenges to the evolution of the PCCCs are also discussed. The following section elaborates on the functionalist model of the PCCC, employing the concept of a fusion centre and checking its viability against the capabilities and experiences of cross-border cooperation. Section 4 seeks to evaluate critically the functionalist model of the PCCC on the example of the multinational EPICC centre. In the conclusions, some critical remarks are offered regarding the tensions provoked by the tendency to develop PCCCs towards an intelligence-led fusion centre model.

2 Police and Customs Cooperation Centres: Legal and Organisational Background

The Police and Customs Cooperation Centre is a cross-border institutional network structure for information exchange which aims to support operational activities carried out by national agencies responsible for police, border and customs tasks in the internal border area (Council of the EU 2011: 5). PCCCs bring together staff from the authorities responsible for internal security: customs, police and other law enforcement services. Officers and experts from the respective agencies of the collaborating states are stationed in a single location, mostly in a joint border facility kept operational under Schengen requirements with respect to the procedure of control and supervision and temporary restoring of internal border checks.

The PCCCs within the Schengen area as an important institutional arrangement seeking to develop ways and means of cross-border law enforcement. The effects of the Schengen agreements for internal borders of the countries having their territories incorporated into the common free travel area were manifold. The logic of Schengen cooperation consisted in the opening of internal borders between the countries making up the Schengen zone for the regular flow of persons and goods. The abolition of checks at internal borders was accompanied by the introduction and development of the so-called compensatory measures, entailing visa policies, integrated external border management as well as technological and administrative reinforcement of the frontiers. In addition, police and customs cooperation between relevant services of the Schengen countries was considerably remodeled, enhanced and focused on the prevention and combating of transnational criminal organisations which were eager to take advantage of the relaxation of controls at internal borders. Indeed, numerous representatives of law enforcement and criminal justice as well as some politicians and local activists believed that the abolition of checks and controls at internal borders would be a factor facilitating the expansion of cross-border criminal networks (Bevers 1993: 83–84).

PCCCs became the core part of the systemic institutional cooperation between law enforcement and customs authorities in the countries integrated with the Schengen area. Title III of the Convention implementing the Schengen Agreement (CISA) stipulated in Article 39.1 that the contracting parties ensure that their police authorities shall assist each other for the purposes of preventing and detecting criminal offences. It was also provided in Article 39.4 that cooperation in border areas may be covered by arrangements between the competent ministers of the contracting parties. Moreover, it was underlined in Article 39.5 that "The provisions of this Article shall not preclude more detailed present or future bilateral agreements between Contracting Parties with a common border." (Schengen 2000).

The establishment and subsequent development of PCCCs reflected an interplay of the two models: realist and functionalist. The former was highlighting the importance of national interests and saw the Schengen agreements as a source of potential difficulties in terms of internal security and public order. So, the realist approach to the PCCC was centred on international law enforcement cooperation as far as it was complying with national laws and requirements. The functionalist model was based on a presumption that the Schengen area should foster a spillover effect with respect also to cross-border cooperation, including information exchange and analytical support. A PCCC was expected to transform into a cooperation node integrating national officers around common security needs and EU-wide projects. The issue of information management was particularly contested by the followers of both models. Either information was considered to be "a national property", and thereby guarded and controlled by the originators, or it was treated as an openly available resource which should be used and processed with the aim to contribute to transnational security arrangements.

The implementation of the CISA in March 1995 brought about numerous contending issues, concerning mainly practical effects of the abolition of internal borders and the introduction of specific mechanisms tackling defiant transnational criminal organisations. The CISA created police powers in the fields of cross-border surveillance, hot pursuit and controlled delivery as one of the compensatory measures accompanying the proclamation of the free movement across internal borders. Given the differences in organisational and administrative structures (federal versus centralised systems), contrasting security cultures, varied experiences of cross-border police cooperation and—last but not least—different sense of territorial sovereignty, the governments were not enthusiastic about a quick implementation of the novel regulations and mechanisms of cross-border operations. Such variety of attitudes towards cross-border policing activities had a direct impact on capability and willingness to adopt and develop new forms of cooperation without debilitating effectiveness and administration of national law enforcement services (Aden 2001: 105–106).

Therefore, governments with a long impressive record in cross-border cooperation, like in the Benelux countries, smoothly adjusted to Schengen regulations whereas France had certain reservations and doubts with regard to possible consequences of the abolition of border controls, especially with Belgium and, to a lesser extent, with Germany. As a result, France initially had maintained controls at the border with Belgium and Luxembourg and also opposed hot pursuit on her territory (Giraud 1999: 37; Hufnagel 2013: 51; Zaiotti 2011: 95–98). In the face of difficulties in the implementation of Schengen rules and mechanisms, France and Germany, the "engines" of European integration in the 1990s and originators of the Schengen agreement, decided to strengthen cross-border security measures through the creation of common police stations on internal borders. In December 1995, France and Germany concluded an administrative agreement on a formal long-standing cooperation in the field of cross-border policing. A similar arrangement was reached in June1996 between France and Spain enabling the establishment of the common border police station in Le Perthus—La Jonquera (Vallar 2009: 136).

The experiences and preliminary assessments of effectiveness and contribution of joint police stations to security and public order brought about mixed reactions. Generally, the arrangements were considered as insufficient to handle properly the growing number of issues resulting from free movement across Schengen internal borders. As a result, in 1996 the Council's Coordinating Committee for EU justice and home affairs put forward a proposal for a standard model of cross-border agreement on police and customs cooperation. That model put emphasis on security matters (prevention and fight against illegal immigration, cross-border crime, threats to public order, illicit trafficking in drugs, arms and human beings). It also stressed the importance of gathering and exchanging information (Polner 2011: 59). It also recommended the conclusion of new agreements enabling the creation of cross-border police and customs centers fulfilling the primary tasks related to internal security and public order.

The first ever bilateral agreement that set a formal basis for the establishment of a PCCC was an accord between France and Italy related to cross-border police and customs cooperation, signed in Chambery on 3 October 1997. However, a model agreement for police and customs cooperation centres was the Franco-German agreement on cross-border police and customs cooperation signed on 9 October 1997 in Mondorf-les-Bains (Hufnagel 2013: 52). It provided for closer cooperation between police and customs authorities in order to prevent threats to security and public order and to promote the prevention and prosecution of criminal offences, including in cases of the temporary reintroduction of checks on persons at the common border, in accordance with relevant provisions of the CISA. Article 3 provided for the establishment of "joint centres" where police and customs services would ensure, within the existing structures and competences, their operational cooperation. Joint centres served mainly for information exchange on a permanent basis (24/7). They were organised around common premises where officers of all police and customs services, seconded by respective national authorities and acting within their respective powers, worked closely together for the purpose of exchanging, analysing and transmitting information related to matters relevant to the border area. They were also entitled to participate in the coordination of cross-border interventions in cases where several different authorities, belonging in different sectors, were concerned (Daman 2008: 203). It was underlined, however, that joint centres must not perform autonomous operational activities. Coordinating activities of the joint centres included harmonisation of the measures of investigation and surveillance in the border area, as well as support for the technical implementation of cross-border surveillance and hot pursuit, as stipulated in Articles 40 and 41 of the CISA (République Française 2000: 14967; Maguer 2002).

The first joint centre for police and customs cooperation opened in the German city of Offenburg on 10 May 1999. Three years later, in December 2002, it was moved to the French-German border, to Kehl, neighbouring with Strasbourg (GZ Kehl 2007: 8). The 1997 Chambery and Mondorf agreements on police and customs cross-border cooperation encouraged other EU countries to negotiate and conclude similar agreements on a bilateral or a multilateral basis (see Table 1). As a result, more and more police and customs cooperation centres were established throughout the Schengen area.

Since their inception, the PCCCs were generating a number of questions referred to the improvement and refinement of their performance. Initially, several member states that had already established such centres were interested in a quick evolution towards the functionalist model. They promoted the creation of joint police stations or police and customs cooperation centres. They drafted, in 2002, a relevant recommendation for the Council but it was not adopted (Council of the EU 2002). The Commission, in the Communication on enhancing police and customs cooperation in the European Union issued in 2004, called for the extension of these forms of cross-border cooperation and the drawing up of a catalogue of best practices, which could encourage more member states to establish PCCCs. Moreover, the Commission opted for the institutionalisation of such cooperation (Commission of the EC 2004).

Table 1 Selected agreements on cross-border police and customs cooperation based on the CISA

	Contracting parties	Place of signing	Date of signature
1.	France–Italy	Chambéry	3.10.1997
2.	France–Germany	Mondorf-les-Bains	9.10.1997
3.	France–Spain	Blois	7.07.1998
4.	Spain–Portugal	Albufeira	30.11.1998
5.	Belgium–Germany	Brussels	27.03.2000
6.	Belgium–France	Tournai	5.03.2001
7.	Luxembourg–France	Luxembourg	15.10.2001
8.	Luxembourg–Belgium–Germany	Luxembourg	23.02.2003
9.	Luxembourg–Belgium–The Netherlands	Luxembourg	8.06.2004
10.	Germany–The Netherlands	Enschede	2.03.2005

The debate preceding the big reform of European integration and rebuilding of EU architecture also took into account the matter of intra-EU cross-border cooperation. PCCCs, despite their small number within the EU, arose a considerable interest of politicians and practitioners. The idea of a strengthened practical (operational) cooperation between adjacent countries, assisted by relevant EU agencies and institutions, like Europol and Joint Investigation Teams, was actively propagated by Germany during its 2007 Presidency of the Council. On the initiative of Germany, the high-level advisory group on the future of the European home affairs policy (so-called Future Group) was formed.[1] The group aimed to address the issues of justice and home affairs cooperation at EU level with the view at ensuring greater cooperation, more beneficial for the member states and more viable for EU institutions and agencies. It sought to debate the future orientation of EU home affairs cooperation ahead of the negotiations on the new multiannual programme in the area of freedom, security and justice for the years 2010–2014.

The issue of joint police and customs centres attracted considerable attention from the participants of the Future Group. France appeared as the strongest advocate of the functionalist model. The French contribution to the final report was overtly enthusiastic about the centres. France, the most active in the development of such forms of cross-border cooperation, praised the PCCCs as an "essential tool for police cooperation in border zones" pointing out that they "represent an innovative approach to cross-border information exchange in crime fighting." The French paper also contained a reference to a "model PCCC" which should be "integrated into the acquis of the Union and used extensively" (Future Group 2008: 2–4). Linking the importance of PCCCs with territorial enlargement of the Schengen area, France suggested a revaluation of the structure and missions of PCCCs towards making them genuine crisis management centres ready to tackle negative effects of international movement of persons.

In the final report announced by the Future Group in June 2008, titled "Freedom, Security, Privacy—European Home Affairs in an open world", PCCCs served as an example of an innovative approach to cross-border information exchange in crime fighting. The Group suggested that the European Union should establish a model of Police and Customs Cooperation Centre applicable to all member states regardless of legal differences, technical barriers and other negative determinants. The structure and missions of PCCCs could be regularly evaluated, in order to maintain their

[1] The group was integrating ministers representing countries holding "trio Presidencies" in the years 2007–2009 (Germany, Portugal, Slovenia, France, Czech Republic, Sweden, and one delegate from the troika composed by Spain, Belgium and Hungary), a representative of the common law area (UK) as an observer, and experts from individual Member States as needed. EU institutions were represented by a delegate from the General Secretariat of the Council, the Chairman of the LIBE (Civil Liberties, Justice and Home Affairs) Committee of the European Parliament, as well as the Commissioner for Home Affairs (German 2007; Crosbie 2007; German Federal Ministery of the Interior 2011).

position as real police-customs centres of crisis management capable of handling events on an international scale. Especially in the border zones, PCCCs should become a model of future police cooperation (Council of the EU 2008a: 8).

Following the publication of the Future Group's recommendations, the French Presidency in the Council forwarded a draft of European Best Practice Guidelines for Police and Customs Cooperation Centres (Council of the EU 2008b) which was further elaborated by national experts and forwarded to the Council's appropriate working groups. It was adopted by the Council in October 2008 and contained practical recommendations for setting up and operating PCCCs. The guidelines constituted another small step towards the functionalist approach to the cross-border law enforcement coordination. They underlined the importance of best practices and standardized solutions to practical problems faced by national authorities in everyday operational cooperation across internal borders. Moreover, the above mentioned document contained outlines of model cooperation agreements and operating regulations of the PCCC. Thus, it drew up a blueprint for the establishment of more PCCCs, especially in the expanded Schengen area (following the 2007 "Eastern" enlargement).

Another important step in the development of PCCCs was an annual conference organized jointly by the Presidency and the Commission. The first conference took place in 2010 on the initiative of the Belgian Presidency, subsequently becoming a wide platform for discussing ongoing issues, evaluating hitherto experiences and putting forward new proposals with regard to conceptual framework and practical recommendations. During the second conference, held in Brussels in October 2011, the roadmap of PCCC cooperation development within the EU Member States was discussed and endorsed (Polish Presidency 2011). The conferences were attended by representatives of the Commission, Europol, Frontex, CEPOL as well as national PCCC coordinators and other member states' officials (Council of the EU 2012, 2013). Annual conferences at EU level have enabled experiences to be shared and common approaches to be discussed. The participants of the meetings drew certain guidelines and set priorities for the practical performance of the existing PCCCs, especially with regard to crime prevention, criminal analysis, information exchange and intelligence sharing.

One of the issues discussed at the PCCC conferences was an IT-platform for non-operational communication. It was raised during the first conference in 2010 and followed up in subsequent discussions. The Polish Presidency in 2011 proposed, during the second PCCC conference held in Warsaw, to create an IT-platform dedicated for the PCCCs. The Information Management Strategy (IMS) for EU internal security also foresaw in its action point 7 to provide PCCCs with an e-platform for non-operational communication (Council of the EU 2013, Annex 1). In a roadmap adopted by PCCC officials from 17 member states gathered at the 4th Conference on Police and Customs Cooperation Centres in October 2013, a proposal was formulated to enrich cross-border crime analyses of PCCCs and Europol through structural communication and cooperation (Council of the EU 2013, Annex 2). No formal decisions, however, have been taken in this regard due to the lack of unanimity. Given that some member states use sTESTA (secured Trans European Services for Telematics between Administrations) network and others prefer SIENA (Secure Information Exchange Network Application) application, the question of an overall EU standard for information exchange among the PCCCs has been stalled and remained subject to the existing bi- and multilateral arrangements.

The review of the evolution of the PCCCs shows that over time there has been not only a considerable numerical growth of the centres across the Schengen area, but also increasingly substantial efforts of standardisation and networking, including advanced IT systems, were made by EU institutions and the member states. The rapidly increasing number of information and data drawn from diverse sources was the main driver of this tendency. As a result, the functionalist model of PCCC has become a clear point of reference for both skeptics and followers of intensified cross-border cooperation.

3 The Functionalist Approach to the PCCCs

In today's security environment, the demand for updated, precise and comprehensive knowledge about factors and drivers of stability and uncertainty, order and disorder, security and insecurity is stimulated by rapidly proliferating risks and growing threats. Security policies and strategies have been increasingly depending on selected information and specialist knowledge as the prerequisites of an effective strategic planning and decision making. However, any final analytical output delivered to decision makers was made up of materials prepared in different institutional and organisational settings, often with specific methods and approaches of information management and varied access to information sources and data banks. The design and architecture of complex bureaucratic organisations may cause that their segments are often internally disconnected and poorly inclined to a structured collaboration (Pfeifer 2012: 1). This also may create information asymmetries and communication bottlenecks resulting in a declining effectiveness of knowledge management for decision-making support.

Law enforcement services have been well aware of the key role that intelligence plays in anticipation of threats, identification of risks and effective prevention in case of serious incidents or adverse impacts on public order or internal security. Effective intelligence sharing is indispensable for crime prevention, preparedness and response. Ability to acquire timely and accurate information about main threats and factors endangering the individual safety of citizens, the public order and national security interests largely depends on identification, assessment and access to various, often dispersed and diversified, sources. A real challenge for law enforcement is posed by obstacles to integration and collation of scattered sources of information and data. These sources often fall under different jurisdictions, are subject to various procedural and organizational frameworks, and are protected by specific measures.

The implementation of intelligence-driven policing in many countries in Europe in the 1990s and early 2000s stemmed from the assumption that the application of criminal intelligence analysis would facilitate crime reduction and prevention (Ratcliffe 2003; Gruszczak 2013). Moreover, it should provide an organisational framework linking law enforcement agencies with intelligence services, thus contributing to new relationships between the intelligence community and local authorities as well as other relevant public actors (O'Brien 2009: 910). The necessity of "connecting the dots", i.e., demonstrating ability and capacity to draw a knowledge-loaded materials from segmented institutions and out of dispersed sources was the cause of the eternal headache of law enforcement services.

The latter feature of cross-border cooperation within the Schengen area reflects the rationale behind the emergence and development of the PCCCs. Transnational cooperation entails an intensive exchange of information for both operational purposes and a strategic assessment of major security threats and criminal activities. The need for a common bi- or multinational coordinating body monitoring cross-border movement of persons and goods seemed plainly evident for the original states-parties to the Schengen agreements.[2]

The flow of information originating in varied and scattered sources required a centralised management through the establishment of a cross-border criminal information hub enabling fast, timely and effective exchange of data provided by the member states. As one police officer said: "From the beginning, the building of the *Lagezentrum* (data centre) itself, with its 24-hour service, proved to be the main pillar of cooperation in the border region." (Felsen 2011: 79).

Police and customs cooperation centres are a valuable local tool for the direct cross-border cooperation between law enforcement agencies, especially regarding information exchange. Collecting and processing information is still all in the domain of national services and institutions. However, multinational units, upon fulfillment of certain requirements, can be entrusted with analysis and intelligence crafting. A PCCC may act as a "broker" and a "facilitator" of information exchange between the representatives of the collaborating states seconded to the PCCC. The bi- or multinational staff stationed in a common centre also maintains a permanent link with respective national customs and law enforcement authorities. They are encouraged to consult data files stored in dedicated bases and protected under national legislation (Council of the EU 2011: 7).

Due to their role defined within the Schengen regime, the PCCCs serve mainly the purpose of the 24/7 exchange of information between the member states

[2] Article 46 of the CISA provides that:

"1. In specific cases, each Contracting Party may, in compliance with its national law and without being so requested, send the Contracting Party concerned any information which may be important in helping it combat future crime and prevent offences against or threats to public policy and public security.

2. Information shall be exchanged, without prejudice to the arrangements for cooperation in border areas referred to in Article 39(4), via a central body to be designated. In particularly urgent cases, the exchange of information within the meaning of this Article may take place directly between the police authorities concerned, unless national provisions stipulate otherwise. The central body shall be informed of this as soon as possible." See Schengen Schengen 2000.

contributing to the PCCC. In the great majority of the cases, the PCCCs provide information requested by relevant customers (mainly appropriate national services as mentioned in the basic agreement on cross-border police and customs cooperation). They seldom work as a channel for the exchange of operational information. It usually happens in an emergency situation at the local level where a PCCC may be involved as a point of contact for the local police or customs services or as a unit providing information support for officers on duty (Unisys Belgium 2007). In the biggest PCCC in the Schengen zone, the *Gemeinsames Zentrum* (GZ) Kehl in Germany, 17,758 requests were received in 2013. Only 80 applications for cross-border surveillance were processed (Wenda 2014: 51). The Polish-German PCCC in Świecko, a more recent centre than the one in Kehl, got in 2014 four thousand requests (Gazeta Wyborcza 2015). In a longer span of time, covering the period 2007–2012, the centre amassed 15,000 requests but only 400 were related to urgent cases requiring operational support (Konieczny 2012).

Information collected in the PCCCs deals with various cases that fall within the remit of the center as defined in the founding agreement. It may concern both petty and serious crime, persons and groups violating public order, road and water traffic safety, illegal migration, missing persons and other. The staff of the PCCC can request information from various national police and customs computer files and databases through law enforcement officers of the member states owning the data. The searches conducted in national databases result in an immediate transfer of results to the centre. Information reaching the PCCC basically refers to:

- vehicles (identification numbers, registration marks);
- persons (selected categories of personal data, including in some cases DNA profiles[3], missing persons, drivers and passengers in vehicles);
- documents (identity cards, driver's licenses; also verifications of the acceptability and authenticity of these documents).

The data goes through information analysis cycle, entailing collation, comparison, analysis and production of knowledge and—if appropriate—criminal intelligence. The PCCC may hold an integrated database storing information delivered to the centre with the consent of individual stakeholders. All data held in the bases maintained in the PCCC is made available online to the counterparts, except for customs information linked to tax privacy issues (Felsen 2011: 79).

The PCCC can do statistical analysis and data mining and check them against available operational information bringing about enriched analytical products covering various aspects of cross-border criminality (Council of the EU 2011: 8). These products are delivered to relevant national authorities and used either as a valuable professional expertise input or as an analytical tool supporting operational planning

[3] For example, German and French authorities agreed in 2004 to exchange dactyloscopic data and then, following the entry into force of the Prüm treaty, also DNA records. See Felsen (2011: 80).

or conduct of the activities by the police, customs or border guards (Council of the EU 2011: 7).

The workflow of data and information is subject to national and international regulations and arrangements. As already mentioned, there is no standard IT platform for information exchange with the PCCCs although the Council, Europol and some member states decisively prefer the Europol-led SIENA application. It allows the exchange of messages through secure channels for data transmission. Nevertheless, some PCCC officials take SIENA as an overlay devoid of real functionalities and definitely less useful than the sTESTA network service.[4]

The functionalist approach to the PCCCs is legitimized by the mounting quantity of information flown to the centres and deemed relevant not only for local border areas but also for national interests of the participating states and even for EU internal security. PCCCs are nodal sites where information and data can be collated, compared, processed and shared with relevant authorities in the Schengen area. So, the functionalist model is based on the presumption of not wasting the opportunity to manage information exchanged in the centres through the use of data fusion mechanisms and tools.

4 Towards a Fusion Centre Model PCCC: A Critical Assessment

As concluded in the above section, the functionalist model of the PCCC entails an extensive information exchange and data management through an active workflow typical for an intelligence-led fusion centre. The fusion method is often seen as a remedy for shortcomings of intelligence sharing among law enforcement agencies. It responds to the need for a holistic approach to intelligence based on an all-source information collection and analysis (Connable 2012: 1; Monahan and Regan 2012: 301–302). Data fusion, according to Buede and Waltz (1998: 51), means

> an adaptive knowledge creation process in which diverse elements of similar or dissimilar observations (data) are aligned, correlated, and combined into organized and indexed sets (information), which are further assessed to model, understand, and explain (knowledge) the makeup and behavior of a domain under observation.

Information obtained from a variety of sources should be pooled together in a single physical location where correlation, combination, assessment and fusion can take place in a secure, stable and professional environment. A fusion center offers relatively comfortable working conditions for a variety of law enforcement agencies that have traditionally operated as separate entities, without any knowledge and experience of interagency efforts to generate intelligence and knowledge concerning the main threats to security and public order (Joyal 2012: 60–62). In an institutional perspective, a fusion centre is a physically located collaborative effort

[4] An anonymous PCCC official. Author's interview, June 2015.

of several agencies that provide resources, expertise, and information and pool them together in the centre with the goal of maximizing their ability to detect, identify, prevent, investigate, and respond to public security threats. It is a large data clearinghouse where information is collected, collated, securely stored, scrutinised, interpreted and analysed and converted into intelligence. Analytical reports (risk analyses, threat assessments, situation trends, critical evaluation) and other intelligence products (e.g., biographic files, security screening lists, alerts, link and network visualizations, matrices, charts, maps, graphs and other deliverables needed by law enforcement services) are subsequently disseminated to authorised users and stored for a further analytical or operational use.

The whole concept of a fusion centre is framed by the need for an effective integration of varied and heterogenous streams of information and intelligence acquired from the whole range of sources and repositories: governmental, public and private (Rollins et al. 2008: vii–viii). It is focused on both strategic requirements of early warning and risk awareness as well as operational tasks, especially with regard to quick and efficient prevention and response to threats and hazards suddenly emerging in the area of individual and public safety as well as national and international security.

The management of huge amount of varied information and data raises serious doubts as to oversight and accountability of fusion mechanisms and practices. We know from experience of fusion centres in certain European countries and world-wide, especially in the United States and Canada, that this is a sensitive and problematic issue (Belgian Standing Intelligence Agencies Review Committee 2010; Newkirk 2010; Monahan and Regan 2012; Regan and Monahan 2014). The critique is focused on the deficit of transparency of law enforcement agencies, the insufficient oversight, risk of errors in information exchange, wrong data management, misuse (even abuse) of personal data (Monahan 2010: 44–48; Monahan and Regan 2012: 307–313). There is a functional similarity between fusion centres in the US and the PCCCs in the Schengen area. As Regan and Monahan (2014: 480) wrote, they "operate as decentralized network nodes that are connected by information-sharing systems and practices". However, there is a crucial legal and administrative difference that determines the issue of accountability and oversight. While US or Canadian centres fall under a single national jurisdiction, European PCCCs work on the basis of relevant bi- or multilateral agreements and within national legal frameworks. Hence, there is a double (or multiple in the case of tripartite or multilateral PCCCs) accountability within a PCCC. Every national stakeholder is responsible for the daily management of information and data according to national laws and subject to appropriate oversight mechanisms. It does not say that protection of information is thereby guaranteed, nonetheless officers representing the collaborating parties in a given PCCC perform their duties in a relatively clear-cut operation area and are bound by strict legal rules.

An interesting, and specific, example of a functionalist PCCC is Euroregional Police Information and Cooperation Centre (EPICC), established in 2005 in Heerlen by the three countries participating in the Euroregion Meuse-Rhin, namely Germany, Belgium and Luxembourg (Spapens 2008: 238). Several dozen police officers stationed there can work together on a single IT-platform called ESLI (Exchange System for Legal Information) system, which is used by the PCCC in Heerlen between the Netherlands, Belgium and Germany. The application runs on three national servers used by EPICC in order to handle information requests: it registers a request for information (concerning the three basic categories of data: people, vehicles, documents) and transmits it to an appropriate counterpart in another office via a secure ISDN line. Only an authorized national law enforcement officer can access the data stored in the servers, retrieve the needed information and possibly deliver it to the requesting officer (Unisys 2007: 89). A feasibility study prepared by Unisys in 2007 contained a critical assessment of the ESLI system:

> According to its users, ESLI is quite heavy to use, and LE officers of the PCCC in Heerlen (EPICC) are looking for a system, which would be more straightforward. A drawback of the ESLI system is that there is no automated way to transfer information from national systems to ESLI. Collected data should be re-written in ESLI. [...] As the name states, ESLI is meant to manage legal information, and is therefore not adapted for exchange of information during a crisis. For the reasons mentioned above, we would not recommend the use of ESLI for the exchange of information during a crisis. (Unisys Belgium 2007: 91)

The critical account of the information exchange system led to a further discussion on availability and plausibility of standardized solutions for EPICC. Finally, the exchange of information since the beginning of 2014 has been carried out by the SIENA application. Therefore, law enforcement officers with on-site access to the content of their respective national databases can quickly deliver accurate, complete and reliable answers to requests for information via SIENA (Council of the EU 2015: 42). As a tool dedicated to secure and rapid information transfer to Europol, SIENA enables a constant exchange of files and data sets between Europol and EPICC.

This brief description of EPICC points at some aspects of the PCCCs as regional information management nodes serving not only local operational purposes but also responding to the need of an efficient management of the exchanged information. The technical functionalities available at the PCCCs allow for a large-scale processing of information and data. However, formal (legal and sometimes political) impediments to data fusion weaken the functionalist features of the PCCCs. In some PCCCs there is a clear tendency towards data fusion. As one of French officers stationed in a PCCC said: "We do data fusion in our PCCC." But he also added that administrative limits and the complex law-enforcement organizational structure effectively reduce the chances to advance with a more developed information management.[5] Formally, the standard agreement on the PCCC contains a provision on analytical support for national authorities, especially in the areas of crime prevention, risk management, joint situational assessments. So, some patterns of intelligence-led policing are practiced in the PCCCs but there is still a wide room for progress.

[5] An anonymous French PCCC official. Author's interview, June 2015.

Obviously, a fusion centre model is demanding both in technical terms and for political reasons. It seems inadequate for the traditional cross-border cooperation for it demands the launching of transnational patterns of criminal analysis and intelligence-led policing. It fits, however, the framework long elaborated in some PCCCs that have focused on local border issues keeping in mind a wider security picture and contemporary challenges to transnational security cooperation. The scattered sources of information, secured by national "guardians", are subject to the increasing connectivity. How to handle the available data is the real challenge for effectiveness and accountability of the PCCCs. Fear of "disclosing" information held by national representatives at a PCCC often prevails over the will to share and deliver valuable inputs for a further criminal analysis and intelligence-driven operational support (see Cordeel 2010: 110–111). Analytical capabilities are often underdeveloped at a PCCC and would require the establishment of an intelligence unit, which is basically unacceptable for the participating governments. The realist prerequisites hamper the progress in data fusion and knowledge management due to the fact that they are strongly embedded in national security interests of particular member states. They also address the question of the customers of analytical products originating in the PCCCs. The realist model legitimates exclusively national authorities. The functionalist approach allows the sharing of expertise with transnational units, especially with Europol as an EU agency. Owing to the fact that Europol's intelligence-driven support has received recognition in many EU member states, the prospects for data fusion in the PCCCs seem to raise the general problem of Europeanization of law enforcement cooperation. This also has to address the sensitive issues of data protection, institutional accountability of the PCCCs and the mechanisms of oversight. For the member states opting for the realist model, these questions are just awkward.

A general overview of information exchange confirms that data fusion processes do take place in the PCCCs, although in a variegated manner and often limited scope. Legal and sometimes political obstacles do not facilitate the flow of sensitive data and access to classified information. Nonetheless, the PCCC has a considerable potential in the area of data handling and intelligence production for the purposes of law enforcement and criminal justice.

5 Conclusions

The several dozen PCCCs established across the Schengen area have proven the need for a well-organized, effective and accountable institution of cross-border law enforcement, policing, customs and criminal justice cooperation. As is widely known, the PCCCs have worked as information sharing centres yet they have also developed knowledge management and intelligence capabilities, at least in some areas and to the extent permitted by the member states. It must be added that information and intelligence shared through the PCCCs is of a very particular kind. It is focused on cross-border local phenomena and engages directly law enforcement and criminal justice issues. Although the centres function as local information channels, they also contribute to general crime pictures and overall situational assessments.

The PCCCs as fusion centres operate on a relatively small scale. They are fairly autonomous yet at the same time they have limited capabilities of acquiring, collecting, collating and analyzing information and intelligence owned by national authorities and relevant EU agencies and units (like Europol, Frontex or the EU Intelligence Analysis Centre). Their utility and potential input in law enforcement cooperation is acknowledged by EU institutions, like the European Commission and the Council, nonetheless one has the feeling that the PCCCs are treated instrumentally by these institutions, as sources of valuable local criminal analyses. Such stance is clearly visible in the new European Agenda on Security, an official position of the European Commission with respect to the renewal of the Internal Security Strategy, announced in April 2015. The Commission underlined that:

> Although most of the information exchanged in PCCCs does not concern serious and organised crime, it is important that information on such cases is passed up to the national level and, where appropriate, to Europol. (European Commission 2015: 10)

Although the Commission unambiguously prefers Europol as a would-be EU law enforcement fusion center, it leaves no doubt that the chances for opening channels of information sharing by the member states with Europol via PCCCs are minimal.

The latter remark refers to a wider critical assessment of the role the PCCCs have played in EU internal security governance. The centres have emerged and proliferated across the Schengen area as international, mostly bilateral, institutions acting as a broker between the national law enforcement machineries of the participating states. They were tasked with rather modest functions, limited to support for local neighbouring police and customs stations in the border areas. The exchange of information was reduced to the necessary support upon clear request sent by one of the parties. Analytical capabilities were practically nonexistent. This formula, named in this chapter the realist model, has been applied by many PCCCs and there is little chance to change it. Therefore, this type of PCCCs has had little to contribute to EU internal security. It is clearly focused on security interests and sometimes enhances a silo mentality of the participating member states. The functionalist model sticks to transnational patterns of EU internal security, welcoming the increasing involvement of EU-led institutional and technical arrangements and looking forward to developing analytical capabilities. It is nonetheless limited by national regulations and hostage to the unanimity principle at EU decision-making level.

The tensions between the two types of PCCCs do exist but they do not bring about an open divide because of the weak interconnectivity and the lack of a Schengen-wide network architecture embracing all the centres. They can be noticed at the meetings of PCCC officers, international conferences or within the relevant EU institutions in charge of internal security (home affairs). For the sake of greater effectiveness of EU internal security governance, especially in its preventive aspect, the functionalist model has been supported by the European Commission and those member states whose PCCCs have operated in well integrated border areas and got considerable experience in cross-border cooperation. It leads, however, to a fragmentation of the PCCC community across the Schengen area and to a negative impact on the overall cooperation in EU internal security field. The lack of accountability at transnational level, due to the decision-making stalemate in the relevant EU institutions, additionally complicates the intergovernmental cooperation at the meso-level of internal security governance in the EU.

The functionalist model employing data fusion capabilities in the PCCCs provides an opportunity to break the deadlock produced by the two competing types of the PCCCs. A greater connectivity and closer direct contacts between the PCCCs across would strengthen analytical capabilities in criminal intelligence and facilitate the existing flow of information at local and regional level (ICMPD 2010: 70–71).

Many PCCCs have already garnered enormous and impressive experience in cross-border cooperation and assistance. These assets could be used for the purpose of improved cross-border information exchange and intelligence sharing. A bolder and more resolute approach is needed on the part of the member states and EU institutions. The PCCCs, linked in an EU-wide network, could make a notable contribution to the EU's internal security policy.

References

Aden, H. (2001). Convergence of policing policies and transnational policing in Europe. *European Journal of Crime, Criminal Law and Criminal Justice, 9*(2), 99–112.

Belgian Standing Intelligence Agencies Review Committee (Ed.). (2010). *Fusion centres throughout Europe. All-source threat assessments in the fight against terrorism.* Antwerp: Intersentia.

Bevers, H. (1993). Police observation and the 1990 Schengen Convention. *European Journal on Criminal Policy and Research, 1*(4), 83–84.

Bonnefoi, S. (1995). *Europe et sécurité intérieure. TREVI—Union Européenne—Schengen.* Paris: Delmas.

Buede, D., & Waltz, E. (1998). Data fusion. In *McGraw Hill Encyclopedia of science and technology.* New York: McGraw Hill.

Commission of the EC. (2004, May 18). *Communication from the Commission to the European Parliament and the Council. Enhancing police and customs co-operation in the European Union.* Document COM(2004) 376 final. Brussels.

Connable, B. (2012). *Military intelligence fusion for complex operations. A new paradigm.* Santa Monica, CA: RAND Corporation.

Cordeel, G. (2010). Europe's police information exchange: An exercise in information management. *Journal of Police Studies, 3*(16), 107–120.

Corrado, L. (1999). L'intégration de Schengen dans l'Union européenne: Problems et perspectives. *Revue du Marché commun et de l'Union européenne, 428*, 342–349.

Council of the EU. (2002, April 5). *Draft Council recommendation on joint police stations and police and customs cooperation centres.* Document 7585/02. Brussels.

Council of the EU. (2008a, July 9). *Freedom, security, privacy—European Home Affairs in an open world—Report of the informal high-level advisory group on the future of European Home Affairs Policy ("The Future Group").* Document 11657/08. Brussels.

Council of the EU. (2008b, October 3). *European best practice guidelines for police and customs cooperation centres.* Document 13815/08. Brussels.

Council of the EU. (2011, April 15). *European best practice guidelines for police and customs cooperation centres*. Document 9105/11. Brussels.
Council of the EU. (2012, November 30). *Outcome of the 3rd Conference on Police and Customs Cooperation Centres (PCCCs) on 6 and 7 November 2012, Brussels, Belgium*. Document 16879/12. Brussels.
Council of the EU. (2013, November 21). *Outcome of the 4thConference on Police and Customs Cooperation Centres (PCCCs) on 21 and 22 October 2013, Brussels, Belgium*. Document 16249/13. Brussels.
Council of the EU. (2015, April 23). *Draft manual on law enforcement information exchange*. Document 7779/15. Brussels.
Crosbie, J. (2007, May 31). Frattini: Scrap vetoes or face two-speed Europe. *European Voice, 13* (21). Accessed June 1, 2007, from http://www.europeanvoice.com/current/article.asp?id=28158
Daman, M. (2008). Cross-border Hot Pursuit in the EU. *European Journal of Crime, Criminal Law and Criminal Justice, 16*(2), 171–207.
Den Boer, M. (Ed.). (2000). *Schengen still going strong: Evaluation and update*. Maastricht: European Institute of Public Administration.
European Commission. (2015, April 28). *Communication from the Commission to the European Parliament, the Council, the European Economic and Social Committee and the Committee of the Regions. The European Agenda on Security*. Document COM(2015) 185 final. Strasbourg.
Felsen, O. (2011). European police cooperation: The example of the German-French Centre for Police and Customs Cooperation Kehl (GZ Kehl). In S. Hufnagel, C. Harfield, & S. Bronitt (Eds.), *Cross-border law enforcement. Regional law enforcement cooperation—European, Australian and Asia-Pacific perspectives* (pp. 73–85). Abingdon: Routledge.
Future Group. (2008, March 28). *Future Group Police Cooperation. French Contribution*. Accessed April 28, 2008, from http://www.statewatch.org/news/2008/jul/eu-futures-apr-police-cooperation-2008.pdf
Gazeta Wyborcza. (2015, February 12). Policja ponownie koordynatorem Polsko—Niemieckiego Centrum w Świecku. *Gazeta Wyborcza*. Accessed June 2, 2015, from http://wyborcza.pl/1,91446,17398703,Policja_ponownie_koordynatorem_Polsko___Niemieckiego.html#ixzz3bwVFRwr4
Gemenisames Zentrum für Polizei- und Zollzusammenarbeit Kehl (GZ Kehl). (2007). *Rapport annuel—Jahresbericht 2006*. Kehl: CCPD/GZ Kehl.
Genson, R. (1998). The Schengen agreements—Police cooperation and security aspects. *Hume Papers on Public Policy, 6*(1–2), 137–139.
German Federal Ministery of the Interior. (2011). Information on the meetings of the high-level advisory group on the future of European Home Affairs Policy. *BMI News*, 27 June 2007. Accessed June 30, 2007, from http://www.bmi.bund.de/cln_012/nn_211020/Internet/Content/Themen/EuropaInternationales/DatenundFakten/Future__Group__engl.html
German Presidency. (2007). *High-level group on the future of European home affairs policy after 2010 meets for the first time*. German Presidency Press Release, 21 May. Accessed June 30, 2007, from http://www.eu2007.de/en/News/Press_Releases/May/0521BMI.htm
Giraud, P. (1999). L'expérience de la France dans le mise en oeuvre de Schengen. In K. Hailbronner & P. Weil (Eds.), *Von Schengen nach Amsterdam. Auf dem Weg zu einem europäischen Einwanderungs- und Asylrecht* (pp. 31–41). Köln: Bundesanzeiger.
Gruszczak, A. (2013). EU intelligence-led policing: The case of counter-terrorism cooperation. In M. O'Neill, K. Swinton, & A. Winter (Eds.), *New challenges for the EU internal security strategy* (pp. 16–39). Newcastle upon Tyne: Cambridge Scholars Publishing.
Hufnagel, S. (2013). *Policing cooperation across borders. Comparative perspectives on law enforcement within the EU and Australia*. Farnham and Burlington, VT: Ashgate.
International Centre for Migration Policy Development and European Public Law Organization (ICMPD). (2010). *Study on the status of information exchange amongst law enforcement*

authorities in the context of existing EU instruments. Vienna: International Centre for Migration Policy Development and European Public Law Organization (ICMPD).

Joyal, R. G. (2012). *State fusion centers: Their effectiveness in information sharing and intelligence analysis*. El Paso: LFB Scholarly Publishing.

Konieczny, S. (2012). *5 rocznica utworzenia Centrum w Świecku*. Accessed June 2, 2015, from http://www.lubuska.policja.gov.pl/serwis-informacyjny/aktualnosci/item/1154-5-rocznica-utworzenia-centrum-w-%C5%9Bwiecku

Maguer, A. (2002). La coopération policière transfrontalière, moteur de transformations dans l'appareil de sécurité français. *Cultures and Conflits, 48*. Accessed June 2, 2015, from http://conflits.revues.org/901

Monahan, T. (2010). *Surveillance in the time of insecurity*. New Brunswick, NJ: Rutgers University Press.

Monahan, T., & Regan, P. M. (2012). Zones of opacity: Data fusion in post-9/11 security organizations. *Canadian Journal of Law and Society, 27*(3), 301–317.

Newkirk, A. B. (2010). The rise of the fusion-intelligence complex: A critique of political surveillance after 9/11. *Surveillance and Society, 8*(1), 43–60.

O'Brien, K. A. (2009). Managing national security and law enforcement intelligence in a globalised world. *Review of International Studies, 35*(4), 903–915.

Pfeifer, J. W. (2012). Network fusion: Information and intelligence sharing for a networked world. *Homeland Security Affairs, 8*. Accessed March 27, 2015, from https://www.hsaj.org/articles/23217

Polish Presidency. (2011). *The last DAPIX group plenar meeting during the Polish Presidency*. Accessed March 27, 2015, from http://prezydencja.policja.pl/pen/events/events-coverages-forme/1181,The-last-DAPIX-group-plenar-meeting-during-the-Polish-Presidency.html

Polner, M. (2011). Coordinated border management: From theory to practice. *World Customs Journal, 5*(2), 49–64.

Ratcliffe, J. H. (2003). Intelligence-led policing. *Trends and Issues in Crime and Criminal Justice, 248*, 1–6.

Regan, P. M., & Monahan, T. (2014). Fusion center accountability and intergovernmental information sharing. *Publius: The Journal of Federalism, 44*(3), 475–498.

République Française. (2000, September 23). L'accord entre le Gouvernement de la République française et le Gouvernement de la République fédérale d'Allemagne relatif à la coopération dans leurs zones frontalières entre les autorités de police et les autorités douanières (ensemble une déclaration), signé à Mondorf-les-Bains le 9 octobre 1997. *Journal Officiel de la Ré publique Française, 221*.

Rollins, J., O'Neil, S., & Masse, T. (2008). *Information and intelligence (including terrorism) fusion centers*. New York: Nova.

Schengen Acquis. (2000, September 22). Convention implementing the Schengen Agreement of 14 June 1985 between the Governments of the States of the Benelux Economic Union, the Federal Republic of Germany and the French Republic on the gradual abolition of checks at their common borders [Special Issue: The Schengen Acquis]. *Official Journal of the European Communities*.

Spapens, T. (2008). Policing a European Border Region: The case of the Meuse-Rhine Euroregion. In E. Guild & F. Geyer (Eds.), *Security versus justice?: Police and judicial cooperation in the European Union* (pp. 225–241). Aldershot: Ashgate.

Unisys Belgium. (2007). *Study of EU cross-border crisis networks (CBCN)* (Study Report 2007). Accessed March 27, 2015, from http://www.straz.gov.pl/data/other/jlscbcn_study_reportv1.00.pdf

Vallar, C. (2009). La coopération policière frontalière bilatérale: les centres de cooperation policière et douanière. L'exemple de Vintimille. *Cahiers de la sécurité, 8*, 135–140.

Wenda, G. (2014). Polizeiarbeit ohne Grenzen. *Öffentliche Sicherheit, 5–6*, 49–52.

Zaiotti, R. (2011). *Cultures of border control: Schengen and the evolution of European frontiers*. Chicago: The University of Chicago Press.

Towards More Security? The Involvement of the National Parliaments in the Reform of the Schengen Agreements

Angela Tacea

1 Introduction

The European Justice and Home Affairs (JHA) area touches upon two fundamental issues: on the one hand the national sovereignty and the State's capacity to control and to manage its territory and its population, and on the other hand the protection of fundamental human rights and civil liberties. Thus, the balance between liberty and security is at the core of the Area of Freedom, Security and Justice (AFSJ), which requires public debate and scrutiny. Until the Treaty of Lisbon, however, most policies in this area were adopted as primary legislation, with no parliamentary debate. As a result, the third pillar's decision-making procedures were considered lacking in terms of transparency and democracy. Moreover, the absence of parliamentary actors was seen to facilitate restrictions on civil liberties (Ludford 2004) and human rights protection (Peers 2011).

This argument is based on the well known "venue shopping" thesis (Guiraudon 2000, 2001), which remains an important line of analysis to European JHA policies despite increasing empirical challenges (Bendel et al. 2011; Bendel and Servent 2015). To recall, the hypothesis is that national governments have shifted control-oriented policies to the European level in order to escape domestic pressures and obstacles (Kaunert 2010; Bendel et al. 2011; Joppke 1998; Boswell 2003, 2008). So whereas, Interior ministers and administrative officials may tend to perceive questions of immigration and asylum with little regard to appeal rights or appellate authorities (House of Lords 1989: 16), from a long-term historical perspective parliaments were established in order to protect individuals from the "oppression

A. Tacea (✉)
Centre d'études européennes, Sciences Po Paris, ATER, Université Paris 2 Panthéon-Assas, 12 Place Panthéon, 75005 Paris, France
e-mail: angela.tacea@sciencespo.fr

R. Bossong, H. Carrapico (eds.), *EU Borders and Shifting Internal Security*,
DOI 10.1007/978-3-319-17560-7_10

of those who govern"[1] (France 1973). Consequently, if at the national level, parliaments may limit the infringement of fundamental rights by the executive branch, the lack of parliamentary accountability of European Justice and Home Affaires measures is likely to aggravate the security bias nature of the EU's Area of the AFSJ (Huysmans 2000; Bigo 1992, 1996; Guiraudon 2000, 2001; Bendel et al. 2011).

However, the Lisbon Treaty transforms, at least on paper, national parliaments into the 'winners' of the institutional reshaping of the EU's decision-making process (De Capitani 2010). National parliaments should actively contribute to the "good functioning of the Union" by staying informed on European policies, by ensuring that the subsidiarity and the proportionality principles are respected, by contributing to the Treaties' revisions, and by participating in the inter-parliamentary cooperation (European Union 2007). Moreover, the Treaty of Lisbon offers national parliaments the specific means and instruments to increase both ex ante and ex post accountability in the ASFJ. Before the formal policy-making in the Council of Interior Ministers, a facilitated Early Warning Mechanism[2] can be activated to check far-reaching proposals, such as envisaged creation of a European Public Prosecutor. After policy-making or when considering the implementation of EU measures in member states, national parliaments can use special evaluation rights, which could counteract executive empowerment and thus support a more balanced approach to a hitherto security-oriented policy field. But are national parliaments genuinely eager to use those new prerogatives? And is their activity really bringing a more human rights and civil liberties oriented perspective?

To address these questions, the chapter connects two bodies of literatures that rarely communicate with each other. The first one deals with national parliaments and European integration, and the second one with European policies of Justice and Home Affairs. Thus, the chapter develops two theoretical concepts, namely that of parliamentary scrutiny and that of frame, in order to explain the activity and influence of national parliaments in the Area of Freedom, Security and Justice. The reform of the Schengen agreement proposed by the European Commission in September 2011[3] serves as a rich case study for the purposes of this analysis. Beyond the renewed debate over the viability of Schengen in 2015, two reasons

[1] Own translation.

[2] The 'Early Warning Mechanism' entitles national parliaments to contest European draft legislative acts within a period of 8 weeks, if they consider the proposal breaches the principle of subsidiarity. Each parliament is assigned two votes divided between the two chambers in bicameral systems. Where reasoned opinions—the instrument through which national parliaments express their disagreement on a draft legislative act's non-compliance with the principle of subsidiarity—represent at least one third of all the votes allocated to the national parliaments, the draft proposal must be reviewed or if it is maintained its author shall justify the reasons for maintenance ("yellow card"). If the reasoned opinions represent at least a simple majority of the votes allocated to the national Parliaments the proposal must be reviewed. After such review, the Commission may decide to maintain, amend or withdraw the proposal ("orange card"). In the Area of Freedom, Security and Justice, this threshold is set at one quarter of the votes.

[3] COM/2011/559 and COM/2011/560.

motivate this choice: firstly, because the reform of the Schengen agreement has been a salient issue for national parliaments, a high degree of mobilisation is expected; secondly, the Schengen governance package refers to a broad range of issues, such as border control, immigration, and asylum. This breadth should allow one to make broader statements about the security orientation of the entire AFSJ field.

From a methodological perspective, the analysis adopts a most similar cases' approach, which can control for many alternative explanations. In particular, the role of the French and the Italian parliament are compared with regard to the same Schengen reform. Moreover, the two countries share many general parliamentary features, which can help to isolate specific factors for explaining observed differences in scrutiny work and policy outcomes. Both countries have bicameral parliaments and operate committee and document-based scrutiny systems. Parliamentary involvement in EU affairs and control of the executive is generally considered weak when compared to a number of other national parliaments. Finally, at the time of scrutinizing the Schengen package, both countries had right-wing governments, which allows assessing the influence of ideological and partisan variables on the framing of the parliamentary scrutiny.

The chapter proceeds as follows: the first section reviews and integrates the literatures on parliamentary adaptation to European integration and on parliamentary involvement in the AFSJ. Section 2 presents the theoretical model and hypotheses, which are then applied to the case study of the 2011 Schengen reform packaged in Sects. 3 and 4. In conclusion, it is argued that the new constitutional and institutional prerogatives of national parliaments introduced by the Lisbon Treaty have reduced the general predominance of the executives in shaping AFSJ policies. However, they have not significantly affected the security orientation of policies. In parliamentary democracies, national parliaments—or at least governmental majority parties in the parliament—do not act autonomously from their governments. Rather, their main role is to legitimize governments' actions in EU affairs.

2 'Bringing Back' the Lost Sovereignty: Parliamentary Scrutiny of the Area of Freedom, Security and Justice

The role of national parliaments in the European decision-making process has attracted increasing attention in recent years. Several studies dedicated to single national parliaments or to groups of parliaments (such as the Nordic or the new member states) analyzed the respective impact of European integration (Bergman and Damgaard 2000; Karlas 2011). More recently, a series of theoretical and comparative empirical studies classified national parliaments according to their institutional position in European affairs and explained their institutional variation (Maurer 2001; Bergman 1997, 2000; Winzen 2012, 2013; Karlas 2012; Raunio 2011; Auel et al. 2015a, b).

Meanwhile, the ASFJ has attracted increasing attention from both political sciences (Monar 2010; Bendel et al. 2011; Kaunert 2010; Trauner and Lavenex 2015) and legal perspectives (Peers 2011). Many studies have also sought to explain the trajectory of individual policy sectors, such as immigration (Guiraudon 2000), asylum (Boswell 2003; Bendel 2010; Reneman 2014), police cooperation (Bigo 1996; Fijnaut and Ouwerkerk 2010; Brown 2010) and data protection (Cammilleri-Subrenat and Levallois-Barth 2007; Brouwer 2009; Boehm 2012). However, to date very few studies have been dedicated to the involvement of national parliaments in the Area of Freedom, Security and Justice (Mitsilegas 2007; de Garibay 2010; Lodge 2001). Given the importance of national parliaments for the democratic legitimacy of EU policies and the progressive constitutionalisation of the AFSJ, this is an urgent and important research gap.

Moving back to the general literature on national parliaments, the first decades of the European integration were characterized by their absence from European decision-making. In the 1990s scholars attested a loss of power and sovereignty, and even feared a "de-parlamentariation" of the European governance (Norton 1996a). National parliaments seemed to have lost on a double level: constitutionally, through the transfer of their sovereignty to European institutions, and politically, as executives and administrative officials, dominate the European decision-making process (Raunio and Hix 2000: 147). This trend was even more striking in the AFSJ, which, until the abolition of the Pillar structure, remained in most of cases intergovernmental, allowing "national executives to agree on AFSJ measures without the usual level of control exercised by national parliaments and national courts" (Peers 2011). The ratification of conventions was the only role the European treaties foresaw for national parliaments under the old Third Pillar regime. Even if national parliaments could indeed veto a convention or an inter-governmental agreement, they would have not much of a say before that stage. In addition, they would have had no right in scrutinizing regular third pillar measures. This long-standing intergovernmental policy-making approach had deep consequences for policy outcomes. Instead of liberalizing the substance of this policy field, like some scholars had predicted (Favell 2001), the AFSJ developed "as a disruption to attempts to build an inclusive and tolerant Europe."(Bendel et al. 2011: 11).

However, national parliaments progressively regained their powers, first by means of national institutional reforms and the creation of European affairs committees (Norton 1996b; Maurer and Wessels 2001). Moreover, in some countries standing parliamentary committees, including Law and Home Affairs committees, developed an interest in European affairs and started to scrutinize European draft legislation in their area of competence (Raunio 2005). Since then, national parliaments have gained more formal rights, such as the right to information; the right to issue formal opinions on EU documents; the right to prevent ministers to vote in the Council until the parliamentary scrutiny has not been completed; or even the right to bind the ministers to the Parliament's position (Auel and Benz 2005; Maurer and Wessels 2001; O'Brennan and Raunio 2007).

As outlined in the beginning, the validity of intergovernmental explanations in the AFSJ field has been also increasingly questioned. While various areas the ASFJ, in particular migration policy, had been gradually communitarised before, the formal abolition of the pillared structure by the Lisbon Treaty extended regular decision-making and oversight further to police, crime and borders control.[4] Beyond the increasing accountability of member state governments, the Treaty of Lisbon expanded the opportunity of national parliaments to act as autonomous European actors in the AFSJ.[5] Those provisions should, at least in theory, have reduced the predominance of national executives (Bendel et al. 2011: 24), and should have triggered a higher protection of fundamental rights and civil liberties. Yet these remain largely empirically untested assumptions. In order to better understand the concrete effect of the Lisbon Treaty and how national parliaments act in the AFSJ field, the following develops more detailed analytical framework on parliamentary scrutiny and on the partisan framing of security issues.

2.1 Enforcing the Security Objectives Through Parliamentary Committees

Parliamentary scrutiny is defined as "the exercise of power by the legislative branch to control, influence, or monitor government decision-making." (Holzhacker 2002: 462) This definition sets a clear difference between the legislative, which has a "negative" role (Le Divellec 2011) of "controlling, influencing or monitoring" the government, and the executive, in charge of the elaboration of the decision-making. However, as it has been argued by the academic literature, this executive-legislative relation is more complex than a pure two-dimensional separation (King 1976). Most of the European parliamentary democracies are based on party government (Blondel and Cotta, 2000), thus it would be mistaken to talk about "parliaments" as an individual actor. The main line of contestation is usually placed between opposition parties and governing parties together with the government, and not between the parliament and the government (Miklin 2013: 26). While government supporting majorities would rarely want to go against the government in the parliamentary arena (Auel 2007), as this would be considered as a failure to reach a compromise between ministers and government backbenchers (Saalfeld 2005: 247), opposition parties that lack in informal ties with the government need a closer oversight of the government (Winzen 2013: 301). Opposition parties may have incentives to use the parliament as "one of the several public arenas, in which they

[4] Although the Treaty of Lisbon integrates police cooperation and criminal law to "community method" and extends the ordinary legislative procedure to legal migration and most criminal law and policing issues, unanimity in the Council is still maintained for certain sensitive issues. A "special legislative procedure" applies for some cases of criminal law, policing, family law and the adoption of measures related to passports. Peers S. (2011) *EU Justice and Home Affairs, Thrid Edition*, Oxford: Oxford University Press. In the same time, as regards policing and criminal law a joint right of initiative between the European Commission and Member states may apply and the Council benefits of an "appeal clause".

[5] Article 69 of the Lisbon Treaty establishes a lower threshold for the Early Warning Mechanism in AFSJ and the Europol and Eurojust activities shall be submitted to parliamentary scrutiny (Article 85§1 and 85§2 of the Lisbon Treaty).

expose and criticize governments in a continuous attempt to become government parties themselves", while governmental parties have more cooperative incentives and see themselves as part of the same team as the ministers (Saalfeld 2005: 345; Tacea and Thomas 2015). Thus, the conflict between the opposition, on the one hand, and the governmental parties and the government, on the other, will be expressed mainly at the plenary level.

However, when it comes to decision-making in European affairs, scholars show that they have been based on a rather "permissive consensus" (Lindberg and Scheingold 1970) that did not generate a high level of contestation within the parliamentary arena. The traditional cleavage between majority and opposition did not play any role with regards to the scrutiny of European affairs (O'Brennan and Raunio 2007). This idea is reinforced by the fact that EU matters rarely reach the plenary (Strøm et al. 2003) with the exception of very salient issues like financial frameworks, treaty reforms or European Council Meetings (Auel and Raunio 2014: 15). EU affairs are mainly dealt with at the committee level, where agreement is easier to reach. This point will be elaborated further below when turning to the detailed case study. Yet it might be argued that, when it comes to AFSJ measures, parliamentarians see themselves as representatives of the citizens and protectors of their rights against the executive (of whichever party), which would lead them to investigate the respective performance of the executive (King 1976: 19; Barbé 2009). In contrast, when the issue under scrutiny becomes electorally salient, the conflict between opposition and majority parties could still play an important role. Taken together, this lead to the following hypothesis

Hypothesis 1: If parliamentary scrutiny of EU affairs is conducted at the committee level, agreement between the majority and the opposition is facilitated. This supports the preferences of the executive, including security measures that affect civil liberties.

2.2 Partisan Framing of AFSJ Measures: Between Security and Civil Liberties

Policy images represent the ways in which a policy is understood and discussed (Baumgartner and Jones 1993: 25). In this sense, the AFSJ can be understood both in security and in liberty terms. Because policies are multi-dimensional, different policy actors focus their attention on different aspects of the policy (Baumgartner and Mahoney 2008: 436) and they can develop different policy frames by "selecting and highlighting some features of reality" while "omitting" or minimizing the importance of others. Selective framing can follow ideological and partisan motivations and can be used as a strategy against opponents to gain political advantage.

Conflict over European justice and home affairs clearly follows this pattern. Law and order issues appear to have more credibility in the manifestos of the right, which they therefore use in their competition with the mainstream left (Alonso and da Fonseca 2011; Green-Pedersen and Krogstrup 2008; Meguid 2005). Moreover, the more to the right a party stands, the more sceptical its attitude towards immigration typically is (Fischer 2003: 25). Mainstream right parties have often used anti-immigration feelings of the electorate as a means of maximizing votes (Alonso and da Fonseca 2011: 3; Brug and Spanje 2009), whereas the electorate of the left wing parties is more divided on the issues of immigration. Consequently, when immigration issues become "hot", left wing parties prefer either to adopt a position close to the median voter, to ignore the debate issues or to reformulate it in order to emphasize its own values (Alonso and da Fonseca 2011: 4). When radical right wing parties threaten the electoral stability on issues of immigration, law and order, social democratic parties experience further pressure to maintain their regular position on migration (Alonso and da Fonseca 2011; Akkerman 2012) and often accept a more restrictive approach, following the logic of "if you can't beat them, join them" (Bale et al. 2010: 413). However, this is not inevitable and left wing parties may also hold their position or diffuse the salience of the immigration and security issue (ibid.). Based on these considerations, we expect that:

Hypothesis 2: When right wing parties hold the executive power, the outcome of the parliamentary scrutiny in AFSJ area is security oriented. The position of the left wing parties depends on the level of conflict between the opposition and the majority parliamentary parties.

3 The Case of the Schengen Governance Package

The reform of Schengen governance was the direct consequence of a Franco-Italian conflict during spring 2011. Following the events of the Arab spring, migratory movements from North Africa to the geographically close Italy surged. In April 2011, approximately 25.867 (Maroni 2011) Tunisian migrants arrived on the Italian island of Lapedusa. Following an unsuccessful call for 'European solidarity' and to share the burden across the EU, the Minister of Interior, Roberto Maroni, unilaterally decided to issue 6-month temporary residence permits for humanitarian protection (Ministri 2011) to those North African immigrants who had arrived in Italy between the 1st and the 5th of April 2011. This allowed the respective migrants to travel around the Schengen area (Maroni 2011: 10). French authorities responded by reintroducing border controls and by blocking the trains travelling from Ventimiglia, the last Italian town before the French border (Guéant 2011).

Although the Franco-Italian dispute was resolved at a bilateral summit on 26 April 2011, its political impact was greater than expected. Following the summit in Rome, the Italian prime minister, Silvio Berlusconi, and the French president, Nicolas Sarkozy, addressed a joint letter to the European Commission and to the European Council, in which they asked for an "in-depth revision" of the European law regulating passport-free travel. In particular, they urged to consider amendments to emergency measures. By early summer, this initiative reflected in Council conclusions (European Council 2011) and led to a Commission proposal for two binding regulations. Taken together, they amounted to "a Union-based mechanism for the reintroduction of controls at the internal borders, where a Member State is persistently neglecting its obligation to control its section of the external border, and insofar as the circumstances would be such as to constitute a serious threat to public policy or to internal security at the Union or national level" (European Commission 2011a). The proposals would also transfer the competence to decide over the reintroduction of border control at the internal borders from the Member States to the European Commission (2011b).

It has been argued that the standoff between France and Italy over the Tunisian migrants was only the pretext for Schengen member states to vent their frustrations and to kick off reforms (Brady 2012: 33). However, during the negotiations over the Commission proposals, Italy was irritated by the lack of solidarity from its Schengen partners and was supportive of the proposed communitarisation. In contrast, the French government recoiled at empowering the European Commission in this manner and underlined the principle of subsidiarity, arguing that only member states could evaluate whether a given situation would qualify as threat to their national security, which would justify the re-introduction of border controls. In short, the Italian government wished for a complete transfer to the European Union, while the French government aimed at strengthening the Schengen governance without transferring sovereignty over border controls. Still, both countries framed the debate in security terms: in the Italian case, it mainly revolved around law and order, whereas in the French case, the focus was on selective immigration.

In light of the foregoing hypotheses on parliamentary control and scrutiny, this gives rise to the following question: To what extent did the French and the Italian parliaments follow the security oriented approach of their respective governments when considering the Schengen governance package? To address these questions, the following sections presents the insights from an extensive qualitative analysis of parliamentary debates as well as from interviews with involved parliamentary actors (MPs, rapporteurs, committee chairmen and administrative staff), which were systematically coded with AtlasTi.

3.1 The Impact of the Institutional Setting on the Politicisation of the Schengen Governance Reform

Most of the activities of the French and Italian parliaments for scrutinizing the proposed Schengen reform took place at the committee level. From a theoretical point of view, the analysis of committees is important because "parliamentary procedures may affect political outcomes and that is therefore desirable to shed light on the organization and functioning rules of legislatures" (Neuhold and Settembri 2009:129) Thus, the following section substantiates hypothesis 1 by showing that both the European affairs committees and the Constitutional/Law committees favoured a consensual decision over a very highly politicized issue. Two explanations for this finding are spelt out in detail. The first is proportional representation on committees. Minority parties are given the right to express their views, but the government strictly controls its committee majority and it tries to avoid any defeats at the committee stage (Strøm and Mattson 1995: 276). The second is the role of committee chairs and rapporteurs for particular dossiers who exercise leadership role during the scrutiny process.

3.1.1 Committee Procedural Aspects

While the overall size of committees varies across the countries and parliaments under investigation—i.e., two countries with two chambers each—the distribution of committee seats is always proportional to the relative size of the party groups. The party that holds the majority in the house also holds the majority in the committee (Table 1). While a difference in party composition exists between the French lower and upper house due to a difference in the timing of elections, legislative elections take place simultaneously in Italy, which leads to a clear domination of the governing party coalition in all parliamentary committees. At the same time, individual parliamentarians can serve in several committees, or specifically the European Affairs Committee (EAC) and the Law or Constitutional Affairs Committees that are of relevance to the Schengen governance reform. This applies to six MPs in the Assemblée Nationale and nine members of the French Sénat, as well as to of five Italian senators.[6] The practical result is their heightened role in the scrutiny process, whereby they become Europe specialists in the Law and Constitutional Committees.

Within committees, both the proceedings and the substance or output are shaped by two major positions of authority: the chairman and the rapporteur (Neuhold 2001; Mamadouh and Raunio 2003).[7] Although it is not explicitly regulated by the standing orders of the parliaments, majority parties control chair appointments. Committee chairs belong to the group that holds the majority in the chamber, thus they belong to the Union pour le Mouverment Populaire (UMP) in the Assemblée Nationale, to the Socialist group in the Sénat and to the government coalition in the Senato and Camera dei deputati.[8]

[6] Comparing to the French institutional rules, the Italian members of the Camera dei deputati cannot be in the same time members of the EAC and of another standing committee. On the contrary, the Senato's standing orders allow for double membership and five senators belong to both committees.

[7] Other key players may be highly influential, as party coordinator or vice-presidents, but they are not relevant for our case studies.

[8] While the committee chairs' distribution is proportional to the parliamentary party groups in the Senat, in the Assemblée Nationale, they are monopolised by the majority parties. The sole exceptions occurred in 1988 and in 2007 when Nicolas Sarkozy assigned the Finance Committee to the opposition party.

Table 1 The distribution of committee seats, chairman and rapporteurship among the parties within the European affairs and the Law Committees in 2011 in Italy and France

France

Committee	Total[a]	Party		Chair		Rapporteur		
		Opposition (PS)	Majority (UMP)	Name	Party	Name	Expertise	Party
Assemblée Nationale								
EAC	48	17	27	Pierre Lequiller	UMP	Didier Quentin	Diplomatic councillor of two Interior Ministers	UMP
Law	70	26	38	Jean-Luc Warsmann	UMP			
Sénat[b]								
EAC	36	14	18	Simon Sutour	PS	Catherine Tasca	No	PS
Law	49	25	23	Jean-Piere Sueur	PS			

Italy

Committee	Total	Party		Chair		Rapporteur		
		Opposition (PD)	Majority (PdL, Lega Nord, MpA)	Name	Party	Name	Expertise	Party
Camera dei deputati								
XIV—EAC	44	14	19	Mario Pescante	PdL	Annagrazia Calabria and Donato Bruno	No	PdL
Ist—Constitutional Affairs	47	15	24	Donato Bruno	PdL	Isidoro Gotardo	No	PdL
Senate								
XIV—EAC	47	13	22	Rossana Boldi	Lega Nord	Irene Aderenti	No	PdL
Ist—Constitutional Affairs	39	10	20	Carlo Vizzini	PdL	Filippo Saltamartini	Police officer	Lega Nord

Source: Author's compilation-houses' websites
[a]Six MPs belong both to the EAC and the Law Committee
[b]At the moment of scrutiny for the Schengen reform proposal, the opposition socialist party dominated the French Senate (senatorial elections took place in September 2011 and resulted in a reshuffle of the former UMP majority)

While expertise can constitute a significant stand-alone criterion for the appointment of a rapporteur,[9] in both the Italian and the French parliament the rapporteurs for the case of the Schengen governance package also belonged to the majority party (Table 1). Two rapporteurs, Didier Quentin for the Assemblée nationale and Hon Filippo Saltamartini for the Ist Committee of the Italian Senate, hold relevant expertise. The first one worked as a diplomatic councillor for two Interior Ministers, Charles Pasqua and Robert Pandraud, both of them important figures during the negotiations of the Schengen agreements and the implementation of the Schengen Convention. Hon Filippo Saltamartini was trained as a police officer and is a member of the Comitato parlamentare Schengen, Europol e immigrazione (Parliamentary Committee on Schengen, Europol and Immigration). In contrast, the French rapporteurs in the Sénat and the Italian rapporteurs in the Camera dei deputati did not have any specific expertise and were presumably selected for party political reasons. Yet this should not lead straight to the conclusions that rapporteurs can simply impose themselves and orient the policy outcome towards the majority party's and government's direction.

3.1.2 Reaching Consensus Through Committees

It is necessary to trace how scrutiny of the reform of the Schengen governance was actually conducted, in order to understand the contrasting tendencies for consensual decisions and party-political orientations. This will focus primarily on the French Assemblée Nationale, as it is the only example where a consensual committee decision contrasted with a politicized plenary debate. The analysis then turns to the Italian chambers, where a strategic use of the negotiations and consensus building behind the closed doors could be observed.

The two European Commission proposals for reforming Schengen were submitted to the Assemblée Nationale in September 2011. By the end of the same month, Didier Quentin, the rapporteur, submitted a report arguing that the proposal for common emergency rules on the temporary reintroduction of border controls breached the subsidiarity principle. He maintained that:

> Member States are better placed to assess the need for the reintroduction of border controls and should be able to re-establish them, subject to a verification *a posteriori* of the European Commission. (Quentin 2011)[10]

The European Affairs Committee unanimously approved the report. As the members of the Law Committee did not raise any objections, the reasoned opinion was considered as adopted by mid-October, before being debated on the 8th of November in the parliamentary plenary. The reform of the Schengen agreement

---

[9] A rapporteur is the MPs responsible for drafting the report on the issue handled by the committee. He/she plays an important role because he/she must compromise in order to accommodate the sometimes-divergent positions of the party groups in the committee Mamadouh V and Raunio T. (2003) The Committee System: Powers, Appointments and Report Allocation. *Journal of Common Market Studies* 41: 333–351.

[10] Own translation.

was a very salient issue for the Assemblée Nationale, not least it would be the first time that the full house debated a reasoned opinion on a European document. After meeting no contestation from the opposition in the respective scrutiny committees, the reasoned opinion and the attitude of the French government towards the Schengen governance received sharp criticism from Socialist party members in the open parliamentary debate.

This creates the puzzle why the attitude or political positioning of the same party could change so quickly and drastically from one stage of the legislative process to the next. The literature on legislative committees considers that allowing consensual committees to predetermine decisions could diffuse divided feelings about contentious issues (Strøm 1997: 162). The French case shows that the opposite tendency of deliberate politicisation after the committee stage. The minutes of the committee stage do not provide sufficient information to capture the extent to which there was no real opposition from the socialist party to the governing UMP, or simply a lack of interest. However, research interviews[11] with, as well as public statements by,[12] opposition politicians reveal a resigned attitude when being outvoted within a majority-controlled committee.

Aside from influencing the final contents of a report, antagonistic relation between majority and opposition parties often entails an oral and public expression (Cox and McCubbins 1993), which is frequently present in public parliamentary debates. So aside from control over policy outcomes, party leaders tend to politicize an issue when they see an appealing potential for their electorate (Hooghe and Marks 2009). Immigration policies are highly salient for the French voters (Dehousse and Tacea 2015), thus the criticism of the socialist party could be seen as a strategic partisan positioning, which shows their electorate that the party actually sticks to its electoral manifesto. This explains why the socialist party not only openly criticized the position of the government during the plenary session, but it also submitted three amendments that had not even been mentioned during the committee stage. The diverging pro-European position of the socialist party, which, to recall, also held the majority in the Sénat, was aptly summarized by this intervention to the debate:

> This conflict revealed the image of a malleable Europe, controlled by the will and interests of specific Member States. It is regrettable that the European Commission, the guardian of the treaties, has agreed to accept the French position rather than oppose it, as the European Parliament did. (. . .) It is time for our government—as for others—to understand that the issue of immigration in its many facets deserves a real European policy, a policy that is not limited to security measures, and does not designate the other as the enemy. (Braouezec 2011)[13]

[11] Interview with Jérôme Lambert, member of the EAC of the Assemblée Nationale and subsequent co-rapporteur on the Schengen dossier, Paris, 2 July 2013.

[12] Mathias Fekl, socialist MP in the Assemblée Nationale, intervention during the radio debate "L'Atelier du politique", 20 August 2012 "Godillots ou frondeurs; les élus de la majorité ont-ils le choix?", France culture.

[13] Own translation.

The Italian case provides the contrasting, but more regular case, of sustained consensus in committee deliberations. Here, the scrutiny of the Schengen governance reform started in the Camera dei deputati on October 2011, whereas the Senato became involved in September 2011. Except for some minor details, such as the duration of the autonomous reintroduction of border controls in case of emergency or the scope of the evaluation visit, all parties supported the proposed reforms within the Ist Committee (Constitutional law) and the XIV Committee (European affairs), both in the Camera dei deputati and in the Senato.

> Taking into account that the measures suggested in the proposal submitted for scrutiny are designed to address phenomena, such as illegal immigration and cross-border organised crime that exceed the scope and responsiveness capacity of the Member states; for reasons of effective control of the above-mentioned phenomena a coordinated action at the level of the European Union is required, which actively involves not only the national but especially the European institutions, so that Member States, such as Italy, which for geografical reasons are most exposed to migratory flows, may rely on the concrete solidarity of the European institutions and on a fair sharing of responsibility, including financial responsability;[14] (Camera dei deputati 2011)

So the high degree of consensus was not only due to the working style of the Italian EACs—where "conflicts are normally very low-key and nonpartisan and they engage in dialogue with the executive in an informal and cooperative atmosphere" (Bindi 2011: 95)—but reflected broader Italian interest in securing more European support for border and migration management. In particular, both chambers voted in favour of the Commission proposals to stave off a yellow card procedure for subsidiarity control:

> We made our plans because we were very, very close to a blocking minority threshold [in the Council] . . .there were two or three votes missing, so there was very easy for France and Germany to retrieve some countries[15]

What might be surprising is that the Northern League party group, well known for its anti-EU discourses (Ignazi 2008: 99) did not publicly oppose the communitarisation of the Schengen regime. According to Umberto Bossi, leader of the Northern League party (La Repubblica 2011), this would be the only way to "drain the bathtub and close the water tap". Similar views might have held by MPs beyond the far right:

> This proposal of the European Commission, according to which the reintroduction of border controls would no longer depend on individual member states but it would be collectively decided at the EU level, was seen by some MPs as a possibility to send those migrants away from the Italian territory[16]

[14] Own translation.

[15] Interview with a clerk from the European Affairs Committee of the Italian Senate, Rome, November 8, 2012.

[16] Interview with a clerk from the European Affairs Committee of the Italian Senate, Rome, November 8, 2012.

Moreover, the Northern League MPs involved in the scrutiny of the Schengen reform refused to speak about the negotiations because "the negotiations took place behind closed doors and too many details are delicate to tell and all was done informally."[17] Committees thus clearly favour a consensual decision and bridging of partisan antagonism. When sensitive issues are at stake, informal negotiations might take place even before the committee stage.

3.2 Partisan Identity of the Executive and the Balance Between the Freedom and Security

The final empirical part explores the second analytical hypothesis, and assesses the extent to which right wing parties in the parliament adopted a more security-oriented approach regarding the Schengen reform. At the same time, it will be traced whether left wing parties reframed the reform in more humanitarian terms or whether, pressured by the nationalistic discourse of the right wing parties and of the radical parties, they either avoided the debate or adopted the same restrictive discourse. To recall, in 2011 right wing parties/coalitions dominated the political dynamics in both the Italian and the French systems.

In a context of a 'security crisis' amplified by the media, debates in the Italian chambers revealed that Berlusconi's coalition parties framed their position regarding the reform of the Schengen governance in terms of law and order. The restrictive immigration and border control policies implemented through legislation were meant to create safe and peaceful conditions for the Italian society. Both the Il Popolo della Liberta (PdL) and the Lega Nord (LN) had made immigration a central issue in their electoral manifestos. The salience of immigration in the electoral manifestos was at 7.8 % for the LN, 3.58 % for the PdL and only 1.7 % for Partito democratico (PD) (de Carvalho 2014: 155). Both parties argued for more restrictive immigration measures and equated new arrivals with illegal immigration and criminality:

> ...this PD is the party that supported Prodi's government. The government that has opened the door to illegal immigrants decreasing the security of citizens and increasing crime and that has denied funding to the police. (La Repubblica 2008)[18]

During the parliamentary debates on the Schengen reform, PdL MPs refer to "tensions", "administrative difficulties", "safeguard of public order and internal security", "conflicts with the locals" to frame the need for transferring competences for border management to the European Commission. Moreover, both the rapporteur of the Ist Committee in the Camera dei deputati, Donato Bruno, and Hon Filippo Saltamartini, the rapporteur of the Ist Committee in the Senate, framed the issue of border controls in terms of control of "illegal immigration" and "cross-

[17] Discussion with one MP member of the Northern League, Rome, 12 November 2012.

[18] Own translation.

border organised crime and terrorism". Since Hon Filippo Saltamartini is a police officer, this security bias may appear obvious and confirm arguments that individual rapporteurs are key to the adoption of positions on European acts (Mamadouh and Raunio 2003: 344). However, it is also clear that PdL's rhetoric of criminalising illegal immigration follows the line of the government. Spurred by the LN, the PdL had previously introduced the "crime of irregular migration" (Italy 2009), which foresees a hefty fine between 5000€ and 10,000€ and expulsion, unless the accused applies for asylum (Art.10-bis). Although, the Constitutional Court criticised some aspects of the law, it did not question the framing of irregular migration in security terms, so that the PdL and LN could regard their position as mainstream.

In contrast, the centre-left party, PD adopted a more human rights oriented approach during the debate on the reform of the Schengen governance package. PD MPs referred to "democratic control of fundamental human rights", "free movement of persons", "fundamental values of liberty and security". Nevertheless, both mainstream parties, i.e., the PdL and PD, reached a consensus "on the frame of the management of inflows as temporary social phenomenon and irregular immigration as law and order issues" (de Carvalho 2014: 157). Thus, the final resolutions of the two chambers mainly reflect the security-oriented discourse: an assumed increased risk of organised crime and terrorism due to illegal migration should trigger European cooperation and solidarity. Independently from partisan affiliation, "European solidarity" is the leitmotiv of the parliamentary debates as well as committee reports on the reform of the Schengen governance, as Italian external borders are the external borders of the European Union and they should not be managed only at the national level.

Similar to Italy, debates on the reform of the Schengen agreements in the two chambers of the French parliament took place in the context of a hardening security discourse of the mainstream right. Since 2005, Nicolas Sarkozy appropriated issues that had commonly been raised by the far-right Front National (FN). However, contrary to Berlusconi and to the PdL-LN coalition, Sarkozy's and the UMP's immigration policy was not framed in terms of law and order, but rather in terms of national identity and selected labour immigration (de Carvalho 2014; de Carvalho and Geddes 2012). In the Assemblée Nationale UMP MPs dominantly used terms such as "national competences", "national sovereignty", "national security services", "border surveillance", "public order and internal security", or "subsidiarity breach". Whereas Italian MPs asked for European solidarity to manage migration flows that were seen as generators of public disorder and local tensions, UMP asked for complete discretion of EU member states in choosing their own migrants, and rejected the proposals of the European Commission. This reflected French governmental policy that sought a balance between "unwanted inflows" and "selected immigration".

Meanwhile, the socialist party kept a low profile regarding immigration and security issues. While Ségolène Royale criticized Nicolas Sarkozy's association between immigration and national identity, the party lacked a strategic position and distinct agenda on this topic (de Carvalho 2014: 117). Yet, the previous section already underlined the contrast between the lack of opposition at the committee level and the parliamentary plenaries, where socialist MPs reframed the discussions on the Schengen to challenge the right wing majority. For instance, Patrick Braouezec, member of the Socialist group in the Assemblée Nationale accused the government and its partisan majority of "restriction of the free movement of persons", of "fight against the immigration by police interpellation", of "irregular and discriminatory controls targeting a specific population: Tunisian immigrants". Moreover, he argued that the security framing of border controls is only an electoral strategy:

> Let's not be mistaken: this escalation of the migration policy of the Government aims, in essence, to allow a recurring display of strength vis-à-vis foreigners in an electioneering purpose. (..) From a value judgement, the responsibility of those who are the artisans of those measures is growing: sending a human being to a country at war or into poverty is not a trivial administrative act. (Braouezec 2011)[19]

In contrast to the consensual Italian case, the French socialist also used the terms of "European solidarity" as an opposition to the government, namely as an ideal of "real European immigration and asylum policy that shall not be limited only to security considerations". Yet in spite of those rhetorical arguments, the final reasoned opinion of the Assemblée nationale reflected dominant right-wing position on the nationalisation and the security framing of border controls, which also reflects the previous consensual reasoned opinion at the committee stage. Only the final resolution of the French Senate, where the socialist party held a majority, reflected a more rights oriented approach, according to which "an amendment to the Schengen border code cannot rely on an automatic assimilation of migration to a serious threat to public order and internal security" (Tasca 2011). Moreover, the resolution underlined that it would be a mistake to focus exclusively on border controls without aiming for common European policies on immigration and asylum.

4 Conclusions

This chapter shed light on the involvement of national parliaments in the scrutiny of AFSJ measures after the Treaty of Lisbon. Contrary to dominant assumptions in the academic literature, national parliaments do not necessarily limit the security-oriented policies of Interior ministers and do not necessarily bring a more human rights oriented approach to policies dealing with police cooperation, border controls and immigration. The Italian and the French parliamentary scrutiny process of the Schengen reform showed that governments can use the support of their parliaments to legitimize security-oriented policies, rather than trying to escape parliamentary accountability via the EU. In other words, parliamentary majorities tend to use the scrutiny instruments created by the Treaty of Lisbon in a cooperative manner with the executive.

[19] Own translation.

Opposition parties, however, may make the opportunity to publicly criticise the government, even if scrutiny outcomes remain dominantly shaped by the majority and dynamics at the committee stage—as set out in hypothesis 1. In both France and Italy, consensual institutional parliamentary settings provided the opportunity for governmental right wing majority parties to impose their views. This was accentuated by the leadership of certain MPs in the functions as committee chairman and rapporteurs. The analysis also confirmed standard assumptions about political parties and security issues, as specified in hypothesis 2. Right wing parties remain the main promoters of issues of law and order in their competition with left wing parties. Their security stance is reinforced by the presence of radical parties. Although left wing parties may reframe security policies using human rights and civil liberties arguments, in the cases under investigation they did not have enough resources or power to substantially modify the final resolutions of the chambers.

In sum, the Treaty of Lisbon may indeed have reduced the predominance of the executives by communitarising large parts of JHA cooperation. But, the granting of special rights to national parliaments has not automatically led to a modification of the substance of policy outcomes. However, in order to claim that the involvement of national parliaments do not bring a more balanced approach to the Area of Freedom, Security and Justice, further cross-country analysis is needed, something that will remain subject to extensive analysis of a future research.

References

Akkerman, T. (2012). Immigration policy and electoral competition in Western Europe. A fine-grained analysis of party positions over the past two decades. *Party Politics, 21*, 54–67.

Alonso, S., & da Fonseca, S. C. (2011). Immigration, left and right. *Party Politics, 18*, 865–884.

Auel, K. (2007). Democratic accountability and national parliaments: Redefining the impact of parliamentary scrutiny in EU affairs. *European Law Journal, 9*, 73–504.

Auel, K., & Benz, A. (2005). The politics of adaptation: Europeanisation of national parliamentary systems. *Journal of Legislative Studies, 11*, 372–393.

Auel, K., & Raunio, T. (2014). *National parliaments, electorates and EU affairs* (Series RPPS). Vienna: Institut für Höhere Studien (IHS)/Institute for Advanced Studies.

Auel, K., Rozenberg, O., & Tacea, A. (2015a). Fighting back? And if yes, how? Measuring parliamentary strength and activity in EU affairs. In C. Hefftler, C. Neuhold, O. Rozenberg, et al. (Eds.), *The Palgrave handbook on national parliaments and the European Union* (pp. 60–93). Basingstoke: Palgrave Macmillan.

Auel, K., Rozenberg, O., & Tacea, A. (2015b). To scrutinise or not to scrutinise? Explaining variation in EU-related activities in national parliaments. *West European Politics, 38*, 282–304.

Bale, T., Green-Pedersen, C., Krouwel, A., et al. (2010). If you can't beat them, join them? Explaining social democratic responses to the challenge from the populist radical right in Western Europe. *Political Studies, 58*, 410–426.

Barbé, V. (2009). *Le rôle du Parlement dans la protection des droits fondamentaux: étude comparative, Allemagne, France, Royaume-Uni*. Paris: LGDJ-Lextenso.

Baumgartner, F. R., & Jones, B. D. (1993). *Agendas and instability in American Politics*. Chicago: University of Chicago Press.

Baumgartner, F. R., & Mahoney, C. (2008). Forum section: The two faces of framing: Individual-level framing and collective issue definition in the European Union. *European Union Politics, 9*, 435–449.

Bendel, P. (2010). Asylum and migration policy. In M. Knodt & H. Heinelt (Eds.), *Policyfields in the European multi-level system. Instruments and strategies of European governance*. Nemos: Baden-Baden.

Bendel, P., Andreas Ette, U., & Parkes, R. (2011). *The Europeanization of control: Venues and outcomes of Eu justice and home affairs cooperation*. Münster: LIT.

Bendel, P., & Servent, A. R. (2015). *Challenging the "Liberal Constraint Thesis" through comparative policy analysis: The role of intra- and inter-institutional relations in asylum policies, border policies and (ir)regular migration*. 22nd International Conference of Europeanists. Paris: Council of European Studies.

Bergman, T. (1997). National parliaments and EU Affairs Committees: Notes on empirical variation and competing explanations. *Journal of European Public Policy, 4*, 373–387.

Bergman, T. (2000). The European Union as the next step of delegation and accountability. *European Journal of Political Research, 37*, 415–429.

Bergman, T., & Damgaard, E. (2000). Special issue: Delegation and accountability in European integration: The Nordic parliamentary democracies and the European Union. *The Journal of Legislative Studies, 6*, 1–174.

Bigo, D. (1992). *Europe des polices et de la sécurité intérieure*. Paris: Editions Complexes.

Bigo, D. (1996). *Polices en réseaux: l'expérience européenne*. Paris: Presse de Sciences Po.

Bindi, F. (2011). *Italy and the EU*. Washington DC: Brookings Press.

Blondel, J., & Cotta, M. (2000). *The nature of party government: A comparative European perspective*. New York, NY: St. Martin's Press.

Boehm, F. (2012). *Information sharing and data protection in the area of freedom, security and justice: Towards harmonised data protection principles for information exchange at EU-level*. Berlin, Heidelberg: Springer.

Boswell, C. (2003). The 'external dimension' of EU immigration and asylum policy. *International Affairs, 79*, 619–638.

Boswell, C. (2008). Evasion, reinterpretation and decoupling: European Commission responses to the 'external dimension' of immigration and asylum. *West European Politics, 31*, 491–512.

Brady, H. (2012). *Saving Schengen: How to protect passport-free travel in Europe*. London: Centre for European Reform Publications.

Braouezec, P. (2011). *Intervention during the Assemblée Nationale's plenary session of 8 November 2011*. Paris: Assemblée Nationale.

Brouwer, E. (2009). The EU passenger name record (PNR) system and human rights: Transferring passenger data or passenger freedom? *CEPS Working Document, 320*, 1–33.

Brown, D. (2010). *The European Union, counter terrorism and police co-operation, 1992–2007: Unsteady foundations?* Manchester: Manchester University Press.

Brug, W., & Spanje, J. (2009). Immigration, Europe and the 'new' cultural dimension. *European Journal of Political Research, 48*, 309–334.

Camera dei deputati, I. (2011). Resoconti Commissioni 1ª Commissione permanente (Affari Costituzionali, della Presidenza del Consiglio e interni), seduta Mercoledi 21 dicembre 2011. In Affari Costituzionali dPdCei (Ed.), *1ª Commissione permanente*. Rome: Camera dei deputati.

Cammilleri-Subrenat, A., & Levallois-Barth, C. (2007). *Sensitive data protection in the European Union*. Brussels: Bruylant.

Cox, G. W., & McCubbins, M. D. (1993). *Legislative leviathan: Party government in the House*. Berkeley: University of California Press.

De Capitani, E. (2010). The democratic accountability of the EU's area of freedom, security and justice ten years on. In E. Guild, S. Carrera, & A. Eggenschwiler (Eds.), *The area of freedom, security and justice ten years on: Successes and future challenges under the Stockholm Programme*. Brussels: Centre for European Policy Studies (CEPS).

de Carvalho, J. M. D. (2014). *Impact of extreme right parties on immigration policy: Comparing Britain, France and Italy*. London: Routledge.
de Carvalho, J. M. D., & Geddes, A. (2012). La politique d'immigration sous Sarkozy: le retour à l'identité nationale. In Y. Surel & J. Maillard (Eds.), *Les politiques publiques sous Sarkozy*. Paris: Les Presses de Sciences Po.
de Garibay, D. R. (2010). *Interparliamentary cooperation in the EU: A case study of justice and home affairs*. 60th Political Studies Association Annual Conference 'Sixty Years of Political Studies: Achievements and Futures'. Edinburgh, UK.
Dehousse, R., & Tacea, A. (2015). Europe in the 2012 French presidential election. In R. Brizzi & G. Goodliffe (Eds.), *France after 2012*. New York: Berghahn.
European Commission. (2011a). *Amended proposal for a regulation of the European Parliament and of the Council on the establishment of an evaluation and monitoring mechanism to verify the application of the Schengen acquis*. COM(2011)559 final. Brussels.
European Commission. (2011b). *Proposal for a regulation of the European Parliament and of the Council amending regulation (EC) No 562/2006 in order to provide for common rules on the temporary reintroduction of border control at internal borders in exceptional circumstances*. COM(2011)560 final. Brussels.
European Council. (2011). *Conclusions of the European Council 23/24 June 2011*. Brussels: European Council.
European Union. (2007). Treaty of Lisbon amending the Treaty on European Union and the Treaty establishing the European Community, signed at Lisbon, 13 December 2007. *Official Journal of the European Union C, 306*, 1–9.
Favell, A. (2001). *Philosophies of integration: Immigration and the idea of citizenship in France and Britain*. London: Macmillan.
Fijnaut, C., & Ouwerkerk, J. (2010). *The future of police and judicial cooperation in the European Union*. Leiden: Martinus Nijhoff.
Fischer, F. (2003). *Reframing public policy: Discursive politics and deliberative practices*. Oxford: Oxford University Press.
France. (1973). *La Constitution française du 24 juin 1973*. http://www.conseil-constitutionnel.fr/conseil-constitutionnel/francais/la-constitution/les-constitutions-de-la-france/constitution-du-24-juin-1793.5084.html
Green-Pedersen, C., & Krogstrup, J. (2008). Immigration as a political issue in Denmark and Sweden. *European Journal of Political Research, 47*, 610–634.
Guéant, C. (2011). Circulaire du Ministre de l'intérieur, de l'outre mer, des collectivités territoriales et de l'immigration à Mesdames et Messieurs les préfets, Monsieur le préfet de police, Monsieur le directeur générale de la police nationale, Monsieur le directeur général de la gandarmerie nationale—Autorisation de séjour délivrées à des ressortissants de pays tiers par les Etats membres de Schengen. In *Ministère de l'intérieur, de l'outre-mer, des collectivité s territoriales et de l'immigration*.
Guiraudon, V. (2000). European integration and migration policy: Vertical policy-making as venue shopping. *Journal of Common Market Studies, 38*, 251–271.
Guiraudon, V. (2001). The constitution of a European immigration policy domain: A political sociology approach. *Journal of European Public Policy, 10*, 263–282.
Holzhacker, R. (2002). National parliamentary scrutiny over EU issues: Comparing the goals and methods of governing and opposition parties. *European Union Politics, 3*, 459–479.
Hooghe, L., & Marks, G. (2009). Postfunctionalist theory of European integration: From permissive consensus to constraining dissensus. *British Journal of Political Science, 39*, 1–23.
House of Lords (1989). 1992: Border control of people. In *Communities SCoE*. London: HMSO (Her Majesty's Stationery Office).
Huysmans, J. (2000). The European Union and the securitization of migration. *Journal of Common Market Studies, 38*, 751–777.
Ignazi, P. (2008). *Partiti politici in Italia*. Bologna: Il mulino.
Italy. (2009). Legge 15 Luglio 2009, n. 94, Disposizioni in material di sicurezza pubblica.

Joppke, C. (1998). *Challenge to the nation-state: Immigration in Western Europe and the United States*. Oxford: Oxford Scholarship Online.
Karlas, J. (2011). Parliamentary control of EU affairs in Central and Eastern Europe: Explaining the variation. *Journal of European Public Policy, 18*, 258–273.
Karlas, J. (2012). National parliamentary control of EU affairs: Institutional design after enlargement. *West European Politics, 35*, 1095–1113.
Kaunert, C. (2010). *European internal security: Towards supranational governance in the area of freedom, security and justice*. Manchester: Manchester University Press, Palgrave Macmillan.
King, A. (1976). Modes of executive-legislative relations: Great Britain, France, and West Germany. *Legislative Studies Quarterly, 1*, 11–36.
La Repubblica. (2008). *Berlusconi, comizio a Milano attacco ai centristi e auguri a Veltroni*. Rome: La Repubblica.
La Repubblica. (2011). *Immigrati: Bossi, chiudere il rubinetto e svuotare la vasca*. Rome: La Repubblica.
Le Divellec, A. (2011). *Vers la fin du "parlementarisme négatif"? Une problématique introductive à l'étude des réformes constitutionnelles de 2008 Jus Politicum*. www.juspoliticum.com
Lindberg, L. N., & Scheingold, S. A. (1970). *Europe's would-be polity: Patterns of change in the European Community*. Englewood Cliffs: Prentice-Hall.
Lodge, J. (2001). Is there a useful role for National Parliaments? *German Law Journal, 2*.
Ludford, S. (2004). An EU JHA policy: What should it comprise ? In J. Apap (Ed.), *Justice and home affairs in the EU: Liberty and security issues after enlargement*. Cheltenham: Edward Elgar.
Mamadouh, V., & Raunio, T. (2003). The committee system: Powers, appointments and report allocation. *Journal of Common Market Studies, 41*, 333–351.
Maroni, R. (2011). *Informativa urgente del Governo sulle misure adottate in relazione all'eccezionale flusso di immigrazione verso l'isola di Lampedusa*. Camera dei deputati Seduta n. 460, XVI Legislatura ed. Roma: Camera dei deputati.
Maurer, A. (2001). National parliaments in the European architecture: From latecomers' adaptation towards permanent institutional change. In A. Maurer & W. Wessels (Eds.), *National parliaments on their ways to Europe: Losers or latecomers?* Nomos: Baden-Baden.
Maurer, A., & Wessels, W. (2001). *National parliaments on their ways to Europe: Losers or latecomers?* Baden-Baden: Nomos.
Meguid, B. M. (2005). Competition between unequals: The role of mainstream party strategy in Niche Party Success. *American Political Science Review, 99*, 347–359.
Miklin, E. (2013). Inter-parliamentary cooperation in EU affairs and the Austrian parliament: Empowering the opposition? *The Journal of Legislative Studies, 19*, 22–41.
Ministri PdCd. (2011). Decreto del Presidente del Consiglio dei Ministri 5 aprile 2011 Misure di protezione temporanea per i cittadini stranieri affluiti dai Paesi nordafricani. In Ministri PdCd Gazzetta Ufficiale n. 81, 8 April 2011. Rome.
Mitsilegas, V. (2007). Interparliamentary co-operation in EU justice and home affairs. In *Fifty years of interparliamentary cooperation*. Berlin: Bundersrat.
Monar, J. (2010). The institutional dimension of the European Union's area of freedom, security and justice. In *College of Europe studies*. Brussels, New York: P.I.E. P. Lang.
Neuhold, C. (2001). The "Legislative Backbone" keeping the institution upright? The role of European Parliament Committees in the EU policy-making process. *European Integration Online Papers (EIoP), 5*.
Neuhold, C., & Settembri, P. (2009). Achieving consensus through committees: Does the European parliament manage? *Journal of Common Market Studies, 47*, 127–151.
Norton, P. (1996a). Conclusion: Addressing the democratic deficit. In P. Norton (Ed.), *National parliaments and the European Union* (pp. 177–193). London: Frank Cass.
Norton, P. (1996b). *National parliaments and the European Union*. London: Frank Cass.
O'Brennan, J., & Raunio, T. (2007). *National parliaments within the enlarged European Union*. London: Routledge.

Peers, S. (2011). *EU justice and home affairs* (3rd ed.). Oxford: Oxford University Press.
Quentin, D. (2011). *Rapport d'information déposé par la Commission des Affaires Européennes sur la conformité au principe de subsidiarité de la proposition de règlement du Parlement européen et du Conseil modifiant le règlement (CE) no 562/2006 afin d'établir des règles communes relatives à la réintroduction temporaire du contrôle aux frontières intérieures dans des circonstances exceptionnelles. Commission des Affaires Européennes AN (COM [2011] 560 final/no E 6612).* Paris: Assemblée Nationale.
Raunio, T. (2005). Holding governments accountable in European affairs: Explaining cross-national variation. *Journal of Legislative Studies, 11*, 319–342.
Raunio, T. (2011). The gatekeepers of European integration? The functions of national parliaments in the EU political system. *Journal of European Integration, 33*, 303–322.
Raunio, T., & Hix, S. (2000). Backbenchers learn to fight back: European integration and parliamentary government. *West European Politics, 23*, 142–168.
Reneman, M. (2014). *EU asylum procedures and the right to an effective remedy.* Oxford: Hart Publishing.
Saalfeld, T. (2005). Deliberate delegation or abdication? Government backbenchers, ministers and European Union legislation. *Journal of Legislative Studies, 11*, 343–371.
Strøm, K. (1997). Rules, reasons, and routines: Legislative roles in parliamentary democracies. *Journal of Legislative Studies, 3*, 155–174.
Strøm, K., Bergmann, T., Müller, W., et al. (2003). *Democratic delegation and accountability: Cross-national patterns.* Oxford: Oxford University Press.
Strøm, K., & Mattson, I. (1995). Parliamentary committees. In H. Döring (Ed.), *Parliaments and majority rule in western democracies.* Frankfurt: Campus.
Tacea, A., & Thomas, A. (2015). The French parliament and the EU "Shadow control" through the government majority. In C. Hefftler, C. Neuhold, O. Rozenberg, et al. (Eds.), *The Palgrave handbook on national parliaments and the European Union* (pp. 170–190). Basingstoke/Hampshire: Palgrave Macmillan.
Tasca, C. (2011). Proposition de résolution de Mme Catherine Tasca concernant les contrôles temporaires aux frontières de l'espace Schengen, 17 novembre 2011. In *Commission des Affaires Européennes S.* Paris: Sénat.
Trauner, F., & Lavenex, S. (2015). A comparative view: Understanding and explaining policy change in the area of freedom, security and justice. In F. Trauner & A. Ripoll Servent (Eds.), *Policy change in the area of freedom, security and justice: How EU institutions matter.* London: Routledge.
Winzen, T. (2012). National parliamentary control of European Union affairs: A cross-national and longitudinal comparison. *West European Politics, 35*, 657–672.
Winzen, T. (2013). European integration and national parliamentary oversight institutions. *European Union Politics, 14*, 297–323.

Overcoming Liberal Constraints in the Field of Migrant Return: Re-establishing Political Control over Borders at the Cost of Fundamental Rights?

Anne Koch

1 Introduction

The recent EU refugee crisis accentuates the long-standing tensions that Western liberal states experience in the area of migration control. While border control measures aimed at deciding who is allowed to enter state territory and who is prevented from doing so are generally accepted as legitimate, the persistent challenge of large migratory flows has long shown the practical limitations of this sovereign power. As a secondary control measure, states therefore deploy instruments to remove undesired resident non-citizens from within their territories. However, deportation, i.e., the enforcement of legal obligations to leave the country, is often considered a "cruel power" (Gibney 2008: 147) on the part of the state. In liberal democracies, return enforcement has therefore traditionally been considered a measure of last resort, rather than a normal policy option.

Yet statistical data on deportations and so-called assisted voluntary returns indicate that over the course of the past two decades, Western countries have become more effective in their return implementation efforts. This restrictive trend in implementation is surprising, given that migrant return is normally considered a stronghold of so-called "liberal constraints" that preclude democratic governments from pursuing overly coercive practices. In general, liberal constraints manifest themselves in the long-term historical development of legal regimes or constitutions that protect individual rights, ensure the accountability of executive actors and pose a non-majoritarian counterweight to populist policies. Third country nationals, while excluded from the rights and privileges that come with citizenship, have benefitted from the evolution of international human rights law and cosmopolitan norms. On the basis of such national and international liberal norms,

A. Koch (✉)
Research Division Global Issues, German Institute for International and Security Affairs (SWP), Ludwigkirchplatz 3-4, 10719 Berlin, Germany
e-mail: Anne.Koch@swp-berlin.org

R. Bossong, H. Carrapico (eds.), *EU Borders and Shifting Internal Security*,
DOI 10.1007/978-3-319-17560-7_11

national courts have repeatedly curbed arbitrary administrative behaviour and created reliable processes for appeal, thereby increasing e.g., the chances of rejected asylum seekers to obtain legal residence status in Western societies. The forced transfer of asylum seekers from one EU member state to another under the Dublin regulation has repeatedly been questioned in court. In the case of forced returns to countries outside the EU, legal and normative obstacles are typically even more prohibitive.

Against this background of deepening liberal constraints, the increase in state-induced migrant returns warrants an explanation. This chapter reconsiders the concept and practice of liberal constraints. In other words, it shows how liberal constraints can operate on a broader practical level than legally defined civil rights. This accentuates the explanatory puzzle at first, as one needs to consider a much greater number of obstacles to the actions of state executives. At the same time, however, this practice-oriented perspective provides an insight into the ways in which public actors can circumvent or reinterpret normative prohibitions by making changes to their administrative practices and programmes. Furthermore, these practices are deeply embedded in international regimes. One example of this embeddedness is the formalized sharing of "best practices" that shapes all areas of modern governance, including migration and internal security. Here the effectiveness of practices, rather than their normative foundation, tends to become the central criterion across multiple layers of governance. These considerations raise new challenges with regard to the accountability of executives in transnational settings, and alert us to the need to pay attention to both local practices and their international diffusion.

This argument is illustrated through an analysis of return-related policy developments of the EU and the International Organisation for Migration (IOM). Responding to the interests of their member states, these organisations have supported a steady extension and institutionalisation of policies aimed at the return of unwanted foreigners, such as readmission agreements or so-called voluntary assisted returns programmes, in international settings. In order to set out the interdependence of several levels of governance in this process, the chapter then turns to the United Kingdom, which—despite its opt-out from the EU Schengen Agreement—illustrates the deep and regular interactions between national experimentation and international frameworks for restrictive migration and returns policies. The conclusion sets out the broader implications of these policy trends, arguing that the observed emphasis on return may over time undermine legal residents' chances of becoming more permanent rights-holders.

2 Liberal Constraints Revisited

The notion of liberal constraints can be traced back to Hollifield's argument that liberal democratic states are constrained in their immigration-related policy responses not just by the demands of markets for foreign labour, but also by an ongoing expansion of non-citizens' rights (Hollifield 1992: 94). Originally developed to explain the observation that states' migration policies are often less restrictive than called for by the public, this liberal constraint hypothesis has since given rise to a nuanced body of literature that highlights a range of factors constraining states' inclination to give in to popular demands in the formulation and implementation of policies aimed at migrants. The principle of *non-refoulement*, for instance, captures liberal democracies' alleged commitment to the right to life, to physical integrity, and to protection from torture. It therefore precludes domestic authorities from enforcing the return of certain vulnerable individuals. In particular, liberal democracies uphold children's rights and therefore typically refrain from pursuing the return of unaccompanied minors.

Against this empirical background, the term liberal constraint can refer to different analytical arguments. Both Boswell (2007) and Koopmans et al. (2012) distinguish between theories that locate the source of constraint at the international level, and theories that look towards the domestic context for explaining liberalizing trends in migration policies. So-called globalists highlight the relevance of international norms and legal frameworks. In particular, authors focus on the development of a global and European rights regime that creates both legal and normative obligations that individual states feel bound by (Jacobson 1996; Sassen 1999; Soysal 1994; Triadafilopoulos 2012).

This international variant of the liberal constraint hypothesis has been criticized by authors who question the independent effect of international norms and legal principles (Joppke 1998). The domestic variant of the liberal constraints hypothesis, put forward by such authors, highlights the constraining power of domestic institutions like courts and administrative agencies (Joppke 1998, 2001; Cornelius et al. 1994; Guiraudon 2002; Guiraudon and Lahav 2000; Hollifield 2000), or of public protests that contest the legitimacy of coercive state action vis-à-vis migrants (Ellermann 2009; Gibney and Hansen 2003; Gibney 2008).

Irrespective of their divergent accounts of where constraints on state sovereignty in the field of migration policy are situated, the different variants of the liberal constraints hypothesis share the assumption that there is an ongoing trajectory towards inclusiveness in liberal democratic states' policies towards migrants. While there is empirical evidence that this has taken place in the field of migrant integration, e.g., through the rights accorded to long-term resident foreigners by courts (Joppke 2001), more recent developments in the realm of state-induced migrant return run counter to this expectation: Statistical data from national authorities implicated in state-induced migrant return indicate that over the course of the past 25 years, the percentage of rejected asylum seekers eventually removed from the country has steadily increased.[1]

[1] Reliable data in Germany reach back to 1990, in the UK to 1992. In 1990, Germany rejected 116,628 asylum applications and returned 21,122 individuals either through force or through so-called assisted voluntary return schemes. In 2012, Germany issued 30,700 negative asylum decisions and returned 15,197 individuals. In 1992, the UK rejected 18,465 asylum applications and returned 6184 individuals. In 2012, the UK rejected 10,853 asylum applications and returned 24,566 individuals. Statistical data on state-induced migrant return from 1990 to 2012 (Germany) and 1992 to 2012 (UK) have been obtained from the UK Border Agency, the German Federal Police, IOM Germany and IOM UK and are on file with the author.

The puzzle is further complicated by the fact that domestic authorities encounter practical obstacles to their implementation efforts when they undertake return initiatives targeted at specific groups of non-citizens. The full range of obstacles to state-induced migrant return is thus broader than is normally recognized by proponents of the liberal constraints hypothesis. It comprises not only courts equipped with strong powers of judicial review and public protests, but also practical matters like uncooperative countries of origin, the sheer cost of return enforcement, instances of absconding, and the fact that potential returnees refuse to disclose their nationality or pretend to be nationals of a different state than their own. These observations call for a reconsideration of the ways in which liberal constraints affect policy-making decisions, and a more nuanced account of when and how they gain traction. In particular, there is a need to complement existing legal and institutional accounts with a practice-centred dimension.

At first sight, the practical obstacles recounted above seem to lie outside the scope of liberal constraints. Yet upon closer consideration, most if not all of the overtly "practical" obstacles encountered by state authorities can be traced back to the rights-based identity of liberal democratic states. Uncooperative countries of origin and difficulties in the identification of potential returnees, for instance, only pose a problem for governments unwilling to simply dump unwanted non-citizens across the border without any further questions being asked. Further, potential deportees have greater chances of absconding in countries where they can appeal against their detention, and where domestic authorities are required to give prior notice before forced return proceedings are initiated. The high cost of return enforcement, in turn, partly arises due to the high standards that return procedures in liberal democracies have to adhere to.

This discussion indicates that the different practical obstacles that liberal democracies encounter in the pursuit of restrictive migration control have a rights-based dimension. Conversely, overtly rights-based obstacles also entail a practical dimension: If appropriate medical care or reception conditions for unaccompanied minors can be established in the country of origin, the legal constraints on sending back children or people suffering from specific illnesses may cease to exist. If safe havens can be installed, the principle of non-refoulement may not apply any more. And if individuals can be prevented from developing social ties in their country of residence, they are less likely to accrue legal claims to belonging.

With regard to this latter factor, the element of time also plays an important role: If overtly practical obstacles hinder the return of individuals for extended periods of time, the likelihood increases that individuals become involved in their local communities, get married, have children, these children go to school and in turn become involved in the community. The ensuing degree of social integration typically amounts to a rights-based obstacle to coercive return. Practical obstacles may thus give rise to or exacerbate legal obstacles.

The different manifestations of liberal constraints are thus interlinked: Not only do they give rise to one another; but practical obstacles can also be reframed as rights-based ones and vice versa. This perspective opens up the notion of liberal constraints to a more differentiated analysis. Rather than being conceptualized as stable entities in response to which authorities in liberal democracies have to back down and abandon their restrictive policy objectives, it presents so-called liberal constraints as malleable phenomena that can be reframed as practical obstacles, and that domestic authorities can thus engage with and seek to overcome at multiple levels of governance.

3 Migrant Return at the International Level

This conceptual discussion allows us to break out of dichotomous discussions over the repressive or fundamental-rights promoting nature of international institutions. Instead, we are directed to the contrast between formal legal frameworks and other, more practice-oriented strategies that seek to reconcile conflicting normative and political demands. In other words, the engagement of international actors in the governance of migrant return can reduce the material and political costs of return implementation for domestic governments. First, international fora, both intergovernmental and supranational, serve as venues for policy harmonization and for the pooling of political resources in the field of migrant return. The EU in particular has driven forward the development of formalized return channels, return-specific funding streams, and a vision of an integrated management of return that stimulates demand for return-specific services. Second, domestic governments' repeated demands for international actors' assistance in return implementation have over time led to the building up of return-specific expertise and capacities at the international level. This is especially apparent in the case of the IOM that relies on project-based funding and whose activities are particularly demand-driven. While a variety of other actors, including intergovernmental consultative forums like the Budapest Process and international organizations like UNHCR are implicated in the regulation and implementation of state-induced migrant return, this chapter therefore focuses on the role of the EU and the IOM's role in the governance of migrant return.

3.1 The European Union: Promoting and Financing an Integrated Management of Return

Driven by the double imperative of stepping up migration control and setting common rights-based standards for implementation, the idea of migrant return has over time assumed a central place in EU member states' and prospective member states' overall migration policy. In this section, I outline the evolution of the EU's competences in the field of migrant return,[2] highlighting in particular its

[2] Cf. Giuffre (2011) for a detailed account of how EU immigration and asylum policy has become progressively consolidated through the treaties of Maastricht, Amsterdam and Lisbon.

role in the negotiation of readmission agreements, its promotion of an integrated return management, and the accordant setting up of the EU Return Fund.

3.1.1 EU-Level Readmission Agreements

Under the Treaty of Maastricht, questions concerning visa, immigration and asylum policy were subject to intergovernmental cooperation under the third pillar of the EU ("Justice and Home Affairs").[3] With the entry into force of the Amsterdam Treaty in May 1999, these matters became Community competence (Léonard 2010; Kaunert 2005). The relevant amendments to the Treaty conferred upon the EU the power to address the issue of "illegal immigration and illegal residence, including repatriation of illegal residents" [article 63(3)b TEC]. Despite not entailing the term readmission, this article was interpreted as equipping the EU with the mandate to conclude readmission agreements with countries of origin (Schieffer 2003: 349; Panizzon 2012: 3).[4] The Tampere Programme of October 1999 set out measures for the implementation of the Amsterdam Treaty and called upon EU member states to increase their efforts with regard to readmission (European Council 1999: A(VI)). Accordingly, negotiations for the first readmission agreements between the EU and Pakistan, Morocco, Sri Lanka and Russia were initiated in September 2000.[5]

The EU defines readmission agreements as "agreement[s] setting out the practical procedures and modes of transportation for the return and readmission by the contracting parties of persons illegally residing on the territory of one of the contracting parties" (European Commission 2002: 26).[6] While early agreements primarily clarified the conditions—e.g., in terms of documentation—that have to be met in order for a country of origin to accept back its own nationals, the conclusions of the European Council in Seville in June 2002 called for the extension of EU-level readmission agreements to third-country nationals:

> readmission by third countries should include that of their own nationals unlawfully present in a Member State and, under the same conditions, that of other countries' nationals who can be shown to have passed through the country in question (Council of the European Union 2002: 9).

The inclusion of third country nationals in readmission agreements constituted a significant innovation vis-à-vis EU member states' existing bilateral readmission

[3] The Treaty of Maastricht, and subsequently the Treaty of Amsterdam, revised the Treaty of European Community (TEC).

[4] Prior to 1999, the EU had included readmission clauses in other treaties with third countries. These clauses, however, were less detailed than the dedicated readmission agreements initiated after the coming into force of the Amsterdam Treaty (Coleman 2009: 1).

[5] As of June 2011, the EU had concluded readmission agreements with 13 third countries, and received a mandate to conduct negotiations with a further six (http://ec.europa.eu/dgs/home-affairs/what-we-do/policies/pdf/eu_readmission_agreements_en.pdf) (last accessed 08/12/12).

[6] Coleman (2009) provides a comprehensive account of the history and the contents of EU readmission agreements.

agreements. It illustrates the increase in bargaining power that came with the EU as an institutional entity leading negotiations in the realm of return: Beyond the EU having greater political weight than individual member states, it was also able to advance unique incentives, e.g., through granting facilitated access to Schengen visa to citizens from countries that have signed a readmission agreement. This has enabled the conclusion of readmission agreements with powerful states such as Russia. A 2011 report by the German Federal Council, for instance, highlights the added value that the inclusion of third country nationals in EU readmission agreements has for domestic governments in saying that while it is generally difficult to identify foreigners' nationality against their will, it is often much easier to find out their last country of residence or transit.[7]

EU readmission agreements have clearly increased member states' chances of returning unwanted non-citizens, and are therefore considered central to their efforts to control irregular migration (Panizzon 2012: 2).[8] However, EU readmission agreements are not the only return-specific instruments originating at the European level.

3.1.2 Towards a Comprehensive European Return Programme

A 2002 Green Paper on a community return policy regarding irregular residents called for a comprehensive European return programme that would entail both voluntary and enforced elements, prioritizing the former over the latter whenever possible (European Commission 2002). In line with this, the early 2000s saw a flurry of European policy initiatives both pertaining to migration broadly,[9] and to the field of migrant return more specifically. Between 2001 and 2005, the following return-related instruments were adopted: (1) Council Directive 2001/40/EC on the mutual recognition of decisions on the expulsion of third country nationals (Council of the European Union 2001), (2) Council Directive 2003/110/EC on assistance in cases of transit for the purposes of removal by air (Council of the European Union 2003), (3) Council Decision 2004/573/EC on the organization of joint flights for the removal of third country nationals (Council of the European Union 2004b), (4) Council Decision 2004/191/EC on financing expulsion measures (Council of the European Union 2004a), and (5) Council Decision 2005/267/EC establishing a secure web-based information and coordination network for member states' migration management services (Council of the European Union 2005). Following on from this, EU-level developments pertaining to migrant return have followed two distinct trajectories. On the one hand, efforts have been undertaken to integrate

[7] Bundesrat (2011), *Mitteilung der Kommission an das Europäische Parlament und den Rat: Evaluierung der EU-Rückübernahmeabkommen*, Drucksache 112/1/11: 2.

[8] However, one of the few existing in-depth case studies of the operation of an EU readmission agreement comes to the conclusion that "the predominant focus of the EU return policy on the effectiveness and efficiency of returns has left little room for safeguarding the human rights of the returnees" (Dedja 2012: 95).

[9] For an overview of EU-level developments pertaining to migration more broadly, cf. Menz (2009: 54–55).

return and readmission into broader EU foreign policy.[10] On the other hand, structures have been developed to facilitate the operational use of existing readmission agreements while adhering to basic human rights standards.

On the first count, the integration of return and readmission into EU foreign policy, the European Commission developed the concept of so-called "mobility partnerships". First outlined in 2006, mobility partnerships do not replace readmission agreements but rather subsume them in a comprehensive package that aims to provide an "overall framework for managing various forms of legal movement between the EU and third countries (. . .) once certain conditions have been met, such as cooperation on illegal migration and effective mechanisms for readmission" (European Commission 2006: 7). This concept is linked to new insights into the developmental potential of migration: Through mobility partnerships, the EU essentially offers countries of origin benefits in form of labour quotas, temporary migration schemes, and reintegration assistance. In return for this, it demands stricter controls of irregular movement and more cooperation in the readmission of both country of origin nationals and third country nationals (European Commission 2007a).[11] So far, the EU has concluded mobility partnerships with six countries (Cape Verde, Moldova, Georgia, Armenia, Azerbaijan and Morocco), and discussions are underway with a number of other countries, including Tunisia and Jordan.

On the second count, the operationalization of existing readmission agreements, the European Council called for the setting up of a separate fund dedicated to return-related activities (both voluntary and coercive), and for the adoption of a directive that would harmonize standards for returning irregular migrants across the EU (European Council 2005). Both of these plans came to fruition in 2008: The European Return Fund, established under the EU's General Programme "Solidarity and Management of Migration Flows", comprised a budget of 676 million Euro for return-related activities in EU member states during the years 2008–2013. The Fund was dedicated to the overall improvement of return management through domestic return initiatives, to joint return operations, and to reintegration assistance in countries of origin. However, its relevance extended beyond its mere financial volume in that it set out and promoted a vision of an "integrated return management" that comprised both assisted voluntary and forced returns (European Parliament and Council of the European Union 2007).

The EU Directive 2008/115/EC on common standards and procedures in Member States for returning illegally staying third-country nationals (EU Return Directive) was adopted in December 2008 (European Parliament and Council of the European Union 2008). While it improves the situation of deportees in countries

[10] This had been called for as early as the 2001 European Council meeting in Laeken (European Council 2001: 11).

[11] For more recent information, cf. also http://ec.europa.eu/dgs/home-affairs/what-we-do/policies/international-affairs/global-approach-to-migration/specific-tools/index_en.htm (last accessed 30 July 2013).

whose laws previously did not stipulate a maximum length of detention, the opposite effect has also taken place: Some EU member states have used the transposition of the directive as a welcome opportunity to increase the maximum length of detention in their national laws (Pollet 2011: 27). Other restrictive provisions include the retention of child detention (article 17) and of re-entry bans following voluntary departure (article 11). Beyond these restrictive elements, however, the EU Return Directive stipulates that under normal circumstances, voluntary return ought to be preferred over forced return (article 7), and that member states have to provide for an effective forced-return monitoring system [article 8(6)]. From a rights-based perspective, the directive is thus a mixed bag. Beyond any normative assessment, however, it arguably makes an important contribution to establishing state-induced migrant return as a policy field governed by EU-level standards. Further, it requires member states to establish administrative and operational structures for the realization of the processes it envisages, e.g., in the field of voluntary return.

Taken together, the different EU-level developments in the field of return and readmission amount to an institutional framework that stimulates new demand for return-related services: On the one hand, the growing number of readmission agreements allows domestic authorities to initiate more removals to countries previously deemed problematic. Second, the prioritization of voluntary over enforced return entailed in EU legislation puts member states under an obligation to offer assisted voluntary return schemes. Further, the legislative requirement of forced return monitoring has created a demand for targeted monitoring services. The implementation of these different objectives has been facilitated through the EU Return Fund, and similar funds have been attributed to the field of return under the new Asylum and Migration Fund that covers the period 2014–2020. State demand and the availability of funding opportunities turned migrant return into an increasingly lucrative business.

3.2 The International Organization for Migration: Promoting the Complementary Nature of Assisted Voluntary and Enforced Returns

The IOM is an intergovernmental organization that offers "migration management services" to governments in the fields of labour migration, refugee resettlement, and migrant return. The IOM's predecessor, the Provisional Intergovernmental Committee for the Movement of Migrants from Europe (PICMME), was established in 1951 in order to arrange for the return and resettlement of those uprooted by the Second World War. A number of subsequent name changes followed, from PICMME to the Intergovernmental Committee for European Migration (ICEM) in 1952, to the Intergovernmental Committee for Migration (ICM) in 1980, and finally the International Organization for Migration (IOM) in 1989. The narrative of the organization's history presented on the IOM's own website links these changes to the organization's transition "from logistics agency to migration agency"[12]—an identity that is actively promoted through the slogan "Migration Management for the Benefit of All" (IOM 2013). While PICMME counted 16 founding members, by 2012 the IOM's membership had grown to 149 states. Unlike UNHCR, it is not based on an international convention and therefore "lacks a clear and consistent migrant protection mandate" (Betts 2013: 196).

3.2.1 Providing an Alternative to Forced Return

The IOM's involvement in migrant return focuses on the administration and implementation of so-called assisted voluntary return (AVR) schemes. These schemes facilitate the return of rejected asylum seekers and in some countries also that of irregular migrants to their countries of origin. They typically arrange return flights, offer cash allowances, and in some cases also provide reintegration assistance upon return to migrants who have no right to remain in their current country of residence. In addition, AVR schemes often entail a temporary re-entry ban. They therefore allow for the "orderly return" of unwanted migrants and avoid the use of outright coercion. Beyond arguably being more humane than forced returns, AVRs are also far less costly. In combination, these two qualities make them uniquely appealing to states wishing to increase their rate of return implementation, and constitute a unique selling point for the IOM.

The IOM piloted its first AVR scheme in Germany in 1979. The service became established in the German context and was copied by Belgium in 1984 and the Netherlands in 1992. During the second half of the 1990s, demand for return services increased dramatically due to the large refugee movements in Europe that arose from the wars in the former Yugoslavia. The large demand for AVRs from German authorities in particular (from 11,500 in 1995 to 76,100 in 1997 and 102,400 in 1998) accelerated the growth of the IOM as a whole. By 2000, the agency spent 34.4 % of its operational budget on return-related activities (IOM 2002).

This increase in AVR took place during a period when the agency's chief executives were committed to overall organizational expansion. In 1995, when the IOM counted 51 state parties, the organization's governing body adopted a strategic planning document that promoted an expansion of the organization's membership base in order to "forge an IOM that is the leading global organization on migration by the year 2000" (IOM 1995). The strategy document singled out irregular migration as "requiring special attention on the part of a migration organization" and identified assisted return programmes as an important response to this growing concern (ibid.). IOM Director General McKinley in 1998 restated IOM's role as a service organization for national governments, and again highlighted its return-related activities:

> Services are the most basic answer to the simple question—one I often hear—"Just what does IOM do?". It was through efficient provision of services (…) that IOM built its

[12] Cf. http://www.iom.int/cms/en/sites/iom/home/about-iom-1/history.html (last accessed 19 October 2012).

> reputation over the decades. (...) IOM intends to make a serious, intensely consultative effort among *all* interested governments to get voluntary return programmes moving. (IOM 1998)

These plans for expansion matched—and were arguably triggered by—the immense demand for AVR in Germany and other European countries hosting refugees from the former Yugoslavia. While Germany, Belgium and the Netherlands expanded their existing AVR schemes to promote the return of Yugoslav refugees, Austria established its first AVR scheme in 1996, and the UK introduced a pilot AVR scheme aimed specifically at Kosovar refugees in 1999, which is discussed further below. Once the majority of refugees from the former Yugoslavia had either been returned or had been granted legal residency status in their respective host country, the previous sharp increase in return demand was followed by a similarly sharp decrease, evidenced by the drop in return budget from 91.5 million USD in 2000 to 26.8 million USD in 2001 (IOM 2002: 4).

The building up of considerable return capacities at the IOM during the late 1990s had included the hiring and training of additional staff. Some of these trained return experts, when no longer needed in countries like Germany, oversaw the setting up of pilot AVR schemes in other European countries. So instead of operating large AVR schemes in a small number of countries, the agency turned to operating smaller schemes in a far larger number of countries. Accordingly, The IOM financial reports for the years 2003–2006 and 2008–2010 list "expanded return activities from Europe" among the key factors contributing to the increase in its overall operational budget (IOM 2004, 2005, 2006, 2007, 2009, 2010, 2011). The number of countries with IOM-administered AVR schemes grew from 5 in 1995 to 13 in 2001 and 35 in 201. Having originally been restricted to Western Europe, the IOM's return schemes now include an increasing number of Eastern European countries and, most recently, non-European states.

Beyond this mere geographical spread, it is worth looking at the institutional set-up of AVR in different states. While in countries that established AVR schemes during the 1970s and 1980s (i.e., Germany and Belgium), assisted voluntary returns and enforced returns are administered by strictly separate branches of the bureaucracy, countries that have established similar schemes more recently (e.g., Canada, Australia and most Eastern European countries) assign oversight responsibilities for both pathways to the same domestic authority.[13] The Canadian government, for instance, openly states that its pilot AVR programme will lead to an increase in the overall return rate of rejected asylum seekers: "By increasing the number of voluntary returns and redirecting these lower-risk cases to the IOM, the AVRR pilot will free up vital Canada Border Services Agency (CBSA) enforcement resources for higher priority removal cases." Rather than AVR constituting an

[13] This analysis is based on overviews of individual countries' migration-related institutions provided by the European Migration Network (EMN). According to this source, the following countries operate forced and assisted voluntary returns under the same institutional umbrella, e.g., their respective Interior Ministry: Austria, Bulgaria, Czech Republic, Greece, Hungary, Ireland, Luxembourg, Netherlands, Slovakia, Slovenia, and the UK.

alternative to deportation, the joint administration of AVR and deportations tends to be used to increase the overall number of returns, including forced ones. This is particularly important in contexts where domestic authorities try to meet publically stated return targets (e.g., the UK and France).

4 Adapting Removal Procedures in the UK

The following part traces developments in state-induced migrant return in a national setting. The UK constitutes a particularly instructive case in that it has long pursued restrictive migration policies while simultaneously constituting a key destination for migrants from around the world. In this context, the question of state-induced migrant return has taken on particular salience. Furthermore, it shows that even the UK that stands out among EU member states as being particularly protective of its national sovereignty and security system is deeply involved in international programmes and transnational exchanges on migration and border control.

4.1 Promoting Alternatives to Forced Return

In 1999, in the context of wider consultations on the return of Kosovar asylum seekers from the UK to Kosovo, the UK government for the first time entered into discussions with the IOM on the topic of voluntary return, and eventually established an IOM-administered assisted voluntary return (AVR) scheme.[14] The first Kosovo-bound return flights left the UK in late July 1999, just over a month after NATO airstrikes had ended. 1570 Kosovars chose to return under this scheme over the course of the next 6 months.[15] The fact that these returns took place before the 1-year Exceptional Leave to Remain that Kosovar refugees had been granted ran out indicates that these early IOM-assisted returns from the UK were of a genuinely voluntary nature.

However, quick returns were also clearly incentivized. On the one hand, the relocation grant offered to participants of the IOM-administered AVR scheme ran out after a 12-month period. On the other hand, the government made it clear that it would enforce the return of those who did not participate in the AVR scheme.[16] This was done with reference to UNHCR's assessment that return was safe for the majority of Kosovo Albanians, and further backed up by the argument that numerous voluntary returns had already taken place.[17] Once the temporary IOM-administered AVR scheme to Kosovo ran out, it was replaced by a general

[14] Cf. House of Commons Debate, 21 June 1999, vol 333 c265W.

[15] Cf. House of Commons Debate, 2 February 2000, vol 343 c600W.

[16] Cf. House of Commons Debate, 18 May 2000, vol 350 cc216-8W.

[17] Cf. House of Commons Debate, 20 June 2000, vol 352 cc146-7W.

and permanent IOM-administered AVR scheme open to all nationalities—the so-called Voluntary Assisted Return Programme (VARP). This constitutes an example of how a return policy tool that had initially been adopted as a measure to address a one-off situation became stabilized and institutionalized.

Beyond this general AVR scheme, the UK adopted further specialized schemes that aimed at incentivizing returns to specific countries, and were typically installed in tandem with new efforts to implement forced returns. This was the case for Afghanistan, Somalia, and Zimbabwe—three countries that around the year 2000, the UK government deemed too unsafe to allow for forced returns. While asylum applicants from Afghanistan had for several years been granted Exceptional Leave to Remain as a matter of principle, this changed during the early 2000s—which stood in stark contrast to the post 9/11 US military campaign against the Taliban, which the UK supported from the outset. As the number of new asylum applications from Afghanistan increased, the government focused on incentivizing voluntary returns prior to the conclusion of asylum proceedings:

> A package of assistance is being introduced for a trial six month period to assist reintegration of those Afghans who return home voluntarily. It will be offered to those who have, on 14 August 2002, asylum claims awaiting decision or appeal, or who have received exceptional leave to remain. Payments of £600 for individuals and up to £2500 for families, to be paid after departure, reflect an equitable payment to make return to Afghanistan sustainable.[18]

In October 2002, the UK government, the Transitional Islamic State of Afghanistan and UNHCR signed a tripartite return agreement. From April 2003 onwards, rejected asylum seekers' returns from the UK to Afghanistan were enforced. Similar to Afghans, rejected Somali asylum seekers were increasingly expected to return, notwithstanding the fact that conditions in Somalia were considered too unsafe to allow for forced returns. In late 2002, a government representative stated:

> Asylum seekers from Somalia who are found not to be in need of international protection following proper consideration of their claim have the option to return voluntarily to Somalia by way of a voluntary assisted returns programme. If they choose not to return voluntarily they will be subject to removal to Somalia as soon as it is possible to conclude negotiations with the relevant authorities.[19]

The fact that AVR was primarily discussed with regard to particularly problematic countries of origin indicates that the UK authorities saw it as a way of circumventing the constraints imposed by the principle of *non-refoulement*: As long as individuals could be convinced—by whatever means—to formally agree to being removed, this principle does not apply. Consequently, the emphasis on quantitative targets that had shaped UK return policy since the late 1990s was carried over into the realm of AVR. According to an IOM UK staff member,

[18] Lord Filkin (Labour), House of Lords Debate, 24 September 2002, vol 638 c214WA.

[19] Parliamentary Under-Secretary of State for the Home office (Bethany Hughes), House of Commons Debate, 3 December 2002 vol 395 c713W.

> it was an obsession with numbers that we had to report on a daily basis, we would have to report by 10 am in the morning the number of people who had departed the day before, so on a daily basis we were reporting statistics. (Interview IOM)

Beyond the basic dependency that came with being financed by the United Kingdom Border Agency (UKBA), staff at the IOM's UK office therefore experienced constant pressure to "deliver" appropriate numbers of returns. While the office remained committed to upholding a basic degree of consent and voluntariness, an interview respondent acknowledged that this situation led to a shift in work priorities: Rather than ensuring that individual returnees were supported all the way from initial contact to successful reintegration in their country of origin, the emphasis lay on recruiting a constant flow of new returnees (interview IOM).

Beyond making returns to individual countries more likely, the introduction of a general AVR scheme open to asylum seekers and irregular migrants of all nationalities had wider policy implications. Up to 2002, individuals qualified for Exceptional Leave to Remain if their return was prevented through no fault of their own (e.g., because the lack of a secure return route, or because their country of origin refused to accept back deportees). This changed when the Minister for Citizenship and immigration announced the replacement of Exceptional Leave to Remain—that had often been granted on a country basis—by Humanitarian Protection and Discretionary Leave to Remain,[20] both of which applied much more rarely than had previously been the case for Exceptional Leave to Remain. This new system allowed the government to uphold return expectations for longer periods of time:

> It is our policy not to grant a person discretionary leave simply because they cannot be removed from the United Kingdom. The great majority of failed asylum seekers can reasonably be expected to return to their countries voluntarily even if they cannot immediately be removed.[21]

This had immediate consequences for individuals from Zimbabwe. For a number of years prior to this policy change, the UK had abstained from enforcing returns to this country on principled grounds, and had habitually granted Exceptional Leave to Remain to affected individuals. Following the introduction of the new Discretionary Leave to Remain and Humanitarian Protection status arrangements, the government's line of argument changed:

> Where a person has not been granted asylum, exceptional leave or humanitarian protection or discretionary leave, it follows that we do not consider that they have demonstrated a protection need or a compelling reason why they should be allowed to remain here. As a result, while we are not enforcing the removal of such individuals to Zimbabwe at present, they have no right to remain in the United Kingdom and are expected to return voluntarily.[22]

---

[20] Cf. *House of Commons Debate, 1 April 2003, vol 402 c54WS.*

[21] Parliamentary Under-Secretary of State for the Home office (Bethany Hughes), House of Commons Debate, 15 April 2003, vol 404 cc65-6W.

[22] Parliamentary Under-Secretary of State for the Home office (Bethany Hughes), House of Commons Debate, 10 June 2003, vol 406 cc 808W.

Once again, this had wider implications. As early as June 2004, for instance, Iraqi nationals not eligible for asylum were refused complementary protection and instead encouraged to register with the IOM to return as soon as possible in practical terms. While their return at this point in time could not be enforced, their eligibility for housing support under section 4 of the 1999 Immigration and Asylum Act was made conditional on their registration for assisted voluntary return.[23] In effect, this meant that individuals not signing up for assisted voluntary returns preemptively, i.e., at a point in time when safe returns were not yet feasible, were left destitute under UK law—and the government justified this situation with reference to the availability of the IOM's assisted voluntary return services.

4.2 Softening the Return of Families and Unaccompanied Minors

In 2010, the UK government commissioned the IOM to initiate a specialized family AVR scheme. From April 2010 onwards, both families and unaccompanied minors returned under the newly established Assisted Voluntary Return for Families and Children (AVRFC) programme. When the detention of minors for immigration purposes was ruled unlawful in 2011, the UK Border Agency (UKBA) was devoid of a key instrument in the forced removal of families. At this point, greater emphasis was placed on family AVRs. Building on the existing AVRFC scheme, the UKBA established a new process that includes a so-called "family conference" and aims at including all affected family members in the planning of their eventual return. Outlined in a 69-page operational guidance document, [24] the process then unfolds as the stepwise opportunity to return in an "assisted", "required", or "ensured" manner.[25] While still amounting to forced return as a measure of last resort, this is presented as a more humane way of handling the potentially traumatizing experience of removal and is highly valued by UKBA staff who claim that "what we have lost through the detention ability to remove, we have kind of gained through the AVR [family] programme" (interview UKBA). The UK's new family returns process constitutes a vivid illustration of a move towards adapting return procedures so as to make them less amenable to public protest, and provides evidence in support of the argument that AVR is often used to complement forced returns rather than constituting a genuine alternative.

While obstacles to the return of families have thus been addressed, the return of unaccompanied minors towards whom states hold special duties of care remains an as of yet unsolved problem. Given that during the late 1990s and early 2000s, the number of unaccompanied minors applying for asylum in the UK increased steeply

[23] Cf. House of Commons Debate, 15 June 2004, vol 422 cc855-7W.

[24] Cf. http://www.ukba.homeoffice.gov.uk/sitecontent/documents/policyandlaw/enforcement/oemsectione/chapter451?view=Binary (last accessed 03 August 2013).

[25] Cf. http://www.ukba.homeoffice.gov.uk/sitecontent/newsarticles/2011/march/03new-family-returns-process (last accessed 03 August 2013).

(from 631 in 1996 to 2733 in 2000 and 6200 in 2002),[26] UK authorities have made efforts to remedy this.

In early 2003, the government confirmed that unaccompanied minors were not to be returned unless suitable reception conditions in the country of origin were ensured.[27] Contrary to the implicit prior consensus that this required safe reception by family members, however, the 2005 strategy paper "Controlling our Borders: Making Migration Work for Britain", set out a broader interpretation of this principle that included a notion of safe reception centres without family support. Subsequently, a pilot programme in Albania was planned:

> We have been developing a returns programme for some time for unaccompanied asylum-seeking children (UASCs) who are under 18 years of age and whose asylum or humanitarian protection claims have been refused. The programme will be piloted in Albania. (. . .) UASCs will be either returned to their family, where tracing has been possible and reunification is appropriate, or given a tailored package of reception, care and support in Tirana, to be provided by contracted non-governmental organisations with considerable international expertise in childcare and welfare issues.[28]

Due to resistance from Albanian authorities, this pilot project was never implemented.[29] A year later, the UK government again engaged in the development of a "returns programme to a number of countries for unaccompanied children who have been refused asylum in the UK", allegedly aimed at Vietnam, Angola, and the Democratic Republic of Congo.[30] Once again, the project failed to be implemented, this time due to vocal critique from UK-based children's rights NGOs.[31]

More recently, however, the UK has joined forces with other EU member states also trying to return unaccompanied minors. Under the Framework of the European Return Platform for Unaccompanied Minors (ERPUM) project that was initiated by the Swedish Migration Board in 2010, Sweden, the Netherlands, the UK and Norway (plus Denmark and Belgium acting as observers) are working together to "develop methods and contacts in order to find the parents of the minors who must return home, but also to find safe and adequate shelter in the country of origin".[32] The project draws on the 2011 EU Action Plan on Unaccompanied Minors, and is partially funded through the EU Return Fund. Currently, ERPUM-negotiations are under way with the governments of Afghanistan and Iraq. While initially, the target

---

[26] Cf. House of Commons Debate, 23 January 2002, vol 378 cc942-3W.

[27] Cf. House of Commons Debate, 7 January 2003, vol 397 c139W.

[28] Minister of State for the Home Office (Baroness Scotland of Asthal), House of Lords Debate, 1 March 2005, vol 670 cc13-4WA.

[29] Cf. http://www.theguardian.com/uk/2006/aug/18/immigration.immigrationandpublicservices1 (last accessed 10 February 2013).

[30] House of Commons Written Answers 31 October 2006: Column 403W.

[31] Cf. http://www.theguardian.com/uk/2006/aug/18/immigration.immigrationandpublicservices1 and http://www.irr.org.uk/news/deportation-targets-trump-childrens-rights/ (last accessed 10 February 2013).

[32] Cf. http://www.migrationsverket.se/info/4597_en.html (last accessed 23 February 2013).

age group was listed as minors between 10 and 17 years of age, this specification has since been removed from the ERPUM website (Lemberg-Pedersen et al. 2013: 3). Lemberg-Pedersen notes the project's potentially misleading emphasis on family reunification:

> The project consistently highlights family tracing as a key component. This has the effect of downplaying central questions concerning another component: the reception facilities. These are framed as secure locations offering care and education where returned children can be placed temporarily while tracing efforts for their families are ongoing. However, one may ask, what happens in the event that it proves impossible to locate their families? (Lemberg-Pedersen et al. 2013: 4)

While the UK government has assured that "Decisions as to whether it is appropriate to return unaccompanied children are always made on a case by case basis",[33] neither the ERPUM coordinators nor the UK government have so far addressed this question. In sum, the issue of unaccompanied minors shows the extent to which some of the most sensitive and controversial aspects of returns operations can be packaged into seemingly technical and pragmatic administrative programmes, which span multiple levels of governance. As such, it becomes harder to establish who exactly should be answerable and held accountable for maintaining central liberal rights and norms. The successful opposition by NGOs to several UK pilot projects mentioned above shows that resisting these developments is possible—but it should not be taken for granted as a structural manifestation of "liberal constraints".

5 Conclusion: The Rise of Temporal over Spatial Control

If forced and so-called voluntary returns are pursued in combination, their efficacy for reaching an overall political objective or a publically formulated return target increases. At the same time, the notion of voluntariness becomes compromised and safeguards against forced returns may be undermined. This points to a broader restrictive shift, not only in public debates on migrant return, but also in the de facto enforcement of this previously exceptional policy choice.

Viewed from this perspective, the capacity-building efforts and subsequent building up of stable domestic and international implementation structures described in this chapter have implications beyond allowing for greater efficiency in state-induced returns. Instead, the fact that the implementation of legal return obligations is more feasible now than it used to be in the past opens up new avenues for policy-making. Whereas earlier temporary labour recruitment schemes became discredited partly because their temporary nature could not be enforced (Castles 1986), the new feasibility of return enforcement may put similar schemes back on domestic authorities' menu of legitimate policy options.

[33] House of Commons Written Answers, 13 February 2013, Column 756W.

There is indicative evidence that this is indeed taking place. Various authors have recently pointed out the rise of new guest worker programmes (Ruhs and Martin 2008; Castles 2006; Rajkumar et al. 2012). Furthermore, in my own research, while focusing on questions of return, I repeatedly encountered references to newly established or planned temporary labour migration schemes. Many of these schemes feature under the label "circular migration", a term first introduced in a strategy paper presented by Wolfgang Schäuble and Nicolas Sarkozy during an informal meeting of the interior ministers of the six largest EU member states in 2006 (Angenendt 2007). A year later, the European Commission issued a communication that linked the notion of circular migration to development policy. The communication proposed a number of "incentives (...) to promote circularity", among these "a written commitment by migrants to return voluntarily to their countries of origin once their contract expires", and "the conclusion and implementation of readmission arrangements to ensure the effective return of the national in the case of an illegal stay within EU territory" (European Commission 2007b). These provisions indicate what a German interview respondent referred to as the strong return objective of circular migration schemes (interview BAMF). Respondents at the International Labour Organization (ILO) confirmed that they witness a renewed interest in temporary labour migration under the label circular migration (interviews ILO). Emphasizing that the differences between these schemes and traditional guest worker programmes are negligible, they called into question the appropriateness of the label circular migration:

> Of course there is a return or at least move-on expectation—perhaps that the innovation with the circular migration schemes, it doesn't have to be return, it's a move-on expectation—as long as you get out of here when we don't need you anymore. (Interview ILO)

This is in line with a recent report by the UK Home Office that states that the UK government is open to circular migration schemes, provided they are "compatible with the UK's commitment to limit net migration (...), and clarify how temporary routes to work and study may help facilitate the circular return of migrants" (Pendry 2011: 53).

Developed countries' continuous demand for cheap foreign labour persists (Winters et al. 2003), as do the migratory movements triggered by this demand. At the same time, local populations in countries of destination are unwilling to share the benefits afforded to them by social welfare systems. Given the trend of an extension of rights that were previously restricted to citizens to long-term residents, this creates a tension that can only be resolved through an emphasis on temporariness and return (Vertovec 2007: 7): It is through upholding strong and credible return expectations that governments in contemporary liberal democracies can legitimately withhold access to important societal resources from non-citizens.

Once again, this credibility has taken on a new level of importance in light of the apparent break-down of conventional border controls. The increasing feasibility of migrant return implementation opens up a new space for temporary and precarious residence titles that run counter to the liberalizing trend in legal provisions pertaining to non-citizens' security of residence that we have witnessed over the past decades. What this outlook points towards is a classic feedback effect of policies affecting politics (cf. Mulvey 2010; Ingram et al. 2007: 95; Pierson 1993), i.e., an instance in which practical developments in the realm of migrant return may over time influence political actors' manoeuvring space on questions pertaining to integration and citizenship rights.

Overall, I propose that there is a broader normative shift in migration policies, which has wider repercussions on our notions of what is considered acceptable. Scholars highlighting the resonance of liberal norms with liberal democratic states tend to neglect states' corresponding power to reshape the international consensus on which these norms are based. In particular, this reshaping can take hold through the normalisation of routine administrative practices and lower-level agreements, rather than depending on a reformulation of general standards of protection or asylum. In this sense, the development of "best practices" is very likely to have an impact on the scope of legitimate policy options among the peer group of liberal democracies. The UK's most recent focus on the return of unaccompanied minors—that arguably constitute the group most thoroughly protected by international law—indicates the extent of this shift. If we follow Triadafilopoulos in treating broader global norms and ideas as resources influencing domestic politics (Triadafilopoulos 2012: 16), this has far-reaching implications for the prospects of future immigrants. The strict enforcement of temporal limitations that this shift allows for matches the requirements of our times where human mobility is cherished due to a continuous need for foreign labour, yet is met by little societal will to integrate large numbers of newcomers. While entry may be facilitated, permanent residence—constituting the presumed endpoint of all return expectations—remains carefully guarded, ensuring that only those deemed worthy by the state attain permanent membership in the society. The ensuing scenario can be described as a rise of temporal over spatial control, in that the focus of control no longer lies on physical access to the territory, but rather on the length of residence and the entitlements this encompasses. This trend has so far largely remained hidden in the seemingly routine and obscure practice of national and international migration bureaucracies. In order to install appropriate mechanisms of accountability, it needs to be recognized and politicised.

References

Angenendt, S. (2007). *Zirkuläre Migration. Ein tragfähiges migrationspolitisches Konzept?* Berlin: Stiftung Wissenschaft und Politik.

Betts, A. (2013). *Survival migration. Failed governance and the crisis of displacement.* Ithaca and London: Cornell University Press.

Boswell, C. (2007). Theorizing migration policy: Is there a third way? *International Migration Review, 41*(1), 75–100.

Castles, S. (1986). The guest-worker in Western Europe—An obituary. *International Migration Review, 20*(4), 761–778.

Castles, S. (2006). Guestworkers in Europe: A resurrection? *International Migration Review, 40* (4), 741–766.

Coleman, N. (2009). *European readmission policy. Third country interests and refugee rights*. Leiden and Boston: Martinus Nijhoff Publishers.
Cornelius, W., Martin, P. L., & Hollifield, J. F. (1994). Introduction: The ambivalent quest for control. In W. Cornelius, P. L. Martin, & J. Hollifield (Eds.), *Controlling immigration: A global perspective* (pp. 3–41). Stanford: Stanford University Press.
Council of the European Union. (2001). *Council directive 2001, 40, EC on the mutual recognition of decisions on the expulsion of third country nationals*. Brussels: Council of the European Union.
Council of the European Union. (2002). *Seville European Council presidency conclusions*. Brussels: Council of the European Union.
Council of the European Union. (2003). *Council Directive 2003, 110, EC on assistance in cases of transit for the purposes of removal by air*. Brussels: Council of the European Union.
Council of the European Union. (2004a). *Council Decision 2004, 191, EC setting out the criteria and practical arrangements for the compensation of the financial imbalances resulting from the application of Directive 2001, 40, EC on the mutual recognition of decisions on the expulsion of third-country nationals*. Brussels.
Council of the European Union. (2004b). *Council Decision 2004, 573, EC on the organisation of joint flights for removals from the territory of two or more Member States, of third-country nationals who are subjects of individual removal orders*. Luxembourg: Council of the European Union.
Council of the European Union. (2005). *Council Decision 2005, 267, EC establishing a secure web-based information and coordination network for Member States' migration management services*. Brussels: Council of the European Union.
Dedja, S. (2012). Human rights in the EU return policy: The case of the EU-Albania relations. *European Journal of Migration and Law, 14*(1), 95–114.
Ellermann, A. (2009). *States against migrants. Deportation in Germany and the United States*. New York: Cambridge University Press.
European Commission. (2002). *Green paper on a community return policy on illegal residents (COM(2002) 175 final)*. Brussels: European Commission.
European Commission. (2006). *The global approach to migration one year on: Towards a comprehensive European migration policy*. Brussels: European Commission.
European Commission. (2007a). *Communication on circular migration and mobility partnerships between the European Union and third countries*. Brussels: European Commission.
European Commission. (2007b). *Communication on circular migration and mobility partnerships between the European Union and third countries (COM(2007) 248)*. Brussels: European Commission.
European Council. (1999). *Presidency conclusions*. European Council Meeting in Tampere.
European Council. (2001). *Presidency conclusions*. European Council Meeting in Laeken.
European Council. (2005). The Hague programme: Strengthening freedom, security and justice in the European Union (2005, C 53, 01).
European Parliament and Council of the European Union. (2007). Decision 575, 2007, EC establishing the European Return Fund for the period 2008 to 2013 as part of the General Programme 'Solidarity and Management of Migration Flows', Brussels.
European Parliament and Council of the European Union. (2008). *Directive 2008, 115, EC on common standards and procedures in Member States for returning illegally staying third-country nationals*. Strasbourg: European Parliament and Council of the European Union.
Gibney, M. J. (2008). Asylum and the expansion of deportation in the United Kingdom. *Government and Opposition, 43*(2), 146–167.
Gibney, M., & Hansen, R. (2003). *Deportation and the liberal state: The forcible return of asylum seekers and unlawful migrants in Canada, Germany and the United Kingdom* (New Issues in Refugee Research Working Paper no. 77).
Giuffre, M. (2011). The European Union readmission policy after Lisbon. *Interdisciplinary Political Studies, 1*, 7–19.

Guiraudon, V. (2002). The Marshallian triptych reordered: The role of courts and bureaucracies in furthering migrants' social rights. In M. Bommes & A. Geddes (Eds.), *Immigration and welfare: Challenging the borders of the welfare state* (pp. 72–89). London and New York: Routledge.

Guiraudon, V., & Lahav, G. (2000). A reappraisal of the state sovereignty debate: The case of migration control. *Comparative Political Studies, 33*(2), 163–195.

Hollifield, J. F. (1992). *Immigrants, markets and states: The political economy of postwar Europe*. Cambridge, MA: Harvard University Press.

Hollifield, J. F. (2000). The politics of international migration: How can we 'bring the state back in'? In C. B. Brettel & J. F. Hollifield (Eds.), *Migration theory: Talking across disciplines* (pp. 137–185). New York and London: Routledge.

Ingram, H., Schneider, A., & DeLeon, P. (2007). Social construction and policy design. In P. Sabatier (Ed.), *Theories of the policy process* (pp. 93–126). Cambridge: Westview Press.

International Organisation for Migration (IOM). (1995). *IOM strategic planning: Toward the twenty-first century*. Geneva: IOM.

International Organisation for Migration (IOM). (1998). *Statement by the IOM Director General, IOM External Relations and Information Department*. Geneva: IOM.

International Organisation for Migration (IOM). (2002). *Financial report for the year ended 31 December 2001 (MC, 2079)*. Geneva: IOM.

International Organisation for Migration (IOM). (2004). *Financial report for the year ended 31 December 2003 (MC, 2140)*. Geneva: IOM.

International Organisation for Migration (IOM). (2005). *Financial report for the year ended 31 December 2004 (MC, 2172)*. Geneva: IOM.

International Organisation for Migration (IOM). (2006). *Financial report for the year ended 31 December 2005 (MC, 2196)*. Geneva: IOM.

International Organisation for Migration (IOM). (2007). *Financial report for the year ended 31 December 2006 (MC, 2223)*. Geneva: IOM.

International Organisation for Migration (IOM). (2009). *Financial report for the year ended 31 December 2008 (MC, 2277)*. Geneva: IOM.

International Organisation for Migration (IOM). (2010). *Financial report for the year ended 31 December 2009 (MC, 2293)*. Geneva: IOM.

International Organisation for Migration (IOM). (2011). *Financial report for the year ended 31 December 2010 (MC, 2313)*. Geneva: IOM.

International Organisation for Migration (IOM). (2013). *The International Organization for Migration in brief*. Geneva: IOM.

Jacobson, D. (1996). *Rights across borders: Immigration and the decline of citizenship*. Baltimore: John Hopkins University Press.

Joppke, C. (1998). Why liberal states accept unwanted immigration. *World Politics, 50*(2), 266–293.

Joppke, C. (2001). The legal-domestic sources of immigrant rights. The United States, Germany, and the European Union. *Comparative Political Studies, 34*(4), 339–366.

Kaunert, C. (2005). The area of freedom, security and justice: The construction of a 'European Public Order'. *European Security, 14*(4), 459–483.

Koopmans, R., Michalowski, I., & Waibel, S. (2012). Citizenship rights for immigrants: National political processes and cross-national convergence in Western Europe, 1980–2008. *American Journal of Sociology, 117*(4), 1202–1245.

Lemberg-Pedersen, M., Schuster, L., Stern, R., Gibney, M., & Allsopp, J. (2013). *The deportation of unaccompanied minors from the EU. Family tracing and government accountability in the European Return Platform for Unaccompanied Minors (ERPUM) project, Refugee Studies Centre, Oxford Department of International Development*. Oxford: University of Oxford.

Léonard, S. (2010). EU border security and migration into the European Union: FRONTEX and securitisation through practices. *European Security, 19*(2), 231–254.

Menz, G. (2009). *The political economy of managed migration. Nonstate actors, Europeanization, and the politics of designing migration policies*. Oxford: Oxford University Press.
Mulvey, G. (2010). When policy creates politics: The problematizing of immigration and the consequences for refugee integration in the UK. *Journal of Refugee Studies, 23*(4), 437–462.
Panizzon, M. (2012). Readmission agreements of EU Member States: A case for EU subsidiarity or dualism? *Refugee Survey Quarterly, 31*, 101–133.
Pendry, E. (2011). United Kingdom annual policy report 2010, European Migration Network.
Pierson, P. (1993). When effect becomes cause: Policy feedback and political change. *World Politics, 45*(4), 595–628.
Pollet, K. (2011). The negotiations on the return directive: Challenges, outcomes and lessons from an NGO perspective. In K. Zwaan (Ed.), *The returns directive: Central themes, problem issues and implementation in selected Member States* (pp. 25–38). Nijmegen: Wolf Legal Publishers.
Rajkumar, D., Berkowitz, L., Vosko, L. F., Preston, V., & Latham, R. (2012). At the temporary-permanent divide: How Canada produces temporariness and makes citizens through its security, work, and settlement policies. *Citizenship Studies, 16*(3–4), 483–510.
Ruhs, M., & Martin, P. (2008). Numbers vs. rights: Trade-offs and guest worker programs. *International Migration Review, 42*(1), 249–265.
Sassen, S. (1999). Beyond sovereignty: De-facto transnationalism in immigration policy. *European Journal of Migration and Law, 1*(2), 177–198.
Schieffer, M. (2003). Community readmission agreements with third countries—Objectives, substance and current state of negotiations. *European Journal of Migration and Law, 5*(3), 343–357.
Soysal, Y. N. (1994). *Limits of citizenship: Migrants and postnational membership in Europe*. Chicago and London: University of Chicago Press.
Triadafilopoulos, T. (2012). *Becoming multicultural. Immigration and the politics of membership in Canada and Germany*. Toronto: University of British Columbia Press.
Vertovec, S. (2007). *Circular migration: The way forward in global policy?* Oxford: International Migration Institute.
Winters, L. A., Walmsley, T. L., Wang, Z. K., & Grynberg, R. (2003). Liberalising temporary movement of natural persons: An agenda for the development round. *World Economy, 26*(8), 1137–1161.

Justifying Control: EU Border Security and the Shifting Boundaries of Political Arrangement

Julien Jeandesboz

1 Introduction

In recent years, EU border control has experienced a double condition of being constantly criticized and perpetually justified. Controversies have unfolded over just about every possible aspect of border control activities. As accounted in other chapters of this volume, questions of financial viability and technical feasibility have meshed with debates over effectiveness and legality, and with foundational issues related to necessity, proportionality, challenges to fundamental rights and freedoms, or humanitarian requirements to save lives. Border control set up as a security concern is also pitted against European and international obligations to uphold fundamental rights, or humanitarian commitments flowing from the EU's core values. Alternatively, it is argued that a balance needs to be struck between security concerns and fundamental freedoms and rights.

These controversies are nurtured by a constant flow of opinions, impact assessments, feasibility studies, activity reports and hearings that address entangled concerns with budgetary discipline, practicality, political opportunity, or that fit with the core principles and values, the spirit or the letter of EU law. In other words, a lot more goes into the shaping of EU border control measures that meets the eye. Practitioners of EU security politics appear to operate on uncertain grounds, and the question arises of how this contingency can be examined in security scholarship.

Such an examination can in fact be done in several ways. In the first instance, these controversies can be taken at face value and assessed as a matter of "problem-solving" (Cox 1981) where security scholarship joins in the work of impact and feasibility assessing and reporting in order to evaluate the extent to which border control measures, activities or plans are reliably designed and/or live up in their unfolding to expected outcomes. Alternatively, these measures can be examined as

J. Jeandesboz (✉)
Université libre de Bruxelles, REPI, Avenue F.D. Roosevelt 39, 1050 Bruxelles, Belgium
e-mail: julien.jeandesboz@ulb.ac.be

R. Bossong, H. Carrapico (eds.), *EU Borders and Shifting Internal Security*,
DOI 10.1007/978-3-319-17560-7_12

a manifestation of hypocrisy, where the interplay of budget calculations, technical assessments, humanitarian and human rights concerns conceals the work of power and interests, whose unveiling becomes the key challenge for security scholarship. Both analytical possibilities share a focus on whether a given security measure is justified or not, in relation to various principles or values, be it cost effectiveness or effectiveness tout court, "fit" with international and European legal obligations or purported fundamental values. They also tend to take the work of justifying (border) security measures for granted, at face value: a measure is either justified or not, but the ways in which it is justified are not considered in themselves to be a matter for investigation.

The third possibility, which this chapter embraces, is precisely to examine controversies over EU border control measures in terms of justification, by asking how, rather than whether, such measures are justified. As the chapter argues in the next section, thinking in terms of justification has conceptual implications and involves looking at (EU) security politics in terms of practice. Examining how security measures are justified builds on the critical literature in security studies (c.a.s.e. collective 2006), whose main characteristic lies in the attention dedicated to understanding how a particular development is given meaning as a security issue. What is of further interest to this literature is the transformative effects that security meaning-making might have, which involves paying attention to the "specific kind of [political] ordering" that security practices perform (Huysmans 1998: 232) and to the "place" that security practice occupies within the broader political order (Jeandesboz 2015).

Asking how, rather than whether, a given measure is justified shifts the scholarly discussion on EU borders and security more generally in two ways, explored in the remainder of the chapter. First, it highlights the political work that mundane and proliferating policy practices such as parliamentary hearings, impact assessments or feasibility studies do. It draws attention to the efforts put into building equivalence between a specific measure and broader practical repertoires of justification. In so doing, thinking in terms of justification also unveils the repertoires that are not, or are very marginally mobilized, and thus renders visible the alternatives to existing measures that are ignored or silenced. Second, thinking in terms of justification highlights the ways in which EU border control is not only about adopting the "right" measure—the efficient, proportionate or acceptable measure—but also involves shifting the boundaries of what is considered justifiable.

2 Security, Practice, Justification

Asking how a security measure is justified contributes to unsettling the notion that security policies are a functional response to externally given and objectively defined threats. The question builds on a now sizeable literature of critical scholarship on security that holds as its core the premise that security receives its meaning (what is to be secured, from what and how) from the definitional practices of security actors, operating in specific contexts, drawing on distinctive social resources and ways of doing, knowing and reasoning, as well as ways of saying (Balzacq et al. 2010). This scholarship draws attention, in other words, to how meaning is constructed and performs what is to be secured, from what and how. In so doing, critical approaches to security have broadened and deepened discussions on security among students of international relations and security, in particular beyond longstanding claims that equate security with the survival of the state in war (Herz 1950; Huysmans 1998: 226). Europe and the EU as well as border and migration control have featured prominently as empirical grounds in this endeavour (e.g., Bigo 1996, 2002; Huysmans 2006; Neal 2009), reflecting the foregrounding of new security concerns beyond inter-state conflict with the end of the cold war, and the development of transnational internal security arrangements in the context of the Schengen agreement and the "third pillar" on EU justice and home affairs.

For all its commonalities however, the critical literature on security also foregrounds diverse concerns when it comes to making sense of the "meaning making" practices involved in the conduct of security. This is often communicated in terms of distinction and contention between "schools" and "theories" among critical approaches to security (Waever 2004, 2011). Debates have however been more fluid than the use of "school" labels implies, and focused on foundational and political matters rather than on the validity or scope conditions of alternative frameworks of interpretation for security analysis. These debates have involved, firstly, the ontological and epistemological role of language, enunciation and discourse relative to the role of doing or making things. Should the making of an issue into a security problem be explained chiefly by how security is enunciated or "said"? This is the claim furthered through the original securitization framework of analysis, which emphasizes how security practice involves the rendering of insecurity through discourse (Waever 1995). Should security "meaning-making", on the other hand, be explained but by the dispositions and the competence to speak of security actors? Works involved in this line of inquiry have studied, alternatively, the conditions of possibility of security speech acts—the perlocutionary dimension of speech (Balzacq 2005) and context effects (Ciută 2009)—and the dispositional grounding of security practices, be they rendered through the social dispositions of agents (Bigo 2011; Bigo 2014) or in dispositifs and devices, modes of knowing and reasoning as well as instruments (Amicelle et al. 2015; Aradau and Van Munster 2007; Huysmans 2006). Second, these claims are associated with distinctive interpretations of the shape of contemporary security politics. Security politics on the one hand is interpreted as consisting of decisive actors and acts that through the enunciation of existential threats to a referent object elevate a matter above the realm of normal politics into the realm of exceptional politics. On the other hand, it is increasingly found to involve a constant reengineering of what 'normal' politics consist of through the dissemination of unease and insecurities across a broadening range of social universes, including but not exclusively through invocations of survival and exception (Bigo 2002, 2008; Huysmans 2014). In the latter perspective, the practice of security is a much more open-ended and messy process: actors think, say and do a great variety of things in different circumstances and multiple ways in the name of security, as well as enter in struggles over the 'right' way to do or avoid doing security.

Asking how a security measure is justified amounts to a specific way of dealing with the 'constructedness' of security, with how an issue is made into a security problem, and anchors security analysis within the growing scholarly conversation on how security measures are 'normalised' and transform politics. Thinking of security in terms of justification here draws attention to the fact that actors 'do not necessarily seek to invent false pretexts after the fact so as to cover up some secret motive, the way one comes up with an alibi: rather, they seek to carry out their actions in such a way that they can withstand the test of justification' (Boltanski and Thévenot 2006: 37). Justifying a course of action—Boltanski and Thévenot's 'imperative to justify'—is a practical requirement rather than a rhetorical effect. Justifying security involves a combination of ways of speaking, reasoning and doing derived from the 'practical repertoires' (Bigo 2014: 211) accrued by security agents throughout their professional trajectories. Looking at security politics in this way enables the analysis to embrace both the diversity and 'messiness' of practice and the regularities and patterned action that underpins it, as well as the conditions that make possible and successful some ways of doing security rather than others.

To say it more conversationally then: actors say and do many things in constructing security, which may not only involve invoking existential threats and survival. This should already be obvious to the attentive reader of this volume. Passing and implementing measures such as "smart borders" or Eurosur requires constant and continuous labour from professionals of politics, bureaucracy, and security. This labour is not only "speech" work, but involves the whole practical paraphernalia of governmental work:

> The eminently technical ways in which the world is represented by means of little things like charts, tables, graphs, numbers, diagrams and reports [. . .] the materials through which the world is made visible, calculable, and amenable to practices of rule (Haahr and Walters 2005: 7).

Understanding justification in relation to the practical repertoires of social agents, then, is useful in a first way, as this understanding cuts across the "ontological" binaries and divides, through which parts of the critical scholarship commonsensically builds security analysis (Schouten 2014), between what is said and what is done, between events and routines, between people and "things". The focus is on controversies and how different persons and objects are brought together in a given situation to justify a particular course of action.

The study of justification in sociology builds on the work of pragmatic sociology developed from the late 1980s onwards within the Groupe de sociologie politique et morale (GSPM) of the Ecole des Hautes Etudes en Sciences Sociales (EHESS) in Paris. While at least one of its leading figures (Boltanski) had worked with Pierre Bourdieu, pragmatic sociology initially worked to differentiate itself from Bourdieusian critical sociology. It engaged with the apparent disregard of this body of work for the 'critical capacity' of social actors, particularly in ordinary situations of everyday life (e.g., Boltanski and Thévenot 1999), a disregard grounded in the 'preponderant weight [...] given to the dispositional properties of actors, at the expense of the properties inscribed in the situations into which they are plunged' (Boltanski 2011: 21).

Pragmatic sociology, then, is a sociology of criticism rather than a critical sociology.[1] The emphasis of studies in the imperative of justification, then, is on critical moments or situations when a dispute arises, and their interest lies in how agreement is established in such situations, that is in how human action ends up being coordinated. This scholarship interprets the social world as a trial (procès) where uncertainties about the status, value or meaning of an object, a person or a situation require actors to consciously justify their positions and submit these justifications to various tests (Lahire 2012: 313; Boltanski and Claverie 2007; Boltanski and Thévenot 1999, 2006). To do so, social actors build "equivalences": they connect a local situation to larger principles or orders of worth, which are derived from classical philosophical principles and modelled as "polities" (Boltanski and Thévenot 2006: 63–123). Qualifying objects of dispute through the building of equivalence in relation to orders of worth grounds the settlement of a dispute in one or several social worlds, such as the "domestic world", the "market world" or the "civic world" (Boltanski and Thévenot 2006: 130–133; Jagd 2011).

There are several issues with this take on justification that impact on the way it can be used to think about security, and which a focus on practical repertoires of action helps address. The main point should certainly be that not all of social relations should be interpreted through the model of the trial. Actors do not systematically question the foundations of their actions, and in most cases, certainty rather than uncertainty predominates in the unfolding of social life. As a consequence, it is mostly in specific circumstances that uncertainty is foregrounded, and it also takes particular dispositions and competences to engage in controversies over the principles and values that underpin social life (Lahire 2012). The sociology of critique goes too far in disregarding the role that systems or patrimonies of dispositions play in shaping practice and the degree to which foundational notions about the shape of social and political relations are pre-reflexive. The capacity for critique both pertains to specific patrimonies of dispositions and is activated by specific contexts. In the "civic world" of pragmatic sociology, which is of central interest for this chapter, this capacity is arguably mostly (but not exclusively) located among agents who have made a career and profession out of politics and bureaucracy. The former dealing in "principles of di-vision", that is in "instruments for perceiving and expressing the social world" (Bourdieu 1991: 172). For the latter, Bourdieu highlights the work of bureaucracies as "great producers of 'social problems'" and solutions (Bourdieu 1994: 2) and the historical 'ambiguity of the

[1] A move rooted in the specific sociopolitical context in which this scholarship initially emerged: Bourdieu's work originally unfolded during the Algerian war and under the successive conservative governments of the French Fifth Republic, while pragmatic sociology formed in the context of the first socialist presidency and government of that period and in a context of societal liberalization (Didier 2014).

specialist and of technical competency (techné) as principle of a virtually autonomous and therefore potentially dangerous power' (Ibid: 24) for professionals of politics.

A particularly valuable contribution of students of justification nonetheless remains their interest in querying and studying the 'construction of agreement' (Boltanski and Thévenot 2006: 32) grounds on which an agreement is both found and founded in a controversial situation, and the specific scope and quality of this agreement. The quality of agreement in the sociology of justification comes in three different versions: a dispute or controversy can either be clarified in one specific world at the detriment of others, or can be settled through compromise or local arrangement (Jagd 2011: 347). While a compromise is consolidated through a common justification and across different worlds, a local arrangement is a temporary set up around a specific decision (Idem). In other words, a local arrangement does not signal an end to dispute or controversy, but rather simply an occasional stabilisation of struggles among social actors.

Rather than presenting a ready-made theoretical "package" to be applied, then, we should take justification as a tool enabling inquiries into security practice to ask a subset of specific questions. To what extent is a given situation problematic and characterized by radical uncertainty? What is the scope, depth and breadth of disagreement or agreement on a given matter? What is it that controversies or disputes reveal, by contrast, about shared habits of thinking and doing and the ways in which this bedrock of sedimented, layered practice shapes the behaviour of agents involved in security politics? The remainder of the chapter asks these questions about EU border control. In so doing, it draws on the tools of the sociology of justification, in the following way. First, the analysis unfolds from the study of specific situations and how the different actors involved in these situations construct equivalences between the issue at hand and broader general principles or orders of worth. Second, these situations are selected within the 'policy life' of EU border control, in circumstances that do resemble more closely those of a trial—where reasons for undertaking a specific course of action are tried, in the two meanings of the word, as an attempt and as scrutiny. Third, the analysis pays attention to the practical repertoires activated by the situations examined, and relates the mobilization of specific equivalences to these repertoires. Finally, and this is the discussion taken up in particular by the last section of the chapter, it probes the quality of the agreement being shaped in these situations and the political effects of these coordination efforts.

3 The Labour of Justifying EU Border Control

Asking how a security measure is justified first highlights the political work that mundane and proliferating security policy practices do. It draws attention to the efforts put into building equivalence between a specific measure and broader practical repertoires of justification, and reveals both the diversity and selectivity of how a security measure is given meaning as an object of dispute. In this section and the following, two recent situations in the policy life of EU border control are used to unpack this labour of building equivalences between border control measures and broader principles of worth. In both situations, justifications of EU border control measures take place in the "civic polity", but draw on different dimensions and orders of worth within this polity.

The first situation involves a discussion in the European Parliament's Committee on Civil Liberties, Justice and Home Affairs (LIBE) on 3–4 September 2014.[2] Such hearings have become a regular feature of EU security politics with the growing influence of the European Parliament in measures related to the Area of Freedom, Security and Justice, particularly since the entry into force of the Lisbon treaty. Committee members first hear external speakers, who are subsequently questioned by Members of European Parliament (MEP). While not exactly modeled on a tribunal, then, such hearings come closer to the situation of a trial than most everyday interactions. This particular meeting unfolded over 2 days. On 3 September, the Committee held an exchange of views with the outgoing Commissioner for Home Affairs Cecilia Malmström, meant in particular for the benefit of the newly appointed members of LIBE following the May 2014 European elections. On the morning of 4 September, the Frontex Deputy Executive Director, Gil Arias, took the floor and answered questions of LIBE members.

Malmström's presentation on 3 September was meant as an overview of the work done over the previous year and more broadly during her term in office. The Commissioner's address is accordingly sweeping, but a third of it focuses on the question of borders, immigration and asylum. It emphasizes the "extraordinary situation" at the EU external borders and the "demands and pressures" put on Europe as a result in particular of "terrible conflict [...] and poverty and other situations that are difficult", in Iraq and Syria and beyond:

> We see a lot of pressure, dramatic pictures from Greece, Ceuta and Melilla, Malta, but of course mainly the hundreds of thousands of people who have tried to cross the Mediterranean reaching the shores of Italy.

Malmström's address does not only build equivalences between the dramatic situation it stages and questions of security and threat. It lauds Mare Nostrum, the search and rescue operation launched unilaterally by the Italian authorities and conducted by the Italian Navy following the death of more than 350 persons after a shipwreck off the coast of Lampedusa on 3 October 2013, connecting border control with the humanitarian imperative of saving lives. It is in this view that the address also asks what would follow Mare Nostrum, and tentatively evokes a "Frontex Plus" operation that "could become active in November". Malmström further highlights the work done by the Commission, and establishes a second equivalence:

[2] A video recording of the discussion is available from the website of the European Parliament. All quotes are excerpts from the author's transcript of these hearings.

> Also, we have to take into account not only international obligations and conventions and the values that we all stand for, but also the demographic situation in Europe, is such as we do need people coming, and we should see migration pressures as an opportunity rather than the threat that they are sometimes portrayed as. And that is why I am very happy that we have made substantial progress when it comes to providing legal ways to Europe.

The focus here is on "people who seek work", related to the adoption of a directive on seasonal workers (adopted in February, 2014) and the intra-corporate transferee directive (adopted in May, 2014). Security does nonetheless come back in at a later stage, when the Commissioner outlines issues related to organized crime and cybercrime, and returns to border control matters through the question of passenger name records (PNR, see De Hert and Bellanova 2011 for an overview). The 'terrible images and events from Iraq and Syria' are again brought up, to underscore that the Commission and the Justice and Home Affairs Council "have given [...] a lot of attention to the issue of so-called foreign fighters. They do represent a real threat in Europe", requiring that progress be made on the establishment of an EU PNR database "that has been on the table for quite some time".[3]

Despite the wider scope of Malmström's address, it is the question of border control, the situation in the Mediterranean and the particular course of action outlined by the Commissioner in relation to Mare Nostrum and "Frontex Plus" that take center stage in the first round of questions, by LIBE group coordinators. These questions are critical to some extent, in that they disrupt or shift the system of equivalences underpinning the presentation given by the Commissioner. "Coming from Malta", MEP Roberta Metsola stresses "that Member States need to move from vocal solidarity to concrete solidarity". The order of worth involved here involves the conduct of states and inter-state relations, placed above concerns with search and rescue, the handling of movements of persons, or security, and despite the questioner's status as a European elected representative, it is on behalf of Malta that the Commissioner is being queried. The conduct of states is also one of the key themes in the intervention of MEP Timothy Kirkhope, albeit in different terms. "A lot of money has been actually committed to the Mediterranean in particular", he states in his intervention,

> but I do think it's important that with that money we should be actually making the behavior or the fundamental rights obligations of these Member States a little more clear to them [...] we are having some unacceptable treatment, conditions for refugees and asylum seekers. I do say that rules are rules, the abuse of rules whether it be by criminal gangs or individuals must not be acceptable or allowed to take us away from the real priority of genuine refugees, genuine asylum seekers, and those who wish to move legitimately across Europe for the purposes of work but not for the purposes of abuse.

The conduct of states invoked in the first place by Metsola is here equated less with inter-state solidarity than with responsibility in the organization of movements of persons. While Malström's address, furthermore, associated movements of persons

[3] The European Commission first introduced a legislative proposal on EU PNR in 2007 (see e.g., Bigo et al. 2011: 28–56).

mostly with humanitarian concerns, on the one hand, and socio-demographic preoccupations, on the other, the equivalence built in Kirkhope's comments associates a concern with human rights and law and order, the purported "abuse of rules" by some being framed as an obstacle to the upholding of international obligations regarding 'genuine refugees, genuine asylum seekers'.

The building of equivalences between EU border control measures and diverse and diverging orders of worth unfolds throughout the questions and answers session. MEP Cecilia Wikström's intervention brings up again the issue of international obligations associated in Kirkhope's statement with law and order, asking

> when will the operational plans for Frontex Plus be available for us in this Committee in order for us to study for example the safeguards put in place when it comes for instance to fundamental rights? I find this very important and as soon as possible, we need to take part of that, because after all it was us, we amended the Frontex regulation, and we added substantive matters just on fundamental rights.

In contrast with Kirkhope and Metsola, the order of worth alluded to here involves parliamentary oversight and the accountability of Frontex itself to the European Parliament. This is a theme that also comes strongly across in the points raised by MEP Ska Keller, who

> question[s] the ability of Frontex to fulfill the task of Mare Nostrum. Frontex as we all know, and we've all been part of writing and re-writing the mandate, is an agency that's there for border guarding, for stopping people from coming in, whereas what we really need is a humanitarian mission in the Mediterranean, to rescue people's lives. That's not Frontex's task, of course they also rescue people when they find some, or so we've been told, very good, but still that is a big difference, and I don't see how a border agency can all of the sudden turn humanitarian, for me that, this is a big issue and it's going to be very very complicated.

Where Wikström (and Kirkhope, to some extent) underline the human rights aspects of the Mediterranean situation, the equivalence interrogated in Keller's standpoint is between border control and humanitarian principles and requirements.

The unfolding of the situation recounted so far calls for two remarks. First, the way in which various equivalences are built and challenged highlight the degree of uncertainty surrounding what justifies the course of action embraced by EU border control towards the Mediterranean. This is not uncertainty due to imperfect or inaccurate information, but uncertainty over what border control stands for, the proliferation of values and orders of worth it can be associated with, and their compatibility. Second, this uncertainty and the apparent messiness of the discussion of 3 September 2014 are nonetheless patterned, in two ways. They are patterned, on the one hand, because the discussion recounted here is embedded in past or parallel debates and disagreements: the revision of the Frontex mandate to include rescue at sea operational aspects and make explicit human rights commitments, the controversies over the question of "foreign fighters", or over the issue of PNR. On the other hand, this specific situation in the policy life of EU border control is structured by the patrimony and repertoire of practices available to the actors involved, all of whom are professionals of politics. The inaccuracy of some of the interventions in the discussion, the lack of clarity about what Mare Nostrum does or did, and what a Frontex operation would contribute, do not really matter because the key stake here is the articulation of a "principle of di-vision" of the world of EU border control, of what it stands for—whether it is associated with human rights, humanitarian or law and order concerns, or preoccupations with the proper behavior of Member States (and the principle this behaviour should be grounded in—territorial sovereignty, solidarity, or responsibility to name a few).

This last point is further confirmed when examining the way in which the actors involved in the 3–4 September meeting relate to a relative outsider, in this case the Frontex Deputy Executive Director, Gil Arias. A career bureaucrat with prior responsibilities in the Spanish Ministry of Interior and the Spanish National Police Force, as well as EU-related duties in various Schengen secretariat and Council of Ministers working groups, Arias has remained in the same position with the agency since its inception, despite the change of Executive Director.[4] He starts his intervention on the morning of 4 September 2014 by framing it as an effort to deal with the inaccuracies and lack of clarity of the discussion with Malmström, noting that

> since I have been watching yesterday the debate with the occasion of the presentation made by Commissioner Malmström, and some questions remained unanswered, I would like to start by briefly explaining what is Frontex and how it works so some of those questions might be answered already now, and also for people who is not familiar with Frontex it might be worth to have this brief explanation.

The first few minutes of his talk are technè at work, dedicated to summarizing what it is that Frontex does, outlining its role 'primarily to support the Member States in such a task [control of the external borders] by coordinating operational cooperation at the external borders, mainly but not exclusively through joint operations' and emphasizing what has come to be one of the most common misunderstandings in the public debate about the agency, namely that it 'does not possess its own technical equipment, planes, vessels, etc., nor does it have border guards to carry out the actual border controls'. In further contrast with Malmström's address, a key technique in Arias' presentation is the invocation of numbers. For more than 5 min, he outlines key figures drawn from his agency's reports, comparing totals and trends in different years—outlining for instance key detection figures and trends:

> at the end of July [2014], the detections were two and a half time larger than last year. In just 7 months, the Member States reported more than 121,000 detections compared to approximately 107,000 for the whole year 2013. In fact, comparing the situation, compared to the situation in previous years, at the end of July we were already well above the annual total for the entire year 2009 and 2010. If the trends continue, as it is likely, the detections of irregular border crossings in 2014 will be higher than in 2011, the year of the Arab Spring when more than 141,000 detections were recorded.

[4] The first executive director of Frontex, Illka Laitinen, was replaced in January 2015 by Fabrice Leggeri, a French official with a career mostly in the national Ministry of Interior dealing mostly with migration and border control matters.

This reliance on numbers and the comparing of trends marks a difference between the practical repertoire mobilized by Arias and the repertoire mobilized both by Malmström and LIBE MEPs, and make it tempting to consider the former's presentation as more 'objective' or evidence-based. Examining this address in terms of justification, however, suggests that this address, while delivered by a career bureaucrat rather than by a professional of politics, is part and parcel of the controversies over the course of action to be adopted in EU border control. In the second part of his talk, Arias explicitly puts numbers aside to deliver a criticism of the Italian government's actions and of Mare Nostrum, by setting up a tension between border control objectives and search and rescue: 'But besides the numbers', he points out,

> it is also important to bear in mind the following. First that the journey of migrants departing from Libya is now considerably shorter than it was before the operation Mare Nostrum, as many boats are rescued in its operational area. Consequently, facilitators provide migrants with less fuel and water on board. The consequence is that if not rescued on time, this increases the risk for migrants. The boats are in poor condition and sometimes the accidents happen not far from the Libyan coast, and frequently migrants depart in waves, trying to take advantage of short windows of calm sea. The Italian authorities sometimes report up to 50 boasts per day, and this also increases the difficult to rescue all of them.

The point argued here is that the increase in search and rescue capabilities increases both the numbers of persons looking to cross the Mediterranean, and the risks they face. This prepares the ground for Arias to introduce the planned operation discussed as 'Frontex Plus' on the previous day by Malmström and the LIBE Committee, which Frontex in fact calls Triton, and to justify its scope. As he remarks,

> what is already clear and I want to stress it, is that first joint operation Triton will not replace Mare Nostrum. Neither the mandate, nor the available resources, allow for that replacement. The operational area of this new joint operation will cover the current operational areas of Hermes and Aeneas [...] Therefore, this operation will be closer to EU shores than Mare Nostrum.

It is the claims that Arias made "besides the numbers", as he himself highlighted, that MEPS pick up on in the questions that follow. Italian MEP Kashetu Kyenge challenges these claims by pointing out the necessity of the actions undertaken by the Italian authorities through Mare Nostrum and drawing on the principle of Member State solidarity. She notes

> a lot being said about the technical details but I can't see any wide ranging political message on migration and asylum policy as such. Up until now Mare Nostrum made a difference in terms of the change in the approach to bringing people back and search and rescue operations. It is a cultural shift required here, looking at the goals of migration. So here's my question then: Frontex, Frontex Plus or Triton, whatever you call it, is it going to change its goals from simply patrolling the borders to an approach where the human element lies at the heart of your work?

MEP Sylvie Guillaume on the other hand, picks up on the tension between border control and humanitarian action, and considers that the launching of Triton

> shows the somewhat ambiguous role of this agency which is controlling the borders, I suppose to search and rescue operations, and thank you for picking up some of the perverse effects of S&R. When you have a lot of people picked up, then the people traffickers get more active [. . .] Now are you going to return to Frontex's more core role of controlling the borders?

In yet another intervention, MEP Keller asks,

> If it's [Triton] supposed to be an operation of rescue, how are you as a border agency going to provide that service, because you are a border guarding agency which is not exactly a humanitarian mission, so how does this go together?

These three interventions—and the queries raised by other MEPs—engage not with the factual, numbered information provided by Arias, but with the values and principles of worth that can, or should, be connected to this information. Where Kyenge effectively argues for a shift to a humanitarian focus, Guillaume invokes the question of law and order, the reference to traffickers, while Keller challenges the very possibility that border guards can be trusted with humanitarian and search and rescue operations.

The response of the Frontex Deputy Director to these challenges shows the workings of the different practical repertoires available to actors involved in the policy life of EU border control. The opening point in his response involves

> the difference between Mare Nostrum and Triton [which] is fundamentally the nature of the two operations. While Mare Nostrum is clearly a search and rescue operation, Triton will be with a main focus on border control, border management, although as it is obvious saving lives is an absolute priority, and in fact very frequently the control operations, the border control operations coordinated by the agency turn into search and rescue operations, and this is how it works in practice. As I said it will also be closer to the EU shores, covering the current operational areas of Hermes and Aeneas, and also because of the nature of, sorry, of the type of assets that are available to the border guards. Normally the vessels that the border guards in the EU countries are not capable to transport, to drive so many migrants as normally travelling on these migrant boats, so one normal patrol boat cannot host 300 persons on board. This can be done by a military ship, but not by a border guard or a patrolling vessel of border guards.

In response to the effort of building equivalence between the Triton operation and broader principles and orders of worth, this reaction reflects a fall-back on technè, on the technical repertoire mobilized by Arias at the onset of his talk.

Examining this first recent situation involving EU border control measures outline the uncertain, shifting grounds on which such measures are based, and the fact that these grounds are hardly ever cleared before a measure is adopted. Actors constantly reformulate the equivalences between a specific measure ("Frontex Plus"/Triton here) and broader orders of worth, the value of past decisions and anticipated courses of action, on the basis of the practical repertoires available to them. This is not a mechanistic process: a bureaucrat such as Arias can attempt to make claims "besides numbers", for instance, but will be challenged by actors whose very profession is to articulate broad principles of vision and division of the social world. Identifying the kind of decisive action underpinning "classical" securitization analysis proves difficult in these circumstances. What the policy life of EU border control measures consists of, then, is different actors muddling through and justifying this muddling through on the basis of their respective dispositions to act. The politics at work here, then, are that of a local, temporary arrangement between mutually controversial positions rather than a politics of general agreement or unanimity. What remains to be clarified, however, is what these politics do.

4 EU Border Control and the Boundaries of the Justifiable

Examining security practice through the lens of justification reveals the political work that this practice does, in two ways. The first way discussed so far involves the confrontation of different practical repertoires of justification and the manifold equivalences built between specific measures and broader orders of worth. The second way in which justification does political work is through the progressive shift in the boundaries of what is considered justifiable. Said differently, practices of justification do not simply unfold in relation to fixed political coordinates, but contribute over time to changing these coordinates.

To continue unpacking the labour of justifying EU border control, this section focuses briefly on a second situation, a policy meeting organized in early May 2015 by the services of DG Home to discuss the "smart borders" legislative package initially introduced in 2013 (European Commission 2013a, b, c) with a selection of representatives from "civil society organisations".[5] The aim of the package is to establish two new databases for the purpose of border control, the Entry/Exit system and Registered traveller programme (EES and RTP, see also Bendel, this volume). "Smart borders" is a fairly recent terminology (European Commission 2011) but some of the core measures envisaged by the package have been circulating in EU border security discussions for more than 10 years. The EES, in particular, was initially examined as an alternative to the introduction of the EU Visa Information System (VIS) in early debates about this latter system and rejected on grounds that the EES would in particular be very costly and have a significant impact on fundamental rights (European Commission 2004: 12–14). This is the case in particular because the EES foresees the recording of all entries and exits of non-EU travellers crossing in or out of the Schengen area.

The meeting involved representatives from various organisations including PICUM, COFACE or Solidar, and the legal and policy officers from DG Home in charge of the smart borders package. The head of unit chairing the meeting introduced it as a "very informal and open exchange [...] so we can discuss

[5] The author was invited and participated in the meeting due to earlier involvement in two studies, written on behalf of the LIBE committee, examining the smart borders initiative (Bigo et al. 2012; Jeandesboz et al. 2013). All descriptions and quotes are excerpts of field notes. The meeting was meant to prepare the grounds for a public consultation, which has just been opened at the time of writing (see http://ec.europa.eu/dgs/home-affairs/what-is-new/public-consultation/2015/consulting_0030_en.htm)

every issue you think is relevant" and as one in a series of "targeted meetings with groups of stakeholders". The repertoire mobilized by the officers leading the discussion is intensely technical in comparison with the previous situation, accompanied by diagrams and graphs displayed on the room's screen. Their audience is told about "process accelerators", "self-service kiosks" where a key concern is "how much time [it takes] for a good digital picture" and "MRZ—sorry, machine-readable zone [on passports]". Participants are "presume[d to] know the difference between verification and identification, verification is one to one whereas identification is one to many", and so on. Yet at the same time a lot of the labour unfolding in the room is about justification. Smart borders are about "the enforcement of Schengen immigration rules" and there will be "no new rules" created by the package. In fact, according to the head of unit present in the room, "[t]he only improvement would be to increase the speed of crossing external borders" and as such smart borders is "about border control, not to manage border surveillance. It is to help the border guards controlling travellers at the external borders".

This last point references the controversies over the package, criticized by migrant and civil rights groups (some of which had representatives in the meeting) as well as policy experts and think tanks. Looking at the 2013 legislative proposal, The European data protection supervisor (EDPS) argued in no ambiguous terms that

> [t]here is no clear evidence that the Commission Proposals to create a smart border system for the external borders of the EU will fulfil the aims that it has set out… [O]ne of the stated aims of the proposals was to replace the existing 'slow and unreliable' system but the Commission's own assessments do not indicate that the alternative will be sufficiently efficient to justify the expense and intrusions into privacy (EDPS 2013).

The smart borders package also led two Green MEPs, Jan Albrecht and Ska Keller, to launch a "smash borders" campaign denouncing the fundamental rights implications of smart borders, including the mass surveillance dimension.[6]

The equivalence built by the Commission officials presenting at the meeting is in this regard twofold. It is on the one hand between the smart borders measures and public virtue, in relation with the quality of legislation and the good use of public money. When asked about the rationale for re-examining the 2013 legislative proposal and consulting with "stakeholders", one of the Commission officials points out that it is "the first time the Commission admits a proposal is not good enough. That is a bit of an innovation which is I think is a sign of better regulation", and proceeds to refer to Commission Vice-President Franz Timmermans' call for "smart regulation". Another point emphasised is that the envelope now proposed for smart borders is, at 791 million euros, "at least 22 % cheaper" than in previous iterations of the package. Budgets had been another key item of controversy about the smart borders measures, which had initially been costed at a little over 100 million euros in 2008, before increasing a 100-fold to 1.3 billion euros in the

[6] The campaign website can be found at http://www.smashborders.eu/en/ (accessed September 2015).

Commission's 2011 impact assessment, with a possible saving of "about 30 %" (European Commission 2011: 32; Jeandesboz et al. 2013: 18). The second equivalence built with questions of values, and particularly of European values and how they can be upheld. A key interrogation raised by participants to the meeting, informed in particular by the parallel debate over the establishment of EU PNR, is whether the data collected by the smart borders systems could be used for purposes of predictive analysis, or profiling. Asked informally about this issue during the coffee break, one of the participating Commission officials reacted strongly, by bringing up U.S. border controls, in particular the US VISIT programme (for a discussion see e.g., Amoore 2006; Epstein 2007). "To me", he argues, "the US is exactly what we are not supposed to do, should not do [. . .] We went there recently, it is insane what they do! For everyone, they can print out a 25-page profile, from all their databases". He reiterates the claim after the break, by pointing out that "what is happening is not only in the EU, it is happening on a global scale", with the examples of the US and Russia being foregrounded—"what they're interested in is getting the data [. . .] The US is asking us every second day"—while insisting that the EU approach is different, "not a dragnet profiling approach."

What unfolds through the situation briefly recounted so far is twofold. On the one hand we find a group of actors labouring to justify a certain course of action related to EU border control, that has in the past proven controversial, by drawing on a specific patrimony of dispositions—here rooted in the realm of technè. Given the specifics of the situation—European Commission officials engaging with actors that have been highly critical of their work so far—it is useful to think of this labour in terms of an effort to establish a local arrangement, rather than a compromise or clarification. Through this effort at establishing a local agreement, on the other hand, we see how the terms through which the issue under discussion is deemed justifiable shift. Challenges to smart borders framed in terms of fundamental rights and concerns with necessity and proportionality are addressed through references to public virtue, to the need for, and effort to deliver, better regulation, as well as ensuring the good use of public money. The question becomes not whether smart borders measures should be put in place, but how to put them in place, how to make them feasible. Measures that would amount to systematically recording data about all foreigners entering and exiting the Schengen area are further justified on grounds that they are less extreme or intrusive than what others are doing, and therefore consistent with a European way of doing things that is more acceptable than the purported US or Russian way. What is being shifted here, then, is not simply the way in which these measures are being justified, but the political coordinates according to which they are considered justifiable. Through the work of justification and equivalence unfolding in this specific situation, questions of rights are relocated as issues of feasibility and cost-effectiveness on the one hand, and as a "least bad" option, so to speak, in view of what is done outside of the EU. Justification, in this sense, is not simply a matter of argumentative reason, of what mainstream constructivists have come to call persuasion or suasion (e.g., Zürn and Checkel 2005), but political work that can shift the boundaries between orders of worth.

5 Conclusion

This chapter started with outlining three possibilities for the study of EU security: the "problem-solving" perspective, the hypocrisy option, and justification. It argued that asking how, rather than whether a security measure is justified offers a further possibility to destabilise functionalist renderings of security, according to which security measures are deemed to respond to threats. Focusing on justification, as has been shown throughout the discussion of two situations in the policy life of EU border control, is also a way to question ready-made categories and claims about changes in the shape and scope of such measures. In the context of the so-called (and on-going at the time of writing) refugee crisis, it is indeed tempting to interpret inflections in policy orientations as a leaning towards a "humanitarian" posture in the case of the Mare Nostrum/Triton discussion or towards a more privacy-oriented approach in the case of smart borders. Thinking in terms of justification foregrounds the fact that actors of EU security politics are hardly as clean-cut in their categories that security analysis may make them to be. At the same time, thinking through justification in the modified way suggested here, that is by correlating specific justifications with patrimonies of dispositions, is a way to ensure that the categories of actors are not just taken at face value, and examined reflexively. Asking how a measure is justified is not simply about following the actors and what they say, as some versions of the "practice turn" in international relations (Adler and Pouliot 2011), of pragmatic sociology or its actor-network theory variant, might argue. It is on the other hand a way to interpret security politics as shaped by the muddling through of actors rather than decisive action, and to show that security as an object of analysis is more unstable and less homogenous than it might appear, including through the work of security scholars.

What is more, thinking through justification also engages with the limits of the labour of justification. In particular, it renders the way in which practices of justification evacuate other dimensions to the discussion. Juxtaposing the two situations examined in the chapter is useful here, since at no point during the May 2015 meeting were the issue of deaths at sea or the early stages of the so-called refugee crisis of the summer mentioned. It is only at the very end of the session that the lead official, pressed to comment on how smart borders measures would impact the situation at the external borders, stresses that by providing information on over-stayers, the EES in particular could contribute to an appeased political debate about foreigners in the EU: "with smart borders you might end up in a real political debate in Europe, because you cannot ignore it anymore, because you have statistics". Justifying security, in this regard, involves drawing lines between what can be debated and when, what is a political question and what is not in the context of shifting EU internal and border security politics.

References

Adler, E., & Pouliot, V. (2011). International practices. *International Theory, 3*(1), 1–36.

Amicelle, A., Aradau, C., & Jeandesboz, J. (2015). Questioning security devices: Performativity, resistance, politics. *Security Dialogue, 46*(4), 293–306.

Amoore, L. (2006). Biometric borders: Governing mobilities in the war on terror. *Political Geography, 25*(3), 336–351.

Aradau, C., & Van Munster, R. (2007). Governing terrorism through risk: Taking precautions, (un) knowing the future. *European Journal of International Relations, 13*(1), 89–115.

Balzacq, T. (2005). The three faces of securitization: Political agency, audience and context. *European Journal of International Relations, 11*(2), 171–201.

Balzacq, T., Basaran, T., Bigo, D., Guittet, E.-P., & Olsson, C. (2010). Security practices. In R. A. Denemark (Ed.), *International studies encyclopedia online*. Wiley-Blackwell: Malden, MA. doi:10.1111/b.9781444336597.2010.x.

Bigo, D. (1996). *Polices en réseaux: l'expérience européenne*. Paris: Presses de Sciences Po.

Bigo, D. (2002). Security and immigration: Towards a critique of the governmentality of unease. *Alternatives, 27*(Special issue), 63–92.

Bigo, D. (2008). Security: A field left fallow. In M. Dillon & A. W. Neal (Eds.), *Foucault on security, politics and war* (pp. 93–114). Houndmills, Basingstoke: Palgrave Macmillan.

Bigo, D. (2011). Pierre Bourdieu and international relations: Power of practices, practices of power. *International Political Sociology, 5*(3), 225–258.

Bigo, D. (2014). The (in) securitization practices of the three universes of EU border control: Military/Navy–border guards/police–database analysts. *Security Dialogue, 45*(3), 209–225.

Bigo, D., Carrera, S., González Fuster, G., Guild, E., de Hert, P., Jeandesboz, J., & Papakonstantinou, V. (2011). *Towards a new EU legal framework for data protection and privacy*. Brussels: European Parliament. PE 453.216.

Bigo, D., Carrera, S., Hayes, B., Hernanz, N., & Jeandesboz, J. (2012). *Evaluating current and forthcoming proposals on JHA databases and a smart borders system at EU external borders*. Brussels: European Parliament. PE 462.513.

Boltanski, L. (2011). *On critique: A sociology of emancipation*. Cambridge: Polity Press.

Boltanski, L., & Claverie, E. (2007). Du monde social en tant que scène d'un procès. In N. Offenstadt & S. Van Damme (Eds.), *Affaires, scandales et grandes causes: De Socrate à Pinochet* (pp. 395–452). Paris: Stock.

Boltanski, L., & Thévenot, L. (1999). The sociology of critical capacity. *European Journal of Social Theory, 2*(3), 359–377.

Boltanski, L., & Thévenot, L. (2006). *On justification: Economies of worth*. Princeton: Princeton University Press.

Bourdieu, P. (1991). *Language and symbolic power*. Cambridge: Polity Press.

Bourdieu, P. (1994). Rethinking the state: Genesis and structure of the bureaucratic field. *Sociological Theory, 12*(1), 1–18.

c.a.s.e. collective. (2006). Critical approaches to security in Europe: A networked manifesto. *Security Dialogue, 37*(4), 443–487.

Ciută, F. (2009). Security and the problem of context: A hermeneutical critique of securitisation theory. *Review of International Studies, 35*(2), 301–326.

Cox, R. (1981). Social forces, states and world orders: Beyond international relations theory. *Millennium—Journal of International Studies, 10*(2), 126–155.

De Hert, P., & Bellanova, R. (2011). *Transatlantic cooperation on travellers' data processing: From sorting countries to sorting individuals*. Washington: Migration Policy Institute.

Didier, E. (2014). Introduction: Alain Desrosières, savant essentiel et homme de qualité. In A. Desrosières (Ed.), *Prouver et gouverner: Une analyse politique des statistisques publiques*. Paris: La Découverte.

Epstein, C. (2007). Guilty bodies, productive bodies, destructive bodies: Crossing the biometric borders. *International Political Sociology, 1*(2), 149–164.

European Commission. (2004). *Proposal for a Regulation to the European Parliament and to the Council concerning the Visa Information System (VIS) and the exchange of data between Member States on short stay-visas—Extended impact assessment.* Brussels: European Commission, SEC. 2004. 1628.

European Commission. (2011). *Smart borders—Options and the way ahead.* Brussels: European Commission, COM. 2011. 680 final.

European Commission. (2013a). *Proposal for a Regulation of the European Parliament and of the Council establishing an Entry/Exit System (EES) to register entry and exit data of third country nationals crossing the external borders of the Member States of the European Union.* Brussels: European Commission, COM. 2013. 95 final.

European Commission. (2013b). *Proposal for a Regulation of the European Parliament and of the Council establishing a Registered Traveller Programme.* Brussels: European Commission, COM. 2013. 97 final.

European Commission. (2013c). *Proposal for a Regulation of the European Parliament and of the Council amending Regulation (EC) No 562/2006 as regards the use of the Entry/Exit System (EES) and the Registered Traveller Programme (RTP).* Brussels: European Commission, COM. 2013. 96 final.

European Data Protection Supervisor. (2013). *Smart borders: Key proposal is costly, unproven and intrusive.* Brussels: EDPS. Press Release 2013/08.

Haahr, J. H., & Walters, W. (2005). *Governing Europe: Discourse, governmentality and European integration.* London: Routledge.

Herz, J. (1950). Ideational internationalism and the security dilemma. *World Politics, 2*(2), 157–180.

Huysmans, J. (1998). Security! What do you mean? From concept to thick signifier. *European Journal of International Relations, 4*(2), 226–255.

Huysmans, J. (2006). *The politics of insecurity: Fear, migration and asylum in the EU.* London: Routledge.

Huysmans, J. (2014). *Security unbound: Enacting democratic limits.* London: Routledge.

Jagd, S. (2011). Pragmatic sociology and competing orders of worth in organizations. *European Journal of Social Theory, 14*(3), 343–359.

Jeandesboz, J. (2015). Putting security in its place: EU security politics, the European neighbourhood policy and the case for practical reflexivity. *Journal of International Relations and Development.* doi:10.1057/jird.2015.11.

Jeandesboz, J., Bigo, D., Hayes, B., & Simon, S. (2013). *The Commission's legislative proposals on Smart Borders: Their feasibility and costs.* Brussels: European Parliament. PE 493.026.

Lahire, B. (2012). *Monde pluriel: Penser l'unité des sciences sociales.* Paris: Seuil.

Neal, A. (2009). Securitization and risk at the EU border: The origins of Frontex. *Journal of Common Market Studies, 47*(2), 333–356.

Schouten, P. (2014). Pragmatic sociology and competing orders of worth in organizations. *European Journal of Social Theory, 14*(3), 343–359.

Waever, H. (1995). Securitization and desecuritization. In R. Lipschutz (Ed.), *On security* (pp. 46–86). New York: Columbia University Press.

Waever, O., (2004, March 17–20). *Aberystwyth, Paris, Copenhagen: New 'schools' in security theory and their origins between core and periphery.* Montreal: Annual Convention of the International Studies Association.

Waever, O. (2011). Politics, security, theory. *Security Dialogue, 42*(4–5), 465–480.

Zürn, M., & Checkel, J. T. (2005). Getting socialized to build bridges: Constructivism and rationalism, Europe and the nation-state. *International Organization, 59*(4), 1045–1079.

MIX
Papier aus verantwortungsvollen Quellen
Paper from responsible sources
FSC® C105338

If you have any concerns about our products,
you can contact us on
ProductSafety@springernature.com

In case Publisher is established outside the EU,
the EU authorized representative is:
Springer Nature Customer Service Center GmbH
Europaplatz 3, 69115 Heidelberg, Germany

Printed by Libri Plureos GmbH
in Hamburg, Germany